Environmental Impact Assessment

United Nations Economic Commission for Europe

Some other titles in this series from Pergamon Press

NOTICE TO READERS

Dear Reader

If your library is not already a standing/continuation order customer to this series, may we recommend that
you place a standing/continuation order to receive immediately upon publication all new volumes. Should
you find that these volumes no longer serve your needs, your order can be cancelled at any time without
notice.

ROBERT MAXWELL
Publisher at Pergamon Press

Environmental Impact Assessment

Proceedings of a Seminar of the United Nations Economic
Commission for Europe, Villach, Austria, September 1979

Published for the
UNITED NATIONS

by
PERGAMON PRESS

OXFORD · NEW YORK · TORONTO · SYDNEY · PARIS · FRANKFURT

U.K.	Pergamon Press Ltd., Headington Hill Hall, Oxford OX3 0BW, England
U.S.A.	Pergamon Press Inc., Maxwell House, Fairview Park, Elmsford, New York 10523, U.S.A.
CANADA	Pergamon Press Canada Ltd., Suite 104, 150 Consumers Rd., Willowdale, Ontario M2J 1P9, Canada
AUSTRALIA	Pergamon Press (Aust.) Pty. Ltd., P.O. Box 544, Potts Point, N.S.W. 2011, Australia
FRANCE	Pergamon Press SARL, 24 rue des Ecoles, 75240 Paris, Cedex 05, France
FEDERAL REPUBLIC OF GERMANY	Pergamon Press GmbH, 6242 Kronberg-Taunus, Hammerweg 6, Federal Republic of Germany

First edition 1981

British Library Cataloguing in Publication Data
United Nations. *Economic Commission for Europe*
Environmental impact assessment. - (ECE seminars and symposia)
1. Environmental impact analysis - Congresses
I. Title II. Series
304.2   TD194.6
ISBN 0-08-024445-9

In order to make this volume available as economically and as rapidly as possible the authors' typescripts have been reproduced in their original forms. This method unfortunately has its typographical limitations but it is hoped that they in no way distract the reader.

Printed in Great Britain by A. Wheaton & Co. Ltd., Exeter

Contents

Part I
Methodologies for Environmental Analysis

A. General Methodological Approaches

B. Methods and techniques for environmental analyses

Part II
Integration of Environmental Considerations into the
Planning and Decision-Making Process

Contents   vii

Introduction

Impact assessment is a concept that evolved in the search for ways to render development and protection of the environment compatible in the complex and interdependent world of today. The speed, scale and character of contemporary technological and economic development, which has permitted material standards of living to reach high levels in the ECE region, has also led to unforeseen effects on the very environmental assets that constitute the basis for sustained socio-economic development. It is becoming clear that air, water and soil must, of necessity, be treated as precious natural resources requiring careful management. Simple cures for pollution problems are no longer sufficient. Comprehensive policies for preventive action to avert environmental damage before it occurs are becoming imperative. In this context, the wide application of procedures for the assessment of environmental impact has become a promising instrument to prepare for public decision-making on development action.

The Economic Commission for Europe (ECE) has long been alert to the value of co-operative government efforts to promote the application of environmental impact assessment in the ECE region. It was of great significance that in the Final Act of the Conference on Security and Co-operation in Europe ECE was designated as an appropriate inter-governmental forum for the study of related methods and procedures.

It was against such a background of interest and concern that the Seminar on Environmental Impact Assessment took place in Villach (Austria) in 1979, at the invitation of the Government of Austria. Delegations from 23* countries in the ECE region took part along with representatives of countries participating under article 11 of the terms of reference of ECE.** Participants from two United Nations bodies as well as various specialized agencies and inter-governmental and non-governmental organizations were also present. Mr. H. Pindar (Austria) and Mr. V. Vinogradov (USSR) were elected chairman and vice-chairman, respectively.

Delegates were welcomed by the Director-General of the Austrian Federal Ministry of Health and Environment who presented an address on behalf of the Minister. He recalled that during the United Nations Conference on the Human Environment, held in Stockholm (Sweden) in 1972, ECE member Governments had pledged their support of a number of basic principles for the protection of the environment. While preventive measures were seen as an encouraging feature, the need for international co-operation, as defined in the Stockholm Declaration, was deemed increasingly urgent. Following the Conference on Security and Co-operation in Europe, the decision of the thirty-fourth session of the Economic Commission for Eurpe to hold the High-level Meeting within the Framework of the ECE for the Protection of the Environment in 1979 was viewed as another sign of the importance attached to the subject. An appreciation of the environmental activities of ECE, as well as an increasing awareness of resource limitations and the need to weigh short-term economic interests against long-term environmental considerations had led the Government of Austria to offer host facilities for the Seminar.

Participants were also welcomed by the Director of Physical Planning and Construction who, on behalf of the Provincial Government of Carinthis, pointed out that the authorities were closely following the effects of development activities on the environment in the Province . In his greetings, the Mayor of Villach reminded delegates of an earlier ECE seminar on environmental problems held in Villach and expressed the wish that the city might become a centre for such gatherings.

---

* Austria; Belgium; Canada; Czechoslovakia; Denmark; Finland; France; German Democratic Republic; Germany, Federal Republic of; Greece; Hungary; Ireland; Netherlands; Norway; Poland; Portugal; Spain; Sweden; Switzerland; Union of Soviet Socialist Republics; United Kingdom; United States of America; Yugoslavia.

** Brazil, Indonesia and the Republic of Korea.

The Seminar was opened by the Executive Secretary of the Economic Commission for
Europe, Mr. Janez Stanovnik, who drew attention to the mandate set out in the Final
Act of the Conference on Security and Co-operation in Europe, which had boosted
ECE activities on environmental impact assessment. He referred to the breadth and
quality of the papers submitted to the Seminar as bearing proof of the great interest
in the subject of the Seminar. Allowing for the complexity of the interdisciplinary
tasks involved, he pointed out that, thanks to increasing experience, impact assessment was becoming a useful policy instrument to safeguard the environment for both
present and future generations.

Some of the difficulties of promoting proper concern for the environment stemmed,
he believed, from prevailing economic conditions. Impact assessment procedures,
for instance, were often seen as delaying investment activities. However, such arguments could no longer be considered valid. In the mature economies of the ECE region,
investment planning had to be sufficiently comprehensive to include social costs.
Moreover, recent economic investigations had indicated that the costs of damage from
neglect of environmental impact would, in most instances, exceed the expenditures
for environmental protection and that for such problems as unemployment and the
increasing demand for energy, environmental protection measures would bring relief
rather than worsen the situation.

Using statistical data, the Executive Secretary illustrated how inappropriate use of
physical resources today could pre-empt future choices. A plea was voiced for
efforts to integrate economic and environmental concerns at different levels and
time horizons of socio-economic planning and management. More humanistic approaches
were necessary also. In quoting great leaders from both developed and developing
countries, the Executive Secretary pointed out that it had been recognized for some
time that growth of material production and consumption could not serve as a goal
in itself nor could one ignore that human aspirations have a very broad spectrum.
It was important that environmental impact assessment become part of a procedure
for comprehensive planning of human activities. The objective of such planning
would focus on sound development rather than on a definite rate of growth. In the
world today there was a need for new approaches to development and for the establishment of a new international order. In that context, he drew attention to another
ECE seminar, organized in conjunction with the United Nations Environment Programme,
on Alternative Patterns of Development and Lifestyles. In concluding, the Executive
Secretary referred to the High-level Meeting within the Framework of the ECE on the
Protection of the Environment and the Convention on Long-range Transboundary Air
Pollution, which give a prominent place to the subject of environmental impact
assessment.

The first plenary session was devoted to a general debate on Procedural and
Institutional Questions of Environmental Impact Assessment. A background document
had been prepared by the secretariat reviewing significant issues on this topic*.
The discussion was led by Mr. F. Hurtubise (Canada) who drew attention to:
procedures for including environmental impact assessment in the planning and decision-
making process; types of impacts; range of environmental considerations to be
considered; field of application of environmental impact assessment; allocation of
responsibilities for environmental analyses and review; information requirement;
allocation of environmental assessment costs among parties concerned; means for
effective public information and involvement; possibilities of legal appeal against
decisions taken on the basis of environmental impact assessments, etc.

During the discussion which followed, reference was frequently made to the background
paper, which was considered to have brought together the major features, concepts

---

* This paper appears in extenso later in this volume.

and approaches of environmental impact assessment in the ECE region. Although the
differences between countries were considerable, it was generally felt that it would
be desirable, and even possible, to elaborate some general principles for impact
assessment and thereby broaden the basis for international co-operation, especially
in respect to transboundary pollution problems.

Flexibility was considered a prime requirement, as experience had shown that an
effective and well-functioning procedure of assessment could be developed only
progressively; the degree of flexibility needed would of course depend on existing
institutional settings and environmental conditions. It was pointed out that
environmental impact assessment should be introduced at all levels of the planning
and decision-making structure; the approaches at these levels could well differ,
however, for instance between a federal and provincial level. The advantages and
disadvantages of various means for introducing assessment procedures were discussed.
Whereas a legislative basis seemed to be an appropriate solution in some countries,
administrative regulations were shown to be better suited in others; in many
instances, the integration of environmental impact assessment into existing physical,
land use or specific sectoral planning systems was considered a satisfactory framework for viewing environmental concerns.

Many participants urged that the assessment procedures have a comprehensive character.
In general, more attention should be given to the inclusion of socio-economic factors
and to the development of mechanisms for broad and continuous public participation.
Mention was also made of the need for appropriate screening and monitoring systems.

It was felt that environmental impact assessment would increasingly have a role to
play at the international level and suggestions were made that attention should be
paid to problems of assessment in the context of development action beyond national
boundaries, in particular with regard to investments in developing countries.

Representatives of international organizations referred to their current work in the
field. Activities elaborated were: adaptive environmental impact assessment and
management procedures; methodologies for assessing industrial environmental impacts;
environmental health impact assessment, and links between agriculture and the
environment. The seminar then examined four specific issues which served as foci
for debate. Governments had prepared papers on the various topics in advance of
the seminar. These were introduced and summarized for discussion.

I.   METHODOLOGIES FOR ENVIRONMENTAL ANALYSES

A.   General methodological approaches

The first specific topic was introduced by Mr. K. Weiner (United States) who presented a summary of the main issues as transmitted by the Governments of Canada, the
Netherlands and the United States. Emphasis had been placed on the need for flexibility and diversity as desirable characteristics of environmental impact procedures,
in order to permit review and revision. Reference was made to the experience of the
United States where, during the last decade, procedures established under the National
Environment Policy Act had evolved into a flexible approach without legislative
amendment. A promising feature was the new "scoping" process, which permitted the
narrowing of issues and the divising of alternatives. As for costs of assessment
for major construction projects, they now rarely exceeded 1 or 2 per cent of total
project costs.

Comments were made on the attempt to distinguish between so-called "process" or
"subject matter" methodologies and the question of defining minimum requirements.
Particular interest was shown in the various methods for generating and evaluating
alternatives. The need was stressed for the interpretation of scientific findings

of environmental impact in terms comprehensible and meaningful to decision makers and the public.

Mr. V. Vinogradov (USSR) then presented a basic report on methodology and comprehensive monitoring programmes for environmental pollution. Comprehensive ecological monitoring constituted the basis for an adequate evaluation of anthopogenic effects on the environment and of the reaction of natural systems to these effects. It should also provide the necessary data for predicting changes in environmental parameters resulting from the growing intensity of human activities. Monitoring was thus seen as an information system for national authorities to use when adopting specific decisions affecting environmental protection and public health as well as the rational use of natural resources.

In the discussion, it was pointed out that two types of monitoring could be distinguished: measurement of local impact, which should be considered an integral part of environmental impact assessment; and the provision of base-line data at regional and global levels, for use in long-term, large-scale analysis or planning at the national level.

B. Methods and techniques for environmental analysis

The six basic reports on this subject were introduced by Mr. B. Clark (United Kingdom). Reports on this particular topic had been prepared by the Governments of Spain, the United Kingdom, the Union of Soviet Socialist Republics and Yugoslavia. They revealed that there were many definitions of environmental impact assessment and consequently a large number of diverse methods being developed for impact studies. The methods utilized a variety of conceptual frameworks and approaches to data presentation and analysis. Both quantitative and qualitative methods were used. While each approach had a role to play, it was suggested that the quantitative method was mainly applicable to technical assessment. In general, there appeared to be a move towards qualitative methods of environmental impact assessment.

Questions raised for discussion included the following: reliability of methods of prediction; need for post-development audits; and utility of methods for evaluating programmes, policies, plans and projects. Several participants offered practical examples of methods used. In the discussion attention was also drawn to some difficulties connected with the flow of information during the process of environmental impact assessment. It was thought that an educational programme should form part of the process. Responsibility for informing the public did not rest solely upon government but was also a duty of the development proponent.

II. INTEGRATION OF ENVIRONMENTAL CONSIDERATIONS INTO THE PLANNING AND DECISION-
     MAKING PROCESS

A. At planning level

The topic was introduced by Mr. V. Markov (USSR) and Mr. A. Staatsen (Netherlands). Seven basic reports, transmitted by the Governments of the Byelorussian SSR, German Democratic Republic, Netherlands, United Kingdom and USSR, had served as a basis for the analysis.

The reports from countries with a state planning system for socio-economic development indicated that a wide range of environmental considerations were incorporated in the annual as well as the long-term plans. These plans contained special sections on measures for protection and rational use of natural resources. In the elaboration of the plans, such factors as trends in regional changes in the state of the environment were taken into consideration. Stress was laid on comprehensive approaches and the need for consistency and interlinkage of current and long-term plans in order to ensure the implementation of both immediate and prospective goals. It was pointed out that sustained economic growth had, to an increasing extent, become dependent on efficient environmental protection. Forecasting of changes in the environment was, therefore, an integral part of planning for future economic activities. The development of comprehensive territorial schemes constituted a new feature of policy for environmental protection. In the case of large-scale projects with possibly regional or global implications, provisions were generally made for environmental impact assessment studies, including scientific research; decisions on implementation were withheld until assurance of viability had been obtained.

In the course of the debate it was pointed out that, in some countries with centrally planned economies, requirements for environmental impact assessment had been introduced in sectoral legislation. No allocation of financial resources for investment could take place before a satisfactory impact statement had been submitted. Increasing emphasis was being placed on the elaboration of alternatives at an early stage, but lack of information generally constituted a serious impediment to fulfilment of the task. The need for improved methodologies for qualitative impact assessment was also pointed out. Environmental education of planners was considered an important requirement in the immediate future. It was also suggested that specific environmental guidelines for planning authorities should be elaborated.

With particular reference to the basic reports on integration at the plan level in the Netherlands and the United Kingdom, it was pointed out that two different approaches could be observed. Whereas the one required a distinct environmental impact assessment procedure tied to already existing procedures, the other could be characterized as an ad hoc integration of environmental impact assessment into a planning system for development control. In this context, the question of criteria that should be fulfilled in order to establish comprehensive environmental impact assessment was raised. The resulting system should be one in which planning goals could be set, alternatives generated, and decisions on implementation facilitated, in accordance with certain procedural requirements.

Special attention was devoted to the problems and possibilities of integrating environmental impact assessment into various land-use planning systems, some of which were more developed than others. One of the reasons for establishing separate procedures for impact assessment had often been that the physical planning framework in some countries was too narrow in scope and not sufficiently dynamic. It was rather typical that in countries where land-use planning was still at a formative stage, there had been a definite need for giving environmental impact assessment a statutory character. The possibilities of integrating impact assessment into planning at national or regional levels depended obviously on the availability of environmental data at that level. Examples of recent attempts, in several countries, to provide such information in the form of general ecological models for the environment or national environmental surveys were described.

The establishment of mechanisms for the screening of development actions that should be subjected to environmental impact assessment was another question that received attention in the debate. In countries with well-developed land-use planning, the existing institutional arrangements, complemented by special lists of criteria for selection, were normally used for the purpose. The creation of special bodies or panels for review of environmental impact assessments was a topical problem. In the discussion, many questions were raised about the composition and functions of such bodies, and of the need for them to be independent of the group that would carry out the impact assessment.

B. At programme and sectoral level

Under this topic, Mr. M. Giacobino (France) introduced the basic reports transmitted by the Governments of the Federal Republic of Germany, France and Switzerland.
These reports had indicated that it was sometimes difficult to draw a line between
plans and programmes. In many instances there was no planning at programme or
sectoral levels but the need for protection of the environment had been the reason
for bringing such planning into existence. The reports tended to show that techniques existed for environmental impact assessment of certain general sectoral
schemes, e.g. for transport systems, and that the results of such assessment could
serve as a useful basis for choosing among alternatives. Assessment at the scale
of programme and sectors seemed to present certain advantages, as it might allow
the simplification of the procedures at project level. On the whole, it was
considered important to promote greater understanding of the relationships between
development action and environmental quality; and, in order to make environmental
impact assessment an efficient policy instrument, measures should be taken to
establish relevant educational programmes for planners, decision-makers and the
public at large.

On the basis of a case study of a regional development programme in his country,
Mr. K.Lorant (Hungary) reviewed problems of integrating environmental concerns
into planning and decision-making. He referred to the Human Environmental
Protection Act of 1976, the purpose of which was to consolidate sectoral legislation
on environmental protection; he also mentioned a National Office for the Protection
the Environment and Nature that had been created to co-ordinate the activities of
various authorities and to develop guidelines for long-term environmental policies.
Procedures for environmental impact assessment of individual projects had also been
introduced. The question of how to allocate the costs of environmental protection
had received considerable attention; in this context, it was pointed out that the
general approach was to reflect such costs in product prices at the expense of
consumers.

In presenting a case study on the implementation of a programme for ecological
optimization of land use, Mr. M. Martis (Czechoslovakia) stated that the main
purpose of the programme was to consider how to improve the productivity of
ecosystems and to examine alternatives for economic exploitation of natural resources,
while preserving the long-term productive capacity and the ecological stability
of the pilot area in question. A multi-stage assessment approach had been developed
and applied. The results of the programme had provided the basis for a government
decree on the development and management of conservation areas. It was expected
that, in the future, ecological data covering the entire national territory would
be processed and incorporated into the system of socio-economic development planning.

In the discussion, it was noted that national sectoral planning was mostly carried
out in a broad context, a characteristic feature being that it was not site-specific.
The introduction of environmental impact assessment could bring a new dimension to
planning at that level, however. In particular, it would provide opportunities
for consideration of alternatives connected with the choice and mix of technological
systems. A remark was made that sectoral planning was in general interest-biased
and had shown little concern for environmental implications of development action;
it was therefore highly desirable to introduce assessment procedures which would
render the decision-making structure more transparent.

C. At project level

A comparative analysis of four case studies, transmitted by the Governments of
Finland, Ireland, Norway and the United Kingdom, was presented by Mr. R. Turnbull
(United Kingdom). In all the studies, stress had been laid on the need for

environmental impact assessment of major development projects, even if statutory
requirements had not always been considered necessary. The complex responsibilities
and relationships between a central and local government in dealing with the processing of specific proposals were dealt with in the case studies; some problems
had been associated with lack of expertise, resources or commitment at one level
or another. A recurrent feature was the lack of guidance in current development
plans on issues of importance for the national economy or employment at the local
level.

In respect of methodology, difficulties had been experienced in developing and
using techniques expressing qualitative considerations in an unbiased way. The
desirability of base-line data and the importance of monitoring had everywhere
been recognized. In the assessment studies, a distinction had generally been made
between social-environmental impacts and economic-technical considerations. The
former had usually been treated less effectively than the latter.

One of the interesting problems raised by the studies was whether environmental
impact assessment could be used for forward planning to identify potentially
suitable sites for location of projects in advance of need. The cost of environmental impact assessment was another frequently occurring question. The general
opinion seemed to be that the expenditures for assessment usually represented a
very small fraction of project costs - mostly a fraction of a percentage - and
various examples of actual financial benefits from introducing the process were
quoted.

In the course of the discussion, a number of participants referred to the need
for establishing some common basic guidelines for environmental impact assessment
and suggested that attempts should be made to establish a system for exchange of
information at the international level. Many participants also expressed the need
for an agreed definition of terms used in environmental impact assessment, which
would facilitate the exchange of information and experience.

III. PUBLIC INFORMATION AND PARTICIPATION

Basic reports on the topic had been transmitted by the Governments of Canada, the
Netherlands and the USSR. In his introductory statement, Mr. V. Vinogradov (USSR)
highlighted the opportunities for public participation in his country within the
framework of the Society for the Protection of Nature. The activities of the
society included: public information and education to promote awareness of
environmental problems; promotion of public involvement in measures to protect
nature; and direct control - by the public - of correct and rational use of
natural resources, in accordance with existing laws. The general public was also
entitled to submit suggestions to scientific and technical boards preparing comprehensive policy to manage certain environmental problems. Provisions were also made
for participation in the monitoring of the state of the environment and in the
assessment of development proposals that could affect the environment. It was thus
possible to take public opinion into account within the planning and management
process.

In introducing the second basic report, Mr. A. Staatsen (Netherlands), referred to
the increasing desire of the general public to participate in decision-making on
development action affecting their physical and social environment. The environmental impact assessment procedure was an obvious place to make provisions for such
participation. A variety of statutes had permitted the public to intervene in
certain categories of important decisions, but the procedures for participation
were at present being brought into conformity. In this context, considerable
attention had been given to various techniques for public participation and
comparisons of their respective merits. On the basis of recent experience, it

seemed appropriate to suggest that public participation should be a continuous process and that proponents of a development action should communicate with the public
at an early stage of planning.

In presenting the third basic report, Mr. F.Hurtubise (Canada) explained that it
presented an attempt to illustrate, with four case studies, how public participation
had been integrated in the Panel Review Process for environmental impact assessment
in his country. The studies referred to different geographical areas, different
kinds of proposals and different economic sectors. They clearly indicated cases
where the public had influenced the recommendations from the Panel to the policy-
makers.

While participants recognized that public participation should be considered as an
indispensable component in processes for environmental impact assessment, where it
could serve as an instrument for improving socio-economic planning and decision-
making, it was also pointed out that final decisions must be balanced and should
not reflect merely particular individual or group interests.

Attention was drawn to a number of questions concerning effective methods for
communication within the process for public participation, which had to be a two-
way flow of information. Great importance was therefore attached to the use,
throughout the process, of a concise language that was understandable to decision-
makers as well as the general public. This was particularly relevant when the
assessment implied reference to very specific scientific data and relationships.

It was pointed out that an efficient process of public participation implied
serious attention to education. Recourse to professional public relations officers
to animate public meetings had occasionally been taken. Experience had tended to
show, however, that in the long run it was better to rely on the genuine interest
of the public itself, which gradually became more skilled during the course of the
process.

Various opinions were expressed concerning the need for special funding of public
participation. The argument was raised that the public was generally in a weak
position and that funds should be provided as support both to individuals and
environmentalist groups. In this context, the question of juridicial standing of
such groups of societies was discussed. A special recommendation was made that
public hearings should be kept as open as possible, in order to avoid attempts to
manipulate and/or corrupt opinions and decisions.

IV. ENVIRONMENTAL IMPACT ASSESSMENT AS AN INSTRUMENT FOR HANDLING TRANSBOUNDARY
     PROBLEMS

Three basic reports transmitted by the Governments of Norway, the United States of
America and the USSR served as background for the debate.

In introducing the contribution of his country, Mr. M. Markov (USSR) referred to
problems of long-range transport of air pollutants which were becoming increasingly
important as was also reflected in the enhanced attention they were receiving in the
ECE countries. Sulphur compounds were considered to be the most important
atmospheric pollutants. He outlined a methodology for studying long-range transport
of sulphur compounds. It was considered that the following aspects of the problem
should be given particular attention: monitoring transboundary flows of sulphur
compounds; studying the fate of sulphur in the environment; ascertaining effects
on the environment. Approaches to the organization of related research were
proposed. Existing international law seemed to provide possibilities for measures
to limit transboundary transport of pollutants, but although there were indications
of some progress, there were still major problems to be considered.

Mr. T. Lie (Norway) presented a basic report prepared by his Government that was concerned mainly with principles of international law in regard to transnational pollution and the need for international rules on information and consultation. With regard to development activities leading to transnational pollution, he put forward various reasons - some of a legal and some of a non-legal nature - including transboundary effects in the assessment of environmental impact. An international exchange of information might be required in order to facilitate such assessment. One non-legal reason was that transboundary effects normally were not compensated for in the country affected. Furthermore, industries subjected to assessment of domestic impact might tend to establish along borders if there were no corresponding obligation to assess transboundary effects. Information exchange could help to prevent international disputes and claims for compensation and assist an exposed country in taking mitigating steps. Indeed, a State affected would need to be informed of the outcome of the assessment, in order to be able to enter into meaningful consultations with the State of origin. The basic report concluded that it seemed desirable to elaborate further international law on information and consultation, and possibly to establish one or more international conventions on the subject.

Mr. W.H. Mansfield (United States), acting as rapporteur, described approaches to the use of environmental impact assessment in international affairs. He felt that it was a natural step to extend the obligation of impact assessment to include effects abroad, although this might raise some jurisdictional, practical and procedural questions. Steps were now being taken within international organizations and in the United States to promote the use of assessment procedures to ensure environmental soundness of development assistance projects. Turning to the use of environmental impact assessment in a transboundary context, the rapporteur described the activities of international organizations and outlined the basic provisions of the United States Presidential Executive Order, which called for environmental review of effects abroad of certain governmental actions. Pointing to the need for broad international arrangements for environmental impact assessment, he outlined the United States Senate Resolution 49 and confirmed the interest of his Government in international co-operation on the subject.

In the subsequent discussion, reference was made to a number of specific transboundary pollution problems, where the establishment of internationally agreed principles or formalized procedures for environmental impact assessment could be of assistance. To such problems belonged, among others: the siting of nuclear installations in frontier areas; the long-range transport of air pollution causing "acid rain" in environmentally sensitive areas; marine pollution in the Mediterranean and other regional seas.

Representatives of United Nations bodies and specialized agencies, as well as of other international organizations, informed the seminar participants about their activities on environmental impact assessment in a transboundary context. A large body of documentation on scientific research, analytical studies and progress reports on current work were available from these organizations.

Delegates drew attention to problems which could be anticipated and would have to be considered when dealing with international aspects of environmental impact assessment. Such problems were, for instance, increased establishment of international networks for monitoring; increased collection of comparable base-line data for large areas beyond national jurisdiction; elaboration of minimum procedural requirements for impact assessment; and establishment of provisions for equal access to assessment data.

As there were many different interpretations of "environmental impact assessment", before entering into discussion of procedural questions it would be necessary to define clearly what was meant by the term in an international context. As examples of some general difficulties that could arise in applying impact assessment at the international level, reference was made to experience from federal States where the constituent provinces enjoyed large autonomy.

Interest was expressed in new approaches to foreign technical aid and international investments which required prior assessment of environmental impact in recipient countries. Attention was also drawn to various international agreements which included reference to conducting environmental impact assessment and a number of delegations expressed support for developing international arrangements for environmental impact assessment, especially in cases of potential transnational environmental damage.

There was a general feeling that the time had come for defining the role of ECE in furthering the idea of using environmental impact assessment as an instrument for handling transboundary problems.

The meeting adopted a set of conclusions and recommendations which are reproduced in full below.

Conclusions and Recommendations

I. METHODOLOGIES FOR ENVIRONMENTAL IMPACT ASSESSMENT (EIA)

Conclusions

A. General

There is general agreement on the need for a common understanding of the term "environmental impact assessment methodology" and/or a common understanding of the purposes and goals and the basic ingredients of EIA methodologies.

The term "methodology" refers to the general and specific ways in which EIA is conducted; and there are two types of EIA methodologies: process methodologies and subject-matter methodologies.

A methodology for the EIA process refers to the general approaches, procedures or frameworks for structuring EIA; a methodology for EIA subject-matter refers to the ways in which specific environmental impacts can be assessed.

A variety of approaches and techniques for both process and subject-matter methodologies are currently in use. The wide range of experience which has thus been gained can be invaluable (a) to those Governments which already have EIA processes and which are seeking to improve their systems, and (b) to those Governments which do not yet have EIA processes and which are considering how best to design their systems.

B. Purposes and goals

In order to serve the purposes and meet the goals established for EIA, it is proposed, inter alia, that:

(a) Decision-makers should use reliable information on the environmental impacts of proposals and alternatives (including policies, programmes, plans and projects) in order to make decisions which protect and enhance the quality of the environment;

(b) Decision-makers should have the authority to consider all relevant environmental impacts;

(c) It is essential to develop and consider alternatives and to gain a comprehensive understanding of their environmental effects;

(d) EIA should begin at the earliest stages in the planning and decision-making process so that impacts can be evaluated and proposals improved prior to decisions;

(e) The results of EIA should be presented clearly and concisely in a language and graphics which are understandable to decision-makers and the public; unnecessary paperwork, detail and technical jargon should be avoided;

(f) The scope and depth of detail of EIA methodologies and documents should depend on individual environmental situations and be commensurate with the significance of the issues; and

(g) EIA methodologies should be sufficiently flexible to be tailored to the unique
     circumstances of individual proposals and environments, should be applicable
     to different stages of planning and development, and should be continuously
     revised on the basis of monitoring and experience.

C. Elements of EIA methodologies

The essential components (i.e. "minimum requirements") of the environmental impact
assessment process include:

(a) identification of objectives, and reasonable alternative courses of action to
     achieve them;

(b) identification of relevant environmental impacts of alternatives, including
     the "no action" alternative;

(c) estimation or description of the identified impacts and evaluation of their
     importance for protecting and enhancing the environment;

(d) specification of the scope, contents and format of the documentation which
     will be required for conducting the EIA (including required and optional
     reports);

(e) communication with planners, decision-makers, proponents and the public on
     the preliminary and/or final results of EIA, including the independent review
     of environmental documents and the methods by which decision-makers respond
     to consultation and comments; and

(f) description of the final decisions made and actions to be taken, including
     mitigation measures; the reasons for the decision; and the procedures
     for monitoring implementation of the actions.

In addition, the EIA process should include a method for determining, in a reliable
and timely way:

(a) which proposals and actions are subject to, or require EIA, and what level
     of EIA is required (e.g. "screening");

(b) what will be evaluated in a particular EIA (e.g. "scoping");

(c) the usual mechanics of the EIA process, such as: who will be responsible for
     which components of the EIA process; and what time schedules, if any; and

(d) how decision-makers use the results of environmental impact assessment.

D. Further conclusions

Both quantitative and qualitative methods are being used to undertake EIA. The two
approaches have a role to play in an EIA process. Quantitative methods may have
a more important role to play in technical assessment exercises. In an over-all
structure, however, there is now a trend towards more qualitative approaches - a
trend which is viewed as a healthy development. An EIA process, in any case, can
be a useful mechanism for harmonizing many types of assessment techniques.

Different countries use, or plan to use, different types of methodologies, depending
on needs and resource availability. Where a comprehensive EIA system is not yet
practicable, experience is being gained as a result of developing specific types
of impact study, such as air pollution assessment and general experimentation

with assessment methods.

If and when countries consider the introduction of EIA processes, the following factors should be kept in mind:

(a) international agencies are prepared to offer advice and assistance, especially on subject-matter methodologies; and

(b) willingness to experiment is important in developing a system which conforms with national needs and requirements.

Recommendations

(a) Member countries are encouraged to include, as part of their EIA processes, the identification of environmentally sound alternatives and to ensure that these alternatives are considered by their decision-makers.

(b) Governments which have or are initiating environmental impact assessment processes should have mechanisms (i) to determine the effectiveness of their processes, and (ii) to recommend modifications on a continuing basis.

(c) Monitoring of environmental parameters and evaluation of ecosystems should be included as an integral part of an EIA system; this is necessary for providing baseline data, technical assessments and ex post facto evaluation of specific decisions. Monitoring and evaluation are an essential aid to decision-making, in order to protect and enhance the quality of the environment.

(d) Where there are various requirements and divided responsibilities for planning and decision-making subjected to EIA, a procedure should be established for a comprehensive review to ensure that:

   (i) important environmental impacts are not missed;

   (ii) environmental impacts are viewed cumulatively; and

   (iii) EIA is completed and used by decision-makers prior to taking actions which would have an adverse environmental impact or limit the choice of reasonable alternatives.

(e) Governments are encouraged to evaluate and share information on EIA methodologies, techniques and experiences, and to seek the assistance of other member countries and international organizations in the development of their EIA methodologies.

II. INTEGRATION OF ENVIRONMENTAL CONSIDERATIONS INTO THE PLANNING AND DECISION-MAKING PROCESS

Conclusions

A. At policy, planning and programme level

It was generally agreed that environmental impact assessment of policies and plans encompasses such decisions as: the adoption of transportation or energy plans; urban or rural development plans; and legislation and administrative rules regarding activities having potential impact on the environment. Such policies and plans often guide or prescribe alternative uses of resources upon which future actions will be based.

Consideration of a broad range of alternatives is one of the prime advantages of environmental impact assessment at the planning level. Therefore, environmental impact assessment must be carried out prior to a decision which would limit or restrict future options.

Integration of EIA into an existing planning process can be efficient only if this process meets certain minimum requirements, e.g. provides the information required or the ways and means to obtain such information (e.g. goals, objectives, alternatives, baseline information, effects on the environment, mitigation measures, monitoring, input from the general public, etc.).

It is anticipated that the introduction, at an early stage of planning, of environmental impact assessment with emphasis on alternative options will result in lower costs than recourse to mitigating measures after plan implementation.

When appropriate EIA is introduced at the policy, plan or programme level, this may reduce the need for specific EIA studies for individual projects. It is recognized, however, that for certain projects EIA reviews may be desirable and/or necessary.

B. At project level

It is recognized that the scope, organization and emphasis of environmental analysis varies according to the importance and size of the project, whether it is a remote possibility or a highly probable consequence, and whether one proponent or several are likely to be involved. This consideration applies, even more so, to linked proposals extending over large geographical areas and particularly if there may be synergistic effects.

The common element is flexibility of approach and the adoption of an initial process: to determine what level of review is needed; and to identify the degree of effort required to evaluate the effect of a proposal on the environment of the affected areas.

For the preparation of an adequate EIA within a reasonable time, the availability of adequate information about the project and the establishment of baseline data on the affected areas are identified as elements of critical importance. This, in turn, requires the provision of adequate expertise to identify and describe potential impacts through the adoption of a methodical approach to data collection, data bank analyses and consultation with institutions, developers and the public.

The accessibility and availability of information on the national and regional context and on the broad administrative procedure involved is also an important factor to facilitate and enhance the preparation of an EIA.

It is generally agreed that the organization and undertaking of EIA for major projects involve contributions from a wide range of sources; and that it is important to seek and establish mutual co-operation between all concerned. This could lead to a common understanding of the problems faced, and ultimately to the making of a better assessment.

The problem of imbalance between resources and expertise at different levels of interest is recognized; another concern is the initial cost and staff commitments for carrying out an EIA. Efforts should be made to improve knowledge of various financial and other costs and benefits of EIA to all affected, i.e. proponent, government, the public, and the environment. Such efforts can assist in better understanding of how the long and short-term costs are allocated; how they could be most equitably distributed and which are the direct and indirect benefits derived from these expenditures. It is also generally agreed that lack of knowledge about the precise costs of EIA should not preclude the use of EIA, especially for actions which might cause serious environmental damage.

The increasing application of EIA at the national planning level is a valuable trend to help in identifying locations for future development in advance of specific proposals.

Recommendations

It is important to consider all relevant factors, such as health, ecological, socio-economic and other pertinent aspects, in environmental impact assessments; the techniques for the presentation of these factors should continue to be developed and tested in practical applications.

For policies, programmes, plans, and projects, environmental factors should be:

(a) considered in all phases and all levels of decision-making, along with tech-nical, social, economic and other factors;

(b) considered in a systematic and comprehensive way; and

(c) defined in adequate detail to be compared to technical, social, economic and other factors.

It is recommended that environmental considerations should be integrated in all phases and at all levels of planning along with technical, social, economic and other factors. Various environmental factors have thus to be considered in a systematic and comprehensive way in order to enable an evaluation of environmental impacts in the adoption of plans.

To integrate environmental impact assessment, including public participation, into systems of planning and decision-making, it is necessary clearly to determine how, where and why environmental considerations should be treated in relation to other relevant factors.

It is recommended that in adopting policies, programmes, plans and projects, the results of an independent review of the environmental impact assessment studies should be taken into account.

It is recommended that, to avoid damages in areas of special sensitivity or to take into account potential cumulative effects of certain small-scale projects not normally subjected to EIA, these should nevertheless undergo review.

III. PUBLIC INFORMATION AND PARTICIPATION

Conclusions

The public has become increasingly interested in participating in the planning and decision-making process. This interest has been recognized and incorporated into the environmental impact assessment procedures of a certain number of ECE member countries.

It is generally agreed that EIA is an appropriate and desirable means of informing the public of the many environmental issues which must be considered in planning and decision-making.

Experience of some countries shows that public participation is an effective mechanism in EIA, especially when properly organized. Various forms and methods for public participation in environmental protection, environmental education of populations, improved professional qualifications in production and planning, are in fact a means for public control of the environmental impacts of development planning and implementation.

It is recognized that the public increasingly insists on the right to comment on the adequacy of EIA studies, and in particular on the alternatives proposed for decision.

Stress is laid on the advantages of early public consultation in the EIA process. It is also agreed that public participation should be on a continuous basis and take place at the various stages of the EIA process.

Monitoring studies and the dissemination of the results of such studies are indispensable to an efficient EIA process.

In public participation the quality of the input may vary with the availability of resources. Education and funding are important means of providing necessary expertise.

Recommendations

Active public participation in the review of environmental impact assessment should be encouraged.

EIA procedures should clearly identify the persons and groups who may be affected by the proposed activity.

Public participation should occur on a continuing basis, at the different stages of the EIA process, by means of both formal methods (prescribed by legislative or administrative action) and informal methods (established by codes of practice or agreement).

Procedures for public information and participation should include, as a minimum, exchange of information at an early stage; publication and wide dissemination of EIA documents; public meetings and/or hearings; and publication of the rationale for the decision; information concerning the results of ex post facto monitoring; and important documents should be summarized in a manner easily understandable by the public.

Public participation in EIA should be encouraged by means of educational programmes and appropriate funding.

Proponents of proposals should consult with the public at an early stage and during crucial phases of the EIA. The public - including interest groups - should be recognized as a source of information and opinions that can be valuable both for identifying significant impacts and for evaluating possible options.

Programmes on the environment should be given high priority in educational institutions in order to make present and future generations aware and respectful of their environment and to train experts capable of functioning in inter-disciplinary fields necessary for EIA.

IV. ENVIRONMENTAL IMPACT ASSESSMENT AS AN INSTRUMENT FOR HANDLING TRANSBOUNDARY PROBLEMS

Conclusions

The environmental impact assessment process can be a useful and practical tool for identifying, evaluating and considering international environmental effects of development activities which inadvertently could harm the environment of one or more countries. The results of such environmental impact assessments can be used, not only by the State which is originating a given action but also bu a State which could be affected by the action - their primary purpose being to improve understanding of, and to deal systematically with, potential environmental problems. Experience gained in utilizing such international assessment processes may also be useful in strengthening domestic environmental impact assessment procedures.

Among the activities which may usefully be assessed for potential international environmental effects are national actions which may cause transnational environmental damage in areas outside the jurisdiction of any nation or in other countries, especially neighbouring countries. Many delegations recognized the importance of using EIA in connexion with development assistance projects. International organizations, such as UNEP, UNIDO, OECD, WHO, FAO, CMEA, the European Economic Community, the World Bank and some governments have considered or are considering activities and proposals for environmental impact evaluation of activities having potential international environmental effects.

The preparation of environmental impact assessments for international effects will raise certain jurisdictional, practical and procedural issues which are not likely to exist in the evaluation of domestic environmental effects. Consequently, flexibility will be required in preparing environmental impact assessment which include international effects, in order to take account of, _inter alia_, national sovereignty and diplomatic considerations; the need for international co-operation; the possible lack of necessary scientific information; and the need for technical expertise.

Recommendations

It is recommended that ECE member countries consider what measures they might take in their planning and decision-making to ensure that environmental considerations are incorporated into any of their own activities which may (directly or indirectly) significantly harm the environment outside their own jurisdiction.

To assist in accomplishing these objectives, it is recommended that ECE member countries consider the carrying out of environmental impact assessments for such activities.

In the recognition that activities undertaken by member countries, including their assistance to developing countries, may cause environmental damage outside their own jurisdiction, it is recommended that ECE member countries consider ways of:

(a) evaluating, to the extent possible, environmental impacts of their activities to avoid undesirable environmental effects of these activities; and

(b) preparing environmental assessments for the major actions they undertake in their own territories or in the global commons that may cause significant harm to the environment of another country or the global commons.

It is further recommended that ECE member Governments discuss with potentially affected countries or, in the case of the global commons, with an appropriate

international organization, for the purpose of preventing or at least minimizing
environmental harm.

SPECIFIC RECOMMENDATIONS

It is recommended that:

The proceedings of the present Seminar on Environmental Impact Assessment should
be published (if possible in all three ECE languages) and given wide dissemination.
Furthermore, steps should be taken to facilitate a continuing exchange of information regarding environmental impact assessments carried out in ECE countries.

In general recognition of (1) the value of environmental impact assessment for
protecting and enhancing the quality of the human environment; (2) the interest
of member countries which do not yet have an EIA process; and (3) the mutual
advantage of exchanging information on EIA methodologies, it is recommended that:

(a)   each member country prepare and send to the ECE secretariat a document to
      describe its EIA process (if any), including information on how it is struc-
      tured and implemented. If the EIA process forms part of other existing
      requirements, this document should identify where the basic requirements of
      an EIA process are to be found.

(b)   the Senior Advisers to ECE Governments on Environmental Problems decide to
      collect and analyse the above information with the purpose of providing
      reference material to countries considering the application of EIA procedures.

(c)   each member country give early consideration to the adoption of an EIA process
      by legislative or administrative means. (In this respect, it is recognized
      that an EIA process may be a separate requirement – albeit one which is tied
      to normal government planning and decision-making – or it may be incorporated
      as a distinctive feature of other requirements.)

As ECE member countries are developing national energy plans up to the year 2000,
and information on such plans is being compiled within the framework of ECE (by
the Senior Advisers to ECE Governments on Energy), it would be interesting and
useful that the Senior Advisers on Environmental Problems consider undertaking a
preliminary study of these composite energy plans in order to begin to identify
the environmental implications of possible future energy policies.

It is recommended that, in the interest of strengthening co-operation and of
minimizing duplication of effort, steps should be taken (possibly with the assistance of UNEP) to identify the authority and respective responsibilities of the
various international organizations engaged in fostering the development of EIA
acceptance and procedures in the ECE region.

Address on Behalf of the Government of Austria

I. Leodolter

Federal Minister for Health and the Environment

The United Nations Conference on the Human Environment in Stockholm, 1972, was
a first milestone in the formulation of a modern environmental policy. Everyone, who took part in the Conference realised that huge efforts were needed,on
both the national and international level, to preserve the foundations of our
existence in our own interest and in the interest of future generations. On
behalf of our countries we pledged ourselves to a number of basic principles,
which have retained their enormous importance and their topicality to this
very day.

In the years that have passed since the Stockholm Conference, we have become
quite successful in reducing emissions to tolerable levels on the national scale
and first steps have been taken towards a second generation environmental policy,
with the main emphasis on prevention. For various reasons, the environmental
policy in the European area is in urgent need of the international cooperation
mentioned in the Stockholm Declaration. This is another field where it has been
and will be necessary to arrive, step by step, at more precise formulations
of the general principles and to incorporate them into everyday reality. A
passage on environmental protection has been most aptly included in the Final
Act of the Conference on Security and Co-operation in Europe (CSCE); we believe it
ought to be realised in full, in the interest of a continued policy of détente
in Europe. From the very beginning, Austria has, therefore, given her unqualified
support to the initiative of convening an all-European High-level Meeting
treating specific environmental problems, in accordance with the Final Act of
the CSCE. We are glad that the 34th Session of the ECE Commission eventually
reached an agreement on the time and agenda of this High-level Meeting. We are
placing great expectations in this meeting because, apart from the currently
topical declaration on low-waste and non-waste technologies, it will frame the
first all-European Convention - that is to say a legally binding agreement -
in a major field of environmental protection.*

Thus far, socio-economic and technological systems of highly industrialized
countries have been based on two dangerous assumptions, namely that our natural
resources are unlimited and that nature is a bottomless dustbin; these theories
were coined by the notion of maximum material production and consumption as the
objective of economic activities. This philosophy was largely justified by the

---

*The High-level Meeting within the Framework of the Economic Commission for
Europe on the Protection of the Environment took place in Geneva, 13-15 November
1979.

human experience of earlier centuries. In the past one relied   — and often rightly -   on the regenerative power of the ecosystems, which were hardly overtaxed by the pinpoint interference of man. But meanwhile population density and the progress of science and technology have reached a stage where the challenge is no longer how to interfere most skilfully with the natural cycles, but how to preserve existing cycles or to create new ones.

The rate of growth of the gross national product can no longer be taken as the sole indicator of a sound economic policy. On the contrary, one has to pay increasing attention to "negative production", that is to say to waste material production, to the exhaustion of raw material resources and to ecological deterioration, in order to arrive at the best possible decision. The difficulty of reaching an agreement certainly lies in the fact that the economists   — to quote the Declaration of Cocoyoc -   are mostly concerned with the "inner limits" of mankind, while the ecologists concentrate on the "outer limits". This implies that the same situation, regarded on the one hand from the viewpoint of satisfying economic needs on a short-term basis, and on the other hand from the perspective of securing economic existence on a long-term basis, will give rise to different conclusions.

To destroy the ecosystem, by overtaxing it, will in the long run lead to considerable economic damage; let me just point to the economic consequences of erosion and karstification. From the long-term point of view, economic and ecological interests are not necessarily contradictory, but rather complementary. We have to strive for a harmonization of economic and ecological interests with a view to improving the quality of life of our population.

As part of such an extended cost/benefit analysis we need environmental impact assessment.

Sectional and more or less haphazard decisions may lead to misplanning, which very often can only be remedied at enormous cost. Such misplanning will be prevented by environmental impact assessments, which permit an extended optimiz-ation procedure by developing a common terminology and evaluation.

So it was not only our general appreciation of the ECE's environmental protection activities, but also a particular interest in the instrument of the environmental impact assessment which prompted us to request the honour of hosting this Seminar.

In conclusion, I should like to thank all those who have prepared this Seminar with such care and dedication, in particular the ECE secretariat, the rapporteurs and the representatives of the Province of Carinthia and the Community of Villach.

Introductory Statement by the Executive Secretary of the Economic Commission for Europe

The Final Act of the Conference on Security and Co-operation in Europe, which was adopted at Helsinki in 1975, stated, among other things, that the participating States pledged themselves to co-operate within the Economic Commission for Europe in developing the capability to predict adequately the consequences of economic activity and technological development. This was the clearest possible mandate for the Economic Commission for Europe to intensify further its interest in this extremely important field. It gave a great boost to ECE activities, which have since developed dynamically and have led to this Seminar. I think that the number and the quality of papers which have been prepared for this Seminar is evidence of this.

We have in the meantime had a number of other important seminars, such as that at Rotterdam in 1975 on the Environmental Aspects of Economic Development Planning. I will not enumerate all the ECE seminars and expert meetings that have been held following this CSCE decision. But this seminar on Environmental Impact Assessment does represent a synthesis of what has been done so far and at the same time it provides a good foundation for another important seminar which is to follow soon in my home town, Ljubljana just across these mountains, on Alternative Patterns of Development and Lifestyles.* I consider that the two meetings are closely interconnected.

The present seminar deals with an extremely complex subject. However I do not think that the complexity of the problem before us should frighten us, still less paralyse our action. We should not be over-impressed by the fact that we are dealing with subjects on which we do not know everything, and indeed on which it is impossible to know and predict everything. I have been told, for instance, that our chemical industries are now adding about 250,000 new chemicals each year to the environment. If those chemicals had to be tested in vitro, in a laboratory, we would need a laboratory staff two or three times as large as the total human race today. It is impossible to be certain what the synergetic effect of any new chemical will be. But this does not mean that we are so ignorant as not to know from the outset that the direct effects of certain chemicals are very toxic or noxious, and that therefore they should not be put uncontrolled into the ecosystem. Although we are confronted with the unknown

---

*This seminar, organized jointly with the United Nations Environment Programme, took place in December 1979.

and often the unpredictable, this should not paralyse our action. There is a
very broad area where action is possible and, indeed, is absolutely necessary.

Now our difficulty is that we have to deal with this extremely complex problem
at a moment when the general economic conditions in our region are not
particularly propitious for environmental action. Very often it is asserted that
environmental requirements or environmental impact statements delay investment
or increase costs and therefore adversely affect economic growth. It is even
argued that, in the long or medium term, the employment situation may be affected
unfavourably. As ECE is an economic commission, it is natural for me to consider
this kind of attitude. Forgive me if, very briefly and quietly, I examine these
arguments, because they are heard too often, even in some bodies of the Economic
Commission for Europe itself.

Let me first take the argument that environmental impact procedures tend to delay
investments. I asked myself immediately, what about other pre-investment planning?
Geological research, or studies of financial aspects, or marketing surveys must
preceed the implementation of an investment plan. These also take time. One does
not simply invest. I am often told that environmental impact statements amount
to huge books, which must then be examined and re-examined. But why not? Should
we engage in investment without fully considering the consequences in advance?
Do we conduct our economic and business affairs in this way? Of course not. I
therefore feel that this kind of argument does not really have very solid
grounds. It does, however, reflect a little inertia from the past, when public
goods were taken for granted. I very often say that it is not by accident that
pollution occurs always in rivers, lakes, seas and the air: always in the
public sector, very seldom in the private. Profit is made in private, but
pollution is made in public. I feel that we have inherited this kind of habit
from the period of what Marxists call primitive accumulation, whereas today we
have grown into mature industrialized societies. Our investment planning
procedures must become more comprehensive if investment is to make a real
contribution to public welfare, and not only to short-term private profit.

There is another argument: that these environmental procedures add a great deal
to the cost of a project. Here I suggest, we are at the heart of the matter.
What is really the cost? Is it right to consider only that part of the social
cost which is borne by the private investor, or must we consider the social cost
in its totality? I was quite impressed by a document recently produced by OECD,
which argues that at the present rate of economic growth, about 3 per cent per
annum, the cost of environmental damage caused by present techniques is in the
range of 3 to 5 per cent of the annual product, whereas expenditure on pollution
prevention amounts to only 1 or 2 per cent of the GNP in the industrialized
countries   members of that organization. If these figures are anywhere close
to reality, it is something we must think about. What if we permit industrial
development or economic activities to continue in this way? If our rate of growth
is 3 per cent but environmental damage is up to 5 per cent, then this means that
the system is taking more than it is giving. I feel that these are matters to
be considered seriously. Hazards - the damage done to the environment - are
reported all to often, and are an increasing public concern. Public opinion on
inflation, balance of payments deficits and so on may vary, but public opinion
feels very strongly about the protection of the environment.

I come to the next argument, concerning energy, which is certainly heard very
often. They say: what shall we do now? We want to switch to burning coal, but
environmentalists protest because they say that there will be too much CO_2 and too
much smoke in the air if we burn more coal. Or there is the argument that
environmentalists are the ones who (as here in Austria) vote against nuclear
energy; economic progress, it is claimed, is stopped by what is called the

environmental lobby. As very often happens in life not all the truth is on one
side of the argument. I do not want to go into every detail of this argument.
But I am firmly convinced that energy problems are not simply problems of how to
arrange for greater and greater production and greater and greater consumption of
energy. I feel rather that the problem is that we are using too much energy and
that we are wasting too much energy. I feel that every ton of coal equivalent of
energy saved is much better than another ton produced. Unless we devote adequate
and proper attention to the procedures and techniques for energy conservation,
nuclear energy will have to come, and it will have to come before it is fully
tested and fully explored. I think that nuclear energy sooner or later will come.
It is really a question whether, through our behaviour now, we will gain time or
not: enough time to perfect technologies to make nuclear energy completely safe.
Safe for the environment, safe for people, safe for those who work in nuclear
installations; whether we gain time for the waste disposal issue and similar
problems to be properly resolved. To gain this time means saving energy now.

This leads me to the last argument, concerning employment, which I for one find
the least convincing of all. In the United States it seems that up to one
million jobs are being provided today, directly and indirectly, through
environmental protection. It has also been calculated that every billion dollars
spent on environmental protection adds another 60,000 jobs to the US economy.
And, of particular interest for the argument I developed earlier in connection
with energy, it seems that every kilowatt of saved energy per capita in the USA
leads to about one million new jobs. Now the USA at present uses about 80 quads
of energy and each quad of energy saved produces 1 million jobs. So, if the USA
energy-saving programmes brought consumption there down to European levels not
only would there be no unemployment in the USA but there would be very hard
pressure on human resources. The same, of course, is true for us. We complain
that there are 17 million unemployed in the region of the Economic Commission
for Europe. If only energy saving programmes - the best friends of the environmental approach to economic policies - were properly conducted, we would also
solve our employment problem.

Now I must turn to another argument, this time coming from environmentalist
circles, which also gives me some difficulties. I was recently at the seminar in
Stockholm where there was a lot of argument about the so-called "carrying
capacity". I have great difficulties with this phrase, because it suggests that
we know what are the physical limits to resources and, moreover, that there are
physical limits to resources. This I cannot accept. Of course, I am not so
ignorant as not to recognise, for example, that geochemically-stored fossil fuels
are finite. But I would also like to bring out the fact that there is primary,
secondary, and now apparently even tertiary exploitation of resources: we could
get more oil out of the ground if we were ready to pay a little bit more.
Therefore resources, in my view, are very closely related to other parameters
and factors in the economic game, such as investment and the use of human and
mechanical energy. Resources is a relative term.

Although I argue in favour of the so-called relative notion of limits this should
not be taken to mean that I will join those who claim that resources are
unlimited. If we look at what is actually going on in the world we see that there
is a land area that is relatively fixed in extent. We have about 13.5 billion
hectares and we have to live with that. Out of these 13.5 billion, just a little
more than 3 billion are potentially available for cultivation; 1.5 billion are
actually cultivated, but less than 1 billion are actually harvested.

Of this 1 billion hectares, however, we are now losing annually about 5 million
hectares through desertification and the irretrievable and irreversible use of
land for other than agricultural purposes. If we assume that, year by year, urban

sites are irreversibly taken away from agriculture something between 0.5 and 0.8 per cent of the total available cultivatable land, this becomes serious. Our grazing and improper farming methods are increasing desertification, as the United Nations Conference on Desertification has proved. If our economic approach, our way of production, develops in such a way that it is irretrievably takes away the land from certain alternative uses, this means that we are pre-empting the future: taking away our freedom of choice and freedom of decision-making in the future. Much the same is true of water. Studies made in our Water Committee show that water use will triple between now and the end of the century and already we are complaining about the high degree of pollution and the decline in the quality of water. The problems are quite serious and no economist who considers himself a professional can simply shut his eyes and ignore such facts; they are not empty projections but are already being felt in our daily life.

In the light of these arguments, I think that we should not engage in a kind of dispute between idealistic ecologists and materialistic economists. We must come to a unified ecological and economic approach. In passing, may I suggest that the etymology of the two words encourages this unity. Whether it was the Greeks themselves who coined these words or whether we did afterwards, it remains the fact that "oikos" is the root of both "economy" and "ecology" and it means "house". The other root in "economy" is "nomos" meaning manage, while "logos" in "ecology" indicates knowledge. Now, how will you manage and act if you don't have knowledge? Economy must go back to ecology; and ecology, to become truly effective must find its own understanding with the economy. I have some difficulties with the Cocoyoc declaration, on "inner" and "outer" limits because, as you have seen, I personally have great difficulties with limits in general, particularly when they become, in the Club of Rome, "limits to growth". I believe that matters are much more fluid and that therefore it is better to speak about the need to find a common approach.

What form should a common approach take? The French President, M. Valery Giscard d'Estaing, recently said that the ecological movement should not just defend the green pastures, but should go a step further and develop a humanistic approach to the operation of economic and social systems. I think that this is the core of the matter. The problem is that the economic approach is too often dealt with as something sectorally independent. Our societies have become so compartmental-ized that each expert has focused on his own little domain; after a while he has come to believe that the whole world is inspired by a single motivating force. Man is motivated by very many impulses, and unless all of them are adequately taken into account, our approaches and answers are bound to be biased and therefore wrong. When the French President argued for a humanistic approach to economic and social systems, he reminded me of something said by Mr. Julius Nyerere,."production is not the purpose of society. When the demand for efficiency and productivity override man's need for a full and good life, the society is no longer serving man, it is using man". I must emphasize that this was said by a leader of a country which is at a very early stage of its development, where the word development is writ large all over the country. Many years earlier, Mahatma Gandhi said "Every machine that helps every individual has a place. But there should be no place for machines that concentrate power in a few hands and turn masses into machine-minders, if indeed they do not make them unemployed."

This brings me to the central theme of our seminar. When, as an economist I read the title of this seminar - Environmental Impact Assessment - I reflect over it, and ask whether we are conveying the proper impression. Does it perhaps suggest to most people that economic action is making an impact on the environment, and that the environment is here just to absorb the so-called side-effects of this human economic action? I strongly urge that the real content and meaning should be

made clear, because what we are after is not corrective action. It would be wrong
to let it appear as if economic action were primordial and environmental considerations merely secondary, being introduced only to correct any ill-effects
which might occur due to economic action. There must be an integrated and true
inter-action of the two. The problem, in my view, is therefore to find appropriate
procedures for comprehensive planning of all those activities where both both
present and future considerations need to be taken into account; economic matters
should have equal weight with matters of a social, cultural or ecological
character. Only if all aspects which contribute to the fullness of our lives are
appropriately taken into account will we have   sound development. In this
approach, it is totally irrelevant whether the rate, the statistical "rate of
growth", is 1, 2, 3, 7 or 12 per cent. What is relevant is the result in quality
terms. This calls for a new approach to development. I think that if anything
has emerged from the very difficult years of the 1970s, it is clear notion which
is being expressed today by such people as the President of the French Republic.
The notion that we cannot continue in the same way as we did in the past; that
there must be a change.

The question if of course: what form should this new pattern of development
achieve? Very often we say we are for the conserver society, we are against the
wasteful society. If I may refer again to the President of France, he had the
courage to say, when the French students went onto the streets in 1968 to condemn
the consumer society, that they were rejecting not only the consumer society, but
also many social values related to it. It takes great courage to say this publicly.
Similarly, when we speak of the new development pattern, we say it must be less
oriented towards consumerism, but I am afraid this is not sufficient to justify
a new development pattern. Again, I would like to quote two statements by men
whose wisdom is universally acknowledged. Bertrand Russell, in his essay on "The
impact of science on society", has the following interesting passage:

> "Man has existed for about a million years. He has possessed writing
> for about 6,000 years, agriculture somewhat longer, but perhaps not
> much longer. Science, as a dominant factor in determining the beliefs
> of educated man, has existed for about 300 years only, as a source of
> economic technique for about 150 years only. In this brief period it
> has proved itself an incredibly powerful revolutionary force. When we
> consider how recently it has risen to power, we find ourselves forced
> to believe we are at the very beginning of its work in transforming
> human life."

This great philospher is telling us that he is convinced we are at the very
beginning of the transformation of life by science. As to how it will be
transformed, I will quote an equally universally-respected economist, Lord keynes,
from his Essays on Persuasion.

> "I draw the conclusion that, assuming no important wars and no
> important increase in population, the economic problem may be
> solved, or be at least within sight of solution, within a hundred
> years. This means the economic problem is not, if we look into
> the future, a permanent problem of the human race."

Imagine an economist saying to the world, that the economic problem is not a
permanent problem of the human race, but he is right. We are truly in the midst
of a process of very fundamental change, but we are like Molière's hero,
M. Jourdain, who found he had been speaking prose all his lifetime, without
knowing it. We are similarly involved in this transformation without being
aware of what a tremendous process it is. It means that, when we speak of
development, we should abandon the so-called gross domestic product (GDP) and,

more than that, we should abandon the idea that development is only about
economics. Development is only in part economic development; basically, it is
societal development; it is cultural development.

If this is to be the new approach which will emerge out of this difficult
experience of the 1970s, the human race will then engage in what is now being
asked for in the General Assembly of the United Nations by the majority of
mankind: the construction of a new world order. The developing countries, which
are in the forefront of this demand, are asking for the restructuring of the
world economy. They are asking for new rules. Sometimes these demands are met
by smiles on the faces of many people living in our own region of the Economic
Commission for Europe. I would like to tell you that I take this thing very
seriously. I went a little way back into history and I came across the Report on
Manufactures produced by Alexander Hamilton, the first Secretary of Finance of
the United States of America. In this report, 200 years ago, he was also arguing
for a new international economic order. He complained of the monopoly of Europe
in the markets to which he wanted access. Similarly I looked into the writings
of Fredrich List, a close friend of Alexander Hamilton, and again I found that
his writing was full of demands for a new world economic order. This demand for
the new order is not something that has emerged only in 1974. It is a recurring
demand of the world's population to have rules that are more suitable for
everybody. I feel therefore that, in meeting our own internal problem in the
developed countries, we must keep very much in mind what is going on in the rest
of the world. If we try to approach our problems by behaving as wealthy islands
in a sea of poverty, we are not likely to succeed.

This takes me from your seminar directly to what I expect to be the main theme
of the seminar in Ljubljana: new lifestyles. The question of lifestyles is not
solely for day-dreamers; indeed the fact that we in the United Nations today
can talk about such delicate matters as lifestyles shows how much progress
human society has made. In earlier times this would have been a question of the
class war. It would have been the proletariat who would have argued for a new
lifestyle and the possessing classes who would have responded: "What do you
mean? We are against that." Today it is the world community which demands a
scientific examination of what kind of lifestyles we should actually strive to
adopt. For it is entirely illogical to demand new development patterns but not
to consider the lifestyles involved. As long ago as 1972 everybody at the United
Nations Conference on the Human Environment in Stockholm pledged himself to take
new environmental approach to energy conservation and similar matters. But we
have seen very little practical results; we are very vocal when it comes to
defending morality and principles, but we are also very pragmatic when it comes
to our daily life. I do not suggest that an international organization should
become a moralistic, semi-ecclesiastic, body, but I think that unless we take
up the question of our lifestyles we will be unable to resolve the problem of
our development pattern. The two are interrelated.

This brings me to another very central item of your seminar, the subject of
popular participation. This is not just a tool, an instrument to achieve better
decisions on development issues. It is an objective as well as an instrument.
People are not content merely to enjoy the good life; they also want to participate in the decisions which bring it about. It is therefore extremely important
to consider how the information will be shared. This is a very delicate matter,
as I would like to illustrate. A few years ago there was a great public protest
over the fumes discharged when jet planes take off; they left behind them a tail
of black smoke, and people protested against this pollution. The manufacturers
sponsored research, and developed new jet engines which avoid this, but the newer
aircraft emit five times as much nitrous oxides as the earlier ones although the
people do not see this. The example indicates to me that we ought not to mobilize

or defuse public opinion by screening the information flow. How to organize the information flow required for popular action and participation in our societies may deserve close attention at this seminar; it will certainly be a matter of great interest at the seminar in Ljubljana.

Lastly, may I raise the question of the international aspects of national activity. The British have a very nice saying that "charity begins at home". I believe that environmental protection also begins at home. In November we will have in ECE the high-level ministerial meeting on transboundary air pollution, non-waste technology and other matters. After the meeting has taken place, the most important task will be to organize the follow-up: for example, how to organize the monitoring and evaluation of the emissions involved in transboundary pollution. I fail to see how such work can proceed unless there is first a solid domestic basis. Unless there are clear national procedures for monitoring and standardization to ensure that data will be comparable internationally, we will be unable to give life and purpose to the convention which will be so solemnly signed and then ratified by all member countries. I feel therefore that your seminar is expected to make a most important contribution to this matter, which is today in the centre of attention for European Governments. For all these and many other reasons, I wish you every success in your work at this seminar.

Environmental Impact Assessment: Procedural and Institutional Questions

The Secretariat

I. BACKGROUND

At a preparatory meeting for the seminar, the secretariat was requested to prepare a paper on the main procedural and institutional questions related to environmental impact assessment. This paper was intended to provide the basis for general debate at the beginning of the seminar. Governments were invited to submit information to the secretariat to assist in preparing this document 1/

It was found that various procedural and institutional arrangements for environmental protection have been introduced in member countries during the last decade and others are in the process of development. Of necessity, these varied according to national differences in political structures and socio-economic systems and also reflected differing ecological and environmental conditions. Many problems facing ECE Governments when devising appropriate institutions and mechanisms for environmental impact assessment are, however, of common concern. In this paper emphasis has been placed on the following aspects:

  (a) procedures for including environmental impact assessment
       in the planning and decision-making process;

  (b) environmental aspects that need to be taken into account and,
       conversely, the types of development activities for which specific
       impact studies are required;

  (c) allocation of responsibility for environmental analyses and
       their review;

  (d) availability of information, including base-line data and monitoring;

  (e) allocation of environmental assessment costs among the parties
       concerned;

  (f) means for public information and involvement, including the

---

1/Information had been received from the following countries: Austria, Canada, Cyprus, Finland, German Democratic Republic, Greece, Ireland, Netherlands, Norway, Poland, Romania, Spain, Sweden, Union of Soviet Socialist Republics, United Kingdom, and United States of America. Use was made as well of other sources of information available to the secretariat on these and other ECE countries. The secretariat also utilized information submitted by the Government of Australia.

possibility of legal appeal of decisions taken on the basis
of environmental impact analysis.

II. <u>PROCEDURAL AND INSTITUTIONAL ASPECTS OF ENVIRONMENTAL IMPACT ASSESSMEN</u>

A. <u>General</u>

In recent years, awareness of potential conflicts between environmental quality and
the scope, scale and impact of development action has grown rapidly in the ECE region; this has led many Governments to examine whether existing planning planning
procedures and policies for environmental protection are sufficient. In most countrie
of the ECE region, the assessment of environmental consequences has usually been a
normal part of the review process required for development proposals and actions
that need authorization from planning authorities. However, it is becoming more
generally accepted that new and improved procedures with emphasis on comprehensive
approaches may be required if environmental considerations are to be given their
proper weight in the process of planning and decision-making.

Existing environmental impact assessment (EIA) procedures in different ECE countries
can be regarded as based either on informal procedures, often modified or adopted
to the needs of individual situations and proposals, or on formal legislation or
methods, specifically designed to ensure an integrated examination of economic,
social and environmental factors affecting a development proposal. Similarly, the
procedures can be characterized either as explicit, and leading to the preparation
of individual environmental impact statements; or as implicit and forming an integral
part of planning, with emphasis on the impact assessment process rather than on the
end product. (1)

Innovations designed to improve and modify earlier procedures have already been
introduced by Governments in several ECE countries. The experience of the United
States has been of particular interest as the National Environmental Protection Act,
which took effect on 1 January 1970, made the improvement of environmental quality
a national policy and the Act required that an environmental impact statement (EIS)
should be prepared by federal agencies for each action that may have significant
consequences for the human environment. Although the United States' procedures might
not be directly transferable to other countries, much has been learned from experien
in implementing the Act.

In several other ECE countries recent or current legislation declares environmental
protection to be a national priority. This action enables environmental consideration
to be integrated into existing planning and administrative frameworks. In some cases,
environmental impact procedures have been incorporated into various planning and
management processes that are required by legal regulations (e.g. physical planning
processes, water management and planning processes, health protection management);
in others, assessment procedures are essential elements in the various forms of secto
planning (e.g. road construction, agriculture). In several countries, Governments
have adopted procedures similar to those required in the United States, although
these procedures may be introduced through administrative measures or agreement among
the authorities concerned as, for example, in Canada, rather than through legislation.
A few Governments have indicated that a formal environmental impact assessment proces
has not yet been adopted in their countries, but several references were made to the
need to develop more comprehensive legislation for impact assessment.

The central planning systems of eastern European countries provide a broad framework
enabling environmental considerations to be incorporated in planning and management,
from long-term plans (up to 1990) at national and regional levels down to local and
individual projects that are already included in current plans. The annual and
medium-term plans that are established by law as the basis for development contain
environmental indicators and concrete targets covering a wide range of environmental

impacts. Techniques and operational procedures are being developed to apply environmental impact analyses in the preparation of subregional plans for selected areas.

The wide variety of national experience in regard to impact assessment procedures
makes a more detailed comparative analysis desirable, even though precise comparisons
may be difficult or impossible. Among the important questions to be noted in such
an analysis are the following:

(a) Are procedures based on legislation or administrative measures?

(b) Is EIA considered to be an addition to existing procedures, or is
it incorporated more generally in procedures affecting several
broad policy areas?

(c) Is EIA required for both public and private development proposals
and actions?

(d) Is EIA applied to policies, plans and programmes or is it restricted
to individual projects?

(e) At what levels of activity is EIA used: national, federal, regional,
local?

(f) Is the assessment mainly confined to impacts on the physical and
biological environment or are socio-economic concernes also taken
into account?

Increasing attention is being given to the assessment of environmental impacts of
development action beyond administrative and political boundaries. Within national
boundaries, and especially in federal States such as Canada where jurisdiction is
divided between the national and the provincial Governments, different procedures
for environmental impact analyses may be adopted by the various authorities, raising
problems in the compatibility of EIA requirements. In the United States many states
have introduced requirements similar to the National Environmental Policy Act (NEPA);
others are considering legislation based on a model document, the State Environmental
Policy Act. Such developments at the state government level are considered to be of
great potential importance in the extension of environmental impact assessment
procedures to activities beyond those in which the federal Government is involved.

At the international level, environmental impact assessment is considered to be a
powerful tool for handling transboundary problems. EIA procedures have already been
utilized in such situations and their wider application is envisaged.
Reference can be made to relevant activities by many bodies such as: the International
Bank for Reconstruction and Development (IBRD), which examines the environmental
implications of investment proposals; the Council of Europe (CE); the Organisation
for Economic Co-operation and Development (OECD); the Council for Mutual Economic
Assistance (CMEA), through its development of a unified regionally-applied environmental impact analysis procedure; and the International Union for Conservation of
Nature and Natural Resources (IUCN). At the subregional level, several steps have
been taken with regard to applying environmental impact assessment in frontier
areas (in the framework of CMEA and the Nordic Council).

In 1977, the International Institute for Environment and Development (IIED) made a
"Study of the Environmental Procedures and Practices of Nine Development Financing
Agencies". It examined the attitudes and approaches of institutions such as:
the European Development Bank (EDB); the Inter-American Development Bank (IDB);
International Bank for Reconstruction and Development (IBRD); and the United Nations
Development Programme (UNDP). Four criteria regarding development and environment
were put forward: development must be to meet critical human needs; the needs of

future generations must be protected; international development institutions have
a responsibility to propose and encourage the modification of projects which otherwise would harm the health or quality of life of the people involved, unacceptably
deplete resources, or harm the physical systems on which human welfare depends;
institutions should consider reorienting their programmes, and consequently their
projects, to reflect a more conservation-oriented use of resources and more sustainable forms of development.

In addition to the activities of individual member countries, the commission of the
European Communities has had under consideration since 1975 a proposal to create a
broad impact assessment system covering all members of the European Community. In
May 1977, the Council of Ministers sanctioned an updated programme of action on the
environment that authorized the Commission to study "how procedures for assessing
impact on the environment might be applied in the Community and in the Member
States. (2) Several studies have been prepared by consultants to provide a basis for
the determination by the Commission of appropriate actions.(3)

Further recognition of the importance of applying environmental impact assessment in
an international framework is evident in the treaty on international environmental
assessment, now under consideration by the Senate of the United States. One of its
primary purposes is to seek agreement among Governments for the preparation of an
international environmental assessment for any major project, action or continuing
activity that may reasonably be expected to have a significant adverse effect on the
physical environment or environmental interests of another nation or the "global
commons". One provision of the proposed treaty is that parties undertaking major
projects should consult with the affected party or parties (or, in the case of action
affecting the global commons, with the United Nations Environment Programme), in
order to prevent or minimize potentially adverse transboundary environmental effects.

B. Procedures for including environmental impact assessment in the
    planning and decision-making process in selected countries

This section summarizes, country-by-country, the information submitted or available
to the secretariat on existing procedures and institutions in ECE member countries.
Particular emphasis has been placed on the way in which environmental impact assessment has become part of the planning and decision-making process. It also takes into
account at what stage of development action the assessment takes place.

Austria

Several administrative regulations provide for the inclusion of environmental considerations into planning and decision-making processes. Relevant bodies involved
are: the Federal Ministry of Health and Environmental Protection (at the federal
level); and, at the state level, the Working Party on Environmental Protection that
has been created within the framework of the Conference of State Governors. A licensing procedure has been introduced which, in accordance with the 1973 Industrial
Code (section 79), requires that a special permit should be obtained for installations that are likely to cause adverse environmental effects. This procedure also
requires that, prior to the issue of a permit, consultations should be held among
appropriate federal ministries, including the Federal Ministry of Health and Environmental Protection, to ensure that environmental considerations are taken into account
The recent Environmental Bill has been developed to ensure that all institutions
concerned, as well as the public, become more actively involved in environmental
protection procedures.

Several recent studies were commissioned by the Federal Ministry of Health and
Environmental Protection (e.g."Safeguarding Environmental Interests in Low", December
1977, and "Consideration of environmental protection aspects in administrative procedures", December 1976). These studies propose legal, procedural and administrative

measures with regard to environmental impact assessment in Austria.(5)

Belgium

Requirements for assessment are contained in physical planning and pollution control legislation; this also establishes the procedures for authorizing new development projects. The General Regulation for the Protection of Labour, dating back to 1888, has been amended and supplemented to include, among other provisions, a requirement for the supply of information on the pollution aspects of a project, before permission to proceed is given. Separate provisions exist for the environmental impact assessment of nuclear power plants.

The inclusion of environmental considerations in the planning processes is at present based on the 1962 Law on Urban and Regional Planning, which introduced a land-use zoning concept at the national level. A special construction authorization procedure has been established by the Department of Public Works which ensures that zoning conditions are met before a permit is granted. The development of a more formal environmental impact assessment process is at present a priority activity in the Ministry for Public Health and the Environment. It is intended to have draft legislation available for consideration by 1980.

Bulgaria

Increased attention is being given to incorporate environmental factors into operational planning within the general, centralized planning system. At the regional level a comprehensive methodological approach for economic and non-economic evaluation of man's impact on the environment is being used on a trial basis for several regions of Bulgaria.

Canada

A federal Environmental Assessment Review Process (EARP) was adopted by the Government in December 1973 and amended in February 1977. The process does not rely on a legal instrument, but on a firm agreement by federal government ministers that they will accept responsibility for the environmental consequences of activities of their departments, including the incorporation of suitable mitigating measures. EARP refers only to the federal role in environmental assessment; constitutionally, the responsibility for environmental matters is shared between the federal government and the ten provinces of Canada. A Federal Environmental Assessment Review Office (FEARO) has been created to administer EARP; it reports to the Minister of the Environment.

The objectives of EARP are to ensure that federal departments and agencies: take environmental matters into account throughout the planning and implementation of development action; carry out an assessment of potential environmental effects before commitments or irrevocable decisions are made (Assessments of projects which may have significant effects must be submitted to the Minister of the Environment for review.); incorporate the results of these assessments in planning, decision--making and implementation.

EARP is based on the self-assessment approach: departments and agencies are responsible for assessing the environmental consequences of their own programmes, projects and activities, or those which they sponsor, and they must decide upon the environmental significance of the anticipated effects. Consideration of the significance of potentially adverse effects depends initially on the judgement of technical and environmental specialists. The process begins as early in the planning phase as possible, with screening by the responsible department or agency of potential adverse environmental effects of a proposed development or activity. This is intended to reach one of three possible decisions: (a) there are no anticipated adverse effects, or the effects are known and are not considered significant; (b) the nature and scope

of potential environmental effects cannot be readily determined during preliminary
screening; (c) the anticipated adverse environmental effects are considered to be
significant and the project therefore requires a formal review by an Environmental
Panel. In case of category "a", no further EARP action is required, but the department concerned is responsible for implementing measures to prevent or mitigate any
environmental effects identified. In the case of inability to identify the full
environmental consequences (category "b"), the project is subjected to a more
searching examination called the Initial Environmental Evaluation (IEE); Guidelines
issued by FEARO are available to the federal department to prepare this document;
advisory services are available to departments and agencies on a regional basis.
Based on the IEE review, a firm decision is made to allocate the project to either
categories "a" or "c".

For projects in category "c", an Environmental Assessment is established, the panel
for each project having its composition, functions and responsibilities defined in
terms of the particular problems involved. One of the first tasks of the panel is
to develop specific guidelines for the preparation of an Environmental Impact Statement (EIS). This must be a detailed, documented assessment of the environmental
consequences associated with the projects, and it will be prepared or commissioned
by the department responsible for the project. The Environmental Assessment Panel
then reviews the EIS, obtains the public's response to it, and submits a report to
the Minister of the Environment, with recommendations concerning project implementation. The Minister of the Environment and the Minister of the initiating department then decide on the action to be taken.

Cyprus

At present, the Government of Cyprus is considering the possibility of establishing
a central body on environmental problems. However, existing legal and administrative
procedures have so far prevented the occurrence of serious environmental degradation
resulting from development and it is therefore felt in Cyprus that, at present, there
is no pressing need for an obligatory environmental impact statement procedure.

Although no comprehensive legislation on environmental protection exists, there are
provisions and regulations under numerous laws dealing with environmental conservation and control of pollution. An established administrative policy is that the
authorities responsible for various types of physical development should consult
the governmental bodies responsible for protection of particular aspects of the
environment, before issuing a licence or permit for a development project (quarry,
mine, hotel, factory, etc.). In addition to statutory requirements, restrictions
suggested by these bodies are often incorporated in such licences.

Czechoslovakia

Environmental considerations are included in the planning system at various levels.
A detailed evaluation of potential environmental problems must be prepared by the
proponents of a project proposal. A "Methodology for economic and non-economic
assessment of man's impact on the environment" has been prepared under the sponsor-
ship of the Institute of Geography of the Czechoslovak Academy of Science; it has
been applied on a trial basis in several regions among various members of the Council
for Mutual Economic Assistance (CMEA) in countries that are at different levels and
have ranging scales of economic, industrial and social development. The Ostrava
region of Czechoslovakia is one industrialized area where the methodology has been
used.

Denmark

Although no formal procedure for environmental impact has been introduced in Denmark,
various laws contain provisions for evaluating environmental aspects of development

proposals. Under the National and Regional Planning Act of 1973, the regional councils are required, on the basis of information provided by local councils, to prepare regional plans containing alternative proposals. The proposals must include guidelines on future urban development, the location of major technical installations and road systems, and the siting of enterprises. Draft regional plans must be made public; final approval rests with the Minister for Environmental Protection. It is proposed that all regional plans should be approved by January 1980.

One of the basic instruments of environmental assessment is the authorization system under the Environmental Protection Act of 1973 which requires that types of development that may severely affect the environment (listed in the annex to the Act) should not go ahead without an authorization given by local or regional authorities. This authorization system does not include major roads and railways. Decisions made by local and regional authorities may be appealed to the National Agency of Environmental Protection and subsequently to the Environmental Appeal Board. Guidelines have been issued by the National Agency for Environmental Protection to help relevant authorities to operate the authorization system.

The recent Nuclear Power Stations Act contains provisions for environmental impact assessment of nuclear energy facilities.

More generally, attention is being given to the introduction of environmental quality standards and the mapping of ambient pollution and pollution sources as a means to integrate environmental considerations into physical planning.

Finland

Environmental impact assessment procedures are basically incorporated in the physical planning process, established by the Planning and Building Act of 1958. Water management and planning aspects are similarly based on the Water Act of 1962 and health protection management on the Public Health Act of 1965. Comprehensive legislation concerning environmental impact statements has so far not been developed in Finland, but the Planning and Buildings Act is under revision, and one objective is to integrate environmental impact assessment requirements more effectively into planning and building legislation.

On the basis of existing legislation, developers must seek (a) a concession from the Ministry of Commerce and Industry; (b) siting permission from the Public Health Board of the municipality; (c) a permit from the Water Court; and (d) building permission from the Building Board of the municipality. If a detailed town plan or area plan exists an opportunity to comment on proposals before building permission is granted.

France

The 1976 Nature Conservation Act provides a legal framework for the introduction of an environmental impact statement procedure in France. The law requires all planning projects, including urban development plans, carried out by public authorities, or those requiring administrative authorization, to take account of environmental considerations. This general mandate provides an opportunity to incorporate such considerations in most existing decision-making processes. The law also requires impact statements as part of the studies preceding developments which, because of their size or potential influence, could threaten the environment.

The Nature Conservation Act of 10 July 1976 and governmental decree of 10 October 1977 implementing the Act came into force on 1 January 1978. The decree contains a list of activities exempted from statement procedures because their probable impact on the environment is considered to be small. These include maintenance and repair work and new projects which are exempted according to certain technical criteria or with estimated costs under six million francs.

The proponent, in most cases, is responsible for the preparation of an impact statement. When applying for planning permission, the impact statement should include the
following: (a) analytical description of the state of the site and its environment;
(b) analyses of impacts on the environment; (c) reasons why the proposed development
has been chosen, compared to possible alternatives; (d) description of measures that
will be taken to mitigate possible adverse effects on the environment, and the costs
involved.

German Democratic Republic

The state planning system in the German Democratic Republic, together with legal
and economic directives, allow consideration of environmental concerns in planning
the comprehensive development of the national economy. Present laws and regulations
provide a basis for environmental impact assessment procedures.

The law for the systematic implementation of socialist environmental policy established statutory goals for development planning in regard to the relationship
between economic and environmental factors in all branches of the national economy.
"Regulations for the regional distribution of investments" lay down that, for all
central projects (planned by the State Planning Commission) and any local investment in excess of 100,000 marks, the required councils have to prepare site development proposals, taking into account all legal obligations for the protection and
management of the environment. In addition, local authorities may set specific
requirements for the investment contractor concerning environmental protection and
they may require environmental impact statements by experts.

A standard process for preparing comprehensive environmental impact statements in
a uniform form does not yet exist, although research on this is in progress. In the
framework of CMEA several institutes are also working on the "Methodology for
economic and non-economic assessment of man's impact on the environment". The law
provides for comparisons of alternative ways to implement a planning development,
in appropriate circumstances.

Germany, Federal Republic of

The Federal Cabinet of 1975 adopted "Principles for assessing the environmental
compatibility of public measures taken by the Federation". All federal authorities
and agencies are required to examine and take into account at the earliest possible
stage any harmful effects upon the environment caused by activities within their
jurisdiction.

Two essential elements enter into any assessment of environmental compatibility:
(a) a requirement to evaluate the proposed measure in terms of environmental policy;
and (b) an obligation to consult expert agencies where this is necessary. At present,
this process is being extended to the federal states (Länder). Through various
federal laws on regional planning, building and emissions, the Federal Government
has an indirect influence on the assessment of environmental consequences of
development proposals. At the Länder level various plans, including regional,
land-use and zoning plans, create a basis for adequate evaluation of environmental
considerations.

Greece

In recent years there has been a major reassessment of environmental protection
strategies by both public and private sectors in Greece. As a result, the following
major events have occurred: (a) an article on environmental protection has been
included in the country's new constitution; (b) a Secretariat of the National

Council on Physical Planning and the Environment has been created, to co-ordinate and promote activities related to issues of environment and planning; (c) environ- mental protection issues have been included in the recently-prepared Five- year Development Plan for Greece; (d) Law 360/1976 pertaining to environmental and physical planning issues has been ratified recently by the Greek parliament.

The introduction of environmental impact studies into Greek legislation is now under examination by a body sponsored by the Secretariat of the National Council on Physical Planning and the Environment.

Hungary

The national economic plan provides the resources and authority to implement a programme for environmental protection by the competent institutions. In cases where economic development and environmental problems are closely linked, the Government creates bodies to ensure co-ordinated implementation of the economic and the environmental protection tasks. An example of this was the complex development programme of the Balaton region, where the Government created a commission composed of ministers and heads of other bodies with national authority.

Relying on environmetal analyses, the competent authorities work out recommendations or issue instructions regarding the development of individual sectors of the national economy. Governmental decrees stipulate that the possible impact of a project on the environment must be determined at the time of project formulation, and these provisions are now being revised to encourage a more uniform approach to the assess- ment process and to incorporate this procedure into the decision-making process

Ireland

Under Section 24 of the Local Government (Planning of Development) Act, 1963, permission must be obtained from the local planning authority for practically any development. This Act empowers the Minister for the Environment to make regulations requiring applicants to furnish to the Minister, and to any other specified persons, any specified information with respect to their applications. This was amended by Section 39 (a) of the Local Government Planning and Development Act, 1976 so that an EIS is required for all projects costing more than a sum specified in regulations (at present £5 million). Regulations made under the 1963 and 1976 legislation were issued in 1977 to effect this procedure.

An application for permission for development which is likely to pollute, and which is likely to cost more than five million pounds, must be accompanied by an impact study. It is expected that the developer will consult with the Planning Authority which has absolute discretion as to whether or not an environmental study should be done if not already provided. A planning authority may declare that an environ- mental study is unnecessary when the development, though large, would have little or no polluting capacity (or have only a small and well-understood pollution element), or in cases when the development is of a type for which full particulars are already available to the planning authority.

Netherlands

At present there is no general legislation in the Netherlands providing for stan- dardized systematic assessment of the environmental impacts of proposed activities. In individual cases, however, documents with the characteristics of impact state- ments, have been prepared. The requirements of the various environmental protection laws vary a great deal, although all provide for licensing procedures. These proce- dures generally require an assessment of particular expected emissions, e.g. the Nuisance Act, the Water Pollution Act and the Air Pollution Act, the Pesticides Act. These require that potentially harmful effects of new compounds should be analysed prior to the marketing of products. The Nuclear Energy Act requires a safety report, covering the measures envisaged to protect man and the environment. While Dutch legislation on environmentl protection does not cover all activities affecting the environment – such as road planning, urban development or mining – these are covered by legislation whose function is not primarily the protection of the environment. This category shows great variation. A third category of activities is not covered by any law. By 1 January 1980 an environmental protection act will take effect; it will contain uniform provisions on consultation with agencies and public participation in the licencing procedures relating to a number of environmental laws.

In preparation for the introduction of environmental impact assessment in the Netherlands, numerous   trial environmental impact assessments have been carried out by consulting firms under the aegis of the Ministry of Health and Environmental Protection. Both governmental and private plans and projects were selected for these trial runs. The four reports resulting from the runs, and the complementary research which was carried out at the same time, form the main basis for the introduction of environmental impact assessment in the Netherlands. By mid-1979 a document will be completed presenting the governmental standpoint concerning the basic principles for legislation on environmental impact assessment. The bill will be submitted to parliament by January 1981.

Norway

New legislation has been passed, or is proposed, to give clearer guidelines for the environmental impact assessment process. The Establishment Control Act of 1977 provides that decisions shall be taken by central authorities after a collective evaluation of all larger industrial undertakings, for example, irrespective of the planned locality, taking into account social interests, economic balance, the labour market and protection of the environment. Other legislation related to impact assessment includes the Building Act, the Water Pollution Act and the Neighbourhood Act which covers air pollution.

A new Planning Act and a comprehensive Pollution Act, which are at present being examined by the central authorities include regulations requiring impact assessment of measures and enterprises with potential effects on the environment. The Planning Act will include regulations covering the use of impact statements in all sectors. Within this general framework, the comprehensive Pollution Act will give detailed regulations concerning pollution effects.

According to these legislative proposals, environmental impact assessments must be as detailed as necessary to clarify the most important anticipated effects of an enterprise on the environment. The authorities responsible for granting permission for the enterprise will determine the scope and depth of the studies to be performed.

Poland

Environmental considerations are incorporated in the planning system at various levels, national, regional and local. One basic task is to improve co-ordination of economic and territorial planning. With regard to the location of the development proposals, the 1971 decree of the Central Planning Commission requires that applications for site approval must outline the predicted effects on the environment, especially on agricultural and forest lands and on water resources.

Spain

According to regulations of October 1976, the authorities may request an impact assessment before issuing a permit for a development classified as potentially capable of polluting the atmosphere. While impact assessment of air quality for various development proposals is specifically required by legislation, a broader procedure exists called the public review period. During this period, objections may be raised to development proposals that could have adverse effects on the environment especially on water or soil. Proponents must obtain authorization from the appropriate ministry in order to proceed with a given project. In cases where a project relates to the responsibilities of several ministries, the project proposed is forwarded to the "Comision Inter Ministrial del Medio Ambiente" (C.I.M.A.) for examination. The C.I.M.A. consists of representatives from a number of ministries concerned with the environment. If the impact assessment is adequate, and the environmental impacts are acceptable, approval is given to proceed to the Public Review Process. After this period, the ministry responsible decides the conditions to be imposed and gives authorization to proceed with a project.

At present, a general law on the environment and a new water protection law are under consideration by the Spanish authorities. Under this new legisltion comprehensive environmental impact assessment procedures will be introduced.

Sweden

Several acts prescribe environmental impact assessment in Sweden. According to section 136(a) of the Building Act, proposals for new or expanded industrial enterprises affecting the country's environment must be subjected to impact assessment. In developing regional and industrial policies, a comprehensive assessment of conditions for environmental protection and planning is required. Questions of land-use and the more detailed design of industrial areas and their surroundings are governed by other provisions of the Act. A permit will be issued by the Government only if the local community affected by the location of a project is favourable to it. If permission is granted under the Building Act, the application is normally subjected to more detailed and further examination under the Environmental Protection Act, the Water Act, and various other specialized acts. Questions concerning the environmental effects of activities through the discharge of pollutants, etc., are handled under the Environmental Protection Act, while project affecting water in lakes, watercourses or groundwater resources are dealt with under the Water Act. Assessment under section 136(a) of the Building Act has been co-ordinated with other acts in such a way that government decisions under this provision are binding and related to subsequent assessments under the Environmental Protection Act and the other provisions of the Building Act.

Switzerland

The regulations for implementation of the Federal Nature and Landscape Conservation Act 1966 enable the authorities granting concessions, permits or subsidies to request from the Federal Committee for the Protection of Nature and Landscapes expert advice on development proposals and to ask for a statement by the proponent on the way in which nature and landscape protection requirements can be taken account.

The introduction of a formal environmental impact statement procedure is at present under examination. The proposed Federal Environmental Protection Bill contains provisions for impact statements for construction or conversion of facilities which may adversely change the environment.

Union of Soviet Socialist Republics

Environmental Impact Assessment is incorporated at various levels within the State planning system. A special section on environmental protection and rational use of natural resources has been added to State plans for economic and social development by a governmental decree of 1972. During the development of plans for environmental protection by the State Planning Committee, and various Ministries and

Councils of Ministers of Soviet Republics, the following factors are taken into consideration: trends in regional changes of the state of the environment as a result of use of natural resources and pollution; utilization of a system analysis approach to determine necessary measures of environmental protection; integration of planning at various levels; obligatory financial support for planned measures for environmental protection.

The development of plans for environmental protection and rational use of natural resources is made on the basis of 220 different indicators. Plan directives, when approved, must be implemented by the institutions concerned (ministries, local authorities, enterprises and organizations). During the preparation of plans, much attention is given to the problems of development and location and the distribution of activity; a basic criterion is that environmental damage should be as little as possible. Before a decision is adopted on the location of a new enterprise, the planning authorities should take into account the current ecological situation in the region and the potential increase of pollution; this should not exceed permissible levels established by state authorities.

In addition, according to regulations issued by the State Building Committee in 1976 the project design document for construction of industrial enterprises should contain a chapter which considers measures to be taken to mitigate or to avoid environmental degradation.

A new dimension in the field of environmental impact assessment in the Soviet Union is the development and implementation of specific goal-oriented programmes for environmental protection and improvement. Ecological forecasting (both sectoral and regional) will provide a scientific basis for the analysis of possible changes in the state of the environment resulting from development of various branches of the national economy. The USSR Council of Ministers recently created the State Committee on Hydrometeorology and Environmental Control with wide responsibilities in the field of environmental protection. One of the Committee's tasks is the organization and utilization of environmental expertise at the site planning stage. It may be mentioned that the "Methodology for economic and non-economic assessment of man's impact on environment", recently developed in the framework of CMEA, has been tested in the Kursk region.

United Kingdom

There is no statutory requirement for any specific form of environmental impact assessment in the United Kingdom. Consideration of environmental factors is an integral part of the planning process under the Town and Country Planning legislation. The major components of the planning system are: the non-statutory regional strategies produced by the Regional Economic Planning Councils; development plans prepared by local planning authorities; and the development control functions exercised be these authorities. Structure plans are designed to set out the main policies for each county, covering land use and other factors which will influence the future of the area.

This system is designed to ensure the wise use of land for the benefit of the community, taking into account social, economic and environmental factors and balancing the potentially conflicting demands of different land uses. Environmental factors are considered when structure plans and local plans are drawn up or revised. Local planning authorities are obliged to asess, among other things, measures for improvement of the physical environment, and to incorporate them in their plans for development and other use of land. Environmental matters also play as large a part as the planning authority thinks necessary in the examination of proposals for individual development projects. Specific environmental impact assessment may be employed in major developments on the initiative of the developer or the planning authority. The Government encourages their use in appropriate cases together with industrial, employment, social, health and safety, land use and other implications.

To assist in deciding whether formal changes in administrative procedures for authorizing major development project are necessary or desirable, the Government sponsored several reports on environmental impact analysis, and its integration into existing planning and decision-making systems. (Environmental Impact Analysis", DOE research report 11, prepared by J. Catlow and C.C. Thirlwall, 1977; "Assessment of Major Industrial Applications", DOE research report 13, 1976). These reports have been published by the governmental authorities as research papers without commitment. The recommendations in these reports, however, suggest ways in which EIA can be incorporated into the existing planning framework without changing the system as a whole.

United States

In 1969 the United States, through the National Environmental Policy Act (NEPA), established a far-reaching process that requires federal agencies to analyse the impacts of their proposed decisions and alternatives. Before taking major actions with significant impact on the human environment, federal agencies must prepare analyses as part of a public document known as the Environmental Impact Statement (EIS). NEPA has been formally implemented through Executive Order 11514 and guidelines issued by the Council on Environmental Quality (CEQ), which was established by NEPA as an agency in the Executive Office of the President. To date, CEQ has issued several sets of guidelines; the most recent was released in November 1978. Taking into account a decade of experience and problems related to the implementation of NEPA, the new guidelines establish the comprehensive procedural structure for the impact statement process. Federal agencies are required by law to follow these regulations and to issue their own implementing procedures, consistent with the CEQ regulations, which must explain how the regulations apply to their specific activities. This recent CEQ effort has been mainly directed towards making the entire environmental review process more useful to decision-makers and to the public - by reducing delay and papework, by integrating environmental concerns into daily government operations, and by transforming the EIS document itself into a meaningful tool. Some of the major innovative provisions of the regulations include the establishment of: (a) the scoping process; (b) standard forecast for evaluating environmental impacts; (c) pre-decision referral process; (d) record of decision; and (e) overall institutional framework for environmental impact assessment.

The process can be divided into several major stages. A federal agency has to determine whether a proposed action requires the preparation of an impact statement. If an action under consideration may affect the environment, the agency must prepare an "environmental assessment" at the same time as it prepares other feasibility analyses, whether technical, economic or legal. If the assessment shows that the environmental effects may be "significant", the agency is required to prepare an EIS. If not, the agency makes a "finding of no significant impact" available to the public and uses the assessment internally to consider what environmental measures should be adopted to ensure minimum impact.

If an EIS is required, the agency issues a "notice of intent" to prepare a statement and announces the commencement of a "scoping process" to determine the proper content ("scope") of the statement. The scoping process enables other agencies which have expertise, or which share some decision-making authority over the proposal, to join with interested parties. This scoping process is designed to avoid subsequent criticism that essential matters were overlooked in the EIS. The lead agency prepares a draft EIS which is filed with the Environmental Protection Agency and circulated for at least 45 days to agencies and the public for comment. After revising the draft in the light of comments received, the agency files and circulates a "final" EIS at least 30 days prior to making a decision. When a decision is made, the head agency makes available a formal "record of decision" which explains the decision, states any mitigation and monitoring measures to be taken, and identifies the environmentally preferable alternative(s).

A recent Executive Order requires all federal agencies to review the environmental effects of any actions which might affect the global commons or the environment of another nation. The order is understood to include such activities as the export of nuclear reactors, assistance for projects such as a dam in one country which could affect the flow of water in another, and activities that could have an ecological impact on major global resources, as in tropical forests.

C. Scope of Environmental Impact Assessment

In this section, procedural questions related to the scope of environmental impact assessment are considered, including (i) the types of impacts; (ii) the range of environmental considerations that are taken into account; (iii) the field of application of EIA (i.e. the types of development activities that are covered).

(i) Types of impacts to be assessed

From the responses received from Governments by the secretariat, EIA appears to be regarded as a tool capable of being used in the assessment of a variety of impacts of a proposed activity or project. They include both direct and indirect (secondary and tertiary) impacts, and both immediate and long-term impacts is of great importance as they are often not considered, for various reasons, by planners, decision--makers or the local people concerned. The EIA process should also identify and give due importance to possible irreversible effects on environment and society. The destruction of a species, a monument or a work of art or the disruption of the climatic balance, could lead to a significant deterioration of the environment and human well-being.

(ii) Range of environmental considerations examined

One important objective of environmental impact assessment is to foster in the decision-making process a continuing awareness of environmental considerations. This can be achieved if environmental aspects are included in existing assessment procedures. Much attention has been given in ECE countries to the problem of how comprehensive environmental concern can be integrated into socio--economic planning and management. According to the nature, scale and location of proposed actions, a great diversity of environmental factors is potentially relevent; a partial list to illustrate the difficulties of achieving a comprehensive assessment may include: air quality (diffusion factor, particulates, nitrogen and sulphur oxides, carbon monoxide, photochemical oxidants, odours), water quality and quantity (flow variations; presence of suspended solids, oil, thermal pollution, biochemical oxygen demand (BOD); toxic compounds; aquatic life); land (erosion; natural hasards, land use patterns); ecology (animals, both wild and domestic, birds, fish, waterfowl, endangered species, natural land vegetation, aquatic plants); sound (physiological; psychological; communication); resources(fuel, materials, products, aesthetics); and socio-economic and human concerns (employment; lifestyles; psychological and community needs). (6)

Almost all facets of the human environment, therefore, may be affected to a greater or lesser extent by a development proposal. Systematic evaluation and assessment of all such interactions is seldom either necessary or practical. All too often in the past, environmental impact assessments and studies have included as an essential element comprehensive "state of the system" surveys (species lists, soil conditions and the like), often expensive to prepare, but yielding little more than a mass of uninterpreted and descriptive data. Typically also, much emphasis has been given to physical and biological impacts while the effects on communities and social systems have not always received proper attention.

While, therefore, environmental considerations should in principle be taken into account in the widest possible sense, a very practical question is the extent to which the decision-making process can, or should, accommodate the full range of environmental factors. It seems to be agreed that environmental dimensions should be introduced and, as far as possible, defined at the very beginning of the development or policy design process. (7)

In Canada, the Federal Environmental Assessment Review Process is concerned with impacts on the natural environment and its ecological systems including man. Environmental factors are accorded the same degree of consideration as economic, social and engineering aspects. Both immediate and long-term considerations are taken into account.

In Norway, the following factors are the subject of environmental impact analyses: current use and development possibilities of the natural resources concerned; pollution of air, water or soil, including the effects that may be expected as a result both of normal activities and accidents; effects on landscape, local climate and on biological and ecological systems. These requirements will be co-ordinated and made more specific in the forthcoming Pollution Act. According to the new Planning Act, now in preparation, other aspects can also be made the subject of impact assessment requirements, notably socio-economic and regional impacts, including counter-measures against adverse effects.

In the Soviet Union, environmental considerations have been integrated into existing annual and long-term planning systems, so as to develop and adopt anticipatory policies related to prevention of environmental deterioration. These policies relate, inter alia, to water pollution and the rational use of water resources; air pollution; and land use; rational use of forests; establishment of nature reserves; and the determination of the volume of investments required for environmental protection measures.

In land use planning in Finland, the scope of the environmental considerations required is laid down in the Planning and Building Statute and in regulations concerning detailed planning principles. Normally the following elements are included: a general description of the landscape; surface formation; soil, building capacity, groundwater and surface water analyses; climatic assessment, vegetation and fauna analyses. In addition, a land use plan should cover culturally and historically valuable areas; cultural landscape features; recreational areas and sites, etc. The major "disturbance factors" are also taken into account: noise level; soil, air, water and coastal pollution, vegetation disturbance, erosion problems. The scope of environmental considerations regarding both water and air quality planning and management are carefully set out in special regulations.

In the United Kingdom there is no limit to the scope of the environmental considerations that may be taken into account, and the decision-making process is designed to be sufficiently flexible to accommodate all relevent aspects. Each assessment is, so far as possible, tailored to needs, as indicated by the scale, complexity and location of the proposed development. The recent enquiry into the proposed development of plant and associated facilities for reprocessing irradiated nuclear fuels at Windscale provides an illustration of the considerable range of factors that may be taken into account in a major planning decision.

When considering a decision on project implementation in Spain the main emphasis has been on maintaining the required standards of air quality. Air pollution should not exceed the established admissible emission levels. A developer of a project may have to submit information on possible environmental impacts in order to determine that these impacts are within the permitted range.

In Ireland the extent of the environmental study is determined according to Section

39 of the Local Government Planning and Development Act 1976 and Article 28 of the 1977 Regulations; these apply to any development action "which would result in the emission of noise, vibration, smell, fumes, smoke, soot, ash, dust or grit or the discharge of any liquid or other effluent (whether treated or untreated) either with or without particles of matter in suspension therein". Development plans in urban areas must show objectives for rational land use, redevelopment of obsolete or badly laid out areas, and the preservation of amenities, such as parks and recreation areas. In rural areas the plan must also include extension of water and sewerage services. A number of trial environmental impact assessments have been carried out on the advice of the provisional central council for environmental protection. These have been concentrated on the primary and secondary effects of proposed activities on the physical environment, including air, water and soil pollution, impacts on ecosystems, effects of noise and protection of nature and the landscape.

In a contribution submitted to the secretariat for information by the Government of Australia, it is noted that the definition of "environment" in the Environment Protection (Impact of Proposals) Act 1979 includes all aspects of the surroundings of man, whether affecting him as an individual or in his social groupings. Environmental assessments should take into account whether proposed actions may result in: (a) substantial environmental effects on a community; (b) substantial impacts on the ecosystems of an area; (c) diminution of the aesthetic, recreational, scientific or other environmental quality or value; (d) endangering of any species of fauna or flora; (e) pollution of the environment; (f) environmental problems associated with the disposal of waste; (g) increased demands on natural resources which are in short supply; (h) curtailing the range of beneficial uses of the environment, as well as long-term effects on the environment. However, although the Act ensures that these considerations are taken into account in the decision-making process, there is no power to enforce decision-makers to accept environmental recommendations concerning the proposed action.

According to new regulations issued by the Council of Environmental Quality (CEQ) for implementing the National Environmental Policy Act (NEPA) of the United States, the significant issues related to a proposed action must be determined by an open process prior to an assessment. "Human Environment" is interpreted comprehensively to include the natural 2/ and physical environment and the relatioship of people to that environment. Effects taken into account include ecological (including effects on natural resources), aesthetic, historic, cultural, economic, social, and health impacts, both beneficial and detrimental. Economic or social effects should not themselves require preparation of an environmental reasons, related social and economic effects are to be taken into account. (8)

The following environmental amenities are those most frequently protected or enhanced as a result of the NEPA environmental impact statement process: wetlands; floodplains; endangered species (and their habitats); prime agricultural lands; open space and recreatical land; aquifer recharge areas (groundwater); surface water quality or quantity; wild and scenic rivers; historic and archaeological sites; and other amenities, such as the prevention or reduction of urban sprawl.

(iii) Field of application of environmental impact assessment

In order to integrate environmental considerations more completely into socio-economic planning and decision-making, there is a widespread feeling that it is not sufficient to work only at the individual project level. Environmental impact procedures may also be needed for national (regional, sectoral, local and land-use) plans, research and development programmes, as well as for legislative proposals. However, because methodologies for the assessment of the complex plans and programmes are

---

2/ The CEQ's new guidelines clarify what are considered as significant effects that should be included in the preparation of an environmental impact statement.

not well-developed, Governments in ECE countries in many cases currently limit assessment to individual projects.

At the project level, the general trend is to provide for assessment of new development actions which are (a) directly undertaken by public authorities; (b) totally or partly funded by public authorities; or (c) subject to governmental licensing or permit procedures. In some cases, one criterion to identify projects that require environmental impact assessment is the estimated cost of implementation of a proposed project (i.e. national regulations specify a project cost; all projects estimated to exceed this cost usually require EIA). (Ireland; German Democratic Republic.) 3/

Little attention has been given so far to environmental impact analysis of legislative proposals and administrative regulations, although in several countries (United States; Federal Republic of Germany) provision has been made for the assessment of legislative proposals that significantly affect the quality of the environment. Despite the general nature of most proposed legislation and the difficulty of identifying potential environmental effects, EIA can be applied to some forms of legislation, (e.g. bills affecting transportation policy or annual construction authorization). Since administrative regulations are more precise in character, their environmental impact assessment may in principle be easier.

Most ECE countries, especially those with established planning practice and experience, have by now recognized, at least in principle, that the environmental dimension needs to be included in the planning process and that ecological evaluation of plans and programmes at various levels (local, sectoral, regional, national) is desirable. It is increasingly recognized that decisions regarding development actions at the project level logically result from the application of broader plans and programmes; various alternatives for a project design and implementation may therefore be determined early in the planning process, making impact assessment at the programme or plan stage still more important. This in turn raises the question of whether a provisional plan or programme should be developed and then subjected to a separate environmental impact assessment, or whether impact assessment should be integrated into the planning process itself.

The types of development proposals and action that are subject to assessment vary considerably in different ECE countries. In some countries assessment at present is mainly concerned with activities at the national government level. According to the recently-issued regulations for the implementation of NEPA, the environmental statement process in the United States covers "major Federal action" which includes actions with effects that may be major and which are potentially subject to federal government control and responsibility. These actions represent new and continuing activities, including projects and programmes entirely or partly financed, assisted, conducted, regulated, or approved by federal agencies, as well as new or revised agency rules, regulations, plans, policies or procedures and legislative proposals. The EIS process also covers federal actions which tend to fall within one of the following categories: (a) adoption of official policy, such as rules, regulations, and interpretations, treaties and international conventions or agreements; formal documents establishing an agency's policies which will result in or substantially alter agency programmes; (b) adoption of formal plans, such as official documents prepared or approved by federal agencies which guide or prescribe alternative uses of federal resources; (c) adoption of programmes, such as a group of concerted actions to implement a specific policy or plan; systematic and connected agency decisions allocating agency resources to implement a specific statutory programme or executive directive; (e) approval of specific projects, such as construction

---

3/Countries mentioned in brackets are cited only as examples; similar situations may also exist in other ECE member countries.

or management activities located in a defined geographic area. Projects include actions approved by permit or other regulatory decision as well as federal and federally assisted activities.

In several countries, impact assessment of proposed development actions is incorpo-rated into the state planning system, including economic and territorial planning at national, regional and local levels (USSR; Poland; German Democratic Republic). In the United Kingdom, physical development projects are subjected to a wide range of controls. As existing procedures are comprehensive, practically no major physical development project (private or public) escapes some form of control.

In Finland, national and regional physical planning process, as well as water management planning and various forms of sector planning, cover a wide range of proposed activities. Major projects, such as nuclear power stations, oil refineries and power transmission lines, are subject to assessment in the framework of land-use planning. Impact assessment at the stage of developing master plans is, however, not yet so effective as at the project level.

In Norway, the Establishment Control Act provides for environmental assessment of all large industrial undertakings, irrespective of locality. The proposed new Planning Act will also include regulations relating to environmental impact assess-ment of all plans and activities which may have important effects on the environment, socio-economic conditions and regional development.

The Local Government (Planning and Development) Act, 1977 in Ireland requires that environmental impact assessment should apply to any trade and industry (including mining) comprising any works, apparatus or plant "used for any process which would result in a wide range of adverse effects on man and environment".

In Sweden and some other countries, impact assessment are for new or expanded industrial enterprises that affect the national resources of land, water, energy, etc. Assessments usually relate environmental considerations to labour market policies, regional and industrial policies and similar matters.

In some countries, environmental impact assessment is restricted to specific types of projects or to development actions likely to cause adverse effects on a specific environmental element. In Spain, for example, impact studies are required for any activity that may result in atmospheric pollution. Sometimes, special attention is given to the assessment of the environmental effects of nuclear power plant installations (Belgium, Spain).

In summing up this diversity of approaches and current practice, it is worth emphasizing some basic questions. Comprehensive integration of environmental considerations into planning and dicision-making systems enables the examination of a very broad spectrum of development actions at an early stage. At the project level, one critical question is whether certain activities really require a thorough impact study. For some projects, particularly those that tend to arouse widespread public concern (e.g. power-stations, especially nuclear plants, high-ways, airports, electricity transmission lines) the need for environmental impact assessment is almost self-evident. The same is normally true of dangerous, insalu-brious or "offensive" development proposals (heavy polluting industrial establish-ments, quarries, slaughterhouses, etc.). However, for such projects as main roads, drainage systems, housing, etc., that are ordinary in size and effect, strict application of environmental impact regulations could sometimes lead to unnecessary and costly analyses, often of insufficient quality in view of the limited expertise and resources generally available. (9)

In the ECE member countries with centrally planned economies, environmental analyses of plans, programmes and projects are carried out by competent State or scientific bodies under directives of the respective governmental authorities (USSR, Hungary, Poland). In the German Democratic Republic, for example, local councils usually order authorities responsible for regional planning development to carry out comprehensive "site studies" of planned projects. Scientific institution and public agencies, e.g. the National Hygienic Control Authority, may be requested to prepare related environmental impact statements (e.g. effects of air pollution, impact on agriculture and forestry, assessment of noise, etc.). The conclusions of such studies are taken into account when a decision is taken on development proposals.

In Finland, because the impact analyses are integrated into the various planning and management processes, planning authorities are responsible for their preparation. In some cases public agencies or private consultants are asked to prepare impact assessments. In the United Kingdom, responsibility for a specific impact assessment is decided in discussion between the developer and the planning authority. The assessment is directed to and reviewed by the planning authority; in the case of projects of more than local importance, this may be the Secretary of State. In such circumstances, an inspector is normally appointed, so that impact assessments are considered at an inquiry. Decisions on a development action are taken by the local planning authority or in certain instances by the Secretary of State. In other countries (Spain, Ireland) the onus for the preparation of an environmental study rests on the developer. The study is directed to the planning authority, which is then responsible for reviewing the entire application including the environmental study. The authority may decide that it lacks the appropriate expertise and may seek the services and advice of outside agencies.

D. Financial responsibility for Environmental Impact Assessments and their review

The cost of environmental impact assessment is commensurate with the complexity and significance of the problem and the degree of detail required for decision-making. Cost responsibilities are generally similar to the pattern of responsibility for preparation and review of environmental assessment. In many cases, the expense is carried by the proponent of the development proposal; sometimes the cost is assumed by public authorities, which are also normally responsible for the expense involved in reviewing environmental impact assessments (Australia, Spain, Ireland).

In Canada, the allocation of costs is based, where practicable, in accordance with the principle that the polluter, or potential polluter, should pay, and that consequently, where government services are provided in support of a specific project, the proponent should bear those costs that are clearly in excess of a department's normal budgetary expenditure. In general, the federal Government bears the costs of baseline studies, verification and enforcement, and monitoring studies, while the proponent bears the costs of preparing the environmental evaluation reports and the environmental impact statement, including any expertise unique to the authority that is required to prepare these reports, proponent inspection and reporting. The community or national authorities in Finland pay for environmental assessments and their review, including collection of baseline data. Exceptions to this procedure are air quality evaluations, which are usually paid for by the firms involved, and the so-called "shore plans", a form of comprehensive shore line and vacation area planning, which is paid for by the landowner. In the United Kingdom, each party to a development decision - the developer, the planning authority and third party interests - meets the costs of those studies which it undertakes. Planning authorities must therefore pay for any independent work they undertake or commission to assist in their decisions. Third parties have access to published information (e.g. that contained in development plans), but otherwise they meet their own expenses.

D. Responsibility for Environmental Impact Assessment and its review

There is at present considerable disagreement on whether it is appropriate to place responsibility for EIA on the proponent or developer of a particular activity or whether it is more reasonable for the decision-making authority to undertake the analysis itself or to delegate this to an independent body. In either case, it is necessary to establish a clear procedure to ensure that the impact analysis is adequately and objectively reviewed.

The most common practice in ECE countries is for the proponent of a development action to be responsible for the preparation of the impact analysis. One advantage of this approach is that the proponent is well placed to know what an activity involves. The proponent may also be able to utilize environmental information to improve the project design if the environmental assessment is done as part of project planning. An obvious disadvantage is that the proponent may consciously or unconsciously use the impact analysis as a promotional tool. Another drawback is that the proponent may not be able to assess indirect and long-term ecological effects adequately, because of a lack of the necessary scientific knowledge and expertise. Even when the impact study is contracted to a specialized agency, the fact that the agency's work has been funded by the proponent leaves room for doubt concerning the impartiality of the evaluation. In all such cases, whether the proponent is a public agency or private firm, the authority which takes the decision on a development proposal must ultimately satisfy itself about the quality and accuracy of the information in the study. (10)

Alternatively, responsibility for the preparation of an impact study may be assumed by the authorities responsible for allowing a development. A specialized inter-disciplinary team could be created for each particular case, providing more assurance of an adequate and comprehensive evaluation of possible environmental effects. But this procedure places a tremendous financial burden on these authorities, if we take into account the scale and size of economic and technological development in ECE member countries. One modification of this approach is to empower an independent scientific institution to prepare environmental impact analyses, but this of course does not solve the problem of expense. (11)

Practical experience in member countries shows a wide variety of procedures concerning the allocation of responsibility of EIA, reflecting different legal and administrative structures and settings.

In Canada, for example, under the federal process the initiator (which is a federal Government department or agency which intends to undertake or sponsor a project) is responsible for both the environmental assessment and the review of a proposed activity. If it is determined that the effects would be potentially significant, a formal review by an independent environmental impact assessment panel is required. The panel establishes guidelines for the preparation of the environmental impact statement, as described above.

In Norway, the task of assessing a petro-chemical industry development was shared by the national Government and the industrial companies. The companies were given primary responsibility for handling the technical and economic aspects of the projects, while the central authorities made an assessment of such questions as safety and emergency preparedness and various environmental aspects, on the basis of material prepared mainly by the companies. According to new legislation proposals (a new Planning Act and a comprehensive Pollution Act), the obligation to provide sufficient information on all positive and negative effects of the plan or proposal rests with the body or enterprise responsible for the plan. The scope and depth of the impact assessment, as well as the choice of institutions responsible for the analyses will be decided upon by the public authorities.

In countries with centrally-planned economies, all financial responsibilities are usually assumed by the State, since in most cases those who require and those who prepare impact analyses are associated with state-controlled institutions. When an environmental impact statement is commissioned from an independent scientific institution, the costs are met by the territorial planning agency or the local authorities (e.g. German Democratic Republic).

Adequate data concerning the actual level of costs of environmental impact assessments are not yet available in many countries. In those countries which have relatively long experience of impact statements, costs vary considerably (between 0.05 per cent and 1 or 2 per cent of the value of the project) but remain acceptable. (12) More detailed information on cost estimates of impact assessment processes can be found in basic report: "Costs of Environmental impact statements and the benefits they yield in improvements to projects and opportunities for public involvement" (see table of contents).

Even limited experience in the ECE countries has shown that the introduction of environmental impact assessment at an early stage in the planning of development action, with particular amphasis on alternative proposals, is more beneficial in terms of economic and social accounting, than measures post facto to mitigate or eliminate adverse effects on the environment and human wellbeing.

The benefits represented by the impact assessment process have usually not been included in the cost-benefit calculations, because of the difficulty of assigning values in monetary terms to such benefits. Reasonable assumptions suggest that, on balance, the benefits accruing from environment impact studies have outweighed costs. Many environmental amenities are characterized by the permanence of any destruction that could occur. Wetlands, floodplains, endangered species, wild and scenic rivers, historic and archaeological sites cannot be restored once they have been adversely affected. Air and water quality, as well as agricultural and recreational lands can be restored only at a great expense of time and money. Urban sprawl represents an impact that is very difficult to reverse. Hence the value of environmental amenities, over extended time periods, is likely to make the costs of environmental impact assessment seem negligible.

F. Information aspects of Environmental Impact Assessment

A vital feature of environmental impact assessments is the information that is presented to the decision-maker: its character, type, volume, detail and credibility. Important also are the techniques of communication. It seems generally agreed that the information should be presented in a language that is understandable to the planning and decision-making authorities. The environmental assessment information that must be conveyed to decision-makers will normally involve, at least in summary form, (a) the data base, including base-line data, actual measurements and assumptions of impacts; (b) description of technical methods used in the analyses; (c) the results of the analyses; and (d) the conclusions and recommendations. (13) There are some formidable problems involved. The volume of information (e.g. data, alternatives and future scenarios) may be too great for planners or decision-makers to absorb and assess in the time that they can devote to the matter. In some cases data acquisition, synthesis and interpretation may not be sufficient as a basis for firm recommendations or decisions. The links from projects, plans and programmes to economic activities and social well-being may often be poorly defined.

In the German Democratic Republic, for example, as a basis for environmental impact assessments, a number of fixed standards adopted by various laws are usually used, including standards fixed for the condition of soil, air, water, noise, waste products, as well as for hygienic aspects and human health protection purposes.

Regulations in several countries empower the planning authority to seek any

information they deem necessary. In Ireland, the authority, on receipt of a planning
application, may require the applicant to provide any of the following material:
(a) particulars, plans, drawings or maps as may be necessary to comply with
regulations; (b) further information relative to the application, including any
information as to any estate or interest in or right over land; (c) evidence
required to verify any particulars or information given by the applicant in relation
to the application. In the United Kingdom, local planning authorities may similarly
require developers to furnish any information they reasonably need to decide on
applications.

G. Monitoring

In order to confirm the nature and importance of anticipated environmental changes,
continuation of assessment activities is required during and after the period of
construction of a project or implementation of a plan or programme. Monitoring and
surveillance of those environmental effects considered in the impact study provide
an opportunity to validate environmental analyses and to assist with future assessment through the identification of errors and unexpected impacts. It is important,
however, that the parameters to be monitored should be carefully selected.

Some ECE member countries have established procedures for such ex post facto
monitoring within the environmental impact assessment process and have also defined
the technical responsibility for implementation; in other countries, such a process
has not yet been developed or is based on the existing monitoring system, covering
measurement of a relatively small fixed number of environmental variables. In
Canada, the proponent is required to conduct repetitive tests and gather data on
effluents, emissions, wastes and environmental conditions. These stipulations,
which are a prerequisite for project approval, may cover both construction and
operation of the project. In addition, the Government may monitor those environmental systems and components likely to be affected by the activity in question.
This work is regarded as an extension of baseline studies and is, therefore, the
responsibility of the federal Government.

Regulations for implementing the procedural provisions of NEPA in the United States
contain a requirement that agencies may provide for monitoring to assure that their
decisions are carried out and should do so in important cases. The Norwegian
environmental authorities –considering that a basic requirement for adequate
environmental impact assessment is precise and comprehensive knowledge of environmental conditions –have given priority to the development of relevant monitoring
programmes. In Ireland, when granting permission for a development, a planning
authority has wide powers to attach conditions which form an integral part of the
permission and can include environmental standards, discharge of effluents, landscaping, provision of open spaces, etc. The planning authority is responsible for
monitoring developments to ensure that all conditions are complied with and it can
take enforcement action if necessary. Some planning authorities require firms to
install monitoring equipment to measure air quality and effluent discharge.

Among the countries which use existing systems of monitoring are the German
Democratic Republic and Spain. In the former country, after completion of a specific
project, continuous environmental control is performed by the National Hygienic
Control Authority and responsible officials at local and regional levels. In Spain,
an inspection and monitoring service has been established in every province.

In some countries, environmental monitoring is regarded not merely as an important
instrument of environmental impact assessment but also as a means of identifying
possible trends in environmental conditions. The results of such evaluation are
provided to planning authorities, for use at various levels of planning processes,
especially in regard to long-term perspective planning. A comprehensive monitoring
system is now in operation within the National Monitoring Service of the Soviet

Union. Its main tasks are: (a) monitoring and measurement of pollution levels in different environmental media to determine the distribution of pollutants in time and space and to enable evaluation of the state and quality of the environment; (b) assistance to various State authorities concerned with regular or emergency data or changes in pollution levels; (c) providing the competent authorities with information to assist the development of recommendations concerning environmental protection and rational utilization of natural resources for annual and long-term State plans and designing various development activities. These comprehensive monitoring activities give a sound basis for the development of effective and scientifically-based measures for mitigating man's impact on the environment.

H. Public Information and Participation

Effective public information and participation are generally regarded as important elements in the environmental impact assessment process. Planning institutions and decision-makers may not always identify the environmental problems that the public perceives to be serious: public knowledge of local conditions can be a valuable input to the process and can result in improved alternative development. Another advantage is that early and active public participation in the planning of proposed development actions may actually facilitate their implementation as the citizens will better understand the reasons for a development proposal. There are, however, possible problems to be taken into account. Public participation may, in the short term, increase planning and project costs and be time-consuming; the citizens involved may not be competent to judge the technical aspects of plans, programmes and projects; those participating may not always be representative of the community at large and may in some cases take a narrow and biased viewpoint.

One recurring difficulty in many assessment studies has been the need to distinguish between the objective and subjective judgements required in analyses. Subjective judgements are usually essential, as it is often not possible to quantify environmental changes or to assess their significance objectively. To cope with this problem of subjective judgements, knowledge is required of public opinion so as to ensure that plans or development actions are acceptable to the people concerned.

In ECE countries, participatory mechanisms vary according to the nature and opportunities provided within the frameworks of different political and administrative settings. A type of citizen involvement that is successful in one country may not necessarily be the most effective in another. Mechanisms that are frequently used include the establishment of information and education programmes, public consultations, public hearings, commissions of inquiry, etc. There are also various means through which appeals may be made against decisions based on environmental impact assessments.

In Canada, federal departments and agencies have been directed by the Cabinet to provide information on, and to seek public response to, their activities early in the planning stage, before vital decisions have been taken. Public information and participation are especially needed in the case of projects requiring formal EIS. The panel appointed to review the EIS may solicit public comment on the proposed guidelines for the statement before they are submitted to the project sponsor. Environmental Assessment Panels hold public hearings to receive comments on a proposed development and these are normally convened in the immediate area of the project, although hearings may be held in other areas as well. The completed Environmental Impact Statements and the guidelines are made available to the public (at libraries, government offices, etc.) well in advance of the hearings. Environmental Assessment Panel hearings are not legal proceedings and are usually structured so as to provide maximum opportunity for individuals or groups to express opinions or to provide information on the potential impact of the proposals. All briefs made to the Panel, both written and oral, are printed and made available to the public along with other documents associated with the Panel review, including

the report to the Minister of the Environment. However, as the Environmental
Assessment and Review Process is not based on legislation, the public does not have
the option of recourse to the courts.

Provision is made in Sweden for extensive public involvement in a broad spectrum
of questions regarding environmental problems, though the technical complexity of
some proposals may make it difficult to provide for widespread involvement. Members
of the public may present their views in public sessions, or make submissions in
writing during the evaluation process. Individual citizens are entitled to visit
authorities and to examine all applications in regard to proposed developments.
Similarly one of the basic principles in establishing the environmental impact
assessment process in Norway is to provide the general public with information
and the opportunity to comment at an early stage in the planning process. The
forthcoming Pollution Act will provide for public hearings whereby the results
of the impact assessments will be presented to the public in appropriate, non -
esoteric language for discussion and evaluation.

In the United States, the regulations for implementing NEPA provide that agencies
must: (a) make diligent efforts to involve the public in preparing and implementing
NEPA procedures; (b) provide public notice of NEPA-related hearings, public meetings
and the availability of environmental documents; (c) hold or sponsor public
hearings or public meetings, whenever appropriate or in accordance with statutory
requirements applicable to the agency; (d) solicit appropriate information from
the public; (e) explain in their procedures where interested persons can get
information or status reports on environmental impact statements and other elements
of the NEPA process; (f) make environmental impact statements, the comments
received, and any supporting documents available to the public. Materials to be
made available to the public must be provided to the public without charge to the
extent practicable, or at a fee which is not more than the actual cost of repro-
ducing copies required to be sent to other federal government agencies, including
the Council for Environmental Quality.

In Spain, after being reviewed by the Administration, project descriptions and
relevant impact assessment studies are submitted to the municipalities for public
information, so that the public can examine them and present their comments. Each
question or enquiry is answered jointly by the Regional Administrative Delegation
and the proponent. If not satisfied by the results of EIA, people affected can
appeal to the courts, but there is no special procedure for appeals related
particularly to environmental problems. The Environment Protection Act in Australia
provides that a draft EIS must be released for public review and comment for a
minimum period of 28 days unless the Minister is satisfied that this would be
contrary to the public interest. The availability of the draft EIS is advertised
and public comments must be taken into account by the proponent in the preparation
of the final EIS. The final EIS is made available to those who had offered comments
and to the general public. The Act also provides for public participation during
enquiry.

In the United Kingdom, all planning applications for development projects are
recorded in a register kept by the local planning authority. This is open to
public inspection and many local newspapers report new entries in the
register. In addition, applications which are at variance with a fundamental
provision of a development plan must be advertised in a local paper and by means
of a site notice. The planning authority is bound to take account all representations made to it before reaching a decision. A major planning decision usually
becomes the subject of a local enquiry which is open to the public. Parties having
an interest in the land, and the local planning authority, have a right to be heard,
but others wishing to express a view or give evidence may do so at the discretion
of the inspector holding the enquiry. This discretion is freely exercised. On a
broader scale, local planning authorities are obliged to ensure that adequate

publicity is given to the preparation of structure and local plans, and must provide adequate opportunity for interested members of the public to make representations to them.

In Ireland, applications to undertake development, as defined in the 1963 Act, must be accompanied by a copy of a newspaper notice or a site notice stating the applicant's intention. The application, together with any plans, drawings, maps, and environmental studies are available for public inspection. This information is to be available (a) from the time of receipt of the relevant document until the application or any appeal relating thereto is determined, and (b) where any permission or approval is granted, a further period of five years. Anyone may object to the proposed development and if the planning authority decides to grant permission, they must notify the objector within seven days of making the decision. The objector may appeal to the Planning Appeals Board within 21 days. The appeal to the Board must be made in writing, stating the subject matter and grounds of the appeal. Any party to an appeal may request the Board to conduct an oral hearing at which all parties may make submissions. In addition to these procedures, planning authorities must publish a weekly list of planning applications; each list is available for inspection for a period of not less than four weeks.

In the German Democratic Republic, the elected representatives of the population directly receive information on a development action, as decisions on investment projects are made by the local parliaments. The law on public representation provides procedures for regular public meetings and opportunities to obtain specific information on a project concerned. Public participation is permanently assured through the involvement of elected representatives in the decision-making process. Mass media are utilized to disseminate information on environmental problems. The public also can appeal against a decision made on the basis of environmental impact assessment via petitions to the local parliaments.

According to the Law No. 9/1973 concerning the protection of the environment, various public organizations in Romania are invited to undertake actions regarding environmental problems. Public information on environmental issues is a matter of regular concern for the press, broadcasting and television.

In the Soviet Union, large numbers of people are active in environmental protection through the "All-Russian Society for the Protection of Nature" which, through 200,000 local organizations, has 30 million members. The main tasks of the Society include public information and education on environmental matters; development of public awareness on environmental problems; promotion of public involvement in environmental protection activities; organization of public regarding protection of the environment; and organization of public monitoring of compliance with environmental protection laws. The central and local councils of the Society have scientific and technical boards, which prepare proposals for comprehensive solu - tions to various aspects of environmental problems. Public participation in monitoring the state of the environment, as well as organized public discussion of development proposals that effect the environment (including use of the mass media), enable public opinion to be taken into account during the planning process.

III. SUMMARY CONCLUSIONS

In most ECE member countries there is general recognition that environmental considerations should be integrated into existing planning and decision-making processes, but the extent and form of integration is different in each country. The need for institutional structures to give support to the process of EIA has been pointed out.

The way environmental assessments are made depends on the political and adminis- trative structure in a given country. In some countries, EIA is done through

legislative or administrative regulations. In others, it is introduced through
integration into various planning systems (central overall planning; socio-economic,
physical, land-use planning).

There is a trend to develop more comprehensive legislation covering environmental
problems arising at the inter-sectoral level, while some countries have introduced
specific legislation or have included provisions for environmental impact assessment
within the existing regulations.

Many countries are undertaking investigations on how best to proceed with EIA; some
have adopted the idea of establishing a formal system of impact assessment, while
others believe that the existing level of integration of EIA into decision-making
and planning processes is sufficient. The general understanding is that EIA should
be made at a very early stage of the project planning or development of plans; the
importance of considering various alternative development proposals was emphasized.

In the process of planning and evaluating development proposals, environmental
aspects should be given equal status with economic, technical and social considerations; in particular, attention should be given not only to immediate impacts, but
also to indirect, secondary and long-term effects. For types of activities to be
the subject of EIA, it was stressed that EIA should be undertaken not only for
projects, but legislative proposals, plans and programmes as well. Many countries
have already established some sort of definitive list of activities for which EIA
are required.

At present, in many cases the responsibility for the preparation of environmental
impact assessment has lain on the proponent of the development proposal. Such a
situation has some advantages as the proponent may know better what an activity
involves; it also offers the possibility to take into account environmental
considerations at project design level. It has some drawbacks as well; the proponent
may, on the basis of the impact study, present a biased view of the development
action. It was mentioned that another way to proceed would be to place the responsibility for impact assessment on the authorities who take a decision on the
action ;   however, it is important that the assessment procedures should be
separated from the review activities, or the assessment itself could, of course,
be delegated to an independent body.

The need for better understanding and examination of local conditions and community
interests was pointed out, which could be achieved, _inter alia_, by encouraging
more open procedures for public involvement in planning and decision-making processes

One of the difficulties of introducing generally valid EIA procedures is the question
of the availability, acquisition and treatment of data. An efficient process for
communication between project proponents, decision-makers and parties affected by
a development action is another problem requiring attention.

The need for monitoring activities was emphasized and considered to be two-fold:
first, as a continuation or extension of EIA and, second, as a tool for collection
and analysis of data and information needed for more meaningful planning. Due to
the actual lack, at present, of such practices in many ECE countries, there is room
for extension of such activities.

Adequate information on costs of impact studies so far are not available; in some
cases they may seem costly and time consuming. Nevertheless, the long-term benefits
for society which would be directed from impact assessment studies, including the
consideration of alternative project proposals, could far outweigh the costs.

Increasing attention and recognition are given to the fact that public participation
is a vital element of EIA. In some countries such participation is provided for

by special regulations (legal or administritive). In many countries attention is given to the introduction and development of educational and information programmes on environmental problems.

References

(1) Background paper for Preparatory Meeting for the ECE Seminar on Environmental Impact Assessment (document ENV/SEM.10/PM/R.2 p3).

(2) Official Journal of the European Communities 20 (13 June 1977) C 139/36.

(3) Commission of the European Communities "Introduction of Environmental Impact Statements in the European Communities" (Doc. ENV/197/76, Brussels, May 1976); "Environmental Impact Assessment of Physical Plans in the European Communities" (Doc. ENV/730/77-EN, Brussels, December 1977); "Methods of Environmental Impact Assessment for Major Projects and Physical Plans" (Doc. ENV/736/77-EN, Brussels, December 1977).

(4) The United States Congressional Record, Volume 124, No. 111 (21 July, 1978), pp. S 11523-24.

(5) "Safeguarding Environmental Interests in Law". Werner R. Svoboda and Ernest Knoth. Institute of Urban Research, Federal Ministry of Health and Environmental Protection, Vienna, December 1977.

(6) Jain, R.K., L.V. Urban and G.S. Stacey, Environmental Impact Analysis: A New Dimension in Decision Making, Van Nostrand Reinhold, New York: 1977 (p.168)

(7) Holling C.S., ed. Adaptive Environmental Assessment and Management, Chichester, United Kingdom, John Wiley: 1978 (p.37).

(8) Regulations for implementing the procedural provisions of the National Environmental Policy Act, Council on Environmental Quality, Executive Office of the President, Washington, USA, 29 November 1978.

(9) "Analysis of the environmental consequences of significant public and private projects", OECD Group on the Urban Environment, document ENV/URB/76.7/3.1 (p.13)

(10) Corwin,R. and P.H. Heffernan, et al. Environmental Impact Assessment, San Francisco, Freeman Cooper: 1975.

(11) "Model Outline Environmental Impact Statement from the Standpoint of Integrated Management or Planning of the National Environment", European Committee for the Conservation of Nature and Natural Resources, Council of Europe, 1979, (p.75).

(12) "How to include environmental concerns in the decision-making process", OECD, ENV/79/5, 26 February 1979, para. 58.

(13) Holling C.S. ed. Adaptive Environmental Assessment and Management op. cit.

PART I

Methodologies for Environmental Analysis

Environment Impact Assessment Methodologies in Canada

H. W. Thiessen (Canada)

INTRODUCTION

The first part of this paper outlines how the scope and content of environmental impact assessment has evolved in Canada, its status in the context of Canadian public policy, and the issues which are emerging from Canadian experience. The second part of the paper presents a more detailed discussion of selected methodological issues, illustrated by present Canadian experience. The paper is primarily based upon reports prepared for the Canadian Council of Resource and Environment Ministers, which has representation from the Canadian Federal Government and the ten provinces. Some of the more detailed discussion relates to methodological experiences in the Province of Alberta.

The underlying theme of the paper is that the scope, content and the methods used to prepare and evaluate environmental impact assessment depend on the purpose and role of the assessment in determining public policy. While a rather simple and obvious connexion must exist between purpose and methodology, the Canadian experience tends to highlight the fact that environmental impact assessment is used for a variety of purposes and therefore requires different methodological approaches.

THE EVOLUTION OF ENVIRONMENTAL IMPACT ASSESSMENT IN CANADA

Environmental impact assessment in Canada is partially an outgrowth of the inability of project planning and evaluation techniques (including town planning and cost-benefit analysis) to address environmental concerns adequately and to deal with the development of an environmental ethic encompassing non-economic and intangible values.

During the 1950s the introduction of land-use planning concepts often resulted in the creation of inflexible plans. The plans were frequently lacking in technical or biophysical data, seldom incorporated the aspirations of those affected by the plan, and failed to accommodate the rapid rates of growth subsequently experienced by many Canadian communities.

In the 1960s the introduction of project planning and economic evaluation, patterned largely after the American cost-benefit analysis, was developed for western United States public water resource development projects. This process, although relying considerably on engineering economic data, did attempt to take

31

into consideration biophysical and non-economic data as well as public values.
During the same period air and water pollution control programmes to protect
human health were implemented by government regulatory agencies. To many,
however, the emphasis was still on technical and economic considerations.

In the early 1970s there was a greater environmental awareness, a realization
of limited natural resources, a requirement for greater public accountability by
government and industry, and an increased desire by the public to become
intimately and actively involved in the planning process. The need to overcome
deficiencies in project evaluation techniques became apparent and brought about
the birth of the environmental impact assessment process.

At present, the environmental impact assessment process is being redefined to
integrate biophysical impacts, social and community impacts, as well as economic
impacts, into a comprehensive and holistic process which relates human aspirations
to biophysical limitations as well as technical and economic realities. This
process permits decision-makers to determine whether certain developments are
acceptable, and to avoid or mitigate adverse effects. It also requires that the
decision-maker be made more accountable to the public for a particular action.

In Canada, each of the eleven federal and provincial governments has chosen to
interpret and implement an environmental impact assessment process somewhat
differently, depending on location, circumstances, and the specific institutional
framework.

CANADIAN EXPERIENCE WITH ENVIRONMENTAL IMPACT ASSESSMENT

Cultural and institutional variations in Canada have had a significant influence
on how Canadians have approached environmental impact assessment. Canadians have
been reluctant to pass specific laws outlining environmental impact assessment
requirements and processes. Although all eleven governments in Canada have
ministries responsible for environmental matters, including environmental impact
assessment, only two have passed legislation concerning environmental impact
assessment. The nine other governments rely on administrative or executive
decisions requiring individual developers to file an assessment. Consistent with
a general apprehension found in Canadian public administration for legalistic
approaches to emerging policy fields, Canadian governments have generally relied
upon guidelines to provide the required direction.

In the case of some governments, environmental impact assessment is required
only for government developments. Projects initiated by the private sector are
excluded. In other jurisdictions, environmental impact assessment is required
for specified development activities and in some cases, all major developments.
Even though there does not appear to be a universal rule of application, the
nature of the development, its size and scale of impact, its potential hazard, and
its public sensitivity are major factors in determining whether an environmental
impact assessment is required.

The procedures used in the review of assessments and the level at which decisions
are taken on major developments vary among governments. In some instances,
separate and independent review panels are created; in others, interdisciplinary
reviews are undertaken throughout the government. In most cases, elected
officials determine whether a development should proceed, and appointed officials
determine the necessary terms and conditions. The terms and conditions are
usually stipulated in various approvals, permits, or licences and it is left to
regulatory agencies to determine satisfactory compliance.

Environmental impact assessment is seen by many governments as part of the planning process for large-scale development projects. This process integrates initial feasibility studies, design preparation, approvals and permits, as well as monitoring and surveillance during and after implementation. It is seen as a viable tool in achieving a balance between industrial development and maintenance of environmental quality.

There is a trend towards greater standardization of environmental impact assessment across Canada by means of legislation, regulations and guidelines. It is hoped that a loss of flexibility through standardization will not result, and that environmental impact assessment procedures will continue to protect the legitimate concerns of the public.

A.   COMMON TRENDS AND EMERGING ISSUES

The Canadian Council of Resource and Environment Ministers has identified nine trends and issues which have emerged from Canada's collective experiences. These are presented as follows:

(a) Definition of Environmental Matters: a broad definition has been adopted for environmental matters, resulting in a corresponding broad scope for environmental impact assessment. In order that a comprehensive assessment can be made, biophysical, economic, as well as social and community aspects should be included.

(b) Role of the Assessment in the Decision Process: environmental impact assessment can serve as a basis for decisions in principle, as one component of the decision-making process, or as a design tool once the principal decision has been made. Each role has different information requirements as well as different ramifications.

(c) Environmental Impact Assessment for Projects and Programmes: most Canadian environmental impact assessments are being carried out on development projects rather than programmes. Projects, which are of interest to the local public, are generally more specific; programmes are more policy-oriented and consequently are more liable to receive input from public interest groups rather than individual members of the public. A trend is developing which suggests that environmental impact assessments should focus initially on programmes and be followed by project assessment.

(d) Examination of Project Need: although the traditional approach has been to determine the impact of development on the environment, the question of the need for development is being raised more frequently. This evolving issue is resulting in additional information requirements, and more emphasis is being placed on alternative forms of development, and in variations in the review and evaluation process.

(e) Public Participation: the public is increasingly demanding open access to information in order that it can participate in the decision-making process. In Canada, there is a trend to explore and devise ways and means that can accommodate the constructive involvement of the public in decision-making.

(f) Environmental Impact Assessment Review Processes: several review procedures are being followed in Canada. Independent review mechanisms are being used where projects are in their early stages of development, or prior to decisions in principle. In cases where decisions in principle may already have been made or where the project falls within declared policy guidelines, internal government reviews may be carried out.

(g) Financial Responsibility: in general, the "polluter pays" principle applies to the preparation costs of environmental impact assessments. Some governments are now beginning to extend this principle to the provision of financial assistance to those landowners directly affected by a proposed development, at the cost of the proponent.

(h) <u>Legislation versus Policy Guidelines</u>: both procedures are followed in Canada at present; two out of the eleven governments have passed legislation dealing with environmental impact assessment. There is still considerable discussion occurring on the merits of legislation versus policy guidelines. The most important aspect is to ensure a proper balance in the administration of the requirements, regardless of whether they are embodied in legislation.

(i) <u>Opportunities for Co-operation</u>: projects having interprovincial or international ramifications require more clearly-defined guidelines. This also applies to co-ordination between provincial environmental assessment processes and municipal land-use planning and zoning processes. This is a matter currently receiving attention.

SELECTED ISSUE AREAS AFFECTING METHODOLOGY

A.   POLICY FRAMEWORK AND CONTEXT

Taking as an example, a proposed <u>in situ</u> heavy oil sands extraction process for north-eastern Alberta the following four issues are discussed in more detail: (a) definition of environmental matters, (b) role of environmental impact assessment in the decision process, (c) environmental impact assessment for projects and programmes, and (d) examination of project need.

From a narrow biophysical perspective, the major adverse impacts of the project are the withdrawal of relatively large amounts of process water from an interprovincial water body, the disposal of water effluent by deep well injection, and the emission of sulphurous compounds to the air.

B.   DEFINITION OF ENVIRONMENTAL MATTERS

If environmental matters are limited to a narrow biophysical definition, i.e. land, water, air, flora and fauna, then the whole concept of ecological interrelationships, including man and his use of the environment, becomes distorted. The philosophic argument of the environmentalist is that man is an integral part of the environment, and because of his ability to modify it for social or economic reasons, he must bear a responsibility for the consequences. Therefore man's use of the environment and the social and economic factors arising therefrom must be considered as an integral part of the definition of the environment.

With the broader definition, the environmental impact of heavy oil development would include: effects on farmers' crop yields and livestock management practices, trappers' traditional lifestyle, commercial fishermen's annual catch, untrained and underemployed local people competing with technically trained newcomers for technical jobs, and three rural communities doubling or tripling their populations in five years. The relatively simple biophysical parameters have been augmented by a set of socio-economic parameters which add to the complexity of the project.

C.   ROLE OF THE ASSESSMENT IN THE DECISION-MAKING PROCESS

Where the assessment is restricted to that of an environmental design tool after a decision has been made, its purpose is primarily to mitigate obvious adverse impacts. Examples of mitigation would include the recycling of process water to reduce water requirements and hence reduce effluent discharge, or the scrubbing of sulphurous emissions using the best practicable technology.

If the assessment, however, is to be one component of several in the decision-making process, it would still retain its broad definitions but would be complemented by other concerns, e.g.: technical feasibility, economic growth, energy requirements, etc. The emphasis would be placed on prevention of adverse impacts as well as consideration of alternatives, rather than being limited to mitigation. The various concerns would have to be weighed in making a final decision.

In those instances where the assessment is the basis for a decision on whether to proceed, all potential ramifications of the proposal would have to be considered. The level of detail and comprehensiveness would in most instances extend beyond the accepted definition of environmental impact assessment.

D.   ENVIRONMENTAL IMPACT ASSESSMENT FOR PROJECTS AND PROGRAMMES

If one defines "programme" to mean a specific policy objective describing a proposed course of action and "projects" to mean individual actions thereunder, it becomes evident that projects are one component of a programme. The in situ development of heavy oil sands in north-eastern Alberta can be regarded as a programme, whereas one proposal is a project.

Where the assessment is based on the project, the cumulative effects of several projects or the entire programme's environmental affects are not fully considered. The impact of water withdrawal or sulphurous emissions from one project may not be critical; the cumulative effects from four or five projects could, however, have a very serious effect. The effect of the programme could alter the entire community structure from rural to heavy industrial.

E.   EXAMINATION OF PROJECT NEED

Typical questions asked in any environmental impact assessment process related to energy development would include the following: Is the additional energy required? Can other forms of energy be substituted? Are other comparable energy developments preferable? In the example, there was discussion on questions of energy conservation versus consumption; on the technology of in situ development, which was relatively unproven, versus conventional mining development; and on whether energy development at some other location could be further developed so as to alleviate the need for the proposed project.

F.   INFORMATION REQUIREMENTS

Experience has shown that information requirements are directly related to the purpose of the assessment, which may vary from project to project.

G.   AVAILABILITY OF EXISTING INFORMATION

In many instances, available information is inadequate in scope or detail, especially with respect to frontier projects either due to location or technology. Information is frequently lacking on biophysical and socio-economic aspects. Although some data may be available from reconnaissance-level resource surveys carried out by government, it is often necessary to assemble data for each specific project.

H.   GENERATING BASELINE DATA FOR SPECIFIC PROJECTS

Collection of baseline data should be done only after there is a clear
understanding between the proponent and responsible government agencies on data
requirements. Frequently the proponent's concept of baseline data has differed
from that of the review agency. This has led to the collection of redundant data
of little use in the environmental impact assessment review process.

I.   DETERMINATION OF REQUIRED INFORMATION FOR ANALYSIS

This can be achieved during the process itself through constant liaison and
consultation between the proponent, the review agency and the public. Such
consultation is an example of the dynamic capability of the environmental impact
assessment process. It is important to have a flexible process. Each assessment
is unique and will be guided by its purpose, the nature of the project, the
community involved, and the adequacy of information.

J.   ENVIRONMENTAL MONITORING OF OPERATIONAL PROJECTS

Traditionally, environmental monitoring of operational projects has been
considered to be an extension of the regulatory process. Compliance with
approvals, licences, and permits has been the prime objective to ensure that predetermined standards were met. This approach is beginning to be contested. Some
of the review agencies that do not have a regulatory process are requesting
greater involvement in the setting of standards, as well as in the monitoring
of compliance, to ensure continuity between the planning process and the
regulatory process. In this manner, corrective action can be taken at the
operational stage of a project and experience gained can be included in future
assessment procedures.

In addition, many local citizen groups in the affected community as well as
special interest groups requesting information on the specific terms and
conditions of approvals. They also request a role in the actual monitoring
process. Their concerns are based partly on misinformation and mistrust of the
regulatory agencies and partly on a sincere interest and desire to be more
involved in controlling their environment. This heightened interest by citizen
groups may result in modifications to the traditional regulatory process to
accommodate greater public input. This will have direct impact on the traditional
regulatory agency role, especially in the areas of public relations and legal
enforcement.

METHODOLOGY IMPLICATIONS OF ALTERNATIVE POLICIES

The scope and content of environmental impact assessments and the methods used
in their preparation and evaluation depend on their purpose and role in
determining public policy. In Canada, environmental impact assessments are used
for a variety of purposes that require different methodological approaches.
Obviously, different methodological approaches generate in turn their own
particular data requirements.

The basic characteristic of the policies governing environmental impact
assessment in Canada is a priority on flexibility to accommodate the broad range
of situations requiring environmental assessment. For some projects which involve
the application of new technologies in frontier areas, environmental impact
assessment must be very comprehensive in scope, requiring new data collection on
biophysical, social, and economic parameters. In such situations, the
environmental impact assessment becomes the primary basis for reaching decisions
in principle, and often includes analysis at both the project and programme

levels, with particular emphasis on determining and substantiating project need. In such projects, priority is often placed on public participation processes and independent review processes.

In situations involving far less uncertainty, environmental impact assessment is often used as an environmental design tool after a project has received approval in principle. Emphasis shifts to the collection of specific data on known problem areas, and away from major technological alternatives and questions on the need for the project. In such cases the scope of the environmental impact assessment is much narrower and review processes are much less complicated.

Intermediate situations involving a moderate degree of uncertainty and environmental risk are often broad in scope, but with the data collection and review process focused on the expected problem areas, whether they involve reclamation, waste disposal, or controversy surrounding siting and route selection criteria.

In Canada, policy guidelines, issued at the executive and administrative level are the dominant factors determining the purpose, scope, content, and corresponding data requirements for environmental impact assessment. In determining the nature of the environmental impact assessment required for a specific project, emphasis is placed on the processes and decision criteria used. In the absence of specific legislation, a process of negotiation takes place outside the judicial system and involves a compromise between conflicting interests.

Canada has adopted a variety of approaches to the preparation of environmental impact assessments which allows for flexibility. Depending upon the nature of the development, its size, location, scale of impact, perceived hazard and public sensitivity, a specific set of guidelines and procedures is tailor-made to meet the perceived needs, often within broad policy guidelines approved at the executive level of government.

CONCLUSION

Canadian experience has demonstrated the fundamental and yet obvious fact that the purpose and end use of environmental impact assessment in public policy determines the scope and content of environmental impact assessment. Since in Canada, environmental impact assessment is used for a variety of purposes (decisions in principle, environmental design tools, or examination of project need), different methodological approaches are required which in turn generate their own particular data requirements. This basic relationship between purpose and methodology has resulted in the adoption of a flexible approach to the preparation of environmental impact assessments, which can accommodate a broad range of situations.

Methodology for Environmental Impact Assessment Based on Case Studies in The Netherlands

W. Klein

(Netherlands)

INTRODUCTION

During 1977 the Dutch Ministry of Health and Environmental Protection initiated nine "trial runs" on environmental impact assessment (EIA). These experiments had been recommended in an advisory report by the Provisional Central Council on Environmental Protection in November 1976. The Council, consisting of members of different interest groups, confirmed that EIA can play an essential and valuable part in environmental management in the Netherlands and recommended that trial runs be undertaken to develop EIA as an operational system in the Dutch institutional situation (1). After preliminary research, reported in the spring of 1977 (2), the trial runs started in the course of that year. By the middle of 1978 environmental impact statements (EIS) had been prepared for each of the studies. At this stage the experience gathered to date was reported to the Ministry (3), together with recommendations on implementation of EIA in the Netherlands. Since the experiments could only represent a minority of possible activities, it was necessary also to carry out complementary research, parallel to the trial runs, to answer more abstract questions. The recommendations (4) are the combined result of trial runs and complementary research. In the spring of 1979 a further report was published on the procedural experiences gathered in the trial runs up to January 1979. This paper is based on the most recent evidence provided by the above-mentioned trial runs and complementary research.

WHAT IS MEANT BY A METHODOLOGY?

As stated in a background paper in preparation for this seminar, "EIA is essentially a dimension of the planning process rather than a specific product" (5) it has a specific purpose, that is to influence the decisions to be made for "the environment" and its values. The methodology is the complex of procedures, techniques and tools that together help to fulfil this purpose of EIA. The preparation of an EIS is only one element in this methodology; any procedural provision that improves the influence of environmental concerns in the planning and decision-making process can also be part of the methodology. In general one can distinguish:

- procedural provisions (e.g. the obligation to prepare an EIS)
- process elements (e.g. the adaptation of the EIS as a result of comments)
- structural elements (e.g. the basic format of the EIS)
- tools (e.g. pollution transmission models and data bases).

IS THERE ONE BEST METHODOLOGY?

The question could be posed whether there is one best methodology for EIA. Probably the answer is that there is not. Of course it would be very profitable if one method could be prescribed for any EIA, so far as uniformity, reproduceability and comparability are concerned. On the other hand, to have maximum impact on the decision-making process would demand a methodology for EIA that is tailor-made to every specific decision. Any activity, any decision and, most of all, each environment is so unique that a standard methodology would most probably neglect the unique factors.

When proposing methodologies one must therefore choose between two extremes: complete uniformity or complete uniqueness. The choice is hardly a scientific one, but more one of policy. If the emphasis is placed on uniqueness, many deta-iled methodologies must be developed, for all types of activities, decisions and environments. If uniformity of approaches is preferred, only one detailed methodology need be developed; however, it would apply only partially to all the differnet activities, decisions and environments. Between these two extremes, a search is desirable to find a methodology that is uniform up to the point where no real harm is done by the uniformity, i.e. any type of activity, (e.g. large or small), any type of decision, (at the policy-level or at the project-level) and any type of environment can be handled with this same methodology.

One of the purposes of the trial runs and the complementary research was to find such an optimally uniform methodology. It seems probable that further experiences in the Netherlands will give way - as has happened abroad - to specific and detailed methodologies applicable beyond the point reached by the presently recommended uniform methodology.

EXPERIENCES FROM THE TRIAL RUNS

It was found that, if the proponent of an activity (whether in the private or public sector) has to prepare his own EIS, he may adapt his plans in favour of the environment before they are formally proposed. Provision that the proponent (and not the deciding agency) should prepare the EIS will, therefore, improve the effect of EIA on the planning process. In our experience, there is no reason to be afraid of "sweet-heart statements", as long as a well-organized system of consultation and public participation counterbalances the natural tendencies of the proponent.

In our trial runs provision was made for an independent body of experts to advise on the adequacy and contents of the EIS. This body was not expected to give advice on the decision to be made (as, for example, occurs with the review panel in the Canadian process). In some cases, decisions have been postponed because the body identified real shortcomings; in other cases, the decision-maker was unnecessarily embarrassed. Besides pointing out basic shortcomings or errors in the EIS, the panel introduced scientific dilemmas of fundamental discussions that should have been discussed in a broader decision-making context.

Several trial runs provided important experience in the process of EIA, by using a step-by-step approach. In one case this was done very consistently, in what was referred to as a "lattice-approach". Each time the statement was presented to the responsible agencies, the outline (lattice) would be complete but with more details filled in (finer lattice). At the outset the details were primarily about the proposed activity; later on details concerning the environment were added.

EXPERIENCES FROM THE COMPLEMENTARY RESEARCH

Although in none of the trial runs has a decision yet been made based on the EIS, it is not difficult to appreciate that the requirement to state the grounds for a decision would help to prevent decisions that are unnecessarily damaging to the environment. In the Netherlands in some cases such a statement is a rule of proper policy, but an explicit procedural provision seems in all cases to be desirable. As already mentioned, the separation of the body of independent experts reviewing the EISs in the trial runs had many disadvantages. Our complementary research into the "panel process" used in Canada convinced us that the body (or panel) should not review from a distance, but should participate actively in the whole process and conclude with advice on the proposed activity.

The "lattice approach" towards gradually increasing the detail in an assessment makes it possible to go as far as is necessary for a decision to be made. In this respect the method is in line with the general tendency in the United States to "scope" the EIA, focussing on the real issues and omitting irrelevant ones. For a decision to be made, a short appraisal of the real issues is much more appreciated than a scientifically complete document. As far as structural elements are concerned, our complementary research showed that a proper checklist approach (although not used in the trial runs) can be a very good means to structure both the creation and the review of an EIS. The basic structure for the EIS was specified in the preliminary research report (2), which suggested that a number of factors are essential for any EIS:

(a) <u>Description of the proposed activity</u> – The EIS must proceed from a description of the proposed activity, with an indication of the objective and the means, and possible and reasonable alternative ways to attain the objective that has been set.

(b) <u>Description of the status quo</u> – There must then follow a description of the existing state of the environment which the proposed activity is expected to affect.

(c) <u>Description of environmental effects</u> – The next step is to describe the environmental impact of the proposed activity and the alternatives, including both indirect and secondary short-term and long-term effects. Attention must be paid to probable environmental effects which cannot be avoided.

(d) <u>Comparison of alternatives</u> – Finally, a comparison is to be made of the expected effects of the different alternatives, for example in the light of standards relating to the proposed activity, including the normative principles underlying the policy.

(e) <u>Outcome of the consultation</u> – public participation procedure.

This appeared to be an acceptable structure, but in some trial runs improvements were proposed. Particularly valuable was the suggestion that the structure should emphasize the impacts of the proposed activity as being a link in the chain of continuous changes in the environment, from a (mostly man-influenced) history to a (man-influenced) future. This is dealt with again below where an attempt is made to combine all the experiences into one set of methodological recommendations.

One negative factor affecting the experiments was the fact that neither the authors nor the reviewers appeared to use checklists to structure their work or their presentation. Similarly there was, as anticipated, a lack of standard or uniform models and of data bases concerning the environment. To a certain degree this has something to do with a typical Dutch reluctance as regards unification and standardization, but it also points to a more world-wide lack of tools. The lack of environmental data bases seems to be quite universal.

As far as tools are concerned, one can readily find specific instruments such as transmission models that are different even for noise from factories and for traffic-noise, etc. In this respect mention should be made of the very enlightening ECE background paper (6), which cites a number of methods and models, many of which could be called "tools" in the context of this paper. It is clear that most of these models and methods have only limited applicability. So (for the time being) they do not fit within the task we set ourselves.

RECOMMENDED METHODOLOGY IN THE NETHERLANDS

It is appropriate here to give a more systematic view of the methodology for EIA, as recommended by the consulting firms involved. Some (or maybe many) of the recommended elements can be found in regulations in other countries, so not all the material will be new or unexpected to the environmentalist. The recommended methodological and procedural provisions, process elements and structural EIS elements will be outlined; finally the tools will be touched upon very briefly.

A.   PROCEDURAL PROVISIONS

Figures   1 and 2 show the two types of procedures recommended by the consulting firms for EIA in the Netherlands: a normal EIS procedure and panel procedure for very important activities (two procedures were chosen instead of one since a single process would not have been completely satisfactory in all cases). In these procedures there are five provisions that have methodological relevance:

(a) the proponent should be responsible for the EIS; the importance of this provision to accomplish environmental consciousness at an early stage has already been emphasized.

(b) restrictive lists are recommended for defining the requirement of EIA; in the case of more than one competent authority, these lists should define a co-ordinating (or leading) agency and this agency should co-ordinate the information from all agencies to the proponent to make sure that, already at this stage, integration of environmental data takes place;

(c) a thorough report of all comments by other agencies and the public should be made by the co-ordinating agency;

(d) decision-makers should be required to state the grounds for their decisions; (The last two provisions are meant to maximize the possibilities for agencies and the public to counterbalance the possible tendencies of both the proponent and the decision-maker(s) to neglect facts raised by the EIA).

      - in the case of the procedure involving a panel, a group of experts
         with acknowledged environmental competence should guarantee an
         adequate EIS; on the other hand, the obligation for the panel to give
         advice on the decision to be made would prevent a too scientific or
         distant approach.

B.   PROCESS ELEMENTS

The recommendations contain three typical process elements:

(a) at least one so-called "preliminary consultation", in which the scope of the EIS and the real issues on which it should focus are determined (This is to get decision documents and not, initially, scientific documents. The public could participate in this consultation).

(b) a step-by-step conception of the EIS by the proponent in consultation with the leading agency and possibly also with the other agencies and the public; (The preliminary consultation is the first step. In the next steps the activity will be put in focus. At the end of the process, and also in the final statement, the environment must be the focus (see below).

(c) in the panel procedure, the co-ordination of agencies and the holding of public hearings (to learn the real attitude of the public) are very important ways for the panel to develop balanced advice.

C.   STRUCTURAL ELEMENTS

The most important structural element in the recommendations is the basic format of the EIS (see Fig. 3). This format is based on a dynamic view of the environment, especially applicable in a man-influenced environment like the Netherlands (see Fig. 4).

- Originally the environment is determined by climate, rivers mountains, soils, etc. (original abiotic environment)

- Man choses his places to live and uses the abiotic environment according to its original features (use of the abiotic environment)

- Man's influence (direct impact, pollution) changes the original abiotic environment in a dynamic process into the abiotic environment existing at the moment of the EIA.

- In this abiotic environment man, fauna and flora live influenced by man's activities and the resulting pollution (existing biotic environment)

- Man encounters the total environment by feeling joy or fear, serenity, compassion, alienation, etc.

Any proposed activity will take place in what is already a dynamic environment. The activity could have direct impacts on any of the environmental components and indirect impacts on even more of them. The basic format of Fig. 3 should help to describe this process according to the schematic presentation of the flow chart in Fig. 4 .

A second recommended structural element is a checklist, such as that in Fig. 5 . Unlike Figs. 3 and 4, where the dynamics in the environment should be expressed, the checklist should give a complete list of all environmental elements. Furthermore, the checklist should remain complete in every subdivision, so the sum of elements in a more-detailed level should be equivalent to the undivided element in the less-detailed level. The intersection through all elements within the same level should add up to the total environment. The function of the checklist is not as a structure for the report, but for use in the development and review of an EIS, so that no element of the environment is overlooked.

A third structural element is our definition of types of alternatives. We distinguish:

(a) Alternatives resulting from giving different functions to resources and in choosing between different goals (e.g. allocation of space in physical plans)

(b) Alternatives resulting from selecting various ways to reach a set goal, by means of:

    (i)   alternative activities: WHAT to do?

   (ii)   alternative locations: WHERE to do it?

 (iii)   alternative processes or techniques: HOW to do it?

(c) The zero-alternative (i.e., no action)

(For any of these types of alternatives, a scenario-approach could be appropriate in early stages of planning).

We recommended that the EIS should always include those types of alternatives that are relevant in the particular stage of the planning process. One can start at the bottom of the list. The no-action alternative can and should always be included.

Even in very late stages of the planning and decisions making process the "HOW" alternatives can be included, whereas the other alternatives can only be included in earlier stages. This structure may enable the proponent to deal with relevant alternatives. At the same time it could prevent the public from expecting certain alternatives when the stage for them has already passed.

D.   TOOLS

The recommendations only state that much has to done on unifying computation models and data bases. So far we have not seen the need, or the possibility, to incorporate the many existing tools in one uniform methodology for EIA in the Netherlands.

REFERENCES

1. Milieu-effectrapportering
(Environmental impact assessment) (English translation available from the
Dutch Ministry of Health and Environmental Protection).
Advies van de Voorlopige Centrale Raad voor de Milieuhygiëne
Ministerie van Volksgezondheid en Milleuhygiëne 1977, VAR 1977/3.

2. Voor onderzoek inzake proefnemingen milieu-effectrapportage en aanvullend
onderzoek (Preliminary research on trial runs with environmental impact
assessment and complementary research), Twijnstra Gudde nv Management Consultants
en DHV Raadgevend Ingenieursbureau BV.
Ministerie van Volksgezondheid en Milieuhygiëne 1977, VAR 1977/21.

3. Milieu-effectrapportage: proefnemingen.
(Trial runs with environmental impact assessment) Twijnstra Gudde nv
Management Consultants en DHV Raadgevend Ingenieursbureau BV.
Ministerie van Volksgezondheid en milieuhygiëne 1979, VAR 1979/12.

4. Milieu-effectrapportage: aanbevelingen.
(Recommendations on environmental impact assessment) (English translation
available from the Dutch Ministry of Health and Environmental Protection),
Twijnstra Gudde nv Management Consultants en DHV Raadgevend Ingenieursbureau BV.
Ministerie van Volksgezondheid en Milieuhygiëne 1979, VAR 1979/13.

5. Royston, M. Background paper for preparatory meeting of the proposed ECE
seminar on practical experiences in environmental impact assessment, 31 August
1977, ECE document ENV/SEM.10/PM/R.2.

6. Börlin, M. Digest of existing methods and models and of their potentialities
for contributing to environmental impact assessment (ECE, ENV/R.81,
16 December 1977)

7. See Fig. 2   for the panel procedure.

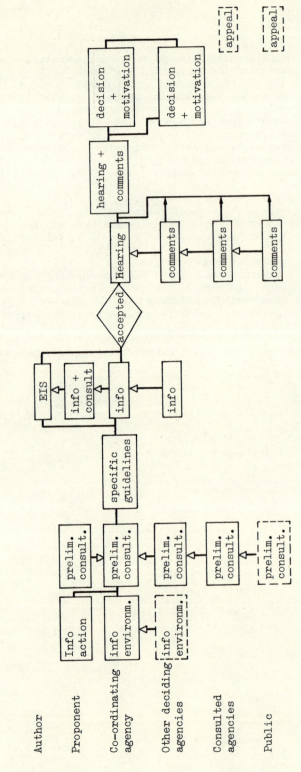

Fig. 1

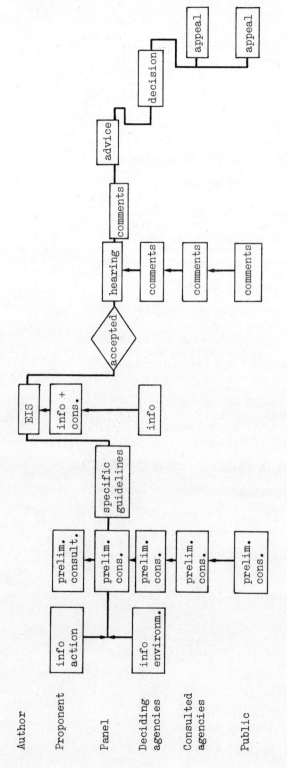

Fig. 2

PANEL PROCEDURE

W. Klein

Figure 3

CONTENTS OF ENVIRONMENTAL IMPACT STATEMENT

    1. Title

    2. Summary

    3. Table of contents

1.   INTRODUCTION

2.   PURPOSE AND NEED OF THE PROPOSED ACTION

3.   EXISTING ENVIRONMENT

    3.1. Original abiotic environment
    3.2. Use of the environment by man
    3.3. Existing abiotic environment
    3.4. Existing biotic environment
    3.5. Environment as experienced by man

4.   THE PROPOSED ACTION

5.   IMPACTS ON THE ENVIRONMENT

    5.1. Impacts on the use of the environment
    5.2. Impacts on the abiotic environment
    5.3. Impacts on the biotic environment
    5.4. Impacts on how the environment is experienced by man

6.   SPOTLIGHT ON THE IMPACTS

    6.1. Unavoidable and irreversible impacts
    6.2. Mitigating measures

7.   GAPS IN KNOWLEDGE AND INFORMATION

8.   COMPARISON

    8.1. Alternatives
    8.2. Standards and Policies

9.   LEGAL PROCEDURES

    4. References

    5. Glossary

    6. Appendices

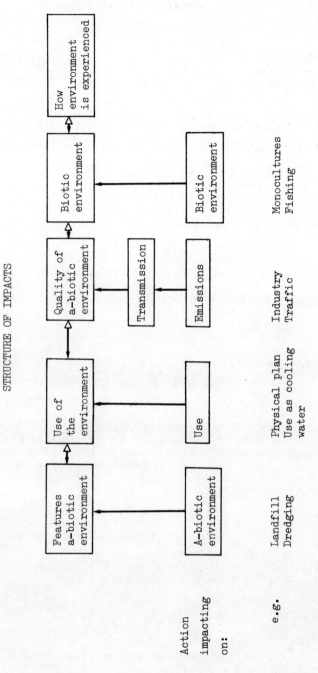

Fig. 4

STRUCTURE OF IMPACTS

Figure 5

CHECKLIST

A.   CONDITIONS OF THE ENVIRONMENT

A.1.   ABIOTIC ENVIRONMENT

A.1.1.   <u>Atmosphere</u>

A.1.1.1.   <u>Structure</u>

                     horizontal and vertical stratification (temperative
                                                   gradient)

                <u>Composition</u>
                     gases
                     particles

                <u>Energetic condition</u>
                     pressure gradient (wind)
                     vibration (sound)
                     radiation (heat, light, X-rays)

A.1.1.2.   <u>Relations</u> (smog, transformations, transportation)

A.1.2.   <u>Hydrosphere</u>

A.1.2.1.   <u>Structure</u>

                     horizontal and vertical divisions (phreatic groundwater,
                     dewatering)

                <u>Composition</u>
                     dissolved matters (phosphates, nitrates)
                     suspended solids (heavy metals)
                     other physical or chemical qualities (pH, COD)

                <u>Energetic condition</u>
                     level
                     radiation
                     stream
                     tidal movements

A.1.2.2.   <u>Relations</u> (between A.1.1. and A.1.2.)

A.1.3.   <u>Lithosphere</u>

A.1.3.1.   <u>Structure</u>

                     layers of sediment or stone with capacity for retention
                     (oil, gas, water)

Composition   Fig. 5 contd.

      stones (granite etc.)
      sediments (clay etc.)
      minerals (coal etc.)
      others (gas, etc.)

Energetic condition

      pressure
      vibration (and shock)
      radiation (temperature, radio-activity)

A.1.3.2.   Relations (between A.1.1. - A.1.3.)

A.1.4.   Pedosphere

A.1.4.1.   Structure

      types of soil
      structure of soil
      geomorphology

Composition

      minerals
      texture
      humidity
      dissolved and suspended solids
      other physical and chemical qualities (pH, C/N)

A.1.4.2.   Relations (between A.1.1. - A.1.4.)

B.   FUNCTIONS OF THE ENVIRONMENT   Fig. 5 contd.

B.1.   PRODUCTION FUNCTION

B.1.1.   Natural production (energy, water minerals, biomass)

B.1.2.   Agricultural production (forestry, agriculture, cotton plantation)

B.2.   CARRIER FUNCTION

B.2.1.   Transport of actions and artefacts (living, infrastructure, recreation)

B.2.2.   Retention (of waste materials)

B.3.   INFORMATION FUNCTION

B.3.1.   Orientation (identification)

B.3.2.   Education (teaching purpose)

B.3.3.   Indicator function (air pollution indicators)

B.3.4.   Scientific information function (fossils)

B.3.5.   Refuge function (genetic information for plant improvement)

B.4.   REGULATION AND PURIFICATION FUNCTION

B.4.1.   Regulation of influences from cosmos, atmosphere and hydrosphere
             (O_3, noise, radiation)

B.4.2.   Soil regulation (erosion prevention)

B.4.3.   Biotic regulation (prevention of insect plagues)

C.   HUMAN REACTION TO THE ENVIRONMENT

C.1.   PHYSICAL HEALTH (physiological, functions, tumours)

C.2.   PSYCHOLOGICAL REACTION
             (aesthetics, fears, annoyance, alienation, happiness)

Costs of Environmental Impact Statements and the Benefits They Yield in Improvements to Projects and Opportunities for Public Involvement

P. L. Cook

(United States)

HISTORICAL DEBATE CONCERNING VALUE OF EISs

Environmental impact statements (EISs) were introduced into the decision-making processes of the United States Government by the National Environmental Policy Act of 1969. The Act requires in Section 102(2)(c) that all agencies of the Federal Government: "Include in every recommendation or report on proposals for legislation and other major Federal actions significantly affecting the quality of the human environment, a detailed statement by the responsible official...". The detailed statement has become known as the EIS.

EISs have been both lauded and defamed. Supporters of NEPA and EISs claim numerous benefits from EISs and the other aspects of the NEPA process. The benefits claimed include:

(a) Reduction of potential adverse environmental impacts of projects both after proposal and during project formulation;

(b) Institutionalization of environmental values in government and corporate planning and decision-making; and

(c) Increased public disclosure and public involvement in decision-making.

In short, proponents of NEPA argue that the statute has brought about substantive changes in decision-making to the benefit of the environment.

NEPA's detractors, on the other hand, argue that these benefits are either illusory or not the result of NEPA. They claim:

(a) Any reduction in potential adverse impacts is a result of sound planning and project formulation, which are improvements in the decision-making process that have been evolving long before NEPA and would have continued without it;

(b) NEPA is principally a procedural hurdle that duplicates existing administrative processes and causes substantial delay in decision-making, which litigation can delay even longer; and

(c) EISs are a paperwork nightmare.

In summary, NEPA's detractors argue that any decision-making improvements measured should not be attributed to EISs or NEPA, and that EISs are principally a non-substantive procedural requirement that results in considerable delay and the generation of substantial paperwork.

PRESSURE OF LIMITED RESOURCES ON ALL PROGRAMMES

The true worth of EISs and other aspects of the NEPA process is not only of great importance to a nation considering the establishment of EIS requirements for the first time, but is also of critical interest to agencies of the United States Government who must spend increasingly scarce resources to comply with NEPA. Even though section 102(2)(c) of NEPA is a statutory requirement, agencies have substantial discretion in deciding which proposed actions need EISs and how they will design their own internal procedures for compliance with NEPA. If agencies perceive that EISs will result in few benefits, they will prepare fewer EISs. This reduction may be tempered by the fact that the agency can be challenged in the courts for not preparing an EIS, but the agency would still be likely to prepare only the bare minimum number of EISs. Similarly, agencies will "cut corners" on the other aspects on the NEPA process, such as reducing the comprehensiveness of the environmental assessment they undertake in deciding if and EIS is necessary.

The problem facing agenices is aggravated when there is intense competition for limited resources. In the United States, the Federal government has recently adopted a form of zero-base budgeting which requires that programmes be re-evaluated each year and that resources allocated be based, at least in part, on their benefits and effectiveness compared with other competing programmes. In this environment all programmes, even those with clear statutory mandates, must demonstrate their worth or suffer loss of resources in the competition with other programmes. EISs and other aspects of the NEPA programme are not exempt from this kind of scrutiny.

ANALYSING NEPA PROGRAMMES

In response to the questions raised concerning the worth of EISs and the pressure of competition for scarce resources, EPA undertook a study of its own EISs to see if it could identify the benefits derived from EISs as well as their costs. Before deciding to limit our study to the benefits and costs of EISs, we took a much broader look at all facets of the programme and measures of performance. An ideal comprehensive programme analysis should include a review of all steps of the NEPA process including:

(a) Submission of a written environmental assessment of the proposed project by an applicant seeking a permit, grant, or other assistance or authorization from the federal government;

(b) Government review of the assessment (or preparation of an assessment on a government initiated project where there is no applicant);

(c) Decision on the need for an EIS;

(d) Preparation of the draft and final EIS if one is needed;

(e) Preparation of negative determination and explanation when an EIS is not needed;

(f) Making the final decisions;

(g) Implementing the decision.

The programme evaluation should answer a number of important questions:

(a) How well is the agency complying with the procedural and substantive requirements of NEPA, the CEQ guidelines, and its own regulations?

(b) What is the quality and quantity of the documents generated (EISs and negative determinations)?

(c) What agency resources are expended in accomplishing the above? A comparison of the resources expended to the quality and quantity of the documents prepared and the extent of the compliance with all requirements will yield a measure of the efficiency with which the agency undertakes its responsibilities.

(d) What are the benefits or merits from all aspects of the NEPA process, including improved decisions, protection of environmental amenities, and project cost reductions?

(e) What are the demerits of the NEPA process, including delays and changes resulting in project cost increases? The net costs of an EIS can be obtained by summing the agency resources expended to prepare an EIS, and the cost increases and decreases in the project brought about by the EIS.

(f) Does ultimate project implementation produce the results predicted in the EIS?

Accomplishing all the above tasks has been a formidable undertaking. Therefore, it was decided to concentrate on analysing the benefits and net costs of EISs prepared by EPA, the reason being that it would make little difference how perfectly one complied with the law and regulations, how many documents were prepared, how perfect the documents were or how efficiently they were prepared if it was not possible to demonstrate that the benefits realized from the EISs were worth the costs incurred. Other aspects of the NEPA process such as assessments, environmental reviews, and negative declarations all could be similarly analysed as to costs and benefits, but resource limitations prevented review of these facets of the programme in the same depth as EISs.

EPA EIS PROGRAMMES

Before discussing the results of the EPA analysis, an explanation is needed of the programmes in which EPA prepares EISs. There are three of these:

(a) Waste water treatment construction grants programme and a few other non-regulatory actions;

(b) New source national pollution discharge elimination system permits (water discharge permits for new sources);

(c) Selected standard-setting regulatory actions (e.g. air, noise, and radiation standards) on which EPA prepares voluntary EISs.

EIS is required by statute to apply NEPA to the first two programmes. This paper will deal with EISs on these two programmes.

The waste water treatment construction grant programme is currently the largest public works programme in the United States Government. Grants to assist municipalities construct public waste water (sewage) treatment works are totalling approximately 2 to 6 billion dollars per year. There are three major steps involved in constructing a treatment work:

Step 1 : Submission by the grantee of a facility plan describing the water quality problems, alternative solutions, the proposed project and the environmental impacts of the proposed project;

Step 2 : Preparation of detailed design drawings and specifications for the proposed projects; and

Step 3 :   Construction of the project.

EISs are generally prepared on the facility plan, early in the development
process, to assure maximum effectiveness of the EIS. EISs are prepared in EPA's
regional offices which are located in each of ten cities in the United States.
The EIS may by prepared in-house by EPA staff, by an EPA contractor or by a
contractor jointly selected by the grantee and EPA and paid for by the grantee
(called a piggybacked EIS). The final EIS must be completed, and the project
modified if necessary, before a step 2 grant can be awarded.

The EPA national pollutant discharge elimination system (NPDES) new source
permit is simply a water discharge permit given to new industrial dischargers.
An applicant for such a permit is asked tp prepare an environmental assessment,
which EPA uses to decide if an EIS must be prepared. If an EIS must be prepared,
it may be prepared in any of the three ways mentioned earlier for facility plan
EISs. The final EIS must be completed before the permit can be issued.

METHODOLOGY OF THE ANALYSIS

To document the benefits and costs of EISs, data were gathered via interviews
with staff and reviews of documents in each of our ten regional offices. A
specific series of questions was asked about each EIS that had been issued in
draft or final form in the past eighteen months to two years. A total of 60 EISs
was evaluated; 51 construction grant EISs and 9 new source EISs. The following
quantitative information was gathered:

(a)   changes that occurred in projects as a result of the EIS;

(b)   environmental amenities protected or enhanced as a result of the EIS;

(c)   public participation activities undertaken because of the EIS; and

(d)   costs of the EIS including project cost increases and decreases
attributable to the EIS.

It is obvious that the first three items represent proxies for the ultimate
benefits that could result from the EISs. The ultimate benefits of the EIS would
include the extent to which EISs result in better decisions, greater public
involvement in decision-making, increased protection for the environment and
reduced project costs. Measuring all but the last of these directly is almost
impossible, so we decided to use the above proxies because they are quantitative,
data for calculating them are available, and they are reasonably accurate
indicators of the ultimate benefits.

For construction grant EISs, the specific project changes that were identified
and totalled were:

(a)   size (capacity) of the waste water treatment plant and/or interceptors
(sewer pipes);

(b)   location of the plant or interceptors;

(c)   level of treatment;

(d)   areas to be serviced;

(e)   sludge disposal;

(f)   hook-up controls;

(g)   method of effluent disposal;

(h)   land use priority.

The categories of change are self-explanatory with the possible exception of
hook-up controls and land use priority. The former refers to zoning ordinance
limitations on access to sewer service for certain areas of the community where
development is not desirable such as flood plains, wetlands, prime agricultural
lands, etc. Land use priority refers to cases where the EIS, which includes
population projections, growth projections and land use planning alternatives,
engenders in the community an awareness of the options for growth and the desire
to ensure that the most desirable alternative is chosen. This increased
awareness is usually characterized by a citizen-initiated effort to develop
(or alter existing) zoning ordinances, subdivision (housing development)
regulations and land use plans.

For new source EISs the following project changes were identified:

(a)   size (capacity) of the treatment plant associated with the industrial
facility;

(b)   location of the facility or transmission corridors (in the case of a
power plant);

(c)   level of treatment of the water effluents and air emissions;

(d)   fly ash disposal.

Most of the EISs on new sources were electric power generating plants, hence
the emphasis on changes relating to power generation.

The second major question answered for both facility plan EISs and new source
EISs concerned the protection of environmental amenities. The study documented
the enhancement of environmental amenities, or the mitigation or elimination of
adverse environmental impacts on:

(a)   wetlands;

(b)   flood plains;

(c)   endangered species (and their habitat);

(d)   prime agricultural lands;

(e)   open space and recreational land;

(f)   aquifer recharge areas (groundwater);

(g)   surface water quality or quantity;

(h)   air quality;

(i)   wild and scenic rivers;

(j)   historic sites;

(k)   archaeological sites;

(l)   other amenities, as well as the prevention or reduction of urban sprawl.

These elements are the environmental amenities most frequently protected or
enhanced as a result of the EIS process. Although they are often directly linked
to the major changes noted earlier, this is not always true. In some instances,
conditions are attached to the construction grant or new source permit which
are indirectly or only remotely related to the major changes caused by the EIS.
Also two or more major changes may, in some cases, result in protection of only
one environmental amenity. For instance, the capacity of a plant, location of an

interceptor and service area could all be altered by the EIS, the principal
benefit being the preservation of prime agricultural lands.

The third area investigated was public participation. Since improvements or
increases in public participation are very difficult to measure directly, the
number of public participation events brought about by the EIS was used instead.
These include public hearings, special meetings, special mailing, and media
supplements. After the draft EISs are issued, public hearings are ordinarily
held to provide for formal public comment. Special meetings are usually held
to provide information to all interested parties, and to receive input from them
during the development of the draft or final EIS. Special mailings serve the same
general purpose. Media supplements are inserts in the newspapers, which may
describe the project and the NEPA process and announce special meetings and
public hearings. Activities noted in the "other" category have included the
formulation of citizens' advisory committees, the hiring of a public relations
firm to disseminate information to the public, and television and radio interviews
with EPA personnel. All the public participation events noted have been conducted
to arouse public interest and then to solicit public input into the decision-
making process.

Finally, costs associated with EIS preparation were studied in detail.
The specific aspects of costs reviewed are listed below:

(a) Delay time: This represents the time span from issuance of the Notice
of Intent (a public notice of the decision to prepare the EIS) to issuance of
the final EIS. In those cases where delays were attributable to other than EIS
preparation activities, appropriate time segments were substracted from the
overall delay time. An example is the case where the EIS preparer (consultant or
EPA employee) must analyse the air quality impacts of a construction grant
project. If the state has not completed air modelling as required by the Clean
Air Act, and such data are required for the EIS analysis, the resultant delay
is not assigned to the EIS in the delay time category. For piggybacked EISs
on construction grants, delay time was established by determining how much
sooner the facility plan could have been approved without simultaneous
preparation of the EIS.

(b) Delay cost: The delay cost is calculated by taking the total project cost
and applying an 8.5 per cent inflation rate compounded annually during the delay
time.

(c) EIS cost savings: The cost saving is determined by comparing the cost of
the project as proposed in the facility plan or proposal by the applicant with
the cost of the selected alternative in the EIS (when the latter is smaller).

(d) EIS cost increase: Any cost increase due to a change from the proposed
project in the facility plan or the project proposed by the applicant to the
project recommended in the EIS.

(e) EIS preparation cost: The cost of the consultant hired to prepare the EIS
and the cost of EPA personnel time in managing the contract, or the EPA personnel
time to prepare the EIS in-house. EPA time is converted to dollars at the rate
of $30,000/man year.

(f) Net cost change: This is the net of delay cost, EIS cost savings, EIS cost
increase and EIS preparation cost.

(g) Total project cost: This is the total capital cost for the construction
grants or new source applicant's project as built or as recommended in the EIS.

(h) Per cent change in total project cost: This is the net cost change
divided by the total project cost.

PROJECT CHANGES MADE AND ENVIRONMENTAL AMENITIES PROTECTED

The study yielded an average of 2.5 major changes per EIS for all EISs. The average for construction grant EISs was 2.7 and the average for new source EISs was 1.1.

Environmental amentiites protected by the EISs averaged 3.1 per EIS overall, 3.3 for construction grant EISs and 1.8 for new source EISs.

All but one of the fifty-one construction grant EISs have caused at least one major change to the original proposal. For environmental amenities protected, eleven construction grant EISs had only one while the rest had between two and ten.

One of the nine new source EISs had no major project changes, one caused three changes and the remainder caused one each. All new source EISs with one exception resulted in protection of one or more environmental amenities.

The lower results for changes and environmental benefits caused by new source EISs is attributed to the smaller opportunity for alteration of new source projects. An EIS is unlikely to influence the level of productivity of a new source industry, the number or location of the recipients or its projects or the land use patterns of the surrounding community. The influence of the EIS is much more closely tied to the treatment and disposal of waste materials, the routing of transmission lines (in the case of a power plant) or the collection and replacement of cooling water.

PUBLIC PARTICIPATION

The average number of public participation events for all EISs was 2.8 per EIS, 3.1 for construction grant EISs and 1.3 for new source EISs. In the opinion of EPA regional personnel interviewed in this study, it was much more difficult to generate public interest in new sources NPDES permits than in the award of grants for waste water treatment plants and systems. Waste water treatment plants seem to generate more interest because they often result in increased service costs to households, and no one wants a treatment plant built near their home. However, where a new source industry requiring a significant labour force is to be located in a sparsely developed area, enthusiastic public involvement might be expected.

COSTS

For fifty construction grant EISs (of the total of fifty-one, one had insufficient cost data for analysis), the average cost was $158,585. The average project cost for those EISs was $82,821,600. Thus, the average ratio of EIS preparation cost to project cost was less than 1/5 of 1 per cent. (.19 per cent).

Of the nine new source EISs reviewed, two had insufficient data for cost analysis. All the EIS preparation and project cost data represent rough estimates, as most of the information came from the various permit applicants who were paying for EIS preparation under a third party agreement. The average project cost was $432,570,000. The ration of EIS to project cost averages is .074 per cent.

The large number of construction grant EISs facilitated a closer look at that programme. The most expensive construction grant EIS cost $1.6 million. The originally-proposed project for which it was prepared, however, had an estimated cost of $865 million. The EIS process on this project resulted in extensive

capacity reductions, elimination of some interceptors and more efficient
dewatering of sludge which rendered existing incinerators sufficient (additional
incinerators had been proposed). The final project, as recommended in the EIS
will ultimately cost $425 million, a substantial reduction. The ratio of the
cost of changes in the project plus EIS preparation cost and delay time cost
to the cost of the project as originally proposed is (-) 50.6 per cent.

The least expensive construction grant EIS has cost $15,000 for a $15 million
project. The ratio between the cost of the EIS and the project cost was a mere
1/10 of 1 per cent. However, the project was delayed for eleven months due
to the EIS. The ratio of the change in the project cost including EIS
preparation and delays and the originally-proposed project cost was +7.9 per cent.

When EIS delay time was factored in to determine total net cost change as a
percentage of the total project cost, nineteen EISs caused net cost reductions
and thirty-one caused net cost increases (only twelve of those were greater than
5 per cent). More significantly, however, the net of all cost increases and
decreases was a saving of $472,937,997 tax dollars. One EIS alone caused a
$438.4 million saving. In calculating the costs of delay attributed to the EISs,
a fairly harsh penalty of 8.5 per cent inflation per year compounded annually
was assessed based on the total project cost. This penalty may be somewhat
unfair, especially on projects financed from annual revenues, since the
availability of funds to pay for the projects are increasing over time because
of inflation at a rate equal to construction costs.

Monentary value of environmental amenities protected and increased public
participation gained as a result of the EIS process have not been factored into
the cost change calculations, because of the difficulty of assigning values in
dollars to such benefits. But reasonable assumptions suggest that, on balance,
all these EISs have been more beneficial than costly. For example, while a
specific value cannot be assigned to wetlands, their value for the remainder of
time compared with their immediate destruction is monumental. Most of the
environmental amenties protected are characterized by the permanence of any
destruction that could occur. Wetlands, flood plains, endangered species, aquifer
recharge areas, wild and scenic rivers, historic sites and archaeological sites
cannot be resurrected once they have been adversely impacted. Air quality,
surface water quality, open space and recreational lands and prime agricultural
lands could be regained only at great expense in time and money. Likewise, urban
sprawl represents an impact very nearly impossible to reverse. Thus the value of
environmental amenitites over extended time periods is likely to make the costs
of EIS preparation and temporary project deferment seem insignificant in
comparison.

CONCLUSIONS

What can one conclude about EPA's EIS activities from these results? It is
obvious that EISs bring about substantive changes in decision-making. Clearly
they are not merely a pro forma paperwork exercise. EISs also bring about
increased protection or enhancement of numerous environmental amenities. The price
one must pay for this in some cases is a slight increase in project costs.
Suprisingly, however, in almost half of the cases studies, there was a decrease
in project cost because of changes made to the project. This demonstrates that
EIS analyses can help improve the cost-effectiveness of projects in addition to
protecting the environment. The EIS process also seems to encourage an increase
in public participation events. While we cannot say that the quality and amount
of public participation increased, it is clear that the opportunity for these
to occur was improved.

These conslusions generally support the claims made by proponents of NEPA rather than the claims made by its detractors. However, this does not mean that NEPA is exclusively responsible for improved decision-making, or that the NEPA process and EISs in particular cound not benefit from critical scrutiny and improvement. In fact a number of valid criticisms such as excessive paperwork, lack of incisiveness of EISs and poor integration into decision-making are the subject of the Council of Environmental Quality Guidelines of 29 November 1978. Hopefully these guidelines and continuous diligence on the part of implementing agencies will make even better a process that one is convinced can stand on its merits.

OTHER RESEARCH EFFORTS

There have been several other recent attempts in the United States to measure the costs and benefits of selected EIS programmes. Most are subjective; a few are quantitative. EPA has conducted a brief survey of Federal and other agencies to determine who had recently done such analyses. Some of the most rigorous and complete studies have been referenced below and synopses have been made of their principal conslusions.

(a) "Effect of NEPA on Corps Studies and Projects (Civil Works) 1970 through 1976" by Office, Chief of Engineers HQDA (DAEN-CWR-P) Washington D.C. 20314, January 1977.

This study was an internal Corps of Engineers document that summarized by category the effect that NEPA has had on 489 Corps' projects from 1970 through 1976. A more specific statement of the effect (the action taken) on each project, the reasons for the action and the origin of the issue was included in an appendix. The results are:

Effect category	Number of projects and studies
Stopped, dropped or abandoned	36
Modified	320
Temporarily or indefinitely delayed	83
Negative reports or studies	10
Board of Engineers for Rivers and Harbours (BRAH) Report midification	28
Reports returned for restudy by BRAH	12

(b) "Effects of Section 102(2)(c) of the National Environmental Policy Act and Section 4(f) of the Department of Transportation Act on the Federal-Aid Highway Program", Report No. DOT-FH-11-9341, prepared for the United States Department of Transportation, Federal Highway Administration, Office of Environmental Policy, Washington D.C. 20590, May 1978.

One of the objectives of this study was to determine the effects on the Federal Aid Highway programme of 102(2)(c) of NEPA (the EIS requirement) and section 4(f) of the DOT Act (a statement of national policy to preserve the beauty of the countryside, parklands, wildlife and waterfowl refuges, and historic sites). Other objectives included a review of the adequacy of regulations and procedures for implementing these requirements, and what improvements could be made to them.

The conslusions reached on the effects of the reulations and procedures are:

- increased project development time;

- increased costs;

- increased environmental awareness;

- better co-ordination and communication with other agencies and the public;

- better planning and decision-making; and

- more attention given to mitigation measures.

Increases in project development time were hard to quantify because most states do not keep records in sufficient detail to isolate the time expended on NEPA or 4(f) matters. The State of North Dakota concluded that the average project planning and development cycle took about five years prior to NEPA and takes about seven years today, although not all of the increase can be attributed to NEPA because of the introduction of other regulatory requirements. Based on Nebraska information, EISs are taking about 230 working days (about one calendar year) for a typical three-mile project on new highway alignment in a rural area. This is about 17 per cent of the time required to advance the project to contract letting. Increases in costs as calculated by Idaho were 1 to 2 per cent, Washington 1 per cent and Nebraska 1/4 to 1/2 per cent for their average rural three-mile projects.

(c) "The California Environmental Quality Act - An Evaluation emphasizing its Impact upon California Cities and Countries with Recommendations for Improving its Effectiveness", prepared for the Assembly Committee on Local Government, John T. Knox, Chairman, November 1975, by Environmental Analysis Systems, Inc., San Diego, California. (This report was being updated as the present paper was being prepared).

This report, sponsored by the State Legislature of California, looks in detail at the effects and costs of the California Environmental Quality Act, which is very similar to the National Environmental Policy Act in requiring environmental impact reports (EIRs) on proposed projects. The report relied upon a number of indirect measures of effectiveness which are stated as questions below:

- Are impacts being identified in EIRs?

- Are changes being made to projects to mitigate impacts?

- Are the decision-makers conditioning or denying projects because of identified impacts?

- Are decison-making bodies changing their procedures to improve environmental protection based on what has been learned in the environmental review process?

- Have the adverse impacts of plans, policies and ordinances been identified and mitigated as a result of the review process?

- To what extent are project proposals environmentally safer?

The answers to these questions were based on an in-depth review of 185 EIRs prepared by twenty-three cities and countries. The review revealed that 57 general types of environmental impacts were identified (pollution, erosion, traffic congestion, loss of open space, etc.). For the 185 EIRs, a total of 1,100 individual impacts were identified and analysed. For 31 per cent of the projects studied, there was at least one instance of mitigation attributable to the environmental reviews. In about 30 per cent of the projects, project approval was conditioned to mitigate an adverse impact. There were no special

conditions in the approval of 53 per cent of the projects. For the remaining
projects, 8 per cent were denied and 9 per cent withdrawn. There was no evidence
of any significant change to the procedures and policies of decision-making
bodies as a result of individual reviews. In addition, there was little evidence
that environmental reviews were identifying adverse impacts of plans, policies
and ordinances, principally because these things are often very general and the
familiar techniques used to review specific projects are not easily adapted to
other areas. While substantial quantitative data were not developed, it appears
that the environmental review procedures are encouraging applicants to submit
proposals that are better from an environmental standpoint, to reduce the time
and expense required to get approval.

Another aspect of this study was an analysis of costs and delays related to
CEQA. The analysis revealed that the incremental costs of CEQA represent about
0.5 per cent of project costs for the State as a whole. Principal costs were
found to be document preparation, carrying costs and delay. Average delay in
reaching a local discretionary decision was three months for projects with an
EIR and one month for projects with a negative declaration.

Finally the study found that some sort of public input occurred on 50 per cent
of the projects. The consultant concluded that the EIR process facilitated public
comment.

(d) "Green Goals and Greenbacks: A Comparative Study of State-Level Environmental
Impact Statement Programmes" prepared by the Institute on Man and Science,
Rennselaerville, New York 12147.

This study focuses on eighteen states which have programmes of environmental
review. Among its findings are: the cost of preparing a state environmental
impact statement averages about $\frac{1}{2}$ per cent of the project cost: state EISs are
prepared on approximately 1 per cent of the state actions: only 20 per cent
encounter delay, litigation or complications. The study makes a number of
recommendations for improving the administrative process and EISs.

"Desegregating" NEPA: A Stronger Role for Alternatives in Environmental Impact Assessment

K. S. Weiner

(United States)

> What is the problem
> What are the alternatives
> Which alternative is best?
>
> John Dewey, 1910

These days it is in vogue to criticize environmental rules of any sort as a burden on private initiative and antithetical to sound economic principle and practice. Some environmental rules, however, not only embody sound business practice, they also encourage the Government to think more like the private economic sector.

Rarely have the concepts of rational economic and environmental conduct coincided more closely than in a well-conceived procedure for environmental impact assessment. The new regulations for implementing the National Environmental Policy Act (NEPA), issued by the Council on Environmental Quality in the Executive Office of the President of the United States, provide a case in point. (1)

Both corporate managers and government bureaucrats are constantly exhorted to identify, choose, and execute practical solutions to real problems. They are pressured to take all relevant factors into account without delay. This basic report examines how the pervasive - and creative - role assigned to alternatives in the environmental impact statement (EIS) reforms in the United States assists in meeting this challenge. The role of "options" or "alternatives" provides a fulcrum for enabling environmental considerations to be lifted up into the mainstream of the planning and decision-making process.

The Business of Making Decisions

The literature of business management abounds with descriptive and prescriptive schemes for managers to employ in making decisions sensibly. Herbert Alexander Simon, who has been venerated by his colleagues "as the man initiating the contemporary study of decision-making", (2) explained in his book The New Science of Management Decision:

> Decision-making comprises four principal phases: finding occasions for making a decison, finding possible courses of action, choosing among courses of action, and evaluating past choices. These four activities account for quite different fractions of the time budgets of executives....

The four fractions, added together, account for what most executives do.

Each business, professor, or management consultant has favourite terms and flow charts to commend to the nation's industrialists. But virtually every theory of decision-making, strategic or operations planning, or executive organization and management that I know includes among its essential components:

(a) the identification and development of alternative choices;

(b) the analysis and comparison of alternatives; and

(c) the making and executing of choices among alternatives. (3)

In short, according to the literature of the business world, if actions are properly planned and executed, the actions will be the result of deliberations which have given a central role to alternatives. (4) The same principle serves as the underlying premise of the environmental impact assessment process in the United States. CEQ's regulations actually say that the comparison of alternatives is the "heart"of an environmental impact statement. (5) Similarly, if managers make their plans and decisions with early and thorough attention to alternatives and the impacts, it is neither an administrative nor economic burden to integrate environmental considerations into planning and decison-making. (6)

The NEPA Process in the United States

A brief recapitulation of the process established by the CEQ regulations may provide helpful background for understanding why the use of the NEPA process corresponds with sensible decision-making and "desegregates" environmental considerations from their historical place at the fringes of planning and decision-making processes.

The process is, at least on paper, simple and straightforward (see Figure 1). An agency begins to consider taking an action. The action may be generated by the federal Government or by an applicant for federal permits, funds, guarantees, and so on. Usually a conscientious official will simultaneously consider not only whether to act (i.e."action/no action") but also how to act (for example, the extent or duration of a grant or permit, conditions which might be attached, other approaches which might accomplish the same objectives better).

If the actions under consideration may affect the environment - whether improving or degrading its quality - the agency must prepare an "environmental assessment" at roughly no later than the time it prepares any other feasibility analyses, (e.g. technical, economic or legal). If the assessment shows that the environmental effects may be "significant", the agency is required to prepare an EIS. If not, the agency makes a "finding of no significant impacts" available to the public and uses the assessment internally to consider the alternatives and their impacts and decides how to proceed. (7)

If an EIS is required, the agency issues a "notice of intent" to prepare a statement and announces the commencement of the "scoping process" to determine the proper content ("scope") of the statement. The scoping process invites other agencies which have expertise, or which share some decision-making authority over the proposal, to join with interested parties, including potential proponents and opponents of the proposal, to identify and sharpen the real issues and to dismiss irrelevant ones.

With the benefit of co-operation from other agencies, the lead agency prepares a "draft" EIS which is filed with the Environmental Protection Agency and circulated to agencies and the public for comment for at least 45 days. After revising the draft, the agency files and circulates a "final" EIS at least 30 days prior to making a decision. This 30-day period provides an opportunity for concerned parties to evaluate the agency's response to their comments and to draw any serious problems to the agency's attention. The 30-day period also provides for the head of one agency to refer the proposal of another agency to CEQ as being "unsatisfactory from the standpoint of public health or welfare or environmental quality." (8) CEQ will review the proposal on the merits and will seek to resolve the interagency dispute. (9) Although its role in resolving "referrals" is advisory, CEQ's views carry great weight. (10)

When a decision is made, the lead agency makes available a formal "record of decision" which explains the decision, states any mitigation and monitoring measures to be taken, identifies the environmentally preferable alternative(s) and explains what considerations were balanced by the agency in reaching its decision.

The entire EIS process may be completed in a time span as short as 90 days, which is a fraction of the time most agencies need to plan proposals with significant environmental impacts. The complete planning of a large public works project or major industrial facility frequently takes 10 to 20 years; major regulations frequently require 1 to 2 years to prepare.

Comment periods may be abbreviated if necessary with the approval of the Environmental Protection Agency. There are provisions for emergencies and modification of time periods. In addition, there are somewhat different rules for legislative proposals, which usually require a single EIS because of legislative schedules and the assurance of public participation through Congressional hearings.

Proposals as Alternatives

In any situation where a proposal for federal Government action could significantly affect environmental quality, the regulations require agency officials to evaluate alternatives and their environmental impact. (11) The regulations explain that there are three basic types of alternatives:

(a) the no action alternative;

(b) other reasonable courses of action;

(c) mitigation measures (not already included in the proposal). (12)

The role of alternatives is so fundamental to decision-making and the EIS that even the notion of a "proposal" - which is a prerequisite for an environmental impact statement - is described in terms of alternatives:

> "Proposal" exists at that stage in the development of an action when an agency subject to the Act has a goal and is actively preparing to make a decision on one or more alternative means of accomplishing that goal and the effects can be meaningfully evaluated. (13)

By defining a proposal in terms of alternative means of achieving a goal, the regulations require decisionmakers to pay serious attention to environmental factors before they have narrowed their choices to a single preferred course of action. By allowing an agency to define its proposals in terms of its objectives and the alternative actions being considered in order to achieve them, the process emphasizes the imperative, stated so frequently in business and management literature, that the solution should be connected to the problem.

The provision also affords protection to government officials who are pressured from within their agencies and by the public to produce a recommendation before the necessary analysis has been prepared. In short, by conceiving a proposal as one of several means to an end, this provision is intended (a) to ensure that alternatives will be fully considered in the early critical phases of agency planning and (b) to set the stage for a genuine assessment of the real choices facing government officials and the public throughout the decision-making process.

There is a world of difference, for example, to higher-level officials and the public in reviewing and reacting to an EIS which describes the agency's "proposal" as:

(a) a dam, which is needed to control downstream flooding of urban areas; or in contrast,

(b) an action to reduce downstreams urban flooding by one of the following means (or a combination of them):

> (1) no federal action required because the local community has sufficient authority to control urban development in the most flood-prone areas;
>
> (2) stricter enforcement of federal flood insurance standards in conjunction with better local environmental zoning laws;
>
> (3) government acquisition of the most flood-prone land so that people living in these areas can afford to move and redevelopment cannot occur;
>
> (4) construction of a dam upstream to halt floodwaters, which is the agency's currently preferred option;
>
> (5) construction of a dike and widening of the existing floodway to improve the flow of water during flood periods.

To express the proposal in the form of (a) above conveys the impression of a fait accompli: the Government has not only made a commitment, for which any discussion of alternatives will smack of pure justification, but the choice was made in a closed-mind fashion ignoring other feasible and possibly wiser alternatives. In addition, the first description of the proposal confuses the problem, the objectives of federal action, and the solution all in one sentence.

The first approach establishes an unnecessarily adversarial stance, and challenges the reviewer to take the extreme position of either accepting or rejecting the proposal. By implying that it will be a tough, uphill fight to produce a different result, opponents are likely to demand no action of any kind in order to establish a strong negotiating position. Such rapid escalation of the debate can easily cause unnecessary controversy, delay and expense.

The second description of the proposal attempts to describe the objective of the action, so that the most appropriate response or technology can be employed. The major drawback of this approach is the opportunity for clever officials to disguise their intentions in a plethora of feasible-sounding alternatives and dissipate the limited resources of reviewers in studying numerous illusory alternatives. In order to minimize this possibility, the regulations also require both draft and final EISs to identify the agency's preferred alternative if one exists. (14) Even the cynic who believes that the chances are unlikely should concede that there is at least a possibility of change - through administrative or judicial review of a capricious decision, if necessary - when

an agency must go on the public record with a responsible analysis of the
various alternatives and their impacts.

The flood control example used above shows how the role of alternatives simply
in defining the agency's proposal can have a profound effect on integrating
environmental consideration with agency planning and decision-making. The
advisability of this approach is even more apparent for proposals which are
not site-specific construction projects. Proposals for new policies (such as
legislation and regulations), programmes (such as a cluster of related actions),
and plans (such as land use plans) are especially amenable to this approach.
Broad policy-oriented proposals are frequently devised because a new or revised
overall attack on a problem is needed, and public debate on the proposal
usually focuses on whether the administrative devices to be employed - whether
grants, loans, regulations, tax credits, or whatever - will be effective in
meeting certain stated objectives.

Alternatives in EISs

Building on the statute, previous guidelines, and case law, the CEQ regulations
require that agencies use the NEPA process to identify and assess all reasonable
alternatives that will avoid or minimize the adverse effects of these actions
upon the quality of the human environment. (15) A decade of experience in the
USA confirms that merely telling officials to integrate environmental
considerations into planning and decision-making is inadequate without specific,
administrative "action-forcing" devices. The regulations provide, for the first
time, a series of specific administrative techniques to connect between
alternatives, EISs, and decisions that are designed to give helpful direction
to policy makers and to ensure compliance with the statute.

The environmental planning and review process can be tied much more closely to
decision-making, and public officials can have an incentive to use these
documents better without unduly limiting their discretion by two simple
requirements: the alternatives analysed in an environmental impact statement
must encompass the range of alternatives which a decision maker ultimatley
considers, and decision makers must consider the alternatives discussed in the
environmental impact statement. (16)

Earlier drafts of the CEQ regulations would have required an environmental impact
statement to cover the same specific alternatives (rather than the range of
alternatives) ultimately considered by the responsible officials. The US Forest
Service suggested the language now found in the proposed regulations, pointing
out that there may be many slight variations and combinations of alternatives.
As long as the range of choices are evaluated, and the impact statement
encompasses the range of choices considered by decision makers, the impact
statement has served the ingenious function of encouraging the creation of
alternatives and at the same time it limits an official's ability to act
without selecting the alternative analysed in the environmental analysis.

An additional incentive reinforces the requirement that the decison maker
consider the alternatives in the EIS; it also helps to ensure the timely
integration of environmental considerations and agency planning and decision-
making: agencies may not commit resources prejudicing the selection of
alternatives before making a final decision. (17)

One of the most effective ways to bring environmental considerations into the
mainstream of the decision process is also one of the most obvious: start the
text of environmental impact statements with a comparative analysis of the
environmental consequences of the alternatives. (18) There are many important

reasons for requiring a comparative analysis of alternatives at the beginning, not the least of which is psychological. Writers tend to pay greater attention to writing their opening lines, and readers tend to give full attention to the opening sections of a report.

More fundamentally, a simplified format which focuses on alternatives from the beginning assists better choices to be made from a substantive viewpoint. The reader gets acclimated to think in terms of options, and an inquiring mind challenges assumptions which often acquire a life of their own as a report proceeds. To combat the situation in which the preferred option is examined in detail while only cursory analysis is provided for the other alternatives, the provision also incorporates a standard for the adequacy of the analysis of alternatives. The regulations require agencies to devote "substantial treatment" to each alternative "so that reviewers may evaluate their comparative merits." An earlier draft of the regulations would have required "substantially equal treatment" for each alternative, but this was rejected as too inflexible. Alternatives may differ in size, complexity, and degree of environmental impact, and it would therefore be inappropriate to imply that each option required the same number of pages in an EIS.

Choice Among Alternatives

The regulations provide that environmental documents, comments, and responses accompany the proposals through existing agency review processes (together with any other relevant documents, of course) and that environmental documents must be part of the record in any formal proceedings. (19) However, the key action-forcing device in the regulations regarding an agency's choice among alternatives is the record of decision. (20)

Like corporate managers, agency officials should be accountable for their choices. In Anglo-American law, public officials making public investments and exercising the public trust are held to standards at least as stringent as those affecting private corporate executives vis-à-vis their stockholders and boards of directors. Public officials should also have the benefit of serious and informed debate in making their choices. The record of decision is intended to promote both these goals by requiring agencies to prepare a concise statement available to the public, which explains the decision in light of the optimal choice from an environmental point of view. (21)

The national environmental policy, enunciated in Section 101 of NEPA, commands the Federal establishment to use "all practicable means and measures" to preserve and enhance environmental quality. Thus, assuming a proposal does not involve conflicts with other values - and many decisions involve choices which are fully consistent with other values - an agency would be required to take the course of action which most furthers the national environmental policy. A shorthand expression for "the course of action which most furthers the national environmental policy," is "environmentally preferable alternative."

It would be not only natural but, one would expect, long overdue for agencies routinely to identify environmentally preferable alternatives. Such a provision serves the dual function of refining our understanding of the national environmental policy in terms of specific actions and of fostering intra-agency and public debate on those actions most in accord with the policy. NEPA is not a "paper tiger" but an effective force; the statute's mandate, as stated in Section 102(1) of the Act, is essentially to ensure that all US policies, regulations, and public laws are interpreted and administered in accordance with the national environmental policy.

Some have argued that this provision in the CEQ regulations will unduly "tilt the balance" toward environmental concerns. But the requirement is a disclosure provision; it does not require the environmentally preferable alternative to be selected. The provision specifically allows agencies to discuss, in addition to environmentally preferable alternatives, preferences among alternatives based on any relevant factors, including economic and technical considerations and agency statutory missions. The provision does focus attention on the substantive merits of agency decisions. In fact, the provision serves precisely the function intended by NEPA's authors, repeated on the floor of the Congress at NEPA's introduction and passage:

> A statement of environmental policy is more than a statement of what we
> believe as a people and as a nation. It establishes priorities and gives
> expression to our national goals and aspirations. It serves a
> constitutional function in that people may refer to it for guidance in
> making decisions where environmental values are found to be in conflict
> with other values. (22)

Many federal officials lament that it may often be impossible to identify an environmentally preferable alternative because the tradeoffs are too difficult to make. Some alternatives involve wetlands, others prime agricultural land, still other virgin timber stands, air pollution, or adequate housing. Yet these are the difficult tradeoffs with which officials are confronted every day. The public deserves to know how their servants, who hold the nation's environment in trust for present and future generations, perceive their obligations; The National Environmental Policy Act makes such a statement obligatory. Except in extreme cases, these judgements fall well within the authority and discretion of agency officials to make. The resulting discussions should contribute substantially to bringing "environmental values to the fore," as intended by NEPA's sponsors. In time, these decisions may establish precedents, traditions and guidelines which will make some of the hard choices a little easier, or at least better informed.

The record of decision also requires specific commitments to the enforcement and monitoring of any mitigation measures, to ensure that decisions are properly executed. (23) By explaining the choices among alternatives and providing a programme to evaluate the subsequent effects of decisions, the regulations force closer attention to the consequences of the options, thereby increasing the likelihood that any tradeoffs to be made between environmental and other factors will in fact be known and considered together.

CONCLUSION

Focusing on alternatives is not merely good management practice or a clever device for making environmental considerations an integral part of agency decisions. A quarter of a centruy ago, at one of the formative international symposia on the environment, Lewis Mumford eloquently articulated the basis for environmental assessment. "For human behavior is not merely purposive and goal-seeking but conscious," he observed, "not merely tied to existing ecological associations but capable of projecting a whole new pattern of relations in which both man's objective knowledge of nature and his subjective projection of dream and wish and imagined purpose modify natural processes and bring them to a different destination." (24)

"Different destinations" are the stuff alternatives are made of. The importance of conceiving a "whole new pattern of relations" leading to a "different destination" has been shown over and over again in nearly a decade of experience in the United States under the National Environmental Policy Act; this may well be the Act's most lasting contribution to our survival as we near the twenty-first century.

REFERENCES

1. Regulations for Implementing the Procedural Provisions of NEPA (hereafter, Regulations; references to the Regulations will use the Code of Federal Regulations section citation), 40 CFR 1500, 43 FR 55978-56007 (29 November 1978). The Council on Environmental Quality (CEQ) created by Title II of the National Environmental Policy Act (NEPA) 42 U.S.C. 4321-4347 (section citations of NEPA refer to P.L. 91-190, 1 January 1970, as amended by P.L. 94-52, 3 July 1975 and P.L. 94-84 (9 August 1975). CEQ's duties are further elaborated in the Environmental Quality Improvement Act of 1970 (42 U.S.C. 4371-4374) and Executive Order 11514 (5 March 1970) as amended by Executive Order 11991 (24 May 1977).

2. Simon, Herbert Alexander, The New Science of Management Decision (1960) p. 40. If the reader is interested in finding some major analogues in CEQ's Regulations, they include Sections 1502.13, 1502.14, 1505.2, and 1505.3, respectively.

3. Ibid.

4. The obvious major "exception" is the theory of "satisficing" decisions, in which the decision maker settles on the first alternative that can apparently succeed, without attempting to "optimize" the decision by finding an alternative which produced the maximum benefits. For further explanation, see Simon's works or Charles E. Lindbloom's article "The Science of Muddling Through" in Dyson and Gore's The Making of Decisions pp. 155 to 156. The theory does not offer a true exception because the decision maker must still develop and compare alternatives until a satisfactory one is found. Simon also does not explicitly include the execution of a choice among his four principal phases because he asserts that the execution requires a reiteration of the four principal phases, this time directed towards implementing the choice. Simon, id. pp. 41 to 42.

5. The other component of decision-making universally present in the literature in some form is the correct identification of the problem that the proposal addresses, or, in Simon's terms "finding occasions for making a decision" (see reference 3). cf. Section 1502.13 of the Regulations: "The [EIS] statement shall briefly specify the underlying purpose and need to which the agency is responding in proposing the alternative including the proposed action." See also Section 1508.9(b) imposing a similar requirement on environmental assessments.

6. Several recent studies have unequivocally confirmed this point, including the final report of the United States Commission on Federal Paperwork entitled Environmental Impact Statements (Washington, D.C., 25 February 1977); a report by the General Accounting Office, the investigative arm of the Congress, entitled The Environmental Impact Statement - It Seldom Causes Long Project Delays But Could Be More Useful If Prepared Earlier, CED-77-99 (Washington, D.C., 1977); and a two-year study by the Council on Environmental Quality entitled Environmental Impact Statements: Six Years' Experience by Seventy Federal Agencies (Washington D.C., 1976).

7. Although an assessment is not necessary if the agency has decided to prepare an environmental impact statement, agencies may and frequently do prepare assessments wherever they are useful to assist planning and decision-making.

Agencies may involve the public in the preparation of environmental assessments.

8.   Section 1504.1(b) and (c). The Regulations represent an improved version of the formal referral procedures, first established by Interim Guidance issued by CEQ on 11 August 1977.

9.   The range of CEQ reponses to a referral are indicated in Section 1504.3(f) (1-7). CEQ does not have veto power over other agency proposals. Neither the referral nor CEQ's response generally treats the issue of the adequacy of an EIS but, rather, the substantive merits and drawbacks of the proposal.

10.   In the case of Alaska V. Andrus, 11 ERC 1321 (D.C., D.C. 1978), the court reviewed a controversial decision by the Interior Department to proceed with an oil and gas sale in the Gulf of Alaska. In upholding the Secretary of Interior's decision but requiring certain mitigating measures, the court noted:

> The Secretary's duty to consider the alternative of delay is underlined by the EPA/CEQ determinations, made pursuant to Section 309 of the Clean Air Act [a NEPA referral] , that the sale was "environmentally unsatisfactory" ... We believe that this requires, at a minimum, that where environmental agencies have concluded that a particular project is "environmentally unsatisfactory," and where a "mission-oriented" agency has none the less decided to proceed with the project, it must articulate clearly its reasons for doing so.
>
> 11 ERC 1329 (ft. 44)

Another case which affirmed CEQ's interpretations of NEPA stated that "they have consistently been regarded with great deference when courts have been faced with problems of statutory construction." Alaska V. Carter, 12 ERC 1486 (D.C. Alaska) at 1493. See, also, Warm Springs Task Force v. Gribble, 417 U.S. 1301, 1310 (1974).

11.   See, for example, Sections 1508.9(b) on assessments, 1501.7(a) on scoping, 1502.14 and .16 on EISs, 1504.2(f) and .3(c)(vi) on predecision referrals, and 1505.2(b) on record of decision.

12.   Section 1508.25(b). Also see Section 1508.20 for a further explanation of "mitigation".

13.   Section 1508.23.

14.   Section 1502.14(e).

15.   Section 1500.2(e). See, also, Sections 1502.14(b) and 1507.2(d).

16.   Sections 1502.2(e) and 1505.1(e).

17.   Sections 1502.2(f) and 1506.1.

18.   Section 1502.10.

19.   Section 1505.1. The Regulations contain several provisions explicitly requiring agencies to consider environmental factors at the same time as other considerations throughout the planning and decision-making process. See, for example, Sections 1500.2(c), 1501.2(b), 1501.7(a)(7), 1502.2(g), and 1502.23.

20.   Section 1505.2.

21. Section 1505.2(b).

22. 115 Congressional Record 14860, 40416 (1969).

23. Section 1505.3.

24. William L. Thomas, Jr., <u>Man's Role in Changing the Face of the Earth</u> (1956) p. 1149.

FIGURE 1

The NEPA Process
Established by CEQ Regulations

ACTION/NO ACTION
(including decision, implementation,
enforcement of mitigation, monitoring)

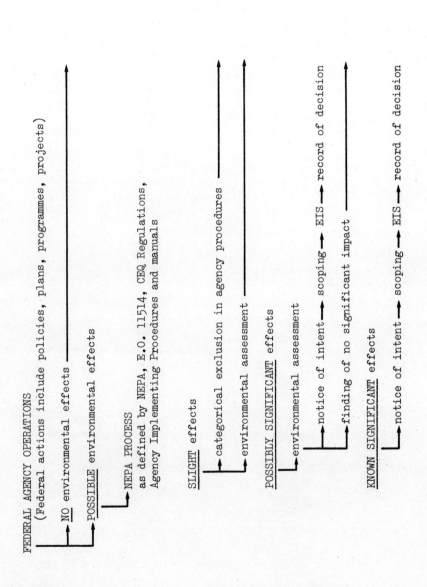

Methodology and Comprehensive Monitoring Programme for Environmental Pollution

Y. Izrael, F. Rovinskiy and L. Filippova

(USSR)

It is of great importance that this ECE Seminar, devoted to environmental impact assessment, should consider the methodology and
programme for integrated ecological monitoring, since this is the
chief means of making an adequate assessment of the anthropogenic
impact on the environment on the one hand, and assessment of the
responses of natural systems to this impact on the other. It is
well known today that the impact made by man on the environment
has reached, in some cases, a significant level and has even a
global scale, i.e, some impacts can be observed in remote areas
where there is no human activity and therefore no direct impact
on the environment. In particular, it concerns environmental
pollution, the monitoring of which is the main concern of this
paper.

In our view (1) monitoring is a system of observations, assessments
and forecasts of the state of the environment under the impact
of anthropogenic factors, and of pollution in particular. This
definition distinguishes between man-made changes in the natural
systems and their natural variability (2,3).

Ecological monitoring, we believe, should be aimed not only at
observation and recording of environmental characteristics but
also at prediction of their variation caused by different degrees
of anthropogenic impact and, still more important, at the assessment
of the observed or predicted state.

The specific feature of ecological monotoring is its comlex nature.
This means first of all that the objects for monitoring should
be simultaneously (1) the whole assembly of natural systems, biota
included, and (2) the assembly of environmental characteristics
(chemical, physical and biological).

Thus the aim of integrated ecological monitoring of environmental

EIA h

pollution is to obtain data on the observed and predicted pollution impacts on natural systems and the observed and predicted
response of natural systems to these impacts. Bearing the latter
task in mind, it is necessary to stress the importance of obtaining
assessments and forecasts of the consequences of pollution at the
level of populations, communities and ecosystems.

Monitoring is therefore an information system. It does not involve
problems of environmental quality control. The product of this
system is information (data or predictions) for the national
administrative bodies to use in making decisions in the interests
of the environment and human health protection, natural resources
management, and of other vital problems facing modern industrialized
and developing countries.

Two types of monitoring should be distinguished, depending on the
level of impact. The sub-systems of impact monitoring (in the area
directly affect by pollution sources) and background monitoring
(in the areas affected by global and regional pollution processes)
are methodologically and technically different and require separate
approaches tu their organization. For obvious reasons, central
importance is now given to the problem of impact monitoring.
Monitoring systems for environmental pollution in cities and industrial centres, where the damage caused by pollution can and sometimes does reach a significant level, are in operation in many
countries. The problem of the background impact of pollutants
may appear to be of less importance, as the damage caused by
this impact is not so evident. There is no well-developed,opera-
tional system for background monitoring in any country as yet.
Nevertheless, we can assert today that this neglect of possible
global changes in the biosphere is not justified (4,5). The
inadequacy of background monitoring development, as compared to
that of the impact monitoring, can be explained partly by the
underestimation of the ecological consequences of environmental
pollution on the regional and global scale; there are, however
also complicated methodological and technological problems to be
solved as well. The assessment and forecasting of the relatively
low pollutant concentrations, and the rather small rates of change
in the state of ecological systems that are bharacteristic of such
background monitoring , is an undeveloped field of research in
many aspects.

The Soviet Union is a highly developed industrial country with
rapidly developing agriculture and growing cities. Its environment
is affected by man's activities and therefore there is a need for
objective assessment of this impact and for information on environmental changes caused by both natural processes and human activity.

In the USSR, the levels of pollution have been observed for about
20 years and the monitoring system of today was established by the
Decree of the CPSU Central Committee and the USSR Council of
Ministers of 29 December I972 "On the Advance of Nature Protection

and Natural Resources Management" which envisaged the creation
of a united State service for observation and control of environmental pollution. The USSR State Committee for Hydrometeorology
and Control of the Natural Environment was designated the lead
agency for implementing this activity together with the control
of atmospheric pollution sources. A number of other institutions
participate in the monitoring system: the Ministry of Health
controls the environmental quality effects on public health; the
Ministry of Water Management and Irrigation keeps under control
sources of water pollution, and undertakes water resources management; the Ministry of Geology and Mineral Resources Conservation
controls ground-water pollution; the Ministry of Agriculture,
Fishery and Forestry controls the state of biological resources.
It is hard to exaggerate the role of the State Committee for
Science and Technology and the Academy of Sciences in coordinating
and carrying out scientific research on problems of environmental
protection.

The principal aims of the State Service are to obtain and assess
data on environmental pollution, in time and in space, as well as
urgent information about sudden changes of levels of pollution
which require protective measures, and to deliver all the information
to users. The Service also produces forecasts and warnings about
probable changes in air, soil, land and sea water pollution.
Observational data on the quality of natural systems also contribute
to the assessment of the efficiency of environmental protection
measures and for long-range forecasts of the state of the environment
in the country.

Together with observations of the level of air, soil fresh- and
sea-water pollution, the observational programme includes accompanying
meteorological, hydrological and hydrobiological observations to
analyse (and forecast) pollution and to identify sources of pollution.
All the water pollution control stations, for instance, are provided
with data on water discharge. This is needed to predict and analyse
the balance of pollutants in a given basin, as well as to study
the fate of pollutants in migration processes.

This principle has been further developed. Due to the fact that
these observations cover soils, atmospheric precipitation and
sea bed sediment in fresh- and sea-water bodies, it is possible
to obtain regular data on the balance and cycle of pollutants,
their transport by different media, accumulation in different sinks,
and so on.

Another principle is the systematic order of observations and
unification of methods of measurements. This envisages observations
at predetermined locations and at fixed hours to detect space
and time patterns of pollutant distribution. To ensure data compatibility, all the methods are uniform and obligotary. Considerable
importance is attached to establishing standards for methods and
means of analysis, as well as to the design pollution control
instruments and the introduction of automatic observation systems.

To provide effective scientific and operational guidance, the
Service is subdivided into: the atmosphere pollution control
network; surface water pollution control network; sea water
pollution control network; soil pollution control network; control
of pollution sources; and the background observational network
(biosphere reserves, regional and base-line stations).

Air pollution control is now being implemented in more than 350
cities. The observational programme involves monitoring such
widespread pollutants as dust, sulphur dioxide, nitrogen dioxide,
carbon monoxide and, if necessary, monitoring specific substances
in individual cities. The list of such substances varies from
place to place and includes sulphuric acid vapour, ammonia hydrogen
sulphide , carbon sulphide, phenol, hydrogen fluoride, chlorine,
methylmercaptan, benzopyrene, ozone, mercury, lead, cadmium, zinc,
arsenic, manganese, chrome, vanadium, nickel, cobalt, and so on.

Surface water control is being implemented in 4 000 sites on over
1 200 most important water bodies of the country (rivers, lakes,
reservoirs). The observational programme involves detection of a
number of factors: temperature, odour, suspended matter, minerals,
Pt units, turbidity, CO_2, pH, eH, dissolved oxygen, BOD_5, COD
basic ions, biogenous components, as well as such widespread
pollutants as oil, detergents, light phenols, pesticides, heavy
metals. The general programme may also include control of pollutants
specific to a certain water body.

The sea water control network comprises 1 700 stations of various
categories covering all the inland and marginal seas. The programme
involves detection of oils, pesticides, heavy metals, phenols,
detergents and, as necessary, detection of dissolved oxygen,
hydrogen sulphide, pH, BOD_5, nitrogen compounds, phosphorous compounds.

Soil pollution control is being implemented both in agricultural
zones and areas adjacent to industrial energy development centres.

Subject to detection in agricultural zone soils are: DDT[1] and
its metabolites, hexachlorocyclohexane, granosane, polychloroprene,
metaphos,[2] cirame,[2] cevin,[2] carbotion[2], heptachlorine, zinc, phosphide,
and some other pesticides. As for the soils near industrial areas,
the elements are mercury, lead, cadmium, arsenic, vanadium, nickel,
cobalt, chrome, zinc, manganese, molybdenum, beryllium, selenium,
benzopyrene, polychlorobiphenyl.

Control of emissions and pollution sources is being carried out
so as to take the most effective measures for reducing environmental
pollution and for assessing information on the state of the environment. Values of maximum permissible discharge (MPD) have been
established to limit pollutant emission to the environment. The
MPD development requires consideration of geophysical factors
that affect the distribution and dissemination of pollutants, of
technological and economical possibilities to limit emissions,

---

[1] Since 1970 DDT has been out of use in the USSR but its residuals
should be controlled due to their high persistence.
[2] References are to the trade names of pesticides.

and of the actual state of the environment. Methods for estimating emission concentrations of various pollutants in the atmosphere and water bodies are used to establish MPD critaria for different branches of industry. Introduction of MPD criteria into various branches of industry and economy, and supervision and instrumental control of their observance have been continuously expanding, for they are an efficient factor in environmental protection.

The basic criteria for assessing air, soil, fresh- and sea-water quality are maximum permissible concentrations (MPC) that are used at present by the State Service. MPC is a chemical compound concentration, the daily long-term impact of which on humans does not cause any pathological changes or diseases detectable by modern methods and does not disturb the biological optimum for man (e.g., occurrence of disagreeable odour or other undesirable organoleptic characteristics in air or water).

MPCs have up to now been established for over 150 substances and 20 of their compounds in air, as well as for 500 substances in water for sanitary-municipal use, 32 substances in sea water, and for a number of substances in soils. MPCs have also been established for 60 substances in fresh water bodies and seas used for fisheries.

This number of substances and indices of MPC has led to problems in optimizing the monitoring programme. Different approaches have been used; the main ones are as follows.

First, substances subject to monitoring are those with considerable emissions; their environmental pollution tends to be widespread or universal. For urban air they are sulphur dioxide, dust, nitrogen oxides, carbon monoxide; for natural waters - oil, phenols, detergents, some metals; for soils - pesticides.

Second, the most toxic substances are also monitored, i.e. substances with very low MPC values, in the locations where their occurrence is confirmed by observational data.

Substances in the third group monitored are those known to be discharged in particular regions. They may not include any of the above -mentioned substances, but may be of considerable local significance.

The information received in the State Service is sorted according to different categories of urgency and then delivered to users. Information on sudden changes in levels of pollution caused either by unfavourable meteorological conditions or by technological or other violations is delivered to the local Party, Soviet or National Economy organizations for immediate action. At the same time it is transmitted to the State Committee for Hydrometeorology and Control of the Natural Environment for delivery to the central Party, Soviet and National Economy organizations.

Routine information includes monthly, quarterly and annual observations. Observations and information analyses are carried out in situ

and the results are transmitted to the State Committee for additional
analysis and comparison, the results of which are delivered to the
governing bodies. Thus, routine information serves also the purposes
of environmental protection planning, implementing the activity of
the State in this sphere, for example long-term forecasting (20 to
30 years) of the national economy and natural resources management.

As well as observations, forecasting of expected pollution levels
is carried out. Industry switches from one mode of operation to
another that has a lower discharge of pollutants on the basis of
forecasts and warnings about the approach of unfavourable meteorological conditions. Some 5 500 forecasts of this type, with a mean
reliability of about 85%, were made in 1978. A significant decrease
in the maximum concentrations of air pollutants was registered in
many towns due to these actions.It should be stressed that this may
be achieved without large additional expenditures.

The Service also participates in long-term forecasting of the state
of the environment . Today, these forecasts are taken into account
when State funds are allocated for environmental protection, and
when annual and 5-year plans and long-range complex programmes for
the national economy are developed. These forecasts enable identification to be made of: (a) the most seriously affected regions
(from the point of view of the anthropogenic load) and branches
of the economy in the country (b) the actual or potential dangerous
impacts (c) the ecological reserves available for use in the national
economy.

The results of observations and assessment testify to the fact
that the state of the environment in the USSR is satisfactory.

Our achievements in the matter of environmental protection have
become possible owing to the great attention and continuous concern
of the Party and the Government. In the last decade Decrees of the
CPSU Central Committee and Council of Ministers been passed that
foresee major actions on nature conservation and resources management. Of great importance is the fact environmental protection is
one of the sections of the State Plan for the development of the
national economy; considerable material resources have been allocated
to this activity.

One of the major achievements of nature conservation in our country,
indicated by the State Service, is the stabilization of levels
of environmental pollution in general and their reduction in some
cases. Taking into account the continuous growth of the national
economy, it is evident that environmental pollution per unit of
production has been reduced.

Special consideration should be given to the development of background integrated ecological monitoring in the USSR. This is a
self-contained subsystem of the State Service, the major aim of
which is to observe and predict changes of the state of the environment on a global scale. For the reasons mentioned in the beginning

of this paper, establishing this system has required the solution
of specific problems and the development of novel approaches to
the construction of a network for background monitoring.

This network has now been created. It consists of base-line and
regional stations, some of which are located within biosphere
reserves so the latter become not only sites for integrated observations but also for fundamental research on the state of the biosphere.

The system for background monitoring of environmental pollution
consists of the following main elements.

(a) Geochemical and Geophysical Monitoring.

This element can also termed abiotic monitoring, because it is
designated to obtain information on the levels of environmental
pollution and on the intensity and character of the pollution that
affects biological systems. It is also designed to predict future
levels of pollution and consequent impact on biota. The main priority
is to detect the most important pollutant concentrations in air,
precipitation, natural waters, soil and biota and to develop and
improve precise methods and instruments for analysing small quantities of these pollutants in natural systems. These methods cannot
however, be used to provide forecasts of environmental pollution.
Therefore, studies of the migration, cycle and transformation of
pollutants in natural systems have received particular attention
recently (6). These involve mathematical modelling of the behaviour
of pollutants in the environment, using experimentally-obtained
coefficients of pollutant transformation and transition. These
mathematical models take into account hydrometeorological and climatological characteristics obtained by supplementary observations.
From these observations and investigations, it may be possible to
assess and predict abiotic conditions of the environment and the
actual intensity and character of impacts on biological systems.

The full programme of background monitoring envisages measurements
of the following priority pollutants:

    - in the atmosphere: sulphur dioxide, suspended particles,
carbon dioxide, nitrogen oxides, ozone, carbon monoxide, active
hydrocarbons, DDT, mercury; aerosol; lead, arsenic,
cadmium, benzopyrene, sulphates, etc;

    - in the seas: as above, plus detection of oil.

Observations biosphere reserves enable data on migration, cycle
and balance of the above substances to be obtained.

(b) Biological Monitoring.

This type of monitoring is designated to assess and predict biotic
response to background pollution. Its principles and programme
have less developed than for abiotic monitoring. Though biological
and ecological studies of natural systems have been carried out

extensively and for a long time, they were not designed to find the
connexions between man-made impacts (pollution) and the response of
ecosystems and their elements to such impacts. The task of detecting
very small effects and of estimating the trend of very minor changes
in the state of the biota of anthropogenic origin is an extremely
complex task compared to situations with very significant impacts
when biotic response is quite evident. Besides, the available ecological methods are not orientated towards the prediction of changes in
the state of populations, communities and ecosystems in response
to anthropogenic factors.

To solve such problems we have developed principles for assessing
and predicting biotic response to the impact of background pollution (7). A mathematical model of exogenous succession, used to
predict ecosystem changes at background levels is the foundation
of these works. The information incorporated into the model consists
of data obtained from the abiotic monitoring programme on observed
and predicted levels of pollutant effect on biota, and of data on
ecosystem and species sensitivity to these effects ("dose-effect"
curves). The changes (experimentally measured for certain species
and then interpolated for the remaining species of a given ecosystem)
are taken as an integral indicator of biotic sensitivity to the background impact of pollution.

From exogenous succession model can be obtained information (forecasts) on the levels of pollutant impact that would cause elimination
of the most sensitive species, the ways and rates at which this
may occur, and similarty information about significant reductions
in numbers of population of individual ecosystems.

Since the seminar is devoted to the problem of assessing impact on
the environment, the focus should be on environmental quality assessment in the light of the problem of creating an optimum monitoring
system.

In using available information on environmental pollution levels
currently and predicted for the future, as well as information on
the qualitative and quantitative changes of ecosystems that would
take place, we should first of all answer the question whether such
levels of pollutions and respective biotic changes are acceptable.
In order to answer this question we should have concept of what is
a desirable or acceptable state of the environment, in terms specific
indicators. Such ideas on an acceptable quality of the environment
have been developed from the point of view of human health and
well-being. These are the touchstones, expressed in terms of maximum
permissible concentrations (MPC), that are used most frequently in
the monitoring system for environmental quality assessment. As has
been pointed out (8), MPC standards are adequate criteria for evaluating
environmental quality in cities and industrial centres where the
environment has undergone significant changes. To assess the state
of the environment, we should first develop environmental quality
criteria within the framework of ecological monitoring and then
develop ecological standards of impact, taking into account the need
for favourable development and functioning of natural systems. These

standards should indicate the maximum permissible ecological load
(MPEL) on an ecosystem, allowing for integrated impacts(1). Such
a criterion should be based essentially on ecosystem stability and
it should take into account the ecosystem's ecological reserve. The
main indicators of a natural system's prosperity are known; their
presence shows that the environmental quality is satisfactory for
this system. We should use integrated indicators (criteria) of the
state of the biological system in ecological monitoring. This concept
has been chosen as the basis for programme and approaches under
development. The ecological requirements for environmental quality
would differ depending on the peculiarities of the region under
consideration, and on the type of man's activities in it (8). Assessment of information on changes of the state of ecological sytems
would also differ. For example, it is evident that in most cases the
acceptability of a predicted disappearance of a species should
be considered on the basis of a comparison of the damage that would
result from its disappearance with the benefit obtained from the
economic activity that caused this impact. This approach, however,
is not applicable in case of unique natural objects and biosphere
reserves, the major aim of which is conservation of genetic resources.
In such situations, maintenance of all species can be accepted as
the criterion for the necessary environmental quality in biosphere
reserves. This is actually impracticable due to existing impacts;
we know that even today there are many species missing from various
ecosystems, though not all of them have vanished as a result of pollution impacts. Maybe we should accept the maintenance of species that
form an ecosystem, starting with a trophic level, as the efficiency
criterion for environmental quality in biosphere reserves to be used
in the ecological monitoring system. In any case, an immediate elaboration of ecological and economic criteria for assessing the acceptability
of observed and predicted loads on the natural environment appears to
be urgently needed. This will enable us to optimize the monitoring
system and, hence, to provide for more efficient environmental quality
management.

REFERENCES

1. Izrael,Yu.A., "Global Observational System. Forecast and Assessment
   of Environmental State Changes. Monitoring Basis." Meteorology and
   Hydrology, No.7, 1974, pp 3-8.

2. ibid. "On the Biosphere State Assessment and Monitoring Stipulation".
   Reports of the Academy of Sciences, Vol.226, No.4, 1976, 955-957.

3. Gerasimov,I.P. Scientific Basis for the Environment Monitoring. In
   "The Environment State Monitoring". Procedings of 1st USSR/U K
   Symposium, 1977, Gidrometeoizdat, Leningrad, 41-52.

4. Rovinsky, F.Ya., L.M. Filippova, Yu.A. Izrael. The Background
   Monitoring: Regional and Base-Line Stations, Biosphere Reserves.
   In "Natural Environment State Monitoring", Gidrometeoizdat,
   Leningrad, 1977, 116-130.

5. Filippova, L.M., Insarov G.E., F. N. Semevsky, S.M. Semenov.
   On the Structure and Problems of Ecological Monitoring. In "Problems
   of Ecological Monitoring and Ecosystem Modeling", Vol.1,
   Gidrometeoizdat, Leningrad, 1978, 19-32.

6. Izrael, Yu.A., I.M. Nazarov, L.M. Filippova, Yu.A. Anokhin, V.M. Ko-
    ropalov, A.Kh. Ostromogilsky, A.G. Ryabopashko. Ecological Approach
    to the Environmental Quality State Control and Regulation. <u>Reports
    of the Academy of Sciences</u>, USSR, Vol.241, No.3, 1978, 723-726.

7. Izrael, Yu.A., L.M. Filippova, F.N. Semevsky, S.M. Semenov, G.E.
    Insarov. On the Ecological Monitoring Principles Under the Conditions
    of the Environment Background Pollution. <u>Reports of the Academy of
    of Sciences</u>, USSR, Vol.241, No.1, 1978, 253-255.

8. Izrael, Yu.A., L.M. Filippova. Assessment and Ways of Achieving a
    Desirable State of the Natural Environment. In "The Environment
    State Monitoring". Procedings 1st USSR/U K Symposium, <u>Gidrometeoiz-
    dat</u>, Leningrad, 1977, 37-40.

A Methodology Used in Spain for Assessing Air Quality Impact[1]

V. Belloch, M. T. Estevan and J. Murais

(Spain)[2]

PRESENTATION OF THE CASE STUDY

In order to describe methodologies currently used in Spain for
environmental impact assessment (EIA) a case-study in the petrochemical industry sector has been chosen. Since 1976 Spanish
industrial regulations have required that assessments be made before
expanding any industrial activity that could be potentially air-
polluting. Accordingly, Spain has considerable experience in the
field of air quality assessment. The study outlines a method
commonly used in such cases, based on estimating air quality through
a simulation model to predict and evaluate the impact of future
sulphur dioxide (SO_2) emissions. The emission of SO_2 serves as a
useful indicator because, besides being one of the larger, more
representative air pollutants in the oil refining industry, the
Spanish air quality surveillance system has established stations
for SO_2 monitoring in the main urban areas.

Most of the environmental impact studies that have been carried out
in Spain have been partial assessments of impacts on air quality
as a consequence of various industrial activities and projects.
Among these studies are several on the impact of oil refineries
on ambient air quality. One which is technically interesting was
a year-long study of a refinery in La Coruña (Galicia) to evaluate
impacts on air quality and find practicable alternatives to meet
the air quality standards if the plant's refining capacity were
enlarged. It is this case that is outlined here.

The region of Galicia where the refinery is located is in the
north-west corner of the Iberian peninsula, north of Portugal.
One of the most attractive natural regions of Spain, it enjoys
a temperate Atlantic climate. Its coasts and rivers are rich in
abundant quantities of fish and shell species. It has considerable
appeal for tourism and each summer attracts many Spanish vacationers

and visitors, as well as foreign tourists. The population is
very sensitive to the issue of pollution; however it is one of
the Spanish regions in need of economic development, being
traditionally an area from which much emigration has taken place
and one which the Government now tries to promote industrialization.

The state-owned refinery lies about 5 km south-west of the town of La Co
Located in the centre of a slight hollow, it is hidden from the
view of the town but is nevertheless close to the gradually
expanding urban area. The refinery has an authorized oil refining
capacity of 3.5 million tons per year, but its potential capacity
is 5 million tons per year. It asked for administrative authorization
to enlarge the plant in order to refine up to 6.5 million tons
per year. Before obtaining authorization, according to Spanish
regulations, the firm must present to the administration a study
on the impact that such enlargement of activity would have on air
quality, with proposals for whatever corrections are necessary
to meet the air quality standards.

The industrial firm appointed consultants with the required
knowledge and technical capability to accomplish the task. The
main features of this study are set out below.

SUMMARY OF THE TECHNICAL AIR QUALITY IMPACT STUDY

The study was intended to determine the dispersion pattern and
the impact on ambient air quality of the SO_2 at present emitted
by the refinery. In addition, a physical-mathematical simulation
model was requested which would facilitate evaluation of projections
of the effect of expansion of the refinery. The study was also
to contain proposals for practicable alternatives to meet air quality
standards conforming to Spanish regulations.

Over a period of two and half month the consulting firm and the
refinery measured the SO_2 emissions of all pollutant sources of
the refinery from 16 emission points, of which 13 were stacks;
an isocinetic sampling device manufactured by the Research
Appliance Company was used. The data collected were: temperature,
velocity and volume of the outflow of gases (including data on
O_2, N_2 and CO, as well as SO_2). From the collected data the SO_2
concentrations in $mgr/m_3 N$ were estimated. Measured at the same
time were the SO_2 emission levels at five monitoring stations
installed between 300 and 2,700 metres from the plant . The
"Thorine method" was used to analyse samples with the aid of a
spectrophotometer (Coleman model 14). The air pollution monitoring
system of the Ministry of Health and Social Security has established
three stations in the area and collected data for this period
which was available on request.

During this sampling period, the plant worked at an average
capacity of 3.4 million tons/year, using oil from Libya which
was its normal staple (1.5 per cent sulphur content). No violations
of air quality standards were observed in these two and a half

months, either by the State or by the private monitoring system.

Meanwhile, a meteorological tower set up in the vicinity of the refinery obtained data on the micrometeorological conditions in the area. The upper level of instruments on the tower for measuring wind velocity and direction were situated at the mean height of the emission stacks. Hourly data were taped of the following conditions: wind direction, velocity, structure and elevation angle, as well as temperature on a vertical gradient. These data were then correlated with the data collected by the National Meteorological Service in the meteorological observatory in La Coruña.

The Pasquill-Gifford model was used as basis for the prediction model. It consisted of a physical-mathematical model that relates the air quality at a given point as a function of the pollutants emmited from one emission point and the physical conditions of such emission. Into these diffusion equations have been introduced the effects of the topography of the area, the plume effects of the different emission points and the reflection effect on SO_2 molecules when contracting the ground surface, causing a small overestimation of the emission levels. Using a computer programme the plume effects were computed for different conditions of atmospheric stability by means of the G.A. Briggs formulae.

With the aid of a table of meteorological frequencies of wind directions and velocities for a four-year period, the cubic matrix of climatological stabilities for the refinery area was obtained. From this could be deduced the probabilities of varying climatological conditions in the area, measured from the frequencies of the probable velocity of the wind from I6 directions. The estimated atmospheric constancy factor, $F_c=0.267$, indicated that, in general, the area studied usually had conditions promoting good dispersion patterns. The prevailing winds blow from the south and west, although the winds having greater mean velocity are those from the north-north-west and east.

Having obtained the cubic matrix of stabilities and the base data and having built the physical-mathematical dispersion model, different situations could then be simulated to obtain values for theoretical concentrations of SO_2 in the air around the refinery for a given set of projected situations and operational capacities. On the basis of results of this simulation, the following conclusions were reached:

(a) When the refinery operated at a 3.4 million tons/year production rate with fuel having I.5per cent sulphur content, concentrations of pollutants remained below the acceptable limit.

(b) If the refining rate were increased to 5 million tons/year and the same fuel were used, violations of standards

would occur during periods of north-north-west and east wind
conditions.

    (c) If the refinery operated beyond the 5 million tons/year
rate and used a fuel with a 3.6 per cent sulphur content (sulphur
content normally used in such plants) the effluent SO_2 emissions
would frequently and substantially violate the air quality
criteria. As a variant, an improvement of the dispersion conditions
was run by simulating an increase in height of the three main
stacks to 80 metres. The results of the simulation still gave
SO_2 concentrations beyond those permissible, indicating that
variables other than those being scrutinized were involved.

    (d) Next examined was the maximum sulphur content of fuel
consistent with each of four refining rates between 4 and 6.5
million tons/year, for meteorological conditions having a probability
above 0.5 per cent. Many values for fuel having a sulphur content
near 0.2 per cent appeared. This was not considered a practicable
alternative. To conform to the air quality standards, the sulphur
content in the fuel, besides being too low, would be almost
unelastic if the rate of refining activity rose above 4 million
tons/year.

In the light of these findings, an optimization study was undertaken
of feasible combinations of regrouping of stacks and elevation
of stack heights in order to obtain better disperation if using
fuel with a 3.6 per cent sulphur content. This alternative is
known as a "supplementary control system". The option of reducing
all I6 emission points to a single stack was also considered.
The conclusions of this optimization study are briefly presented
here:

    (a) An acceptable solution appeared to be one that consisted
of regrouping two of the present stacks into one stack I00 metres
high and combining four other stacks into another stack also
I00 metres high;however, there would remain a 5 per cent probability
of violating quality standards in the air surrounding the refinery.

    (b) In such situations, the solution might be to change
to a fuel with lower sulphur content.

Finally, with this study must also be considered a previous study
done to determine the approximate environmental situation resulting
from enlargement of the refinery.

It will be necessary to carry out a more complete EIA which will
include all the new production conditions when the refinery
processes 6.5 million tons/year. It should include possible
alternatives such as in-site refinery structure reshaping, which
may contribute significantly to decrease the environmental impact
of emissions, the elimination or regrouping of emission sources,
and, for the most unfavourable meteorological conditions, the
use of a fuel with an appropriately low sulphur content.

ADMINISTRATIVE PROCESS OF EIA

When the study of emissions impact is presented to the administration and this one was presented only recently – it is studied
and reviewed. The administration may then ask that the study be
completed or that obscure parts of it be further detailed or
developed. After this information has been completed, a final
decision will be reached in discussions between the administration
and the proponent, in order to establish the best practicable
means to meet environmental standards and to achieve a positive
balance between public interest and industrial or economic development.

Regarding public information and participation, this action takes
place when a firm requests permission for construction from the
municipal authorities. To get this authorization, the firm must
present the project in the Town Hall, for either establishing
or enlarging the premises. The EIA must be included, and the
industry associations must have access to examine and study the
documents; they may make comments or raise questions which,
unfortunately, are not binding upon the administration.

If it is felt that a case has not been satisfactorily considered,
those presenting the brief can appeal to the court; however,
there are neither special procedures nor actions which may be
taken that seem adequate from an environmental standpoint, nor
can appeals be made by parties who are not directly affected by
the environmental impact. Nevertheless, in spite of shortcomings
and the lack of specific procedures, EIA methods are making head-
way and in Spain help considerably to put into operation better
production processes for general economic activities, thus offering
a measure of environmental protection.

Methods of Environmental Impact Analysis in the United Kingdom: Current Practice and Future Prospects

B. D. Clark and R. Bisset

(United Kingdom)

INTRODUCTION

This paper examines the use of methods for environmental impact assessment (EIA) in the United Kingdom. A number of quantitative and descriptive impact studies carried out since 1973 are described and discussed. Themes arising from these studies include the use of quantitative matrices compared with methods involving the provision of information which is descriptive, qualitative and disaggregated.

The role of the method contained in the "Assessment of Major Industrial Applications - A Manual" (DOE Research Report 13), prepared by the Project Appraisal for Development Control (PADC) research group at Aberdeen University under the auspices of the United Kingdom central Government, is emphasized. This is an EIA method which local planners have been encouraged to utilize; two case studies are examined which show how the method can be used to assess both water and urban projects.

Conclusions from the review of current practice in the use of EIA methods in the United Kingdom are considered in the light of trends in both the United Kingdom and the United States relating to the role of EIA in planning and decision-making. The effects of these trends on the future use of methods in the United Kingdom are considered. Finally, a prediction is made concerning the general type of method likely to be used in the United Kingdom in the future.

DEFINITION OF METHODS

The first formally instituted EIA system was introduced in the United States of America with the passage of the National Environmental Policy Act (NEPA) in 1970. This legislation was followed by the development of methods to aid implementation of EIAs. EIA methods developed in the United States of America and other countries display considerable variety in their conceptual framework and their approach to data presentation as well as technical sophistication. All incorporate means of collecting and classifying material for EIA. In addition, methods aid the presentation of results. Generally, all methods share a common objective of ensuring that as many potential relevant impacts as possible are identified, measured and described; some go further and incorporate means whereby impacts from different project designs can be evaluated and compared. These latter methods not only identify impacts, but also quantify, weight and aggregate them. Many methods have been adapted from other subjects and disciplines, but most are

EIA i

useful for some, rather than all, of the activities associated with EIA. It is
generally recognized that an EIA must consider the following subjects:-

(a) Impact identification

(b) Impact measurement

(c) Impact interpretation

(d) Impact communication to information users, including the public.

Recently, the importance of project monitoring has been emphasized (Munn 1975,
PADC 1976). Some methods can deal only with certain of these activities while
others have been developed to cope with all of them.

Conceptually, it is useful to distinguish between EIA methods and EIA techniques.
This paper concentrates on EIA methods. These are concerned with the identification
of impacts and the organization of results, while techniques provide the results.
There is, however, an important linkage between methods and techniques. Impacts
are identified using a method and techniques are used to predict likely changes.
Techniques for EIA can be grouped into a number of subject areas such as
hazard, noise, transport, air pollution, ecology, landscape character and
visual impact. Information and data obtained using techniques can be organized,
presented and, in some cases, evaluated, according to the guidelines of a
particular method.

In discussing the use of EIA methods in the United Kingdom it is important to
distinguish between those studies which were implemented to examine specified
impacts and those concerned with a wide variety of environmental and socio-
economic effects of proposed developments. The latter studies have been the
context in which EIA methods have been used.

RECENT AND CURRENT PRACTICE IN THE UNITED KINGDOM

(a) Introduction

Activities associated with the exploitation of North Sea oil and gas have
provided the impetus for impact studies of specific developments in the United
Kingdom. Since the first of these studies was completed in 1973, approximately
20 impact studies have been undertaken for major contentious development
proposals (see paper for this siminar by R. Turnbull). In addition, less
controversial developments have been subject to some form of environmental
impact assessment by developers, central government or planning authorities.

In the United Kingdom, there is no single method of impact assessment which is
used generally for identifying impacts, information collection and presentation
of results. There has been no central government requirement which specifies a
particular method for assessing impacts. Consequently, local authorities, public
sector developers and privately-owned enterprises have been free to adopt
methods which they consider will help achieve their particular objectives.

An examination of impact studies implemented in the United Kingdom since 1973
shows that there has been considerable variety in methods used. One trend has
been the use of matrix methods accompanied by the quantification, weighting and
aggregation of impacts. Two such methods will be discussed below.

(b) Loch Carron Study

In this study eight potential sites for oil production platform construction in western Scotland were assessed (Sphere Environmental Conslutants 1974). An impact matrix was used to identify and score, on a scale of 0 (very good) to 5 (very bad), the extent of impacts on particular environmental components (Table 1). As an equal weight was applied to each factor, that is, all factors were considered to be of equal importance, an initial ranking of the sites was obtained by adding the figures representing impacts on each factor for each site. Sphere tested the applicability of their initial ranking by altering the weights applied to the fourteen factors.

If different weighting schemes caused large variations in the rankings obtained, it could be assumed that weighting was significant. On the other hand if little variation occurred, weighting would be insignificant and the initial ranking would represent the best ordering of the sites. The fourteen factors were divided into two categories: "environmental" and "engineering". Only the relative weights between factors in different categories were changed. There was no weighting of impacts on factors within these groups, that is, the internal weighting was undifferentiated. A variety of different weighting schemes, changing the relative importance of the environmental category, was used to aggregate the impact scores for each alternative site. Composite scores for each site were then compared to identify the site likely to result in least damage to the environment.

Various comments have been made on the weighting techniques used and the matrix (Clark et. al. in press). The environmental components listed in the matrix are believed to be too broad to be of great analytical value. Also, the weighting schemes are not sufficiently detailed to enable adequate comparisons between sites to be made on the basis of composite scores for each site.

(c) Vale of Belvoir Study

Recently, a major study has been undertaken for the National Coal Board for a major underground coal field development in the Vale of Belvoir (Leonard and Partners 1977). Four main stages can be discerned in the impact assessment. Sieve mapping was used to identify six possible mine sites. The six sites were classified into nine different options depending on the scale of operations at particular sites. Each option was subject to an EIA. However, this EIA covered only four types of impacts; visual intrusion, noise, landscape loss and agricultural loss. For each of these impacts a quantitative index relating to the worst possible case for that impact on a particular site was calculated. Similar impacts were related to the worst case in the form of a percentage which represented the extent to which the worst case score was met.

This method of relating similar impacts from the same development on different sites may be misleading. Using arbitrary "worst cases" assumptions and then comparing alternatives only shows that the scale or importance of impacts varies on the chosen scale. It tells little about the type of impacts, their extent and likely effect on people and the environment. By scoring through percentages a chosen alternative can be made to look attractive because all the rest are so much worse. It does not provide information on the nature, scale and significance of the impacts as the "worst case" reference point is theoretical. Instead they have been converted into "neutralized" numerical values. This results in the loss of a great deal of impact information in the conversion of qualitative information to numbers.

Subsequently, a matrix was prepared showing the relative performance of each option against each of the four impacts. Other matrices were used in an attempt to determine the best combination of sites in relation to least environmental damage. Both weighted and unweighted matrices were used. The former have been questioned, because of the nature of the assumptions involved in the weighting (Williams, Hills and Cope 1978).

This EIA method bears many conceptual similarities to the matrix method used by Sphere (1974) although it is more complex. However, only a limited number of impact variables were used and the degree of quantification and simplicity of the weighting schemes provide results which may be questioned.

(d)   Non-quantitative Impact Studies

In contrast to these studies involving the use of quantification and matrices, other impact studies have been carried out using methods which avoid the quantification and aggregation of impacts. Interaction matrices have been used to structure impact identification, the collection of information and the presentation of results. Matrices such as the Leopold matrix (Leopold et al. 1971) have formed the basis for particular adaptions formulated for specific assessment exercises. Most EIAs have presented information in a qualitative, descriptive manner. Ordinal rankings of alternatives supplementing written descriptions of impacts have been produced as, for example, in the study of alternative oil production platform sites in the Clyde estuary carried out by Jack Holmes Planning Group (1974).

The British Gas Corporation, the United Kingdom nationalized industry responsible for the provision of gas supply throughout the United Kingdom, has been a pioneer in the use of EIA in project planning. The Corporation undertakes a thorough review of a variety of impacts and utilizes a standard interaction matrix form. This matrix provides qualitative assessments of impacts (Dean and Graham 1978). The British Gas Corporation has used this EIA method for a variety of projects involved in the provision of gas supply, for example, compressor stations and storage tank facilities.

(e)   The PADC Manual

In 1974, United Kingdom central government commissioned the PADC research group at Aberdeen University to prepare a manual which would aid central and local government planners in the assessment of the environmental implications of major industrial developments. In 1976, the manual was published by the Department of the Environment as Research Report No. 13. The method contained in the manual was developed to fit the existing planning framework for appraising major developments. In addition, it was formulated in an attempt to resolve two recurrent problems encountered by planners assessing proposals, namely, the difficulty of obtaining sufficient detailed information from prospective developers and the lack of a framework for the systematic appraisal of proposals.

Components of the assessment procedure are grouped into three sets of related activities (Figure 1). While the approach is shown as a sequence of events, many of the activities, may, in practice, be performed concurrently. The approach incorporates certain activities which are already features of the assessment of planning applications in the United Kingdom. However, certain innovations are introduced which for convenience will be considered with reference to identifying potential impacts, predicting impacts and presenting information to decision-makers.

Two elements of the method are useful in identifying potential impacts. These are the Project Specification Report (PSR) and the Impact Matrix. With a planning application, prospective developers are asked to submit a PSR giving detailed information on a proposed plant and its processes to ensure that planners receive a wide range of detailed information at the outset. Potential impacts are identified by relating data on a proposal to the characteristics of the site and its surroundings. It is important to consider both construction and operational phases of the proposal in the matrix (Figure 2). Cells within the matrix representing likely interactions are identified. Each of these interactions is given detailed consideration during appraisal. The categories in the matrix are very general. For example, land and ecological characteristics represent large numbers of potential impacts. If necessary, selected subject areas can be expanded into a number of attributes, using a matrix format, to indicate the range of potential impacts.

The method provides planners with a means of predicting impacts. It advocates the collection of detailed information on the proposed development and data on the existing area. An analysis can be made of the scale and significance of potential changes for each likely impact identified in the Impact Matrix. These predictions can be structured using Technical Advice Notes included in the manual. Ten such notes are included, covering hydrology, visual intrusion ecology, landscale, transport, water pollution, air pollution, noise, employment and immigration. Certain notes contain techniques for making projections of likely changes. In some cases, however, subjective assessments of likely impacts must be made by technical experts based upon previous experience, and the notes contain advice on the range of factors which ought to be considered. Similarly, the manual contains a list of questions identifying the range of factors to be resolved during assessment.

In analysing probable impacts of both the construction and operational phases, it is important to establish both the magnitude and significance of each impact. Each can be assessed to establish whether it would be:

(a) beneficial and/or adverse
(b) short-term and/or long-term
(c) reversible and/or irreversible
(d) direct and/or indirect
(e) local and/or strategic

Whenever possible impacts should be explained in quantified terms, supported by reasoned argument. Quantified assessments, for example, can relate to factors such as the number of people likely to be affected by anticipated changes in noise levels.

Detailed information on potential impacts can be drawn together into an Impact Statement which can be made available to both decision-makers and the public. In an Impact Statement each impact is described briefly and assessed in relation to the five criteria identified above. It is important that the "no go" alternative is also considered. Summary sheets (Figure 3) are useful for presenting information on potential impacts to decision-makers and the public. Two EIAs which used the PADC Manual are discussed below.

(f) Alternative Water Storage Schemes

In 1976, a major comprehensive study of the environmental impacts of four alternative water storage schemes in north-west England was initiated. The study was carried out by a firm of consultants for the statutory organization charged with the control and planning of water resources in the area. Following a review of the available EIA methods, the consultants decided to base their assessment on a modified version of the method in the manual. Since the manual was developed for the assessment of industrial projects, modifications were required to make the method more suited to water resource developments.

The assessment involved the collection of data on the proposed storage schemes by means of a "Project Specification Report", comparison of the sites and development characteristics to identify impacts by use of an "Environmental Assessment Matrix"

and use of summary sheets to describe the characteristics of significant impacts.
The final report containing the findings of the impact study has now been published
(Land Use Consultants 1978). Preliminary reaction to the report from a range of
sources has been favourable. The report is considered to be a comprehensive and
thorough account of probable environmental impacts.

(g) Urban Developments

Birmingham District Council planning department agreed to assess two different
proposals, in an urban context, using the method in the manual and present their
conclusions at a seminar on EIA (Dawson 1978). The proposals were for a supermarket
and a large extension to an existing factory.

Initially, the planning officers who carried out the exercise were sceptical about
the possible success of applying a method, developed primarily for major industrial
developments, to smaller projects in an urban environment. It was felt that the
method was complicated, too long, and would require the time of too many expert staff
Nevertheless, when the method was applied to the assessment of the proposed developments, a number of significant advantages became apparent. It was felt that use of
the manual aided the provision of better and more comprehensive information. This
was achieved because a formalized structure for assessment was provided, which was
lacking in normal assessment procedures. With the co-operation of the developer,
the use of the method might have helped eliminate irrelevant issues early in the
assessment. It was concluded that the manual offered the following advantages:

(a) a more logical approach to assessment;
(b) receipt of more useful information
(c) a more objective approach;
(d) time-saving by allowing shorter reports to be prepared.

Finally, experience gained from using the manual resulted in the planning officers
re-examining their normal practice in assessing development proposals.

FUTURE PROSPECTS

An examination of impact studies in the United Kingdom shows that quantified
approaches to measuring relative impact importance and magnitude have not been
prominent. Most impact studies have considered impact data in a qualitative manner
and have provided written accounts of the characteristics of all likely impacts.
The support given by the United Kingdom central government to the use of the PADC
manual has resulted in this method being used to assess a wide variety of development types in varying administrative and development contexts.

A number of factors would seem to indicate future prospects for the use of methods
in the United Kingdom. Experience gained from utilization of the PADC manual has
been used by the PADC group to update, extend, modify and revise the manual. It
was expected that the revised, extended manual would be published by the Department
of the Environment early in 1980.

The Commission of the European Communities had prepared a preliminary draft directiv
on the introduction of EIA procedures for a wide range of private and public sector
developments. A further draft was produced and a directive, requiring EIAs, may
be introduced at some future date. Should such a directive be introduced there coul
be an increasing number of impact assessments carried out in the United Kingdom.
It is likely that the directive will only specify the broad procedures to be
implemented and that no single method for assessing proposals will be advocated,
the choice of a particular method being left to the discretion of the member
States. However, it would seem probable that the Commission would prefer to see as

much uniformity as possible in methods used. The United Kingdom central Government will be in a favourable position as it will have had three years' experience of assessing the method proposed in the manual. A revised manual, taking account of this experience, will be published at approximately the same time as the directive is promulgated. Thus, qualitative approaches to impact assessment within the existing United Kingdom planning framework - similar in principle to that contained in the manual - are likely to be used in future impact studies in preference to other methods.

This prediction would seem to be borne out by recent developments in the perception of the role of EIA in planning and decision-making. Initially, in the United States of America, EIA was seen as a means of integrating environmental considerations into government decision-making. The variety of methods developed included a large number involving weighting and aggregation of impact scores. Such methods were the product of a particular view of the role of EIA. It was seen as a scientific exercise providing "objective" information to decision-makers enabling "rational", better decision-making to take place based on the provision of accurate, comprehensive information on environmental, social and economic impacts. Consequently, many methods were developed in the context of this view of EIA. They were methods formulated to provide "technical" solutions to planning problems. By structuring the scope of impact studies and by requiring the collection, interpretation and utilization of comprehensive data, these methods were seen as aiding the production of decisions which were thought to be "better" than those which would have been made had impact studies not been required.

This view of the role of impact assessment must be considered in the context of the United States federal planning and decision-making structure. NEPA required the preparation of environmental impact statements for projects, plans and policies initiated by federal agencies only. Private sector development was exempt. Therefore, impact assessments were undertaken by federal agencies and decisions on the future of proposals were made by the same agencies. No external check, apart from the United States President, was provided for in the United States system. There existed a partially closed system in which federal agencies assessed and made decisions on their own proposals. However, environmental groups made use of the judicial system to enforce NEPA and to influence both agency assessments and decisions on particular proposals. Consequently, the EIA system in the United States was opened up to public scrutiny and involvement.

At present, the role of politics in the administrative process has led to a re-evaluation of the role of EIA and this has implications for the types of methods likely to be used in the United States, United Kingdom and, perhaps, in other countries. EIA is seen less as a technical exercise likely to result in "better", more "rational" decisions by the provision of more environmental information. Instead, project, plan and policy formulation, assessment and implementation is regarded as part of a political process involving a variety of different political actors. Impact assessment is now seen as an integral part of the political processes which involve the proponent, local people and national interest groups (Susskind 1978, Wandesforde-Smith 1979).

The use made of the information obtained from impact assessments has important implications for the types of methods to be used. Technical experts and decision-makers in organizations carrying out impact assessments on their own proposals may have preferences for the way in which impact data are presented that differ from those of lay members of the public concerned about the effects of a proposal. Assessment methods which include complex calculations involving the quantification of impact data are unlikely to be easily understood by laymen. Indeed, such methods, because of their complexity, may enable those implementing assessments to determine results by manipulating the assumptions upon which the method is based (Bisset 1978). It is

more difficult for members of the public to comprehend an impact assessment and
involve themselves in debate on a proposal if a complex quantitative method is used.

United States experience seems to indicate that quantitative methods will play a
decreasing role in impact assessment. This conclusion is borne out by the findings
of a research group at Battelle Laboratories, Columbus, Ohio (Duke et al. 1977). In
1971, this group developed one of the first and most comprehensive of the quantitative methods (the Environmental Evaluation System) produced in the United States
(Dee et al. 1972). They have now developed an alternative method, as the Environmental Evaluation System did not find favour with agency personnel, decision-makers
and the public. The new method involves the use of qualitative information only.
Quantification is not involved.

In the United Kingdom, EIA has been seen as a means whereby planning authorities
can assess both private and public sector proposals likely to be located in their
area. Decisions on whether proposals are acceptable or not are made by publicly-
elected planning committees that are part of the local government structure. Consequently, EIA in the United Kingdom, has been considered as part of a local and,
in the case of certain major contentious developments, a national political process.
There has been in consequence an ever-present need for information to be presented
in a manner which is easily assimilated by non-experts. Therefore, the preponderance
of qualitative methods is likely to continue at the expense of quantification.

REFERENCES

Bisset, R. Quantification, decision-making and environmental impact assessment in
the United Kingdom, Journal of Environmental Management, 7 (1), 1978 pp. 43-58.

Clark, B.D., Chapman, K., Bisset, R. and Wathern, P. Environmental impact analysis,
in Lovejoy, D. (ed.), Land Use and Landscape Planning, 2nd ed. London: Leonard Hill
(in press).

Dawson, P. "Environmental Impact Assessment at the Level of Planning Policy".
Paper presented to Seminar on Environmental Impact Assessment at Birmingham Universi
October 1978.

Dean, F.E. and Graham, G. The Application of Environmental Analysis in the British
Gas Industry (General Considerations). Proceedings of the UNECE Symposium on the
Gas Industry and the Environment, Minsk, Byelorussian SSR, June 1977.

Dee, N., Baker, J., Drobny, N.L., Duke, K.M. and Fahringer, D.C. Environmental
Evaluation System for Water Resource Planning. Columbus, Ohio: Battelle Columbus
Laboratories, 1972.

Duke, K.M., Dee, N., Fahringer, D.C., Maiden, D.C., Moody, C.W., Pomeroy, S.E. and
Watkins, G.A. Environmental Quality Assessment in Multiobjective Planning.
Columbus, Ohio: Battelle Columbus Laboratories, 1977.

Jack Holmes Planning Group, An Examination of Sites for Gravity Platform
Construction on the Clyde Estuary. Glasgow: Jack Holmes Planning Group, 1974.

Land Use Consultants, Environmental Appraisal of Four Alternative Water Resource
Schemes. London: Land Use Consultants, 1978.

Leonard and Partners, The Belvoir Prospect London: Leonard and Partners, 1977.

Leopold, L., Clarke, F.E., Hanshaw, B.B. and Balsley, J.R. A Procedure for
Evaluating Environmental Impact. US Geological Survey Circular 645. Washington D.C.:
US Geological Survey, 1971.

Munn, R.E. (ed.) Environmental Impact Assessment: Principles and Procedures.
SCOPE Report 5. Toronto: International Council of Scientific Unions Scientific
Committee on Problems of the Environment, 1975.

Project Appraisal for Development Control The Assessment of Major Industrial
Applications: A Manual. Department of the Environment Research Report 13.
London: Department of the Environment, 1976.

Sphere Environmental Consultants Ltd. Loch Carron Area: Comparative Analysis of
Platform Construction Sites. London: Sphere Environmental Consultants Ltd. 1979.

Susskind, L. "It's time to shift our attention from impact assessment to strategies
for resolving environmental disputes." EIA Review, 2. 1978, pp. 4-8.

Wandesforde-Smith, G. "Trends in environmental policy and law: environmental impact
assessment", in Bothe, M. (ed.), Trends in Environmental Policy and Law. Morges,
Switzerland: International Union for the Conservation of Nature and Natural
Resources (in press).

Williams, K., Hills, P. and Cope, P. EIA and the Vale of Belvoir Coalfield.
Built Environment, 4 (2), 1978, pp. 142-151.

	PORT CAM	CAMAS	RERAIG	W. RUSSEL	RUSSEL BURN	SEAFIELD	ACHINTRAID
1. Visual intrusion	2	4	1	2	3	4	4
2. Potential for re-use	2	2	5	5	5	4	4
3. Reinstatement possibility	1	1	5	1	1	1	1
4. Land use destroyed	1	2	4	0	3	3	2
5. Houses directly affected	0	0	3	0	1	2	5
6. Houses indirectly affected	4	0	0	0	0	2	3
7. Other factors	2	5	0	2	2	3	1
8. Road access	2	2	5	4	3	3	4
9. Rail access	0	5	5	5	5	5	5
10. Sea via rail access	0	3	2	2	2	2	2
11. Suitability for labour camp	2	2	3	3	3	3	3
12. Site workers	1	5	4	5	3	5	5
13. Distance stage 1 – 2	0	2	3	2	2	2	2
14. Ecology	2	1	2	1	1	1	1

Key: 0 = Very Good
      1 = Good
      2 = Moderate
      3 = Quite Bad
      4 = Bad
      5 = Very Bad

TABLE 1: The Sphere Matrix

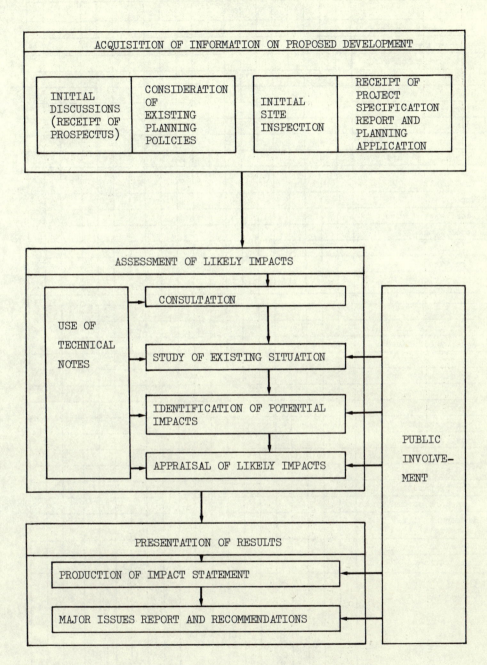

Figure 1. Linked Activities in the Appraisal Method

Phase	Impact	Climate	Land uses	Water quality	Landscape quality	Ecological characteristics	Population density	Tourism	Employment structure	Unemployment	Local economy	Traffic	Water supply	Sewerage	Finance	Education	Health service facilities	Housing	Emergency services	Community structure	Culture
OPERATIONAL PHASE	Hazard		x																x		
	Solid waste disposal			x	x	x															
	Aqueous discharges			x	x									x							
	Dust particulates																				
	Odours										x										
	Gaseous emissions		x		x													x			
	Vibration																	x			
	Noise																x	x			
	Transport of products											x									
	Transport of employees											x									
	Transport of raw materials											x									
	Employment								x	x											
	Local expenditure										x										
	Water demand												x								
	Severance		x																		
	Structures				x																
	Immigration						x								x	x	x	x	x	x	x
CONSTRUCTION PHASE	Hazard																		x		
	Solid waste disposal				x																
	Aqueous discharges			x	x																
	Odours																				
	Gaseous emissions																				
	Noise														x			x			
	Vibration																	x			
	Water demand												x								
	Local expenditure										x										
	Employment								x	x											
	Site clearance		x	x																	
	Site preparation			x	x																
	Transport of employees											x									
	Transport of raw materials											x									
	Severance		x																		
	Immigration													x	x	x	x	x	x	x	x

Figure 2. EXAMPLE OF AN IMPACT ASSESSMENT MATRIX

Figure 3. EXAMPLE OF A SUMMARY SHEET

POTENTIAL IMPACT OF PROPOSED DEVELOPMENT	CLASSIFICATION OF IMPACT	DESCRIPTION OF POTENTIAL IMPACT
Loss of <u>Zostera</u> feeding areas of brent geese	Indicate where appropriate B = Beneficial A = Adverse St = Short term Lt = Long term R = Reversible I = Irreversible D = Direct In = Indirect L = Local Sg = Strategic	The reclamation programme of 56 ha associated with the development proposals would cause disruption of siltation patterns in the estuary. Inundation of <u>Zostera</u> beds in the north bay by water heavily-laden with fine silts would lead to loss of approx. 60% of this important habitat. Expectation: short-term increases in the number of waders in this particular area; once the construction phase is complete, and these silts are not replenished, the number will return to its former level. A thin layer of anoxic mud will cover the beds. These would probably not be reinvaded by <u>Zostera</u>, so that 60% of area would be permanently lost. Wintering brent geese, which constitute 20% of the world population, feed exclusively on <u>Zostera</u> and the reduced area of grazing would not support the present number of geese.

A QUANTITATIVE METHOD FOR THE ASSESSMENT OF EXTERNAL EFFECTS

Report prepared by Messrs. V. D. Fedorov, V. N. Maksimov and V. B. Sakharov (USSR)

At present various quantitative methods are being developed to evaluate external effects on the environment, and on ecological systems in particular. Several difficulties arise in this connexion, and, to overcome them, considerable intellectual and material effort is required.

Methods for evaluating ecosystems concerned with measurements of productivity, the ability of ecosystems to resist negative influence and preserve their characteristics, and their possibilities for exploitation are points where significant problems exist. The situation is aggravated by the urgency of solving these difficulties, if the ecological balance between man and the biosphere is to be retained. Various approaches may be taken to most of the problems, and each has its advantages and disadvantages. The following paragraphs examine some characteristics of one possible method of evaluating the state of ecosystems, a method which has been developed in recent years at the Faculty of General Ecology and Hydrobiology of Moscow State University (USSR).

Let us consider a simple model of an ecosystem influenced by pollutants (fig.1).

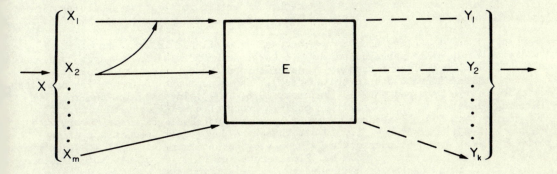

Fig. 1 Influence of pollutants on an ecosystem.

The square in the centre of the diagram represents an ecosystem composed of a totality of populations interacting with each other and with a biotope. Each of them has a heterogeneous internal structure (sex, age, function, etc.) and performs similar or dissimilar functions in a biocenosis.

Within the limits of such an ecosystem the transformation of energy and substances takes place, i.e. the ecosystem is reasonably autonomous and complex, and possesses in a spatially-recognizable form, a number of overall characteristics determined by composition (sets of population), structure (interaction of population) and activity (succession of population, changes in their relationships). To such overall characteristics we attribute indices of stability (conditioned by homeostasis), reliability (conditioned by maturity) and complexity (conditioned by species diversity and variety of relations among populations). On the left of the diagram at the "entry" of the ecosystem, potentially harmful substances are depicted by continuous arrows. It is assumed that for each specific ecosystem their quantity, which is not great could be roughly determined, and that their physico-chemical properties are specific, i.e. the sets of potential pollutants differ from ecosystem to ecosystem.

A priori, we know that among any group of potential pollutants some will interact with others in their influence on an ecosystem. Consequently the effect of an individual pollutant may be considerably weakened or increased through such effects.

On the right of the diagram, at the "exit" from the ecosystem, so-called indices of its state are depicted. They include both biotic and abiotic aspects. Recognising that the number of dependent variables could be infinitely great, some selection is necessary, so as to identify a limited number of indices which show the overall effect on an ecosystem of the influence of all pollutants. Such indices may be considered as indices of environmental quality i.e. the properties of the ecosystem as seen.

The diagram therefore represents a common situation: multiple pollutant influences on an ecosystem, the state of which is defined by a number of responses that are arbitrarily selected in terms of the interests of mankind (e.g. indices of drinking water quality) or in the interests of an ecosystem itself (e.g. maintainance of ecosystem productivity). In this case the task is essentially to investigate the dependance:

$$\vec{y} = f(\vec{x}) \tag{1}$$

In previous papers concerned with the development of a biological monitoring strategy, some specific methods were suggested for establishing priorities among factors affecting the environment. Also demonstrated was the need to set up a multi-factor experiment as one basic method to obtain information regarding the anticipated effects of pollutants on the state of an ecosystem (Fedorov, 1976, 1977)

The selection of factors should take account of available information on the presence of specific man-made pollutants (e.g. heavy metals) in the area concerned, as well as of significant changes in natural substances, harmless in normal concentrations (phosphates, nitrates,etc.). Recommendations on the choice selected variables were provided earlier (Fedorov, 1976, 1977). In designing an experiment to study independently and simultaneously a group of n selected variables, it is suggested that design matrices of orders one and two should be used (Maksimov, Fedorov, 1969; Golikova et·al., 1974). These are now widely used as a routine method for studying complex system with a view to obtaining uncomplicated descriptiv models in the form of a polynomial. Simultaneous examination of about ten factors "suspected" as harmful does not cause any major difficulties and can be easily implemented. Our experience shows that this form of experiment is highly efficient in the solution of multi-variate problems from the optimization of nutrient media composition to experiments in situ for studying the probable effects on ecosystems of different forms of environmental pollution. The question of methods and approaches for the examination of a group of independent variables $(x_1, x_2 \ldots x_k)$ may therefore be regarded as sufficiently well studied and tested in practice.

What should be considered as dependant variables and how are they to be studied?

An ecosystem possesses many characteristics which describe its composition, structure, functioning, development, maturity, stability, etc. For our present purposes these can be considered as dependent variables. Since the number of these variables considerably exceeds the number of factors involved $(k \gg m)$, it is in practice necessary to limit the number of indices characterizing the state of an ecosystem. Whether we are conducting an experiment or whether we intend to use the result of biological observations we have to limit the number of variables, using explicitly and implicitly the criterion of their respective relative importance for the purposes of the task. A certain set of organisms are characteristic indicators of the conditions that have shaped the ecosystem over a long period in the past. "The face of an ecosystem" reflects at every moment the end result of the influence of environmental conditions on the composition and structure of a biocenosis. Nature behaves as if it is continuously conducting an experiment on species survival under the influence of external factors. This effect on the "shape" of an ecosystem has stimulated in hydrobiology the varied use of indicator organisms for the evaluation of the pollution of the aquatic environment. In several European countries the most wide-spread system of indicator organisms is the one of Kolkvits and Marson, as modified by Zelenka and Marvan, Knopp, Pantle and Bukk, Sladechek and others.

It seems likely that any improvements to indicator systems will be of limited value for the purposes of water quality control due to practical difficulties as well as to more general considerations. The set of organisms characterizes the composition of the population of an ecosystem, but by no means does it determine its structure which reflects the types of connexions among elements (individuals of a population) in the system. Therefore basic indices of ecosystem strucure are estimates based on the processes (linked to the variety of types and the forces of interaction among organisms) and on the results of such processes (expressed in correlations of abundance or biomass of the populations forming the "face" of a biocenosis).

At the same time it seems evident that it is necessary to supplement the indicator approach with the recognition of a number of new principles characterizing the structure of natural ecosystems. Let us consider recent attempts to improve the evaluation of the pollution of natural waters.

The first group is composed of indices that can be described as "time integrals" i.e. as the results of actions (functions), at the moment of their observation or measurement. This category includes indices characterizing the quantity of biomass, number of species, their relative abundance, measures of species richness, variety, compatibility, relative abundance, dominance, etc.

The method developed by Woodiwiss for the river Trent (Woodiwiss, 1964), is one of the most popular and successful for the evaluation of water pollution using a number of indices related to the benthos. Woodiwiss introduced the concept of a "group", reducing substantially the list of indicator organisms and, as a rule, using easily defined forms. In some cases these are species, in others they may even be families. At the same time the principle of indicator significance of such taxa is supplemented by the principle of the decrease of faunal variety in a polluted water environment.

The second group of estimates of an ecosystem structure is composed of indices that could be described as "time derivative", i.e. related to the speed of change in certain functions. This category comprises indices of productivity, respiration, assimilation of substances and other characteristics of processes taking place in an ecosystem. The number of such indices is considerable, and the selection of a small number should be made with the help of some discriminating criterion. In an earlier paper (Fedorov, 1977) we formulated the main requirements for

selection among dependant variables, and enumerated some basic indices describing
the state of an ecosystem. A possible situation was considered in which certain
combinations of "norms" and "pathologies" of some indices are specific to
individual pollutants and, consequently, evidence of such combinations can be
considered as a reliable symptom of ecosystem decline.

Contrary and quite feasible situations may arise, when various pollutants do not effect flows of energy and materials in an ecosystem. In this case the study of the
regular behaviour of some characteristics allows them to be evaluated as "good" or
"bad" for the existence and functioning of an ecosystem. Thus, the analysis of
rates of change in available data becomes, in fact, the only information that we
consider convincing in determining whether something is "good" or "bad" for the
ecosystem. A method is needed to combine different indices, some of which describe
"good" environment qualities or states of an ecosystem and others indicate "bad"
characteristics. The solution of such problems implies two consecutive steps:
(a) evaluation of the quality of each dependent variable d_i; and (b) determination
of the quality D, based on the evaluation of the selected d_i indicators.

As one simple approach, the characteristic "1" can be applied to an index that
corresponds to an established norm, and the characteristic "0" to an index which
does not correspond to the norm. Thus, the presence of at least one "0" in a set
of quality evaluations indicates a "bad" condition of the system. Use of discrete
values such as "0" and "1" can probably be justified in assessing the quality of
industrial products. Such an approach, however, is scarcely fruitful when applied
to an ecosystem, if only because the assessment of the quality should be related
to an objective. Thus, for example, water which is suitable for street cleaning
is "good" for this purpose whether or not it can also be used for drinking purposes.

For application to ecosystems it is much more desirable to use a continuous scale
of values from "0" to "1", instead of discrete, either/or values. In this case
a dependant variable, d_i, becomes an estimate of the relative desirability of some
index y_i according to the initial condition:

$$0 \leq d_i \leq 1$$

The relationship between d_i and y_i may be established by "common sense", which
may frequently indicate a non-linear relation between them, since the desirability
of a factor may change abruptly as it departs from the norm. Harrington has
introduced this non-linearity into the continuous scale by means of the formula

$$d_i = e^{-e^{-z_i}}$$

(2)

where Z_i - is a coded variable that could be easily linked with any real variable
y_i by a _linear_ dependance. The general shape of the function 2, resembles a logistic
curve, Fig. 2. It should be noted that a desirability of 0.993 (i.e. very close
to unity) corresponds to $Z = 5$; $d = 0.98$ when $Z = 4$; $d = 0.68$ when $Z = 1$; $d = 0.37$
when $Z = 0$; and, $d = 0.0006$ (i.e. close to zero) when $Z = -2$. In order to determine
the connexion of Z with actual dependant variables y_i, it is sufficient to link the
limits of the normal variability of the latter to a scale of variation of Z from
-2 to 5. Detailed information on a method using Harrington's scale of desirability
for assessing of biological systems has been presented in Maximov (1977).

Harrington's function is not good enough for the assessment of the state of
natural systems because of the monotonic character of the connexion between d_i and
y_i which it describes.

In reality a unimodal shape of a function is normal in biology in general and
ecology in particular. Hence, the curve of a dependant variable should have only
one maximum, corresponding to optimum desirability. This means that the lowest
and and highest values of y_i are less desirable than values located close
to an optimum.

Since the shapes of unimodal curves may vary considerably (symmetrical, left- or
right-hand asymmetry), there is no point in trying to determine their shape by
a particular formula. If we take as a background initial condition, instead of
"the more, the better" the assertion "the more often, the better", then the
desirability of any index could be easily ascertained as a function of the
distribution. Theoretically, the characteristics of the distribution should be
related to the concept of a statistical norm, but this question is quite unexplored
since the concept of a statistical norm rests on a postulate and is perceived only
by intuition (Fedorov, 1977). Nevertheless, desirability equal to "1" could always
be attributed to a value of modal class whatever the character of distribution,
and, in this case, the main difficulty is to decide the intervals on either side
of the value of "1".

If the normal range of variation of a variable is well-known, the value of
desirability equal to 0.63, which corresponds to the lower limit of "good" on
Harrington's scale, may be equated with the limit of this normal range of the index.

In order to determine these limits of normality, many different ways may be used,
two of which are mentioned below.

The first way is taken from medical practice and based on percentiles (Sepetliev,
1968). Any value of a response, lying within the limits from 0.25 to 0.75 per cent
of the total variation, should be considered as normal. In this case comparison
of specific values of these percentiles for each response with the indicated value
of desirability will demonstrate the connexion of a real index to the value of its
desirability.

A second way is based on a knowledge of the law of distribution of the response
indices in an undamaged system and on the assumption that we can estimate correctly
the mean ("a") and the standard deviation from the mean (σ). Then, adoption of the
hypothesis of normalily (if necessary, the results should be treated logarithmically
for the purpose of "normalization") enables identification of the range of values
that are "normal"; they are those that fall within the limits of one standard
deviation either side of the mean, and including about 2/3 of the total number of
responce values (fig. 3). Values of variables that fall within two standard
deviations of the mean include "bad" as well as "good" indications, showing the
disturbed state of the ecosystem.

In order to make a judgement regarding the "bad" or "good" state of an ecosystem
as a whole, it is necessary to refer to a generalized desirability index that
may be calculated as the geometric mean of the totality of d_i evaluations:

$$D = \sqrt[m]{d_1, d_2 \ldots\ldots\ldots d_m,}$$

(3)

where d_i - are the coded values of particular desirabilities, determined by one of
the above-mentioned methods.

In conclussion, the scale that is set by the condition $0 \leq D \leq 1$, should be
calibrated with the help of common sense concerning the well-being of an ecosystem.

Recalling the attractive simplicity of the five-element scale used in school marks
systems, the following is proposed as uncommon common sense:

Table 1

Recommended intervals of the desirability scale for the assessment of the state
of an ecosystem

D	state	marks
1.0–0.8	excellent	5
0.8–0.6	good	4
0.6–0.4	satisfactory	3
0.4–0.2	bad	2
0.2–0.0	very bad	1

Two examples of the assessment of the state of an ecosystem with the help of the
desirability function

We may take as one illustration the calculation of desirability values on the basis of
hydrochemical data given in an article by F. Woodiwiss (1977). In this paper, the
results of the determination of the biotic index on various sections of the Trent
River, and on several tributaries, are compared with values of the principal
hydrochemical indicators measured at the same stations. Woodiwiss discovered that
there was adequate correlation between the assessment of water quality, expressed
as a biotic index (from 0 to 10), and several of these indicators. Among them, in
the first place, are the permanganate oxidability, the contents of dissolved oxygen
and the contents of ammonia nitrogen. By calculating the mean values of these
indicators from observations over five years, Woodiwiss showed that each value of
biotic index corresponded to a definite value of each of the above-mentioned
indicators.

In this connexion, it would seem reasonable, if each value of a hydrochemical
indicator is compared with the desirability value in a manner such that Woodiwiss'
biotic scale (1 to 10) is directly linked to the desirability d_i range from 0 to 1.0.
For example if, in waters with biotic index 4, a concentration of ammonia nitrogen
of 3 mg/l was observed as the average in 5 years, than the desirability d = 0.4
could be attributed to this concentration. The same value of desirability could
be established for a permanganate oxidability of 8 mg/l, and to 7 mg/l dissolved
oxygen. Following this principle, on the basis of the data in the article by
Woodiwiss, graphs have been constructed to show the conversion of the actual values
of selected indicators to their desirability values (fig. 4). These graphs show
that desirability d = 1 for dissolved oxygen requires a concentration above 11 mg/l,
and values for permanganate oxidability and ammonia nitrogen equal to zero.
With such an approach, therefore, the "ideal" water will be saturated by oxygen and
without organic compounds and reduced forms of nitrogen. In the construction of
desirability functions, a value of 1.0 should be considered as an "unachievable
ideal".

Using the graphs in fig. 4, generalized desirabilities have been calculated for 49
stations on the basis of data given in tables 5 and 7 of Woodiwiss' paper. Values
of individual desirabilities for all three indices and values of generalized
desirability D, calculated from them, are given in table 3. In the same table, value
of biotic index, determined by Woodiwiss at these stations, are given for the sake
of comparison. According to his assertion, deviations in the assessment of an index
do not normally exceed one interval on the scale. On that criterion, the desirability values D, multiplied by 10, coincide with the Woodiwiss index in 34 cases, and

only in four cases is the difference between the desirability value and the index greater than two intervals. Such coincidence of the data should be regarded as entirely satisfactory.

It is interesting to compare values of individual desirabilities for each of three selected indices with the value of biotic index. In spite of the fact that there is a clear linear connexion between these values, in accordance with the method of their calculation itself, deviations greater than two intervals are found in 10 cases, if the assessment of water quality is based only on the concentration of dissolved oxygen; in 9 cases, if it is based on the contents of ammonia nitrogen; and in 8 cases, if permanganate oxidability is used. We can agree with the opinion of Woodiwiss, given in the cited article, that there is no way of relying upon discovered relations between biotic index and individual hydrochemical data. The problem, however, is not as Woodiwiss believes, that these relations are indirect in character, but in the fact that the degree of well-being of the aquatic environment from the point of view of the aquatic life and assessed by biotic index, is conditioned by the whole complex of abiotic factors, and each of them, taken separately, the correlation between the level of a factor and the state of a biocenosis be may weak or may be strong. The value of the desirability function is precisely as an assessment of the totality of factors giving a more precise assessment of the state of an ecosystem than would be the case if each of the factors is considered separately.

In the situation just considered, the desirability of each index is assessed in terms of the fitness of the water to support aquatic life. Let us now take a second example, where the desirability function was used to evaluate the effect of various pollutants on an ecosystem. The experiment was designed to determine the effect on plankton in the White Sea of two petroleum products - diesel fuel and motor oil - and a dispersant substance, correxite 7664. The results are given in Table 3. Experiments were carried out in glass bottles with a capacity of 30 litres, exposed 4 days in the surface layer of the sea. The bottles were filled with natural sea water, taken from the open sea, and specific mixtures of these three substances were added to each bottle in accordance with a 2^3 full-factor experiment (FFE) design. At the end of the exposition, the quantity of phyto- and zooplankton was calculated, and the primary productivity of phytoplankton and the fixation of carbon dioxide in the dark were determined by the radiocarbon method. The data on the change in the quantity of five species of algae and four representatives of zooplankton that were dominant at the time of the experiment (July 1975), are given in the Table 3, as well as data on changes of the production indices as ratios of the control figure which was taken as one for all eleven functions of the response.

The dependance of each of these functions upon three examined factors does not coincide, in general, with that of the others. The quantity of diatoms decreases due to the presence of the petroleum products; noticeable stimulation of the growth of blue-green algae is found in the presence of given values of the additives; increase in the primary productivity in those elements of the experiment when diesel fuel is added is connected, evidently, with this phenomenon. Various representatives of zooplankton also differ considerably regarding their sensitivity to petroleum products and correxite.

As a means of providing an estimate of the effect of the examined pollutants on the totality of indices characterizing the state of the plankton, the desirability function could be used. In this case, the main difficulty is the choice of a conversion scale from the concrete values of the response functions y_i to their expression in terms of relative desirability. It is obvious that, when assessing damaging effects of external factors on a system, the most desirable condition is one where damage is not detected at all. This value of the response function should be taken as one on the desirability scale. To establish the value of the response function when the desirability should be considered equal to zero is more difficult. In particular, the decrease of the number of different species in a population to zero, i.e. the total destruction of a population, would of course be an extremely undesirable phenomenon; but decrease to a certain critical value, such that the restoration of a population becomes impossible even after the removal of damaging factor, would be equally undesirable.

Since such critical values for real species in real ecosystems remain at present unknown, one has to choose some other point for the construction of the desirability scales, the location of which point can be established on the basis of some biologically feasible suppositions. In the present case, it might be agreed that the decrease of population to one-half its size, as the result of a single damaging effect, might be considered acceptable in the sense that the population maintains its ability to return to the initial state after the removal of pollutants (e.g. the principle of self-purification). This assumption may be extended to production indices, due to the lack of any other well-grounded hypotheses. For those indices that turned out to be greater in experiments than in the control, i.e. in the case when $y_i > 1$, having doubled in comparison with the control was taken as acceptable.

It should be made clear, that by the word "acceptable" here we mean a deviation from the control that corresponds to an estimate somewhere in the interval between "good" and "excellent" on the desirability scale. In the case mentioned, we chose the numerical value of the desirability $d = 0.85$ for the quantitative expression of this estimate. The value of the conditional variable $Z = 1.9$ corresponds to this value. For the value of y_i in the control we took $Z = 5.0$, giving the value $D \approx 1$, when using equation (2). With such choice of the "strong points" the transition from values y_i to values Z could be carried out by the linear transformation:

$$Z = \frac{p - 0.2}{0.16} \quad , \quad \text{where}$$

$$p = \begin{cases} y & \\ 1/y & \\ \end{cases} \quad \begin{array}{l} \text{when } y \leq 1 \\ \text{when } y > 1 \end{array}$$

The desirability values, calculated by this method, are given in Table 3. The values of the regression coefficients in the same table were calculated on the basis of the values of D for three examined factors and their interactions. The verification of the significance, carried out according to the method of Daniel (1959), showed that, given the above-mentioned assumptions regarding the desirability of changes produced by the admixtures, the effect on the plankton (expressed as the sum of the eleven chosen indicators) of the two petroleum products was considerable, and that the effect of diesel fuel was more noticeable than that of motor oil. The effect of each of them is the greatest in the case of individual action, due to the existence of positive effects in their interaction. Such interaction should be considered as the display of the one-type non-linear dependance "dose-effect" for two substances, and as the result of it, the addition of one of them to a system which is already under deterioration caused by the other, does not lead to an equivalent effect. The case was examined in detail earlier (Maximov, 1977).

The effect of the correxite on the value of the desirability function, as well as the effect of its interactions with the petroleum products, proved to be insignificant, and it may be concluded that correxite in the concentration of 10 mg/litre does not produce any major undesirable changes in the plankton population; nor, however does it change the toxicity of the petroleum products either, if the word "toxicity" is understood as the ability of a substance to cause undesirable changes in a population or in an ecosystem as a whole.

CONCLUSION

In view of the existing arbitrary character of the evaluation of the norm and in the methods used to establish the extreme limits of "good", etc, it does not seem worthwhile to try to improve the proposed system for assessing the state of an ecosystem. The system may be accepted or rejected on the basis (once again) of an entirely subjective views as to whether it is for some reason worse or better than other systems of the assessment. What might be justified would be an attempt to intercalibrate various systems or, conversely, to allow them to exist side by side and independantly of one another, if logical soundness and complete-ness of the construction are recognized as the sole criteria for their existence.

It is unlikely that a single system could be elaborated, that would be better than all the others, and for this reason, would be given preference in the analysis of the state of ecosystems. Methods of assessment would, probably, differ in every case, depending on objectives, specific conditions, and populations. But the number of principles at the basis of such methods of assessment cannot be greater. According to general considerations, if seems that all of them would deal, to a greater or lesser extent, with specifics of functional-spatial structure of ecosystems or with their living components. The integrity of such formation as an ecosystem cannot fail to be based upon specifics of their organization. Methods of the assessment themselves would rather vary slightly depending on types of ecosystems, their maturity and the "reserve of the strength" (stability), when exploited by man. As to toxicological analyses of water quality, despite their desirable simplicity and cheapness, their role in the making of ecologically sound decisions cannot be a determining one.

References

1. Golikova T.I., Panchenko L.A., Fridman M.Z. - Catalogue of the second order plans. Moscow State University, 1974.

2. Maximov V.N. - Specific problems of the study of the complex effect of pollutants on biological systems. Hydrobiological journal, v. 13. No.4, 1977.

3. Maximov V.N., Fedorov V.D. - Mathematical planning of biological experiments. In "Mathematical methods in biology". 1968, VINITI, Moscow, 1969.

4. Sepetliev D.A. - Statistical methods in scientific medical research. Moscow, Medicina, 1968.

5. Fedorov V.D. - Problems of maximum permissible effects of the anthropogenic factor from the point of view of an ecologist. In "Comprehensive analysis of the natural environment". Leningrad, Hydrometeoizdat, 1976.

6. Fedorov V.D. - A problem of the assessment of the norm and pathology of the state of ecosystems. In "Scientific basis for the control of surface water quality using hydrobiological indices". Proceedings of a Soviet-English seminar. Leningrad, Hydrometeoizdat, 1977.

7. Daniel C. - Use of Half-Normal Plot in Interpreting Factorial two-level Experi-ments. Technometrics, 311-341, 1,4, 1959.

8. Woodiwiss F. - The biological system of stream classification used by the Trent River Authority, Chemistry of Industry, 1964.

V. Fedorov *et al.*

Table 2

No. of stations	Total permanganate oxidability mg/litre and its desirability		Ammonia nitrogen mg/litre and its desirability		Dissolved oxygen mg/litre and its desirability		Generalized desirability	Biotic index	Difference
1	2	3	4	5	6	7	8	9	10
1	5.2	0.68	0.4	0.84	9.9	0.88	0.80	7	1.0
2	6.7	0.53	3.7	0.29	7.0	0.37	0.38	4	0.2
3	7.9	0.43	2.1	0.46	8.1	0.46	0.45	5	0.5
4	6.2	0.58	0.4	0.84	8.1	0.46	0.61	6	0.1
5	7.3	0.48	2.4	0.42	6.3	0.32	0.40	5	1.0
6	6.2	0.58	0.6	0.73	9.2	0.64	0.66	6	0.6
7	4.6	0.74	0.2	0.92	10.3	0.92	0.86	8	0.6
8	8.8	0.36	9.1	0.09	6.0	0.30	0.21	2	0.1
9	8.9	0.36	1.2	0.62	7.2	0.39	0.44	6	1.6
10	2.0	0.93	0.0	1.00	11.7	1.00	0.98	10	0.2
11	3.8	0.81	1.5	0.56	6.3	0.32	0.53	6	0.7
12	3.2	0.85	0.1	0.96	12.5	1.00	0.93	8	1.3
13	1.5	0.96	0.1	0.96	12.4	1.00	0.98	10	0.2
14	7.5	0.46	1.5	0.56	9.5	0.74	0.53	4	1.8
15	8.0	0.42	5.4	0.17	6.4	0.32	0.28	2	0.8
16	6.3	0.57	4.3	0.24	10.2	0.92	0.50	7	2.0
17	4.8	0.72	0.4	0.84	11.1	0.99	0.84	8	0.4
18	6.4	0.56	7.4	0.11	9.8	0.86	0.38	4	0.2
19	2.8	0.88	0.0	1.00	13.7	1.00	0.96	7	2.6
20	6.0	0.60	1.2	0.62	9.3	0.68	0.63	6	0.3
21	4.8	0.72	0.5	0.83	9.4	0.74	0.76	8	0.4
22	8.6	0.38	3.8	0.28	5.6	0.28	0.31	3	0.1
23	4.6	0.74	0.2	0.92	9.8	0.86	0.84	6	2.4
24	6.0	0.60	1.9	0.49	7.7	0.43	0.50	3	2.0
25	5.0	0.70	1.5	0.56	7.4	0.40	0.54	5	0.4
26	5.0	0.70	1.4	0.58	7.1	0.37	0.53	4	1.3
27	6.0	0.60	2.8	0.37	6.3	0.32	0.41	4	0.1
28	4.0	0.79	0.2	0.93	10.9	0.98	0.90	10	1.0
29	3.0	0.87	0.2	0.93	10.8	0.97	0.92	10	0.8

Table 2 (contd.)

No. of stations	Total permanganate oxidability mg/litre and its desirability		Ammonia nitrogen mg/litre and its desirability		Dissolved oxygen mg/litre and its desirability		Generalized desirability	Biotic index	Difference
1	2	3	4	5	6	7	8	9	10
30	4.0	0.79	0.2	0.93	9.6	0.79	0.83	10	1.7
31	4.0	0.79	0.3	0.88	10.7	0.96	0.87	9	0.3
32	3.0	0.87	0.3	0.88	18.4	1.00	0.91	9	0.1
33	5.0	0.70	0.3	0.88	9.2	0.64	0.73	9	1.7
34	5.0	0.79	0.8	0.72	9.5	0.78	0.73	7	0.3
35	4.0	0.70	0.8	0.72	9.1	0.62	0.71	7	0.1
36	5.0	0.70	1.6	0.55	8.3	0.48	0.57	6	0.3
37	5.0	0.60	0.9	0.69	8.4	0.49	0.62	4	2.2
38	6.0	0.60	2.1	0.47	6.0	0.30	0.44	4	0.4
39	6.0	0.50	1.2	0.62	8.1	0.46	0.56	4	1.6
40	7.0	0.35	3.0	0.67	7.8	0.44	0.53	2	3.3
41	9.0	0.79	2.7	0.39	6.7	0.34	0.36	2	1.6
42	4.0	0.60	0.3	0.88	10.5	0.94	0.87	8	0.7
43	6.0	0.70	0.4	0.85	9.6	0.78	0.74	8	0.6
44	5.0	0.29	0.5	0.82	10.6	0.95	0.82	8	0.2
45	10.0	0.29	6.2	0.14	6.3	0.32	0.24	4	1.6
46	10.0	0.29	7.7	0.10	6.1	0.30	0.21	2	0.1
47	10.0	0.29	6.2	0.14	7.6	0.41	0.26	3	0.4
48	10.0	0.29	5.3	0.18	7.0	0.37	0.27	3	0.3
49	12.0	0.20	7.1	0.12	6.6	0.34	0.20	3	0.1

Table 3

	1 control	2	3	4	5	6	7	8
Diesel fuel		10	0	10	0	10	0	10
Motor oil		0	10	10	0	0	10	10
Correxite		0	0	0	10	10	10	10
	1.00	0.10	0.09	0.08	0.98	0.17	0.07	0.07
Small flagellates	1.00	0.06	0.12	0.04	0.92	0.06	0.63	0.05
	1.00	0.12	0.28	0.16	0.89	0.21	0.29	0.21
Cyanobacteria	1.00	0.16	0.60	0.12	0.97	0.10	0.16	0.06
	1.00	0.10	0.06	0.11	0.19	0.10	1.00	0.14
	1.00	0.95	0.97	0.86	0.98	0.88	0.93	0.75
	1.00	0.92	0.57	0.32	0.79	0.50	0.19	0.10
	1.00	0.14	0.99	0.14	1.00	0.14	0.99	0.12
	1.00	0.48	0.98	0.41	0.99	0.48	0.98	0.41
Primary production	1.00	0.82	0.82	0.56	0.93	0.32	0.94	0.10
Temp assimilation	1.00	0.25	0.70	0.93	0.92	0.95	0.72	0.34
Generalized desirability	1.00	0.24	0.39	0.22	0.81	0.24	0.49	0.15
Marking of factors	"1"							
Regression coefficients	0.442	−0.230	−0.130	0.102	−0.020	0.002	0.028	−0.045

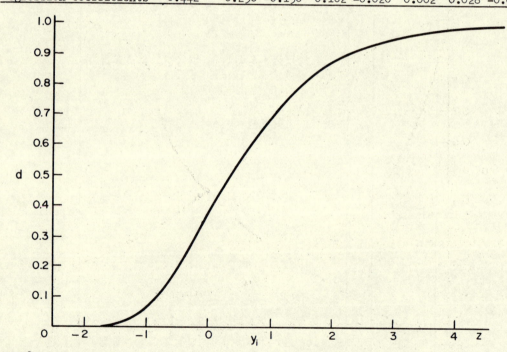

Fig.2. The connexion between dependant variable y_i, coded variable Z and desirability d.

(The second version)

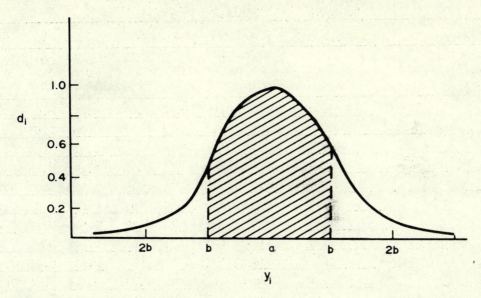

Fig. 3   The connexion between dependant variable y_i and desirability d_i

(The third version)

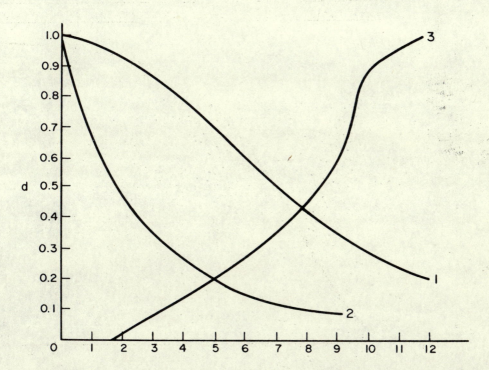

Fig.4   The transition from concrete values of permanganate oxidability (1), concentration of ammonia nitrogen (2) and content of dissolved oxygen (3) to values of the desirability d.

Economic and Non-economic Assessment of Environmental Impact on a Region

M. Lemeshev

(USSR)

The paper notes that the impact of human society on the environment may be either positive or negative. In view of the broad scope of the problem, however, the author does not consider all possible forms of impact but only those caused by economic development. Major attention is devoted to measuring economic damage, in other words, an assessment is made of the losses which can be quantified in monetary terms. The paper gives a classification of types of economic damage in relation to particular objects in the environment. In the author's view, many negative consequences of the development of industry and the growth of consumption go to make up this damage. They include the depletion of natural resources for example, energy and water resources, deforestation, soil degradation, destruction of natural landscapes, environmental pollution, etc. Not all types of negative consequences are discussed in the present paper, however, but only those caused by environmental pollution and, principally, air pollution.

Since the distribution of population and of sources of pollution in any country is extremely uneven, and the natural and atmospheric conditions of different territorial units vary, the author has chosen to consider the regional aspect of the problem. In this regard, the paper describes the methodological approaches to the economic and non-economic assessment of the consequences of atmospheric pollution along regional frontiers.

The main discussion in this connexion is of economic assessment, since the economic interpretation of the consequences of environmental impact can be actively used as a guiding parameter in models for planning processes of nature use and other environmental protection measures.

Prominence is given in the paper to the definition of the concept of economic damage, standardization of the terminology used, a description of the procedure for calculating economic damage and the reasons justifying expenditure on preventing it.

The paper also describes the methodological approaches to the assessment of non-economic damage in its ecological, aesthetic, moral and other forms. As subjects for assessment, the author takes losses in the variety of the genetic stock in biocenoses, the level of destruction of the natural landscape, the degree of pollution in the leisure sector, the presence of unpleasant odours in industrial and residential areas, etc.

In the author's view, a five-point scale including the following deviations from
the normal (desirable) condition of the unit under consideration may be used to
assess the degree of impact: insignificant, weak, very noticeable, strong, very
strong and critical. Obtaining sufficiently representative values for such
assessments and their subsequent processing and interpretation may be used as a
guiding parameter in the planning of social and economic development and of
society's nature conservation activities.

System of Planning for the Study of Interaction Between Economy and Nature

L. I. Mukhina, T. G. Runova, V. S. Preobrazhenskiy, A. M. Grin and L. I. Tatevosova

(USSR)

Since 1975, multilateral co-operation among the member countries of the Council for Mutual Economic Assistance (CMEA) has focused on the problems of conservation and improvement of the environment and on rational use of natural resources. Included in this set of issues have been studies concerned with methods for evaluating human impacts on the environment.

The theme "Methods of econmic and non-economic evaluation of human impacts of the environment" is being pursued within the Institute of Geography of the USSR Academy of Sciences; the topicality of the problem of regulating and managing the interation between man and environment is obvious.

Economic, social and ecological consequences of the human impact on the environment are frequently the object of evaluation. To solve various socio-economic problems it is necessary to employ different types of evaluation, both economic and non-economic, as each has its intrinsic value. The term economic evaluation is taken to mean the amount of basic expenditures for prevention and compensation of damage inflicted upon the economy and the population. It may be concerned with both the value of material assets and the health of the population, the latter being considered as a labour resource. Non-economic evaluation has two aspects: demo-ecological (social) and bio-ecological. The demographic or social aspect is concerned with evaluations of various transformations in nature and their consequences on the economy according to the criterion of human health ("health" being defined in terms of World Health Organization standards). Bio-ecological evaluation deals with the conditions of conservation of the biosphere's genetic fund.

The study of the complicated mechanism of interaction between the economy and the environment may be subdivided by stage and function:

(a) the study of economic impacts and their sources as starting mechanisms in the process of interaction between man and the environment;

(b) the study of transformations in nature caused by these impacts, beginning with transformations affecting the basic socio-economic and natural ecological functions: resources reproduction, environmental reproduction, function of place, function of genetic fund conservation;

(c) the study of consequences, primarily negative, arising from man's activities

123

which make it necessary to regulate interaction between man and the environment.

Establishing the linkages, both functional and spatial, between impacts, transformations and consequences is based on the knowledge of specific economic, natural and social complexes and their components. These linkages and the chain reactions within them mainly account for the pattern of the linkages. Different ranks and levels - from local to global - may serve as objects for study; this paper will be concerned with the approaches to the study of systems at the regional level.

The investigations have proved that, despite the qualitative diversity of impact, transformations and consequences, they may be grouped into several main types; this facilitates their examination, study and modelling, in particular. The following classification of impacts, transformations and consequences is suggested:

(a) Human impacts:

- extraction of material and energy from nature;

- introduction of material and energy into nature;

- transformation of natural material and energy (without extraction and introduction;

- introduction of man-made constructions.

(b) Transformation of nature:

- transformation of reserves, balance, cycles of material and energy;

- transformation of chemical, physical and mechanical properties of material and energy;

- transformation of dynamics (régimes) of natural processes;

- transformation of structures and linkages, of natural complexes;

- quantitative and qualitative reduction of natural resources;

- degradation of the environment - pollution of air, water, soils; desertification, deforestation, soil erosion, etc.;

- reduction of open spaces, including natural landscapes;

- reduction of genetic fund.

(c) Consequences:

(i) Economic

(a) primary: reduction of volumes and deterioration in the quality of the end-product; reduction of duration of equipment exploitation (corrosion, increased wear); reduction of productivity of labour and labour employment in production (increased illness); increase of fluctuations and deterioration of qualification of labour resources (migrations, illness);

(b) secondary (2): emergence of modern enterprises and termination of old ones, modification of transport flows and infrastructure, deterioration of conditions of functions of old enterprises; transformations in structure and specialization of the economy; transfer or modifications in consumption;

(ii) <u>Social</u>

(a) primary: deterioration of human health (increased sickness, death, disablement rates; decreased birth rate); increase of population migrations; reduction of free time; increase of time required for everyday services;

(b) secondary: transformation of the demographic structure of the population, migration and transport flows, distribution of employment.

For the purposes of comprehensive investigation relating to the interaction process between the economy and the environment and for the modelling of this process, the authors have suggested a system of parameters and indices to define "impacts", "transformations", "consequences". These include:

- quantitative characteristics of "impacts", "transformations", "consequences" and their magnitude, determining the scale of the interaction process;

- dynamics of the process: time of origin, its régime, acceleration and tendencies of development; the period between the emergence of impacts and the rise of transformations and consequences; this aspect facilitates forecasts of the development of the interaction process;

- distribution of the process within the territory with specific reference to the directions and areas of distribution, zones with different intensity of manifestation of the process. This parameter makes it possible to distinguish "hot points" or "critical zones", i.e. to make a regional analysis of the territory;

- combination of various types of impacts, transformations, consequences.

In elaborating the system of indices relating to these parameters, much attention was paid to the indices defining the size and scale of the interaction process. Thus, to define the magnitude of the impact of man and his activities on nature, it is suggested that three indices be established in accordance with the main characteristics of this impact:

- "resources intensity": this index reflects the amount of matter (mineral, organic, water, air) and energy extracted from nature;

- "waste rates": this determines the amount of products of human activity introduced into nature, in the form of matter or energy which is often alien to nature. The substances introduced may be of a purposeful character (fertilizers and chemical pest killers) or they may be wastes resulting from human economic activity;

- "land intensity": this index evaluates the size of the territory shaped by man in transforming natural matter and energy – ploughing, felling trees, flooding or draining areas and various changes which take place in the course of developing a territory and constructing such objects as quarries, mines and main transport lines.

Each kind of activity is distinctive in its combination of these basic indices; this makes it possible also to classify them with respect to the scale and mode of their impact on nature. This classification may facilitate preliminary evaluation regarding the conformity of a certain activity to the nature intensity of the region, and help in selecting where a certain industry should be located.

While studying regional socio-economic systems, the following economic structures are treated as sources of impact: industrial nodes, agricultural regions, cities and agglomerations, settlement and transport systems, recreation zones, etc. In this case the total magnitude of the impact depends mainly on the pattern of

spatial distribution of the sources of impact, the pattern of their linkages with
the natural complex and the specificity of this complex. Generally, spatial
distribution of the impacts is reflected in the pattern of land-use. Nevertheless,
this indicator reflects most clearly the scale of the impacts. To consider the
role of the territory and its natural specificity in the magnitude of impact
(with the help of influx and extraction parameters) it is necessary to employ
indices to define the saturation of the territory with linear, point and nodal
sources of impact, taking into account the density and size of the network,
distances between neighbourhood, configuration of this network, its internal
differentiation,etc. It is very important to consider the position of the sources
of impact with regard to various natural objects in terms of their different
stability towards the impacts.

In order to evaluate the ecological, social and economic consequences of human
impacts on nature, these absolute indices should be transformed into relative
ones. First should be tackled the problem of choosing a basis for comparison:
a criterion defining the degreee of transformation of natural and socio-economic
systems that have been subjected to various impacts.

When considering the degree of transformation of the natural systems, the
untransformed state of nature cannot be considered the starting point, for two
reasons. First, our treatment of nature envisages rational utilization but not
preservation from utilization; secondly, nature has already been transformed
almost everywhere. Data on the modern state of nature are often regarded as the
starting point. This popular index is typical in the situation where, within
the context of increasing deterioration of the environment, one of the principles
which governs human activity may be expressed as: "do not destroy that which
still exists".

In terms of such an approach, the relative indices of the magnitude of an impact
is commensurate with the absolute size of natural matter and energy extraction
and the reserves available in the region: the size of transformed lands is
compared to total land area. The amount of matter and energy introduced is
compared to the background content in the natural state of the region in question.
These indices are often treated as the coefficients of resources utilization
(CRU) and land-use (CLU) within a region. To measure the influx of matter and
energy in terms of an area's background content, the index suggested is the
coefficient of influx of matter (or energy) – CIM. Usually these indices are
expressed as percentages.

However, even these indices are not sufficiently comprehensive for measuring
the negative effect of possible consequences. Most suitable for this purpose is
the socio-economic notion of the "threshold state" of natural systems and their
components. Within this state, natural systems and their components meet the
public requirements of resources and environment reproduction and conservation
of the genetic fund. Disturbance of this state results in exhaustion of natural
resources and degradation of the environment and natural cover of the earth.
Although the indices of "threshold states" arise from the socio-economic demands
of society, they are still based on such properties of natural systems as
self-purification, self-reproduction and other forms of self-preservation. These
properties, called "the elasticity of natural systems", determine the stability
of nature towards various impacts and loads. They are widely used in elaborating
concrete indices of "threshold states" of the natural systems and their
components which usually correspond to definite impacts. While elaborating these
indices, one should bear in mind the efficiency of environment-preservation,
nature-protection and land-reclamation measures and aim at facilitating the
natural productive forces.

These indices include, initially, standards of environmental quality represented
by the norms of ultimately permissible concentrations (UPC) of pollutants in the
air, water, soils, food. In the USSR the indices are fixed with regard to
threshold values of danger for human health (at the level of bioecological
danger) and for fishing reservoirs. In several contries, in particular the United
States of America, standards are established for threshold economic concentrations
(TEC); if these concentrations are exceeded material values could be damaged.

Another group of indices comprises the standards of rational functioning of
integral natural objects. At present, such standards are being elaborated for
only some types of objects and depend on the policy of their utilization and
the category of preservation. Included are: natural reserves, zones to protect
water supply sources, green zones around cities, health resort zones. The
authors have had some experience in identifying the threshold states of natural
systems needed to maintain natural resources: agricultural, timber-industrial,
hunting grounds and fisheries, sources of water supply, etc. It is necessary to
co-ordinate the indices which envisage rational functioning of natural activities
(including natural resources) and preservation of their functions of environment-
reproduction and nature-conservation.

The system of indices, in defining the threshold states of natural systems, aids
in determining the degree of natural transformations for the purposes of human
activities. At the same time, it serves as a basis for elaborating the standards
of ultimately permissible loads (within the existing mode of nature-utilization)
which aim at the prevention of negative consequences.

Among these idices should be mentioned standards of ultimately permissible wastes
in air and water reservoirs (UPW), elaborated in order to control the functioning
of enterprises and reduce the level of environmental pollution. For economic
activities, several indices are used to define the dtandards of ultimatley
permissible loads (UPL) on lands used as sources of renewable resournces. These
standards define, inter alia, the projected wood-cutting area, amount of fish and
game caught, pasture of cattle, withdrawal of water from open reservoirs,
application of chemical pest killers and fertilizers. Observance of the standards
ensures normal functioning of these systems according to the requirements of man.

The least elaborated standards are those setting permissible transforming impacts
(ploughing, drainage, irrigation, afforestation, construction) and the standards
relating to optimal correlation of lands with different types of utilization to
regions with various natural conditions. The difficulty of elaborating
quantitative and qualitative indices of UPW and UPL consists in their regional
nature and their dependence on the conditions in a certain region, such as the
hydroclimatic characteristics and geological relief, the modern state of the
natural systems and their stability towards impacts. In addition, indices
depend on the branch and territorial structure of the economy, peculiarities
of the settlement system, transport network, etc.

To define the magnitude of negative consequences in social and economic systems,
a measure of economic and social damage is usually employed. For example,
economic damage is often fixed with regard to the amount of expected production
which has not been forthcoming because of exhausted natural resources, the decrease
of labour productivity and labour employment owing to illness; damage inflicted
upon material values because of corrosion of metals, increased wear, etc.
Similarly social damage may be expressed in terms of data relating to the
decreases of the level of human health (growth of rates for sickness, death and
disablement, reduction of expected lifetimes and birth rate), growth of
population migrations, reduction of free time, psychological and emotional damage.
These and other consequences can cause chain reactions within the socio-economic

systems and can result in indirect and undesirable after-effects.

Within this subject area should be also included the problem of criteria to define the degree of negative consequences arising in social and economic systems and the problem of stability of these systems towards the impacts. To evaluate the magnitude of negative consequences within the economy, Soviet scientists employ indices relating to the provision of a certain level of the total national economic effect of a specific economic complex. With this aim, they then consider the value of differential rent (for the nature-consuming branches); this value is the difference between the final (and ultimately permissible rate for society) and the actual material expenditures for obtaining a certain natural resource. For other branches of the economy they use an index based on defining the value of profit, calculated on the basis of interbranch models. (3) The possible degree of differential rent and profit decrease may serve as the index, thus defining the magnitude of negative consequences. These consequences are evaluated by measuring the amount of public expenditure necessary to prevent them occurring.

A system of suggested indices which promotes an integral study of all the links in the chain of man-nature interactions: source of impact - impact - transformation in nature - consequences in social and economic spheres, represents the first investigation of its kind. It is now clear that many of these links should be studied thoroughly. Such a set of indices should include:

- data relating to the background (modern) state of natural, social and economic systems;

- data relating to the absolute magnitude of impacts, transformations, consequences arising within the interaction process; data on their dynamic and spatial development;

- data regarding the criteria: the starting points, definition of the degree of transformation of natural, social and economic systems;

- data relating to the threshold (ultimately permissible) loads on natural, socio-economic systems;

- data of comparative analysis: relative or evaluating indices which express the degree of transformation of these systems.

REFERENCES

(1) The main results of investigations were published in the following contributions: Geographical aspects of interaction within "man-nature" system. M., Institute of Geography of the USSR Academy of Sciences, 1978; L.I. Mukhina, V.S. Preobrazhenskiy et al. "System approach towards evaluating consequences of human impact on the environment" in Natural resources and the environment: Achievements and perspectives, 5th edition, M., 1978; Mukina, L.I., Runova T.G. "The logic of geographical study of the interaction within the population-environment-economy system", in Izvestiya Akademii Nauk SSSR, geography series, N 4, M., 1977 (translated in Soviet Geography: Review and Translations November 1978); V. Vorachek, I.V. Komar, L.I. Mukhina, T.G. Runova, "problems of elaborating methods of evaluation of human impact on nature" XXIII International Geographical Congress, Moscow, 1976. Symposium on applied geography. (Tbilisi, 20-26 July 1976). Volume of papers of the Soviet geographers. "Metsniereba", Tbilisi, 1976 (also published in English).
(2) Secondary transformations and consequences include those caused by chain reactions; they may be treated as transformations and consequences at the level of integral systems (subsystems): natural, economic, social.

(3) "Preservation of the Environment", M., Economy, 1977.

Indicators for Environmental Impact Assessment

S. Borovnica

(Yugoslavia)

Environmental indicators are tools which can be used systematically to identify and assess the state of the environment and the evolution of conditions and their impact on the environment - not only from a technological and ecological standpoint, but as an integral part of social, economic and cultural development. Consideration for the environment - as an inseparable part of development - should ensure that its values are preserved and that it is protected from damaging effects.

Environmental indicators cannot be confined to individual features viewed in isolation (for example, human settlements, water, air or soil), but should cover the environment as a whole. The environment needs to be an integral part of social, economic and cultural development processes, since the quality of the environment is an essential criterion for the assessment of development, and the environmental indicators are related to causes as well as consequences of such processes.

In accordance with the basic principles established, the Task Force has considered the fields which the environmental indicators would cover along with the choice of indicators.* These basic principles were taken as the starting point for devising the system of indicators adopted in Yugoslavia. Environmental indicators cover the whole subject of the environment and physical planning. They represent not simply a set of indicators of the situation in particular areas - human settlements, water, air, etc. - but an attempt to set up a system of indicators (cross-indicators) which will reveal the state of the environment and of physical planning in the context of development activities and interrelationships.

Methodology for environmental analysis and impact assessment and the reasons for its selection

The system of indicators has as its basis the belief that environment and physical planning should be treated together as a whole because they are inseparable. This approach takes into account the complex realities of the land and the relationship between man and the environment in terms of development. Essentially, it eschews a sectoral approach in favour of one that is integrated.

---

* This report has been prepared in the light of the results of the work done by the Task Force on the study of Environmental Indicators, set up by the Senior Advisers to ECE Governments on Environmental Problems, in accordance with guidelines laid down by Yugoslavia as the lead country of the Task Force.

In order to attain the objectives desired, and in accordance with fundamental principles, it was considered necessary to take as a starting point the basic trends of development that determine the quality of the environment (causes and consequences).Furthermore, it was sought to identify their interaction with natural resources and with the environment and physical planning, as the reflection of, and basic factor in, social, economic, cultural and technological development. The ways and means of inculating in society a positive attitude to the environment also formed part of such considerations.

Investment policy makes it possible to create almost a new environment and to preserve environmental values through careful investment of society's resources in the environment and in physical planning. The limitations of a narrowly sectoral or local investment policy may be overcome by the use of economic instruments (prices, taxation, ground rent) as part of a planned policy, or by interventionist measures. Investments, especially in housing, human settlements, infrastructure, industrial or tourist facilities and landscape planning must be put to use as a complex whole, in accordance with agreed plans of urban and rural development.

The relationship between individual and social benefits in environmental matters and physical planning is of particular importance. If it is accepted that the social benefit of a particular development project – using a part of the land and natural resources – has a positive or negative impact on other possible projects, it is possible to assess its effect in the general context. The cost of activities and the influence of projects on one another, although often unexpected and unsought, are an integral part of production and consumption. The main question is whether those costs can be foreseen, and consequently avoided, or, if they cannot be avoided, whether they can be somehow offset.

In Yugoslavia, two Republics have introduced a mandatory three-stage procedure for controlling all new investment: site permit, building permit, and utilization permit. The Federal Executive Council has also suggested to the authorities of those Republics and Provinces that have not yet introduced such legislation that, for purposes of the construction of new buildings or the reconstruction of existing building for industrial, infrastructural or similar uses, they should require that a study be made to assess the interaction between such construction and the environment. This assessment would form an integral and obligatory part of both investment and technical   documentation required, in particular that related to population distribution, management of natural resources and construction of human settlements. It would thus ensure economic development in harmony with the environment.

Environmental impact assessment is carried out by authorized research institutions specializing in effects on air, water, human settlements and the natural habitat. Comprehensive, long-term assessment of such effects is made by adapting qualitatively the urban and rural development plans (simulation models) which already contain the basic data necessary for such an assessment.

Identification, verification and compilation of data on the environment: chief difficulties and limitation encountered and methods used to compile and analyse basic data

The data processing equipment available in this field is fairly extensive, but dispersed among many different institutions. The basic services responsible are the institutes of statistics, survey institutes, departments in charge of the preservation of national monuments and the protection of nature, hydrometeorological services, public health institutes, geological institutes and others.

Almost all environmental aspects are monitored, with the exception of non-renew-able resources, secondary raw materials and waste. However, there is no clear distribution of responsibility and no co-ordination between the different institutions monitoring the state of the environment nor of physical planning, either within the Republics themselves or between the Republics and the Provinces. The main problem is that the various monitoring units are not coextensive: the survey departments rely upon the local land registries, the statistical services rely upon statistical societies, and the communes depend upon local communities. The creation of a system of indicators for the environment and physical planning represents the first step towards a comprehensive and interdependent system of control in this field.

Specific possibilities of the methodology chosen (for example, for the definition, forecasting, communication and evaluation of risks); other factors, such as time and resources required

Indicators for environmental impact assessment are used for many purposes: environmental and physical planning through medium-term social plans; long-term rural and urban development plans; plans for the development of water and forestry resources; agricultural land-use plans; and plans for building the network of cultural, social, public health and other institutions. Work is now in progress to devise a minimum set of unified indicators for social planning purposes.

Indicators with which to assess the relationships between individual and social benefits are of particular importance for investment policy, in respect of environmental matters and physical planning. Hence, the use of indicators in planning may be the means of avoiding the costs which would otherwise be incurred through the interaction of different development projects. The indicators should serve to ensure that investment policy is not governed solely by direct effects but that it is aimed at the conservation, in its broadest sense, of the environment. Further, they should lead to a policy that becomes - as it can under the political system prevailing in Yugoslavia - a powerful instrument for the conservation of the land, in particular by ensuring that more permanent structures are in harmony with environmental conditions and values, not only from the point of view of location but also in terms of the technological solutions adopted.

Conclusion

Indicators for environmental impact assessment should be developed as an open system that can be adapted to the needs and potentialities of each country and to social, economic, cultural and technological developments.

PART II

Integration of Environmental Considerations into the Planning and Decision-making Process

Assessment of the Use of the Water Resources of the Byelorussian SSR in Planning and Decision-making

A. M. Klybik

(Byelorussian SSR)

The Byelorussian SSR consistently tries to ensure the rational utilization and protection of water resources in accordance with the principles of planning the multi-purpose use of water to the best economic advantage and of providing the best possible working, living, leisure and health conditions for the Soviet people.

The measures taken to achieve these goals depend for their effectiveness on the preparation of inventories of water resources, and are designed to meet long-term economic and household requirements, subject to environmental considerations.

Water resource management is governed by the Water Code of the Byelorussian SSR and by other regulations. Planning organizations and water users draw up and apply, in conformity with these regulations, rational water-supply and waste-treatment schemes providing for the recycling of process water, conversion to air cooling, the maximum removal of pollutants from waste water, the construction of effluent-free production units, multi-purpose reservoirs to regulate runoff, and dual-purpose land improvement systems, etc.

The monitoring and executive body in matters relating to the use and protection of water resources is the State Committee of the Byelorussian SSR for Nature Conservation. The Committee has a say in decisions on the siting of production units and the planning of water resource projects; it reviews hydraulic engineering projects to ensure compliance with requirements governing the rational use and protection of water resources; it also monitors the application of measures relating to the use of water resources, participates in the acceptance testing of facilities, and verifies that they are operated in accordance with the water regulations.

As matters stand, the Byelorussian SSR has sufficient reserves of both industrial-quality and potable water. The drinking-water requirements of the public and of a number of branches of industry are met by the use of ground-water, whereas the demand for water of the quality required for production processes and agriculture is covered mainly from surface water resources.

The measures drawn up by the Republic to provide water of the right quality and in adequate quantities to all sectors of the national economy are set out in forecasts and schemes concerned with the multi-purpose use and protection of water resources and in the annual and five-year plans for the development of the national economy.

The establishment of water balances is an integral part of planning measures for the use and protection of water resources. The balances serve as the basis for developing measures to meet water demand and are used in long-term plans for the development of water resources. The integrated schemes drawn up for the use and protection of the water resources of each river basin make it possible correctly to plan and site economic production units and to design, build and operate water resource facilities.

Under the current five-year plan, water resources are being protected against pollution by the construction of new treatment plants and the modernization of existing ones at industrial undertakings. New comprehensive biological treatment plants serving entire urban areas have also been built in many towns of the Republic. Such plants ensure thorough treatment of effluent before it is discharged into bodies of water. The amount of water that is recycled at enterprises has been increasing each year as new closed-circuit systems are installed.

Household, industrial and agricultural water requirements will be fully met and the rational use and the protection of water resources ensured by the measures being carried out and drawn up.

Experience of Environmental Impact Assessment in the Planning System of the German Democratic Republic

H. Kroske

(German Democratic Republic)

In a socialist society, successful implementation of any socio-economic development strategy requires that possible contradictions between steady, long-term economic growth and the degeneration of natural conditions must be detected and averted early enough to avoid negative impacts on the working and living conditions of large segments of the population and a decline in the efficiency of the national economic reproduction precesses. The resolution and prevention of contradictions between the steady growth rate of a socialist economy and ecological stress in nature must be studied on a long-term basis, and tackled in a complex manner. Early and increasingly comprehensive assessment of the impacts of economic projects on nature and human society may be made on the basis of the current state of knowledge in the natural and social sciences. This forms part of the over-all socio-economic mechanism of management and planning in a socialist system and corresponds to its deeply humanistic basic conception.

During the coming years, the German Democratic Republic will strive for steady, long-term economic growth guided by the needs of the people. Such growth can be maintained only if national resources are used in a rational manner. Otherwise, expenditures for restoring natural conditions will turn out to be a factor with serious consequences for the efficiency of the economic process as a whole. That is why Environmental Impact Assessment, with its complex approach, corresponds perfectly to the fundamental planning mechanism of socialism which attends to the over-all aspects of society as a whole.

The state planning system in the German Democratic Republic, together with effective economic and legal provisions, allows consideration of ecological concerns in planning the comprehensive development of the national economy. However, when assessing the ecological impact of economic projects, it will be increasingly important in the future to take into consideration not only locally-limited aspects or business-biased arguments but, above all, the needs of the entire society and the possible impacts of the proposed projects or technologies on the living conditions of present and future generations.

Present laws and regulations in the German Democratic Republic, as far as environmental and economic problems are concerned, demonstrate the opportunities for applying and realizing complex methods of Environmental Impact Assessment. A recent analysis made by the Institute of Geography and Geoecology of the national Academy of Sciences has shown that the protection and management of the environment,

as fixed by law, already corresponds to such a complex assessment. An example of
the Law of the Systematic Implementation of Socialist Environmental Policy is
presented below.

The general environmental law stipulates that environmental protection is an
over all social task demanding that environmental policy should be planned in a
complex manner. In general, the need for environmental management ought to be
considered early and from a long-term stand-point in the economic decision-making
processes. The national management bodies are obliged by law to take into account
the need for environmental management when planning the distribution of the
productive forces and the corresponding investments.

The regulations for implementing the law also contain a great number of directives
for the management of soil, air, water, noise and waste products, as well as
matters of hygiene and health protection, which serve to avoid, reduce, or
eliminate environmental damage. These directives fix limits for contamination,
especially of air and water. The observance of these limits is controlled
permanently by state and social authorities. Recently, extensive control was
carried out by the Workers' and Farmers' Supervisory Committee of the German
Democratic Republic in checking compliance with these laws.

However, the situation represented in the synopsis in Figure 1 also shows some
deficiencies with regard to the application and enforcement of complex assessment
methods in the planning process. The numbers in the body of the diagram indicate
specific aspects and problems concerning the application of Environmental Impact
Assessment principles in the country, and are explained briefly below.

1. The "Law of the Systematic Implementation of Socialist Environmental Policy in
the German Democratic Republic", dated 14 June 1970, sets out very far-reaching
principal goals for the connexion between the economy and environmental conditions.
The fundamental rule is that rational use and conservation of man's natural
environment, as well as its complex evolution, is an inseparable part of the
formation of a developed socialistic society, and that nature (with its components)
represents an indispensable basis for the development of the national economy and
for the satisfaction of the material, mental and cultural needs of the working
people. On such a basis, compulsory statutory goals are set for the planned
development of the relations between man, production and the natural environment,
for all branches and sections of the national economy. Protection and management
of the environment, (as a rule summarized by the term "Landeskultur" – Land use)
are interpreted here as an over-all national task which goes beyond the particular branches and fields of the national economy. A complex planning system for
environmental management is requested. As a general principle, environmental
necessities have to be considered in time and on a long-range basis, whenever
economic decisions are being prepared.

The regulations issued up to the present for the implementation of this land-use
law deal with particular, specific measures for environmental protection. They
are bound to specific environmental media (air, water, noise, etc.) and aspects
and, in this way, represent starting points for further investigations to clarify
the problems of managing and planning economic-ecological interactions.

2. and 3. The "Regulations for regional distribution of investments" lay down
that for all central projects and any local investment above 100,000 M, micro-
regional proposals should be compiled by the local bodies representing the people.
They have to consider all the requirements fixed by the law for the protection
and management of the environment. In addition, local authorities may give
specific orders to the investment contractor concerning environmental protection
and call for environmental impact statements made by experts.

This regulation, as well as the "Regulation for the reproduction of fixed assets", takes, as bases for consideration, the regional efficiency of the investments and calls for analyses and statements concerning impacts which might pass beyond micro-regional aspects. However, the ecological impacts are not yet taken sufficiently into account. This is not so much owing to a lack of understanding, but more to the lack of feasible methods.

4. Although the law in its principal statements allows comparisons of alternative variants, this point has not yet been fixed in detail. However, in practice alternatives are taken into consideration during the preparatory stage of micro-regional proposals. For example, when planning a great thermoelectric power plant based on lignite in the Cottbus area, the procedure started with 16 possible locations. This number was reduced to six for economic and socio-economic reasons (manpower, housing, migration). For reasons of air pollution (SO_2), three other locations were discarded. The final decision-making process is not yet completed. This example demonstrates that in practice the determination of optimum alternatives, i.e. those with the least environmental pollution, has already advanced much further than the law.

5. This aspect has not yet been provided for in legislation. The procedure works in the following way. Preparatory to management decisions, the local council calls for the elaboration of a complex micro-regional study for the planned project. Complying with this order, the institution charged with performing the study – as a rule it will be the appropriate bureau for regional planning – then requests environmental impact statements (e.g. those concerning impacts on air quality, agriculture and forestry, noise, dust, etc.). These statements are also made by scientific institutions and by the National Sanitary Inspection and other state authorities. They share in the decision whether or not the project in question may be built at the location suggested. Environmental impact statements may be requested, too, from building enterprises which are to carry out the planned project.

In this connexion, it must be stated, however, that such impact statements, drafted by diverse expert bodies, are, as a rule, specifically bound to one respective medium exclusively, i.e. they will consider the consequences for air or water, or housing problems, or waste products, etc., but not others. Complex, synthesizing procedures which Environmental Impact Assessment requires, so far exist only in a rudimentary form. Conflicting target alternatives are decided by qualitative priorities; quantifiable mathematical methods are still at the research level stage.

6. Surveys of the difference in environmental quality between the dates of commencement and completion of projects take place through a State Building Commission. This commission also controls the environmental protection parameters. However, having completed a certain project, National Sanitary Inspection and special officials charged with responsibility for environmental protection within the enterprises and on the regional level, will check for compliance with the approved limits of the environmental parameters.

7. The German Democratic Republic too , is a country which, because of its geographic and climatic conditions, must make great efforts in water management to ensure a steady supply of potable, as well as non-potable, water to the population, industry and agriculture. The critical water-balance is exemplified by the high degree of resource utilization: amounting to about 40 per cent. Owing to the intrinsic conflict between the need to maintain the quality of water as a life-sustaining element and the need to use it in production processes which increasingly cause undesirable effects, a series of laws and regulations were issued concerning the use and protection of water. By these laws (the "Water Law"

of 1963, and the "Land-use Law" of 1970) use and protection are considered to be
an undivided complex and are permanently entrusted to the care of state and
economic bodies. In order to achieve rational utilization of water, the laws
anticipate an all-round, co-ordinated long-range planning policy, to ensure the
water supply, increase its available share, and improve its quality. The national
requirement to obtain authorization for water use, together with the controls
exerted and the orders issued by the water-management authorities enable them to
exert a decisive influence favouring environmental protection. For these reasons
comprehensive economic and ecological assessments of the impacts caused by
economic activities require a long-term and complex analysis of all relevant
factors (physical, chemical, biological, economic, social, socio-economic.

8.   Similar considerations explain why the overall responsibility for the
consideration of water-management aspects within the national economy was assigned
to the State Planning Commission. In addition, an institutional framework was
created under the responsibility of the Ministry for Environmental Protection and
Water Management, which will ensure the collection and processing of data, the
registration of environmental changes, and compliance with the legal rules.

The Chief River Superintendents, the Water Management Boards, and the plants
for water processing and sewage treatment all have their tasks differentiated so
that relevant data concerning Environmental Impact Assessment may be recorded. In
addition to the usual data from water analyses, there are special balance sheets
for water quantity/quality, statements about the efficiency of water use (e.g.
economy of technologies), lists of usable soluble (secondary raw) materials,
relations between evolution of the whole watershed region (development of
population and production).

9.   On the basis of this information, as well as subsequent procedures which are
equivalent to Environmental Impact Assessment, governmental authorization is given
for water use. Increasingly, entire river and water systems are being included in
the optimization process. Likewise, according to the procedures of Environmental
Impact Assessment, long – and medium-term prognoses are worked out for water
management projects. However, after sufficient verification of the simulation
models, there is still a need for appropriate methods to ensure feed-back from
Environmental Impact Assessment to the decision-making procedure. An important
task of basic research for the improvement of Environmental Impact Assessment will
be one that surpasses mere water management issues; it will be a synthesis of
numerous, individual investigations which are usually bound to specific media or
objects. The final aim will be comprehension, modelling and control of economic-
ecological interactions within the entire range of economic development.

One result of applying Environmental Impact Assessment in water management is
the gradually decreasing percentage of heavily polluted waters in the German
Democratic Republic. On the other hand, it must be emphasized that the complex
ecological approach, even for water management, still needs extensive improvement;
also such an approach still lacks application to the other environmental media
besides water.

CONCLUSIONS

From this analysis and review of the extent to which complex economic-ecological matters are taken into consideration within the national planning system and in legislation, the following conclusions may be drawn:

(a) The socialist social order has the necessary socio-economic basis for the protection and management of the environment. That is why the complex approach inherent in Environmental Impact Assessment may be applied on the basis of effective laws and regulations, and the existing institutional pre-conditions.

(b) Complex methods of Environmental Impact Assessment may be applied in an efficient way. The greatest obstacle in doing so, however, has proven to be the lack of a generally-accepted methodology for uniformly elaborating such statements, in order to assess the over-all ecological effects. Research work has begun in order to close this gap.

(c) When contemplating the institutional levels within the decision-making hierarchy of the German Democratic Republic, various governmental and other bodies appear to be appropriate machinery for such complex approaches. This concerns, in particular, the State Planning Commission, the State Bureau for Investments, the Regional Planning Commissions, the bureaus for regional planning, etc. Through these institutions, decisions are prepared and taken which will define long-range developments, and, in doing so, correspond to a multifactor optimization.

A I

Starting points for E.I.A. include the legislative basis of the planning system and its use in the practice of the G.D.R.

#	Operational procedures of E.I.A.	Planning order 1976–80	Order for distribution of the productive forces	Order of reproduction of the means of production	Directive for the 5 year plan	Law of the systematic implementation of socialist environmental policy	Law and orders for management of			
							Water	Noise	Soil	Air
I	Essential and integral part of all planning for major actions		2 →	3 →		1				
2	National goals and policies should take environmental considerations into account									
3	Institutional arrangements for the process of E.I.A. should be determined and made public	10 →					8			
4	Timetables should be established									
5	Study of all the relevant physical, biological, economic and social factors						7			
6	Inventories should be prepared of relevant sources of data and of technical expertise									
7	Study of alternatives, including that of no action	4 ↑	•							
8	Spatial frame of reference should be much larger than the area encompassed by the action						7			
9	Mid-term and long-term predictions of impacts should be included									
10	The difference between the future state of the environment and the state if no action occurred must be assessed	6 →								
11	Estimates of the magnitude and the importance of environmental impacts must be obtained									
12	A methodology for impact assessment should be selected	5 →					9			
13	Recommendation for inspection procedures									

Legend:
- E.I.A. requested by the law
- Possibilities for E.I.A. approach
- E.I.A. principles not yet applied

Environmental Impact Assessment in the Netherlands' Physical Planning Process

M. C. in't Anker and M. Burggraaff

(Netherlands)

INTRODUCTION

The central concern in this paper is whether the physical planning process in the Netherlands offers sufficient opportunities for integration of environmental impact assessments into the process. A brief survey is presented of physical planning in the Netherlands, especially the way in which planning is organized. The characteristics which would enable assessments of environmental impact to be integrated in the planning process are then outlined. This theoretical outline is then used to make a comparison; two particular examples of physical planning are evaluated in terms of this outline. To avoid any misunderstanding, it must be pointed out that, at present, there is no legislation on environmental impact assessment in the Netherlands, nor is such assessment obligatory on other grounds. The Dutch government at this moment is preparing proposals regarding the incorporation of environmental impact assessment in the Environmental Protection Bill (General Provisions).

In physical planning in the Netherlands the accent is gradually shifting from final-state planning to process planning. This shift is clearly noticeable if a comparison is made between the Second Report on Physical Planning of 1965 and the Third Report in 1972 and the following years. These reports present the physical planning policy at the national level. A picture of the expected land-use pattern in the year 2000 is presented in the Second Report. The Third Report is a series of policy reports and consists of three parts. The first section (Orientation) contains a set of goals to be reached by the physical planning policy; the other sections deal with Urbanization and Rural Areas. The national physical planning policy laid down in these reports is further elaborated in the so-called Structural Outline Sketches and Structure Schemes. These reports, sketches and schemes are reviewed once every five years, emphasizing the process character of physical planning.

Structural Outline Sketches concern general physical developments which the National Government wishes to influence in a particular direction. Examples would be urbanization and the development of rural areas. A Structural Outline Sketch consists of a report and map concerning the main structural outline ultimately desired. Thus, a Structural Outline Sketch, as a physical plan, constitutes the general framework for a coherent long-term policy with respect to the various sectors or facilities formulated in Structural Outline Plans. Publication of the Urbanization Report was accompanied by the Structural Outline Sketch for

Urbanization, while the Report on Rural Areas was accompanied by a Structural
Outline Sketch for the Rural Areas.

Structure Schemes are concerned with the long-term policy in respects to a sector.
They have a strong physical planning accent, such as the extensive communication
systems or public utilities. In these schemes the expected size and location of
the facilities concerned are indicated in rough outline on a long-term basis
(20 to 30 years). Structure Schemes for drinking and process water supply,
electricity supply, navigable waterways, traffic and transport, and housing have
been completed. Other Structure Schemes are still being elaborated: airports,
seaports, outdoor recreation, nature and landscape conservations, land reconstruction, military training grounds, and pipelines. By adjusting the Structure
Schemes to the Structural Outline Sketches an attempt is made to achieve
co-ordination between sectoral policy and general physical planning policy.

At the sectoral level the Structures Schemes are elaborated into medium-term
plans and subsequently into project plans. The above-mentioned reports, as well
as the Structural Outline Sketches and Structure Schemes, follow a procedure which
offers facilities for participation to both the public and the lower government
authorities (provinces and municipalities). This is the procedure of the Crucial
Physical Planning Decision.

Apart from reports at national level, physical planning also involves plans at
regional level (Regional Plans) and at local level (Structure Plans and Land-Use
Development Plans). For further information on the organization of Netherlands
physical planning reference may be had to the publication entitled "Planning and
Development in the Netherlands" (Volume IX-2/1977), from which Fig. 1 has been
taken.

The transition from final-state planning to process planning is also reflected
in the approach of physical planning according to systems theory. In this approach,
the physical system (defined as the whole of natural environment, artefacts and
localized activities) is regarded as being in constant interaction with other
systems. The latter systems are the ecological, economic and social aspect systems.
This complex of systems is governed by the control system. Its elements are formed
by the objectives and instruments which society applies when engaging in physical
planning.

With a view to defining the ecological system, a study was undertaken entitled,
"Towards a general ecological model for physical planning in the Netherlands".
This General Ecological Model defines the relations between society and the
environment. A project known as the National Environmental Survey was undertaken
for the purpose fo supplying data to this General Ecological Model. It consisted
of an ecological survey of the natural environment in the Netherlands, chiefly
based on a survey of vegetation (1).

At present studies are in progress in the Netherlands to introduce systematic
environmental impact assessment. As far as physical planning is concerned, the
important question is whether a provisional plan should be first presented and
then put through a separate environmental impact assessment procedure, or whether
such assessment can be integrated into the planning process itself. This question
is raised in a report by Lee and Wood which was compiled on behalf of the
Commission of the European Communities (CEC) (2).

These authors claim that EIA can be built into the planning process, provided
this process fulfils a number of conditions. These condition relate to:

- setting planning goals and objectives
- survey, prediction and analysis
- generation and evaluation of alternative draft plans
- plan decision, implementation, monitoring , etc.
- Procedural aspects.

In more detail, the conditions specified in the report are listed below, more
or less as they appear in the CEC report.

Setting planning goals and objectives

(a) Environmental goals whose attainment could be affected by different kinds of
impact should be articulated at an early stage in the planning process. Measures
should be taken to ensure that these environmental goals are translated into
operational environmental objectives and that these are subsequently refined at
each objective reformulation stage in the planning process.

Survey, prediction and analysis

(b) This stage in the planning process should incorporate a survey of the existing
environmental conditions in the planning area, a prediction of future environmental
conditions over the planning period (in the absence of plan implementation), an
identification of environmental problems likely to arise during the plan period
and revision of goals and objectives in the light of these evaluations.

Generation and evaluation of alternative draft plans

(c) The draft plans which are developed should, inter alia, be formulated with a
view to meeting agreed environmental goals and objectives. For each draft plan
an assessment of the likely impact of its implementation on environment conditions
over the plan period should be undertaken as part of each general plan assessment.
Environmental consideration (including compliance with environmental objectives)
should be incorporated into the process of formulating plan evaluation criteria
for choosing among alternative draft plans.

Plan decision, implementation, monitoring, etc.

(d) Environmental monitoring should form part of the plan implementation monitoring system, in order to establish whether the environmental impacts expected to
result from plan implementation are being realized and whether the environmental
goals and objectives are being achieved. Failure in this respect would justify
a review of plan implementation procedures or plan revision.

Procedural aspects

(e) The procedural requirements for an EIA would be met provided there is
suitable provision in the planning procedure itself. Such provisions should include:

  (i)   publication of the impact assessment, in draft and final form (possibly
        in stages, corresponding to the main stages in the planning process itself,
        but commencing prior to the first significant point of decision);
 (ii)   agency and public consultation; and
(iii)   monitoring of plan implementation.

To what extent does the physical planning in the Netherlands already fulfil these conditions? To provide an answer two practical examples will be examined, viz.: the Urbanization Report and the Structural Outline Sketch for Urbanization (Policy Resolution 1976); and the Regional Plan for East Gelderland (Report on alternative provisional plans, 1975). The Urbanization Report and related Structural Outline Sketch constitute a recent endeavour of physical planning at the national level. Th Regional Plan for East Gelderland may be regarded as an example of the modern method of regional planning. The term environment will be interpreted in the sense of ecological, socio-historic and visual aspects of space and the qualities of soil, water and air.

Urbanization Report and Related Structural Outline Plan

The Urbanization Report comprises the general policy guidelines and the policy instruments with respect to population distribution, urbanization and mobility. The Structural Outline Plan presents the physical structure for urbanization and contains quantitative pronouncements setting objectives in relation to the physical structure of urbanization.

The Urbanization Report is a continuation of the Orientation Report in which the goals for physical planning have been laid down. The Urbanization Report was first presented as a policy resolution. After a period of public participation and administrative consultation, the Government took a decision in regard to the policy resolution, and published its decision. The report contains the following chapters: outline of the urbanization process, the physical development and the problems involved; orientation in respect of the future, when long-term scenarios are drawn up and alternatives for the urban planning policy formulated; policy choice, when the margins and marginal conditions for the policies of the lower government authorities are laid down; and a chapter on instruments.

Goals

Some of the goals in the Orientation Report relate to the environment. Even the basic goal raises the environmental aspect:

"the promotion of such physical and ecological conditions as to ensure that:

a. as far as possible justice is done to the real endeavours of individual persons and groups in society;

b. the diversity, coherence and durability of the physical environment are guaranteed as effectively as possible".

Some aspects encountered in the further elaboration of the goals are: improvement of the quality of life; adaptation of the desires of society to the possibilities of space and environment; reduction of environmental pollution; conservation of environmental hygiene; conservation of the desired ecological conditions; safeguarding nature areas, cultivated landscapes and cultural monuments; and promoting the creation of new forms thereof. The goals relate to a number of aspects of the environment: residential and living, ecological, visual and pollution.

Survey, prediction and analysis

In the planning process of the Urbanization Report the environment survey produced a number of maps, viz.: ecological significance of the natural environment; simulation of the visual effects of urbanization elements; survey of the physical environment, vulnerable land and land unsuitable for housebuilding; water-catchment areas, and, among other things, recreation areas, and areas with high noise load.

The survey of the social and physical developments of the Netherlands resulted in the identification of a number of bottlenecks. One that particularly relates to the environment is the invasion of open areas and of areas of value from an ecological or landscape point of view. Other bottlenecks concern increasing mobility, shortage of recreation facilities, population spill-over from the cities, development of employment in urban areas, etc.

A pattern for future environment conditions is set out in the scenarios for long-term physical development. Four scenarios have been drawn up, based on one set of goals, but with certain goals emphasized more strongly than others in different scenarios. One of these four scenarios may be characterized as "friendly to the environment" and is concentrated on energy-saving. In addition, a "trend scenario" has been drawn up, based on the continuation of current developments.

The scenarios present a description of a future situation and of the developments that lead to this situation. In this way, insight into the consequences of certain developments can be acquired. No direct policy choice was derived from the scenarios; they were used simply as warning signals for likely conflicts within the chosen set of goals.

Generation and evaluation of alternatives

Alternatives have been formulated in response to the bottlenecks identified in the physical development. To this end an indication was given, for each bottleneck, of directions in which a solution might be sought. By combining these possible solutions for the different bottlenecks, alternatives were obtained for the physical development. For example, in regard to the invasion of open areas considered valuable from the ecological or landscape point of view, two possible solutions were indicated: (a) greater emphasis on isolation of high-value areas and conservation of the existing situation by avoiding any interference whatsoever: (b) greater emphasis on integration of environmental values, especially of "green" residential and recreation areas thus reducing the effects of invasion and adding new values.

In all the alternatives, conditions were incorporated with regard to occupation of ecologically valuable areas and of open areas; these areas had been identified on maps. In the case of the alternative placing emphasis on isolation of ecological and landscape values, the area excluded from occupation was greater than in the alternative emphasizing integration. Further, with respect to the environment, allocation demands for house-building were applied to support the alternatives. Areas for occupation were designated on the strength of the map of the physical environment. One solution aimed to prevent house-building in areas where the soil has insufficient load-bearing capacity; the second solution was aimed at integrating house-building and the values of the physical environment.

Alternatives were evaluated in three ways: by checking against the goals; checking against the degree of problems solved and against the scenarios; and checking for possibilities of realization. To check the alternatives against the goals of the Orientation Report, these goals were combined into four groups: urban renewal, conservation of the environment, mobility and environmental differentiation. In checking the alternatives for their contribution towards solving the various bottlenecks, it was indicated which alternatives would involve the greatest protection for nature and for open areas. The check against

scenarios gave some indication of the long-term environmental conditions likely
to result from the choice of a given alternative.

Plan decision, implementation, monitoring

Now that the Government has taken a decision on the Urbanization Report and the
related Structural Outline Sketch (1977), the implementation of the policy can
commence. In order to ascertain whether the actual physical development accords
with or deviates from the desired development, a system of process monitoring
is applied. With a certain amount of regularity it can furnish relevant information
on the physical development. To this end, a set of indicators has been coupled
to the different policy guidelines. The intention is to present annually an overall survey of actual developments and an evaluation of these developments with
their likely consequences for policy. This survey will be presented to Parliament
together with the budget. Once every five years, a more detailed picture will
have to be submitted in respect to actual developments, including those relating
to the environmental aspects. This more detailed information should make it
possible to decide (on specific points) whether the Structural Outline Sketch
requires modification.

Procedural aspects

The procedural aspects of EIA, i.e. publication in draft and final form and
consultation with agencies and the public, are part of the procedure for the
Crucial Physical Planning Decision, which was followed in the Urbanization Report
with the accompanying Structural Outline Sketch. The procedure of the Crucial
Physical Planning Decision is discussed in more detail in the paper in this
volume entitled "Public Information and Participation in the Netherlands" by
A.A.M.F. Staatsen.

REGIONAL PLAN FOR EAST GELDERLAND

The landscape in East Gelderland is small in scale. Situated largely on a surface
layer of sedimentary sand, it is a scenery which farmland, meadows, coppices,
moors, brushwood and brooks.

A regional plan has been prepared for this area in a number of stages. In the first
phase, the programme phase, goals were formulated and subsequently established
after consultation and public participation. This was followed, in the provisional
planning phases by the presentation of a report on alternatives; these were also
subjected to public participation and consultation.

The administration of the Province made a choice among the alternatives. The
preferred alternative was elaborated into a draft regional plan. The next phase
is the establishment phase, when the draft regional plan goes through an establishment procedure laid down in the Physical Planning Act and in which provision
is made for consultations with a number of authorities and for objections to
be lodged by members of the public. The regional plan for East Gelderland is now
in this establishment phase (3). How far the Regional Plan for East Gelderland
fulfils the criteria of Lee and Wood for a planning process into which EIA could
be integrated is explored below.

Goals

Various aspects of the goals of the regional plan relate to the environment. This
aspect is in fact evident in the main goal of the regional plan:

(a) the specific rural character will be the central concern in the regional plan area; elements such as nature, landscape, peace and quiet and limits of scale play an important role in this respect;

(b) within this framework, however, sufficient room should be available for economic, social and cultural development, with special attention to raising the quality of employment and improving the agricultural sector.

other goals include:

(a) conservation of both large nature areas and smaller areas;

(b) conservation and improvement of areas considered to possess landscape value, especially if they are of socio-historic significance;

(c) reduction, to a generally-acceptable level, of pollution of the environment in its various forms;

(d) expansion of overnight accommodation which should, in the first instance, be sought through the extension of existing facilities, provided that landscape and natural science features are not adversely affected.

A number of goals are elaborated in the form of limits set for drawing up alternatives. These goals relate to the ecological, landscape and socio-historic aspects and to environmental hygiene.

Survey, prediction and analyses

In the Regional Plan for East Gelderland, a survey of the environment has been provided in a number of maps. These include maps of the different types of landscape, ecological assets, visual landscape assets and socio-historic assets. Futhermore, a zoning map for outdoor recreation indicates how this type of recreation should be incorporated in the landscape.

The survey of the social and physical developments in the regional plan area revealed three important points:

(a) a great need to increase the volume of agrarian production (expansion of the farming acreage, increased intensive cattle-farming and improvement of the external production conditions);

(b) a need to improve employment opportunities (to reduce commuting and migration);

(c) as a result of its attractive and quiet character, the area is becoming increasingly popular for residential and recreational purpose (resulting in grrater pressure on the area).

Generation and evaluation of alternatives

Before alternatives are formulated, some restrictions and rules are established. These take the form of:

(a) the setting of limits;

(b) determination of variables; and

(c) the working out of a set of rules.

The limits are set in the first instance by the established goals. A further restriction is then imposed by physical and social features and the further elaboration of the goals. The physical features are considered to include those areas which are of great significance from a landscape or natural science point

of view. Such areas are derived from the maps showing the ecological, landscape
and socio-historic features. In this way, the goals relating to nature and
landscape are further elaborated. The other physical features determining the limits
are: buildings, roads and railways; facilities for outdoor recreation; conduits and
other public utility provisions; and agriculture. The social features restricting
the alternatives relate to developments having far-reaching spatial consequences;
these include the future development of the population, the future housing
needs and space for house-building, etc. In principle, alternatives can be
created within the limits thus delineated. In some cases, however, encroachment
on the limits is permitted, if it can be demonstrated that such encroachment
is essential.

The variables in the three alternatives are:

(a) residential areas;

(b) industrial estates and concentrations of services;

(c) installations for outdoor recreation;

(d) traffic infrastructure.

In addition, future land use for agricultural purposes, relating in particular
to landscape and nature values, is formulated separately in each alternative.

Apart from limits and a number of variables, allowance has been made for a
number of rules in drawing up alternatives. With the aid of these rules the
variables concerned are placed in a more detailed physical development pattern.
The rules are derived from the sector goals, as reported in the regional plan.
Thus, supplementary to the limits, several rules are also given with respect to
nature and landscape:

(a) the valuable elements in ecologically less-valuable areas should be protected,
where possible;

(b) landscape structuring, should be used to enrich the areas which are less
important from the landscape point of view;

(c) socio-historically valuable elements should be conserved, as far as possible.

Some rules specified on behalf of environmental hygiene are:

(a) the location, nature and volume of activities likely to disturb the physico-
chemical environment must be carefully studied in relation to the function of
the area concerned and those of adjoining areas;

(b) a distinction must be made between noise-susceptible uses and serious
noise-producing uses.

The description of alternatives takes place for each part of the plan area. This
provides insight into the differences between the physical developments produced
by different alternatives. The alternatives are then checked against the goals
of the Goals Report.

In this regional plan, separate attention has been given to the discussion of the
relationship between agriculture and nature. Many landscape and nature values in
this area are closely associated with a specific form of agricultural management.
This association is gradually disappearing, however, as a result of intensification
of agriculture, often at the expense of landscape and nature values. Weighing the
agricultural values against nature values takes place in the division of the
plan area into three categories:

(a)   area where agriculture has a superior function;

(b)   area where agriculture and ecology function side by side;

(c)   area where ecology has a superior function.

This classification is arrived at by comparing a map of the agricultural values with a map of the ecological values. For the division of East Gelderland into these three categories, three alternatives are presented: an agricultural alternative, a neutral alternative and an ecological alternative.

Plan decision, implementation and monitoring

In the preparatory work on behalf of the regional plan, the adjustment stage is indicated as a separate phase. This phase will come into effect after the regional plan has been established by the Provincial States. As the regional plan has not yet come to this point, this phase has not yet been specifically elaborated. The intention is that a constant, limited, repetition of the previous phases of regional plan preparations will take place (the programming, provisional draft and establishment phases). The results will be put before the Provincial States once every two or four years.

Procedural aspects

With regard to the procedural aspects, it may be noted that opportunities for public participation and consultation are provided for in different phases of regional planning (goals, alternatives, provisional draft, draft). The procedures for submitting the plan for public inspection, for consultations and for lodgement of appeals have their legal basis partly in the Physical Planning Act, i.e. as far as the establishment procedure is concerned.

CONCLUSION

The two practical examples of the Netherlands physical planning process described above enable some conclusions to be drawn concerning the feasibility of integrating EIA within the process. In regard to the characteristics set out by Lee and Wood the following results were found.

Setting planning goals and objectives

(a) Various goals were formulated in regard to the environment. These goals relate to environmental hygiene, to ecological, visual and socio-historic aspects and to the economic use of space. Several of these goals were translated into operational planning objectives, which were used as conditions when drawing up alternatives.

Survey, prediction and analysis

(b) In the survey of the plan, area maps were presented of different environmental aspects (ecological, socio-historic, visual, etc.). The analysis of the physical development gave rise to the identification of problem areas with respect to the environment (deterioration of open areas and of ecologically valuable areas caused by urbanization; problems in the relationship between agriculture and nature). Both plans present a rough forecast of the environmental effects to be expected from the alternatives, within the scope and the limits of the state of science and the scale of the plan.

Generation and evaluation of alternative draft plans

(c) On account of the bottlenecks in the physical development, alternatives were
formulated in the two plans. Several environmental aspects were introduced as
conditions in these alternatives (ecological, visual and socio-historic aspects).
In evaluating the alternatives it was indicated whether they came about entirely
within the range of conditions set or not; an evaluation was also made with
reference to the goals and objectives.

Plan decision, implementation, monitoring

(d) Both plans were drawn within the framework of a cyclic planning process.
Once every five years it will be considered whether the Structural Outline Sketch
will have to be modified (on specific points) on account of divergence between
actual developments and planned developments. The regional plan will be adjusted
by means of a monitoring process, the results of which will be submitted to the
Provincial States once every two or four years.

Procedural aspects

(e) The two plans follow procedures in which public participation and consultation with offical and administrative bodies are ensured, both on behalf of the draft
and the final plan. In this respect the regional plan finds its legal basis in
the Physical Planning Act. The procedure of the Crucial Physical Planning
Decision will also shortly be incorporated in this Act.

The two plans studied – the Urbanization Report, with its related Structural
Outline Sketch, and the Regional Plan for East Gelderland – are regarded as models
for future physical planning in the Netherlands. This comparative study indicates
that these plans fulfil the criteria for integrating environmental impact assessment into the planning process. The conclusion may be drawn that the present
physical planning process in the Netherlands has characteristics that enable
environmental impact assessment to be integrated into this process without a
great deal of change being necessary. The question that may arise, of course,
is whether it is desirable from the physical planning point of view to introduce
environmental impact assessments and thus give specific attention to the environmental aspects. After all, in physical planning one is just as much concerned with
economic and social aspects as with environmental aspects.

It is evident that environmental aspects constitute an important structural
element of physical planning in the Netherlands. It may be concluded, therefore,
that the integration of environmental impact assessment into the planning process
will in any case provide valuable support for physical planning. It may have
a stimulating effect on research with respect to environmental effects of physical
activities, the specific elaboration of environmental goals in the planning
process and the formulation of alternatives. On the other hand, similar introduction of social and economic aspects into physical planning is also important.
In this connexion environmental impact assessment might perhaps be gradually
expanded into an assessment which pays proper attention to environmental, social
and economic aspects alike.

Another question that may arise is in what way should the environmental impact
assessment which is integrated into physical planning relate to the environmental
impact assessment of projects. Without going into detail, it may be said that
environmental impact assessment in physical planning cannot serve as a replacement
for the environmental impact assessment of projects. A project is, essentially,
a further elaboration and specification of a plan, and should, therefore, be
based on a more detailed and more specific description of environmental effects.

Conversely, the environmental impact assessment of a project cannot serve as a replacement for such an assessment in plans. In physcial planning a process of evaluation takes place, which forms the policy outline for the elaboration of projects. This evaluation and weighing of alternatives should also be based on an appropriate description of environmental effects.

REFERENCES

1. Further information concerning the General Ecological Model, the National Environmental Survey and the application of these two studies in the preparation of Structure Schemes was presented in a paper entitled "Towards an Ecological Model for Physical Planning in the Netherlands", the contribution by Van der Maarel and Vellema to the ECE Seminar, "Ecological Aspects of Economic Development Planning", held in Rotterdam 1975, as well as in the contribution of P.G. Meijer entitled, "Structure Schemes for Infrastructure" published in Planning and Development in the Netherlands. Summaries in English of these two studies were issued by the Ministry of Housing and Physical Planning.

2. Dr. Norman Lee and L.M. Wood, Environmental Impact Assessment of Physical Plans in the European Communities, Dec. 1977.

3. For further information on regional plans, their function, their preparation and procedure, refer to the contribution by W.A. van Meel entitled "Regional Plans" in Planning and development in the Netherlands.

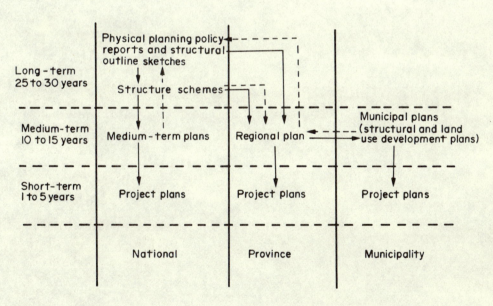

Relationship between physical planning policy reports. Structural outline sketches, structure schemes and other plans.

Integration of Environmental Impact Assessment into the Planning and Decision-Making Process

L. G. Schimmelpenninck

(Netherlands)

INTRODUCTION

This working paper focuses on the integration of environmental impact assessment into the existing planning and decision-making processes. The experience of a few trial runs of procedures for environmental impact assessment which have taken place in 1977 to 1978 in the Netherlands (1) are reviewed. Attention is centred on procedural integration questions, as they have proved to be a major problem in introducing environmental impact assessment.

The way in which environmental assessment is included in existing planning and decision-making processes is first described (2), and then the experiments with environmental impact assessment (3). Finally, some problems and possible solutions with regard to the integration of environmental impact assessment in planning and decision-making processes are presented (4 and 5).

ENVIRONMENTAL ASSESSMENT IN EXISTING PLANNING AND DECISION-MAKING PROCESSES

In most industrialized countries there is a need for environmental protection. In the Netherlands, situated in the heart of one of the densest populated and industrialized regions in the world, the need for an environmental policy is evident. Damage to the environment has to be prevented where possible, or restricted where it cannot be avoided. All actions which may have an adverse impact on the environment must be evaluated very carefully for their environmental consequences before a final decision on their implementation can be taken.

In the Netherlands, as in most industrialized countries, the recognition of environmental values has in the past 10 or 15 years been translated into a great number of legal and other provisions for environmental protection. Generally they comprise the following requirements:

(a) anyone planning a development action, which may have an adverse impact on the environment, requires a permit or other form of approval from a public authority before proceeding with implementation;

(b) public discussion about the acceptability of the proposed development must take place;

(c) specialized environmental protection agencies with decisive or advisory
competence with regard to the approval of the proposed development should be
created.

Generally speaking, this has led to much greater attention being given to the
environmental aspects in planning and decision-making. Public and private
organizations have been forced, some more willingly than others, to integrate
environmental assessments into their existing planning and decision-making
processes. All the procedures for permits, public information and participation
and consultation of environmental protection agencies require the collection and
evaluation of information on the environment. Specialized environmental staff has
had to be recruited in many organizations in response to these requirements.

Change in organizational attitudes and behaviour is always difficult and slow.
Environmentalists have had to fight for a timely and adequate involvement in the
existing planning and decision-making processes. But gradually, under the
influence of changing attitudes and more openness and participation, they have
acquired a more important role in the planning of important industrial or
infrastructural projects as well as in land-use and sectoral development planning.

There are, however, many shortcomings in the present situation. The most
important are:

(a) Regulations regarding environmental protection do not apply to all development actions which may have an adverse impact on the environment. In fact,
there is a wide variety of procedures. For some developments (e.g. developments
which require a permit under one of the pollution acts) there are legal
prescriptions as to the environmental information to be presented, public
information and participation procedures and the consultation of environmental
protection agencies. For other developments, which may have similar or more
important impacts on the environment, there are only internal regulations
(e.g. highway projects) or no regulations at all (e.g. planning a North Sea
island) to safeguard environmental values in the planning and decision-making
processes.

(b) For those actions which are covered by anti-pollution acts, the comprehensive
and integrated collection and evaluation of environmental information are
hampered by the restricted scope of these acts (all are restricted to pollution
aspects and each act is restricted to a certain type of pollution, e.g. air
pollution, water pollution and noise).

(c) There are as yet no prescriptions for integral, systematic study and
description of environmental impacts of developments which may adversely affect
the environment.

(d) Generally, in those cases where a form of environmental assessment is
prescribed, it takes place in a late stage of planning and decision-making, when
important decisions (e.g. a general policy, the choice of certain alternatives)
have already been made and are, in fact, irreversible.

There exists, therefore, a widespread feeling that a more uniform, comprehensive,
integrated, systematic form of environmental assessment should be prescribed so
that better decisions can be made. From the beginning this assessment should
optimally be integrated into the existing planning and decision-making process
(2). It is here referred to as environmental impact assessment.

EXPERIMENTS WITH ENVIRONMENTAL IMPACT ASSESSMENT

Stimulated by the experiences in some countries (particularly the United States and Canada) and pursuant to draft recommendations of the OECD and the European Communities, the Government of the Netherlands has decided to study the introduction of environmental impact assessment. To this end, several trial runs have been selected and experimental assessment procedures have been started.

The trial runs relate to decisions on:

- the acceptability of petrochemical industry in certain areas (Eemshaven, Groningen and Graetheide, Limburg);

- the development of an industrial park (South-East Brabant);

- a highway plan (Valkenswaard, North Brabant);

- the location of a sewage treatment plant and a rubbish tip (Tiel, Ede);

- the sale of land and a permit under the Nuisance Act (Hinderwet) for the expansion of a paint factory (Uithoorn, Noord-Holland);

- sites for the disposal of dredge material from the Rotterdam harbour area;

- the acceptability of constructing an island in the North Sea.

The trial runs have been executed on the basis of a scenario indicating the environmental information to be collected and the procedures to be followed (3). Essentially, the scenario prescribed that:

(a) a comprehensive study of the expected environmental impacts should be made by the proponent ("environment" being interpreted in a restricted sense i.e. no social and economic impacts, other than those caused directly by changes in the environment);

(b) the evaluation procedure concerning this study should be integrated as fully as possible into the existing procedures applicable to the decisions to be made.

In more detail the procedure to be followed is:

(a) a draft environmental impact statement (DEIS) should be prepared by the proponent;

(b) the DEIS should be submitted to the public and to the environmental protection agencies for comment;

(c) the DEIS should be submitted to a panel of independent experts for review, the chairman of this panel being appointed by the Minister of Health and Environmental Protection;

(d) the responsible authority should make the final environmental impact statement (FEIS);

(e) the responsible authority should make a decision on the proposed activity and publish its decision and the FEIS.

In some trial runs step (c) took place prior to, or parallel with, step (b).

Integration of the EIS procedure with the existing procedures to be applied, if any (formal procedures for decision-making do not exist in all cases), was meant to take place in the following basic form:

IA m

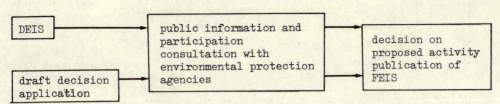

As many decision-making processes regarding activities which may have adverse impacts on the environment already provide for public information and participation as well as consultation procedures, paralled development and evaluation of EIS and other decision-making documents are often possible. In this way environmental assessment, formalized in an EIS procedure, becomes part of an integrated planning and decision-making process, without causing unnecessary delays.

However, in the trial runs, as in experiences with EIS systems in other countries (especially the United States), integration is not always achieved. Several questions concerning integration need to be considered carefully when setting up for procedures for environmental impact assessment.

IS PROCEDURAL INTEGRATION DESIRABLE?

An argument can be made against procedural integration. Some environmentalists argue that a clear-cut separation should be made in the planning and decision-making process. This would take the form of:

(a) a stage of gathering and evaluation of information concerning the expected impacts of a proposed activity,

(b) a stage of decision-making, based on the outcome of (a).

With this approach, discussion about the merits of a proposed activity should not start before optimal environmental information has been presented, evaluated and "approved". There are several ways to formalize this approach. Essentially, the procedure would have the following structure:

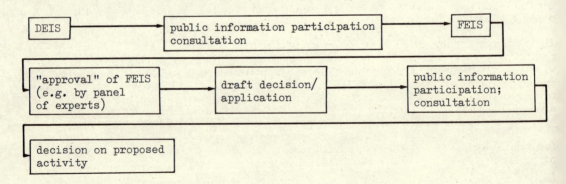

Although in theory this may seem an attractive procedure which guarantees that public discussion on a proposal can be based on "approved" information about the environmental impact of that proposal, it is in most cases impracticable. Its main shortcomings are:

(a) in most cases it is not possible to separate the information and decision-making stages. While discussing the merits of a proposal, amendments are made, new alternatives are presented and mitigation measures are included. All of these change the activity originally proposed and generate new environmental information;

(b) in the trial runs it became clear that it is not possible to limit a first stage public discussion to information aspects (i.e. "is the information presented adequate and correct?"); the public wants to discuss the issue itself (i.e. "is the proposed activity acceptable?");

(c) a consecutive information and decision-making stage is time-consuming.

Apart from exceptional cases, synchronization of the EIS procedure with, or even integration of the environmental impact assessment into, existing procedures would be desirable. This implies that the consideration of environmental information should be combined with consideration of technical, economic and social information at all stages of planning and decision-making (4).

The environmental aspect has often been neglected in the past. It is therefore understandable that there is now a tendency to over-emphasize it in order to redress the balance. In restructuring planning and decision-making processes imbalance should be avoided. Environmental aspects should receive attention that is simultaneous and equal to other aspects of planning and decision-making; not less and not more. Only in exceptional, very important and controversial cases should procedures be set up that guarantee that more attention be given to environmental than to other aspects (e.g. special review procedures before the environmental expert panels).

INTEGRATION PROBLEMS

The main problem with regard to the integration of environmental impact assessment into the existing planning and decision-making procedures is the discrepancy between the need for an integrated and systematic collection and evaluation of environmental information, on the one hand, and the usual fragmented and unsystematic planning and decision-making procedures of public authorities, on the other hand.

In the Netherlands, as in most other countries, public planning and decision-making is a very complicated process, in which many different public authorities, with different areas of competence, take part. For one major activity (e.g. an industrial site) to be implemented, a great number of "approvals" and other forms of concurrence (e.g. on land use or grants) by public bodies is required. These are seldom considered simultaneously, and are seldom based on the same information or subject to the same public procedures.

(a) Some decisions are made earlier, some in later stages of the preparation of an activity;

(b) some decisions are based on very broad and rough information of the proposed activity; some on very specialized and detailed information;

(c) some decisions are based on evaluation of all aspects of a proposed activity; some on a restricted scope of aspects (e.g. only water pollution aspects), hence the scope of the information required varies accordingly;

(d) some decision are subject to elaborate procedures, with guarantees of public participation, expert consultation and the right to appeal; some are not.

In the course of time, and influenced by these procedures, the concept of the activity takes shape, changes, and grows into a final and irreversible form.

In which stage should the environmental impact assessment take place? The desirability of environmental impact assessment at all stages of planning and decision-making process has already been considered. This implies that even in the earliest stages - when policy decisions are made which will have an important influence on the way in which developments will be realized - environmental impact assessment should take place. Although information on environmental impacts will generally be very rough at this stage, what can be made available should be presented to the decision-makers. As experience from some of the trial runs and other studies indicates, it is possible to generate useful environmental information at this stage (e.g. with the use of models and assumptions of possible developments). As "the truth" about environmental impacts emerges mostly in later stages of planning and decision-making, it is essential that feed-back procedures should exist, so that environmental information generated in later stages can lead to a reconsideration of earlier policy decisions.

How is environmental assessment to be integrated into the various existing planning and decision-making procedures? As stated above, integration can take place in all stages of planning and decision-making, from the first policy statements to the ultimate implementation decisions on a specific activity. In the earliest stages, there is the lack or inadequacy of environmental information. Generally, there is no problem as to the integration of this information into the existing procedures. In these stages, for the most part, there are no restrictions as to which aspects should be considered or the scope of the information to be presented (e.g. a sectoral policy or programme decision, a land-use decision). In later stages, however, the integration problem becomes evident:

(a) numerous decisions have to be taken more or less simultaneously regarding the same proposed activity;

(b) some decisions are restricted to certain aspects of a proposed activity (e.g. water pollution) and can only be based on information concerning this aspect.

The first point raises the question of whether environmental impact assessment should form part of all decision-making procedures regarding individual activities. For example, should environmental impact assessment be integrated into planning and decision-making on the lease of land, the provision of a grant and the issuance of a number of pollution permits for one particular industrial project? As these decisions are generally made by different authorities, under different procedures which are generally not co-ordinated, separate assessments would take place which would not necessarily conform.

In principle, there appear to be three different possible answers to this problem:

(a) a seperate environmental impact assessment procedure, preceding the different decision-making procedures. These can then all be based on one set of "approved" environmental information. As this approach fragments the environmental information and the planning and decision-making procedures it does not seem generally desirable;

(b) all decision-making procedures at the same stage are parallel and co-ordinated. i.e. all decisions are based on one set of "approved" environmental information, collected and evaluated in the course of the co-ordination procedure. In view of the differences between most of these procedures, this solution would generally be impracticable;

(c) one or a few closely-related decision-making procedures (e.g. if applicable, the pollution permit procedures) are designated to include the environmental impact assessment.

If the environmental impact assessment is to be integrated into a few closely-related procedures, these should be parallel and co-ordinated. For instance, the seperate decisions under the different anti-pollution acts (e.g. water pollution, air pollution, noise abatement permits) should be based on one set of "approved" environmental information, which would be collected and evaluated in the course of the co-ordination procedure.

As there is a proposal in Parliament for legislation in the Netherlands which would provide for a co-ordinated procedure under the various anti-pollution acts, this solution could be feasible, i.e. concerning decisions in the project stage (5).

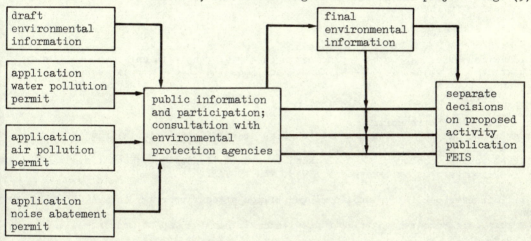

It is essential for environmental impact assessment that all environmental aspects of a proposed activity can be evaluated in an integrated way. The co-ordinated procedure, described above, is in many cases not sufficient to provide for a comprehensive and integrated environmental impact assessment because:

(a) not all environmental aspects are subject to consideration under a public decision-making procedure (e.g. in the Netherlands there is generally no "approval" procedure with regard to landscape protection or energy conservation aspects) and, as a result, information on these aspects will not be integrated into any of the existing procedures for decision-making;

(b) a parallel and co-ordinated procedure for the collection and evaluation of environmental information does not guarantee that decision-making will also take place in an integrated way and several public authorities can, therefore, make their own separate decisions, based on information concerning the aspects which are subject to their authority.

In order to overcome these problems there are two possible solutions:

(a) all public authorities should have legal competence to consider all environmental aspects in their planning and decision-making procedures;

(b) with regard to every individual activity, a leading agency should be
designated and have the competence to consider all environmental aspects which
may not, under the existing legislation, be considered by other agencies. In
addition, this agency should have the authority to ensure that the planning and
decision-making by several agencies takes place in an integrated way within a
co-ordinated procedure.

These organizational devices to promote integrated environmental impact assessment,
in what is very often fragmented public planning and decision-making, are really
only patchwork measures. A much better and simpler way to ensure an integrated
environmental impact assessment would be to provide for integrated public decision-
making: one authority (or a few authorities with a joint decision-making
competence) to evaluate and decide on the basis of the consideration of all environmental aspects of an activity. But this implies a too drastic organizational
change in the present public administration with regard to environmental
protection in the Netherlands.

REFERENCES

1. Milieu-effectrapportage: proefnemingen (Trial runs with environmental impact
assessment), Twijnstra Gudde NV Management Consultants en DHV Raadgevend
Ingenieursbureau BV Ministerie Van Volksgezpndheid en Milieuhygiëne 1979,
VAR 1979/12.

2. Milieu-effectrapportering
(Environmental impact assessment) (English translation available from the Dutch
Ministry of Health and Environmental Protection)
Advies van de voorlopige Centrale Road voor de milieuhygiëne, Ministerie van
Volksgezondheid en Milieuhygiene, 1979, VAR 1977/3.

3. Vooronderzoek inzake proefnemingen milieu-effectrapportage en aanvullend
onderzoek
(Preliminary research on trial runs with environmental impact assessment and
complementary research)
Twijnstra Gudde NV Management consultants en DHV Raadgevend Ingenieursbureau,
Ministerie van Volksgezondheid en Milieuhygiëne, VAR 1977/21.

4. Milieu-effectrapportage: aanbevelingen
(Recommendations on environmental impact assessment)
(English translation available from the Dutch Ministry of Health and Environmental
Protection)
Twijnstra Gudde NV Management Consultants en DHV Raadgevend
Ingenieursbureau BV, Ministerie van Volksgezondheid en Milieuhygiëne,
VAR 1979/13.

5. The Environmental Protection (General Provisions) Bill passed the Lower House
of the States General in March 1979.

The Integration of Environmental Impact Appraisal into the United Kingdom Planning System

R. Lloyd Thomas

(United Kingdom)

INTRODUCTION

This paper deals with development control, i.e. the granting of permission for individual projects in England and Wales. The systems in Scotland and Northern Ireland, though similar, have their own separate legislation and differ in certain respects.

THE PRESENT SYSTEM

All development (defined as: "the carrying out of building, engineering, mining or other operations in, on, over or under land, or the making of any material change in the use of any buildings or other land") requires planning permission. Certain classes of minor developments are given a general permission by Order, made by the Secretary of State with the approval of Parliament.

When considering an application for planning permission, the planning authority, whether the local authority or the Secretary of State, is required to "have regard to the provisions of the development plan, so far as material to the application, and to any other material considerations". This requirement allows the planning authority to have regard to any aspect of the probable effects of a development, including its impact on the environment in the widest sense.

The prospective developer must make his application for planning permission on a form prescribed by the authority. Each application must be accompanied by a plan sufficient to identify the land to which it relates and such other plans and drawings as are necessary to describe the development. In addition, the authority may issue a direction requiring the applicant to provide such further information as it needs to come to a decision on the application.

In practice, firms or individuals wishing to carry out large-scale developments have informal discussions with the planning authority before submitting a planning application and are encouraged to do so by the central government. In this way the officials of the local planning authority have an opportunity to inform themselves of the exact nature of the development to be proposed and also to indicate to the developer the information which the planning authority (i.e. the elected members of the local authority) will probably need before a decision on the application can be reached.

On receipt of an application the planning authority must enter details in a
register which is open to public inspection. Applicants for certain classes of
development (colloquially known as "bad neighbour developments"), e.g. waste
disposal, minerals working, sewage treatment, slaughterhouses, motor racetracks,
cemeteries, etc., are required to advertise their application in a local newspaper
and to exhibit a notice on the site itself. By these means members of the public
are informed of what is proposed and are given an opportunity to make their views
or objections known to the planning authority.

In addition, the planning authority must ascertain the views of a number of public
bodies (the "statutory consultees") including the highway authority, the water
authority, the Nature Conservancy Council and the Ministry of Agriculture,
Fisheries and Food. These bodies are allowed not less than fourteen days to make
their comments before the planning authority proceeds to take a decision.

A fuller description of the existing system is contained in a booklet entitled:
"Planning Permission - A Guide for Industry". This booklet is available free of
charge to prospective developers in the United Kingdom.

ENVIRONMENTAL IMPACT APPRAISAL

It will be clear from the foregoing description of the existing system that the
latter does not provide for environmental impact appraisal eo nomine. But ever
since a statutory system of development control was introduced (about 1947 in its
present form) there has been an obligation on a planning authority to have regard
to the probable effects on the environment of any proposed development. Consequently, planning authorities in the United Kingdom have been conducting environmental
impact appraisals in all but name without necessarily recognizing that that was
what they were doing - rather as M. Jourdain, in Moliere's Le Bourgeois Gentilhomme,
found to his suprise that he had been talking in prose for the past forty years;
Nevertheless, in the United Kingdom consideration has been given to the suggestion
that it might be advantageous to introduce into the existing flexible system a
more formal procedure for incorporating environmental impact appraisal.

In 1974 the Secretary of State for the Environment, together with the Secretaries
of State for Scotland and Wales, appointed two independent consultants to study
and report on the subject of environmental impact analysis. In their final report
published in May 1976,(1) Thirlwall and Catlow concluded that there was a need
to employ a system of environmental impact analyses for some kinds of development
in Great Britain, and that it could be carried out, at least for a trial period,
under the existing planning system. They made recommendations as to how this might
be done. They envisaged that possibly twenty-five to fifty projects in the course
of a year might qualify for this treatment, though they also observed that, with
the present flexible system of planning in the United Kingdom, proposals can be
dealt with as rigorously as the planning authority deems fit.

Earlier, in 1973, the three Departments had commissioned a research study from
Aberdeen University on the subject of project appraisal for development control;
this was eventually published in 1976 as a manual entitled "Assessment of Major
Industrial Applications". (2) The foreword to the manual commended it for use by
planning authorities, government agencies and developers, but stresses that the
views expressed were those of the authors and did not necessarily represent the
views of the Departments. The declared objective of the manual was to combine
the best local authority practice with techniques of impact assessment in a method
which could appropriatley be applied to the appraisal of major planning
applications in the context of the present development control system in the
United Kingdom.

The attitude of the United Kingdom Government was stated in a public speech at Manchester in September 1978 by the Secretary of State for the Environment. After some remarks about public inquiries into major planning applications, Mr. Shore said

"I would like to mention another subject in which there has been general interest - the idea of assessing the environmental impact of significant major developments, as part of the planning process. My colleagues and I have considered how best to pursue this. We fully endorse the desirability, as set out in the Thirlwall/Catlow report, which my Department published in 1976, of ensuring careful evaluation of the possible effects of large developments on the environment. All could agree with that, though we must not forget the unacceptable delays and costs of some environmental assessment procedures used in other countries, nor the strong interest we have as a nation in the success of our industrial strategy.

"The approach suggested in Thirlwall/Catlow is already being adopted with many other public and private sector projects. We should therefore wish to encourage use of this approach in cases where its use is worthwhile in the circumstances; relevant to the decision; and necessary to the total evaluation of the project along with the industrial, the employment, the social, the health and safety, the land use and the other implications.

"Our feeling therefore is that in selected major cases, involving environmentally sensitive areas or circumstances, a more explicit approach should be pursued. In the selection of such cases, the initiative could come either from the developer or form the planning authority. We should expect that the planning authorities and the public or private developers would agree at as early a stage as possible whether environmental assessment was justified; and if so the form of, and methods of preparing an assessment, including the division of responsibility for carrying out the work. It would be helpful also if detailed consideration could be given to informing all interested parties including the general public of the scope and nature of the analysis to be undertaken. The sensible use of this approach, through the co-operation of all concerned, should I believe improve the practice in handling these relatively few large and significant development proposals."

SUMMARY

It would be fair to say that in the United Kingdom there is a long tradition of examining and inviting public comment on the probable effects, including effects on the environment, of all planning applications for development. The present system of development control permits these effects to be appraised with whatever degree of detail is thought necessary, having regard to the importance and the circumstances of each particular application. Nevertheless, there is a disposition to accept that in a small number of major applications there should be a more systematic examination, prepared by the developer and the planning authority in collaboration, and made available for comment by the public. An essential element would be that this examination should be accommodated within the existing system and not be an additional cause of delay in an already intricate and lengthy procedure.

It should be mentioned in closing that this paper has been concerned entirely with development control procedures. It takes for granted that other aspects of environmental concern, such as emissions to the air, discharge of effluents, disposal of solid waste and the safety of buildings and plant (whether in construction or operation) will be dealt with under the appropriate anti-pollution

or safety legislation and also that under such legislation monitoring of the
development will be carried out after the granting of planning permission.

REFERENCES

1.   "Experimental Impact Analysis", a study prepared for the Secretaries of State
for the Environment, Scotland, and Wales, by T. Catlow and C.G. Thirlwall,
Department of the Environment, Research Report 11, 1976.

2.   "Assessment of Major Industrial Applications", a manual, Department of the
Environment, Research Report 13, 1976.

Basic Principles and Methods of Environmental Protection Planning in the USSR

V. A. Markov and V. A. Anikeev

(USSR)

In the USSR the rational use of natural resources and the prevention of environmental pollution form one of the basic tasks of the State, the most important elements of which have been elevated to the rank of constitutional principles of the Soviet State and are embodied in article 18 of the USSR Constitution, which provides as follows:

> "In the interests of the present and future generations, the necessary steps are taken in the USSR to protect and make scientific, rational use of the land, its mineral and water resources and the plant and animal kingdoms, to preserve the purity of the air and water, to ensure reproduction of natural wealth and to improve the human environment."

State economic and social development plans of the USSR include a special section entitled "Environmental protection and the rational use of natural resources". This section assigns to the Councils of Ministers of the Union Republics, and ministries of the USSR, tasks designed to ensure rational use of natural resources, to improve the conditions under which the sectors of the economy operate, to reduce any adverse effects produced on the environment by industrial and agricultural production and by urban public utilities, and to establish the most favourable living, working and recreational conditions for the population. These plans are prepared by the USSR State Planning Commission, State Ministries and the Councils of Ministers of the Union Republics.

Environmental protection measures are planned in terms of the natural surroundings: i.e., to protect water resources, the ambient air, the land, flora, fauna and natural resources against pollution and depletion.

Tasks relating to the protection of the environment and the rational use of resources are binding and individualized: i.e., they are assigned to specific executing agencies (USSR Ministries, Councils of Ministers of Union Republics, local administrative bodies, enterprises and organizations), and are provided with the necessary resources (capital investment, equipment, manpower, etc.). Furthermore, these tasks are framed so as to ensure the continuity and co-ordination of current (annual), medium-term (usually 5-year) and long-term (10-year or longer) plans, thus making it possible to reconcile the solutions of urgent and long-term problems in the best possible way.

In preparing draft plans for environmental protection and the rational use of

natural resources, great attention is paid to the problems of development and
location of the country's productive capacities. For example, in determining the
pace and relative degree of development of different sectors of the country's
economy, provision is made for settling the series of questions involved in
distributing industrial and agricultural production over the country's territory
in such a way as to ensure the rational use of natural resources and to reduce
environmental pollution to a minimum.

The State planning of measures for environmental protection and for the rational
use of natural resources in the USSR makes it possible to ensure that the work of
implementing specific organizational and practical measures to preserve and
improve the country's natural environment is carried on in businesslike fashion,
and to concentrate material and financial resources in areas where the introduction of environmental protection measures is most needed.

The Choice of Main Directions and the Development of Special-purpose Programmes for Activities to Solving the Important Scientific and Technical Problems of the Environment

V. G. Sokolovsky

(USSR)

In accordance with the Constitution of the U.S.S.R., as well as with decisions taken in recent years by the Communist Party of the Soviet Union and the Soviet Government, necessary measures are taken in the U.S.S.R. in the interests of present and future generations, on protection and scientifically-based rational use of the earth and its minerals, water resources, flora and fauna as well as on conservation of clean air and water, maintenance of renewable resources and improvement of the human environment. The necessity for these measures is determined, on the one hand, by the steady growth of overall production in traditional industrial centres and by economic development of new regions, and on the other hand by the ever-growing medical and biological, ecological and other requirements.

The urgent solution of many problems associated with the conservation of the required natural environment quality, as well as the diversity, complexity and inter-disciplinary nature of these problems, predetermine the need for efficient coordination, on a national scale, of basic activities in the field and their orientation in the most promising directions. The Soviet Union possesses all the necessary prerequisites for this purpose.

Since the basis of the U.S.S.R. economic system is the public socialist ownership of the basic means of production and natural resources, including the land and minerals, water and forests, the country's economy is governed on the basis of annual and long-range state plans of economic and social development. These envisage, along with other tasks, measures on environment protection and rational use of natural resources. Such measures may be practical in character or they may be scientific and technical.

The planned practical tasks on nature protection are principally aimed at providing substantial reductions in the negative impact of industry, agriculture, transport and municipal economy on the environment, as well as promoting conservation and increase of the country's resource potential by rational use of natural resources.

In accordance with the above aim, plans on nature protection of each ministry, department and Council of Ministers of all the republics include tasks on:

- protection and rational use of water resources;

-   air basin protection;

-   protection and rational use of lands;

-   protection and rational use of forest resources;

-   protection and reproduction of fish resources;

-   protection and rational use of mineral resources;

-   development of national parks and reserves;

-   operation of facilities, construction and objects for nature-protection
    purposes;

-   volume of capital investments and material and technical means connected
    with the environment protection.

Unlike the above practical measures that use available designs and technological
decisions, standard equipment and materials, etc., the scientific and technical
work provided for in the state plans of economic and social development is mainly
aimed at the solution of long-range problems to prevent natural environment
deterioration and to improve the use of natural resources.

It should be noted that by "deterioration of the natural environment" we imply
both its pollution by anthropogenic toxic wastes such as waste waters, solid
wastes, dust and gaseous emissions, and the undesirable disturbance of large-
scale natural processes, such as the salt, temperature and water regimes of
water bodies, landscape destruction by mining and thermokarst processes, or soil
degradation as a result of erosion, salinization, acidification.

Preliminary work begins with determination of long-range tasks; this stage is
completed when the main directions of activities and the problems to be solved
have been determined. Let us consider preliminary work aspects in more detail,
since the effectiveness of all subsequent labour and material expenditures
and successful practical solutions for environmental problems depend to a great
extent on the correct determination of long-range tasks and, consequentl, the
main direction of activities.

The analysis required to determine long-range tasks in the field of nature use
and environment protection is based on possible changes in the biosphere due to
developing branches of national economy, as well as on an integrated programme
of scientific and technical investigation and its socio-economic implications,
a general long-range scheme of productive forces distribution, and other studies.

Prediction of the state of the environment has become an important tool for
ecological assessment of the implications of planned overall production together
with the chosen plan for the distribution of productive forces, taking into
account the evolving character of the main technological processes, the existing
water, air and soil pollution levels and the consumption of basic natural
resources. It should be considered as an integral element of the environmental
quality control function: the basis for elaborating an extensive programme of
actions that range from organization of the required research to practical nature
protection measures.

The expected natural environment state is determined by the following important
factors:

(a) the initial state of water, air, soils, biological resources, population
health, etc.;

(b) the current level of industry, transport and municipal economy development and planned growth during the period of prediction;

(c) the territorial distribution of enterprises, existing and planned;

(d) the technological level of enterprises, existing and planned, (specific
consumption of appropriate natural resources, composition and amount of toxic
emissions per unit of commodity production);

(e) the degree to which stationary environmental pollution sources are equipped
with the means of waste gas cleaning and effluent treatment, the quality
efficiency of gas cleaning equipment and facilities for effluent treatment, as
well as for industrial and municipal solid waste reprocessing;

(f) hydrometeorological conditions of the regions for which the natural
environment state is predicted, as well as possible changes as a result of
economic activity and other factors;

(g) demographic and other changes;

The analysis performed has two aspects: inter-disciplinary and territorial. While
studying the development prospects of leading branches of the national economy
(e.g. in reference to "Air protection against pollution"), the existing and
expected annual amounts of dust and gaseous emissions are successively considered
for each branch as a whole. Then each branch "contribution" is disaggregated
according to principal and specific pollutants, and the sources (i.e. enterprises)
of the most important ones are identified. For example, by means of such an
analysis it was found that thermal power stations account for almost 50 per cent
of total sulphur dioxide emissions in the U.S.S.R. From this it was inferred that
the solution of the problem of atmospheric pollution by sulphur dioxide emitted
by thermal power stations would make it possible to reduce the total national
emissions of this pollutant by 50 per cent. Thus, the work in this field should
be referred to priority tasks.

To evaluate the urgency for control of an individual pollutant more precisely,
one should take into consideration the number of people exposed to it, as well
as undertaking a complex assessment of its toxicity including both the pollutant
amount and the degree of toxicity.

Since such interdisciplinary analysis does not provide a true picture of the
existing and expected state of the atmosphere over cities and industrial
centres, the necessity arises for analysing the expected distribution of new
enterprises and increase of facilities in each large industrial centre or city,
i.e. an analysis of the integral impact of various enterprises on the environmental quality in each region.

Such a regional analysis introduces significant corrections into the assessment
of urgency of problems, concerning not only air pollution but also water resource
consumption, use of land for non-agricultural purposes, etc.

It should be noted that the principal object of both inter-disciplinary and
regional analyses consists in indentifying the basic expected environmental
problems and the main causes of their occurence and development. The determination
of the main links in the chain of causes and effects is the necessary condition
of such an analysis, which is a prerequisite for solving any problem and
identifying the main directions of research and design work.

The main directions of activities are based, on the one hand, on the established
environmental problems and their causes, and, on the other hand, on the preliminary work on their solution.

Analysis of national and foreign research and development work related to each

problem of nature use and environmental protection makes it possible to
determine the main tasks involved and the appropriate executive bodies.

An important role in determination of basic problems and ways of their solution
is played by the Interdepartmental Scientific and Technical Council on Complex
Problems of Environmental Protection and Rational Use of Natural Resources under
the U.S.S.R. State Committee for Science and Technology.

The whole complex of research and development work carried out to solve general
and specific problems of rational use of natural resources and protection of the
natural environment in the U.S.S.R. can be presented as a three-level system:

- fundamental research concerned with the development of the scientific
  basis of nature use and environmental protection, which is carried
  out by institutes under the U.S.S.R. Academy of Sciences;

- research and development work performed as part of programmes aimed
  at solving important inter-disciplinary scientific and technical
  problems of rational use of natural resources and environment protection, which are coordinated by the U.S.S.R. State Committee for Science
  and Technology;

- research and design work in solving the inter-disciplinary problems
  concerning the improvement of natural resource use and prevention of
  environmental pollution, which are performed within the framework of
  inter-disciplinary plans, as well as according to joint plans of
  organizations belonging to various ministries.

Research organized by the U.S.S.R. Academy of Sciences and related scientific
and technical work coordinated by the U.S.S.R. State Committee for Science and
Technology are linked together at the planning stage. Inter-disciplinary
developments are taken into consideration while generalizing, analyzing and
assessing the advantages offered by different ways to solve particular problems.

Since 1976 the U.S.S.R. has undertaken special purpose-oriented programmes
aimed at the solution of complex environmental problems of a multi-sectoral
character. The activities undertaken in these programmes have included research
and development, and the design, construction, testing and operation of appropriate installations.

Draft programmes are prepared by appropriate U.S.S.R. ministries and departments
responsible for their development and realization, i.e. for the solution of the
problems as a whole.

As a rule, any draft programme of activities is prepared by a specialized
research institute of the branch and appropriate department of the ministry.
All the ministries and departments concerned, as well as their research
institutes, design organizations and enterprises, are entrusted with draft
programme elaboration.

With a clear-cut task in view the leading organization carries out a comparative
analysis of technical and economic indices, i.e. capital and operating costs,
metal and energy consumption, productivity, compactness, ease of fabrication
and maintenance, reliable operation, etc. for all alternative solutions of the
problem.

In choosing the main directions of development, allowance is made for the results
of the following studies:

(a)   intercomparison of ecologic effect indices for each alternative solution, e.g. indices of toxic emission reduction;

(b)   intercomparison of costs required for complete development of each alternative solution;

(c)   time required to develop and introduce each alternative solution on a scale sufficient to accomplish the practical objective by the planned date.

These results make it possible to determine and formulate the objective and the ways of solving the problem which form the basis for programming activities.

Participating agencies, stages and terms of work, its volume and the sources of finance are determined in the programme of activities.

The problems and main tasks aimed at their solution are approved by the U.S.S.R. Supreme Soviet as a part of five-year plans of economic and social development; detailed programmes of activities on the solution of problems are similarly authorized by the U.S.S.R. State Committee for Science and Technology.

At present the U.S.S.R. is tackling many problems and activities on the development of new progressive technological production processes, e.g. low-and-non-waste techniques, the development of more progressive gas-cleaning and water-treatment equipment, systems and instruments for monitoring the environmental state, as well as on the solution of other important problems concerning nature use and environmental protection.

We hope that the implementation of these programmes of activities will create the necessary conditions for the prevention of the deterioration of the environmental state during the period 1990-2000 while maintaining the required rates of national economic development for the same period.

Ecological Models in the Land-use Policy-Making Process

M. Martis

(Czechoslovakia)

Czechoslovakia is a country with a relatively high level of economic and social development, considerable population concentrated in a small area, and rather limited natural resources. Both the acreage of agricultural land and the quantity of water resources per inhabitant are among the lowest in Europe. The exploitation of the ecological systems is nearing the limits of their carrying capacity.

Fundamental to the further economic and social development of the country is the harmonization of requirements for complete self-sufficiency in food and the highest possible use of domestic resources (raw materials) compatible with the need for safeguarding constant, high productivity of the land. Those qualities which make areas attractive for living and recreation must be preserved while maintaining their ecological stability. It is necessary to achieve steady harmony between economic activities and biological production. Serious problems should be averted early, at the stage of scientific and technical development, because only through preventive measures can the negative impacts caused by economic development, which affect the landscape as well as natural resources, be eliminated without great expense.

Czechoslovakia is approaching the problem of ecodevelopment by an extensive scientific and technical project of ecological optimization. This project involves evaluation of land-use and natural resources and is known as the EKOPROGRAM. The objectives of the EKOPROGRAM are to increase the production of ecosystems and to broaden the possibilities of economic exploitation of natural resources, while preserving the long-term productivity, habitability and ecological stability of the landscape. The EKOPROGRAM co-ordinates all scientific, technical and economic studies for "ecodevelopment" in Czechoslovakia. Unlike certain projects aimed at pitting ecology against economic and social development, i.e., "zero-growth", the fundamental aim of the EKOPROGRAM is the gradual integration of ecological knowledge into the technical development of new production technologies and into the system of State and economic administration, regional planning and education.

Research in Czechoslovakia over the past decades has accumulated vast but fragmented knowledge of the processes taking place in nature and of the interactions between man and nature. However as a rule this information is not available in an immediately usable form for planning and decision-making. Economic and social development has often advanced without being significantly affected or controlled by the quality of or need for ecological research. The

main task of the EKOPROGRAM is to synthesize and supplement such partial
knowledge and findings; it therefore affects the choice of further scientific
studies, their specification and subsequent elaboration as tools for decision-
making at central and regional levels.

More than 100 experts from 30 institutes and institutions of higher education,
grouped in specialist teams, drew up the Report on the Effects of Large-scale
Agricultural Production on the Environment for the Czechoslovak Government. The
report objectively evaluates the negative impacts of the development of
agriculture on the ecological stability of the landscape, the usability of
natural resources and the health of the population. It has put before the
sectors of agriculture and food, as well as other sectors, 21 concrete tasks
aimed at improving the current state of affairs and at preventing possible risks.
The fulfilment of targets set by the Government is controlled annually by the
team of EKOPROGRAM experts in agricultural research institutes and production
units; information on the fulfilment of the targets and on new problems is
submitted to the Government's Commission for the Environment. This procedure
effectively secures the continuous incorporation of the latest ecological
knowledge in the development of that production sector which, in Czechoslovakia,
manages more than 50 per cent of the total land area. It also allows for the
regular evaluation of environmental impacts related to the development of
agriculture.

Within the EKOPROGRAM have been incorporated integrated environmental
information systems to cover the territory of Czechoslovakiz, basic data registers
and operational systems for controlling the data bank containing environmental
information. Following up the new law on physical planning have been
methodologies for project designers, criteria for evaluating natural phenomena
with regard to basic social activities and the categorization of the territory
of the Czechoslovak Socialist Republic with a view to the ecological optimization
of land-use. Environmental information is beginning to be used in the routine
practice of regional and physical planning projects, i.e. those which are
Government-controlled.

The current trends of intensification in agriculture, forest management, fuel
and raw material exploitation, as well as in the development of industry, power
production, transport, settlement, recreation, etc., have often led to rapid
simplification of the diversity of species and ecosystems which are the basis
of the ecological stability of the area. The ability of a certain natural
environment to absorb the impacts of economic development without grave and
long-term damage to the ecosystem and landscape should be considered as being
in itself a specific economic resource. On the other hand, a landscape with
disturbed ecological stability, one which is unable to resist or balance the
effects of secondary negative impacts of the development of civilization,
becomes a strictly limiting factor for economic and social development.

The EKOPROGRAM, therefore, focuses primary attention on preserving and
strengthening the ecological stability of the intensively-exploited territory
of Czechoslovakia. A new trend in this respect is the endeavour to create
gradually what is called a "framework of ecological stability" for Czechoslovakia;
this would help preserve, at an acceptable level, ecological stability without
requiring far-reaching interference in the existing, intensive land-use in the
economically most important sector.

The establishment of a network of stabilization zones will increase the capacity
of ecosystems in the most intensely developed areas, thereby reducing the risk
of possible serious ecological failures in the period preceding the adoption of
further environmental control measures. The main stabilization zones are

protected landscape areas, i.e., areas in the Czechoslovak Socialist Republic
where in the past centuries economic development proceeded in harmony with the
natural environment. Around the oases of virgin nature (today's reservations) a
landscape has formed with a secondary ecological balance corresponding to the
potential and capacity of the ecosystems and meeting the economic demands of
contemporary society. This mosaic of conservation areas and national parks
(10 per cent of the territory of the Czechoslovak Socialist Republic) forms the
actual framework of the ecological stability of the Czechoslovak landscape.

The pilot area chosen for the case study was the Trebon district in the southern
part of Bohemia, an area with a great number of ponds where, since the beginning
of its early development in the thirteenth century, no branch of the economy
has developed to the detriment of any other branch. The area has always been
utilized as an integral part of the complex landscape system. By building an
ingenious system of ponds and trenches on what in the Middle Ages was an
inhospitable landscape, this region was transformed into an area which is
excellent for economic, urban and recreational uses.

Currently, the Trebon district is undergoing rapid transformation as a result
of the intensification of agricultural production, fish breeding, forest
management and the expansion of sand and gravel exploitation. With significant
support from the regional and local bodies of the State administration (the South
Bohemia Regional National Committee and the district national committees), the
Federal Ministry for Technical Development and Investments has designed a
project for the ecological optimization of land-use in the Trebon district.

In the first stage of the project, leading specialists were called upon to
elaborate studies on the natural conditions and historical development of the
region, i.e., zoologists, botanists, ecologists, hydrologists, pedologists,
geologists, meteorologists, geographers, historians, hygiene and sanitations
specialists and many others. Information was collected on the current and
anticipated development of agriculture, forest management, fish husbandry, sand
and gravel exploitation, water management, peat exploitation, spas and tourism.
All regional planning documentation was collected as were the data required for
the development of the settlement.

The second stage of the project included a five-day colloquium whose participants
were provided with the above documents well in advance. Using the brainstorming
method, the key problems of the present state and future development of the
Trebon area were discussed and the basic principles of the project drawn up.
Some 50 specialists participated in the compilation of the 300-page document.
A total of 180 specialists attended the individual sessions of the colloquium.

In the third stage of the project, nine 5- to 10-member task forces were set
up to work on the individual tasks of the project. One team to synthesize the
results and one inter-ministerial team to process the documents related to the
project within six months of completion were also established. The problem area
was divided into ten parts: the characteristics of the landscape, water
resources, raw material resources, the forest, farmland, peat lands, ponds,
natural reservations, the biosphere, the settlement structure.

In the fourth stage points of dispute and disagreement were examined and
discussed with representatives of production organizations, ministries and the
central planning bodies, in cases where such action proved necessary.

In the fifth and final stage the project entitled "The Ecological System of
Management in the Trebon Conservation Area" was negotiated with the Council of
the South Bohemia Regional National Committee and, on its endorsement, became

a guiding document for planners of the economic and social development of the
area for the years 1981 to 1985 (see appendix).

During the project, a Government decree declaring the Trebon area a conservation
area protected under the law was submitted for inter-ministerial negotiations.
On the basis of experience with this project, and with projects undertaken in
other pilot areas, it was decided that a Government decree would be issued
in 1981 concerning the development and management of conservation areas; it
will be tested in several other pilot areas and will then become an integral
part of the law on nature conservation. Currently, similar projects are underway
in three other conservation areas and work has started on three ecological models
of areas with high mining, power production and industrial activity. It is
expected that, in the coming decades, ecological data covering the entire
territory of the Czechoslovak Socialist Republic will be processed and
incorporated in the system of planning the economic and social development of
Czechoslovakia.

APPENDIX I

Excerpt from "Ecological System of Management in the
Trebon Conservation Area", Scientific and Technical
Project, Czechoslovak EKOPROGRAM

Utilization of Peat Fields

Peat belongs among Czechoslovakia's valuable raw materials whose uses are
increasing in the country and elsewhere. Czechoslovakia has 31,369 hectares
of peat fields. The function of peat in spas in irreplaceable. Peat is indispensable for securing the fulfilment of planned targets in agriculture, i.e., it
is used in large nurseries, hot houses and modern, large-scale propagating
houses for growing vegetables, mushrooms, etc. Peat is an extremely important
factor in specialized branches of forest management. The growing discrepancy
between demand and supply requires increased peat exploitation.

Many preserved peat fields are ecologically unique and irreplaceable natural
systems with surviving fauna and flora which does not exist anywhere else. They
are also valuable natural archives and sources of information on the development
of the climate and vegetation on our territory over the past 14 thousand years.
Peat fields are extremely attractive areas for tourism. For their scientific and
cultural enlightment and their educational importance they belong among the
most valuable components of our landscape. The inappropriate choice of areas for
peat mining in recent years has resulted in the devastation of several small
peat localities before peat fields which had previously been opened for mining
and which, from the natural science point of view, were less important had
been exhausted. Currently more than 50 per cent of the mined peat is processed
into composts (Vitahum) while ecologically less-valuable raw materials, such as
wastes, tree bark, etc., are not used. Current knowledge allows for considerable
choice among other raw materials and also makes it possible to open for mining
locations where such activity is acceptable from the ecological point of view.

The biggest area of peat is in the South Bohemia Region - 12,461 hectares, of
which 7,590 hectares are in the Trebon basin. The nature reserves cover 550 ha,
natural curative areas, 310 ha, while the remaining part of the area (including
ponds) is used for agriculture or covered with forests.

The effect of peat mining in the Trebon basin has so far often had negative
impacts. Practically all ecologically valuable localities of the Trebon basin
have been damaged. In compliance with the new concepts of the rational utilization

of peat fields and their protection, it will be necessary to look into
requirements for the opening of new deposits and to enforce the mining of deposits
in localities which have already in the past been devastated and where mining
will create better conditions for subsequent reclamation.

In Brannà, Hranice and Príbraz the existing deposits cover an area of 247 ha
with 126 ha for mining. Príbraz is promising while the other localities are
nearing exhaustion. After the deposts are exhausted the area will be reclaimed
with forests planted in one part of the area and a pond established for the
reclamation of part of the Príbraz deposit.

For Branský Forest (72 ha), a mining permit has been issued for expanding the
current mining project. With regard to the prospective drilling of wells for the
Trebon water supply, the designers of the mining project will have to respect
the water management authorities.

For Hrdlorezy (120 ha), a mining permit has been granted for expanding the
current mine. From the ecological and water management points of view there
are no objections to the rational exploitation of the deposit.

The Záblatí (344 ha), deposit has been considered for exploitation. The locality
is situated in the Horusice-Dolní Bukovsko catchment area which supplies the
town of Jindrichuv Hradec with drinking and utility water. A mining permit
would threaten the quality and quantity of the water from the resource. The
emptying of the Záblatský pond would result in considerably reducing retention
capacity and would become a flood risk factor. The locality also comprises the
last compact stretch of pastureland in the Trebon basin with valuable plant and
animal communities. In view of the fact that other deposits in the Trebon area have
not yet been exhausted and that a number of more suitable localities may be found
for peat mining in the area, peat mining in the Záblatí area should be considered
as totally unacceptable.

APPENDIX II

Basic Trends of Ecological Optimization of
Land Use in the Trebon Basin

(principles of optimization model)

  - Priority should be given to the protection and gradual utilization of
water resources in the whole area and further exploitation interests should
be subordinated to the importance of the area for water management in the South
Bohemia Region;

  - sand and gravel exploitation should remain at the current level and
should gradually be reduced; deposits which have already been opened should be
fully exploited and the assorted raw material should be rationally utilized for
purposes set by the Czechoslovak State Standard. Any increase in exploitation
of sand and gravel should be secured outside the ecologically valuable Trebon
area. The requirements for feldspar mining should be matched against its actual
need in Czechoslovakia and against the effective utilization of the deposit with
regard to the future consumption of this raw material in Czechoslovakia;

  - in forest management, timber production should be kept at the current
level and a more rational utilization and efficient processing of pulp should
be ensured (the adequate development of the wood processing industry, the use
of waste from forest exploitation and selective cutting for compost production
and for other purposes); the topography and soil structure of the area does not

favour the use of heavy machinery for tree cutting and forest soil amelioration, so having regard to the considerable amount of foreign currency from the sale of timber from the Trebon area, it will be necessary to import lighter and more operational machinery;

    - in plant production it will be necessary to reconsider the usefulness of the further development of land improvement schemes which are currently restricted mainly to the drainage of temporarily waterlogged plots; it will also be necessary to draw up a water regulation scheme at research and project design level for the Trebon basin which would involve agriculture, forest management and the system of ponds;

    - to give priority to the development of meadow farming in the specific conditions of the Trebon area; to categorize the meadow grasses and to determine differentiated cultivation; to secure light machinery and drying plants;

    - to define adequate protection zones, with a ban on the aerial application of fertilizers and pesticides (the aerial application of chemical substances has the most serious hygienic and ecotoxicological impacts on the area);

    - in case of the further development of livestock production, it will be necessary to observe even more consistently the water management, hygienic and ecological regulations for the construction and operation of large-scale livestock breeding farms; regular checks will have to be made of the equipment of the farms and technical discipline supervised with regard to possible impacts on the ecology of the landscape;

    - in the economic plans of crop production, fish pond husbandry and forest management it will be necessary to harmonize the application of fertilizers to the individual ecosystems (fields, meadows, ponds, forests) with the aim of attaining the maximum utilization of nutrients by the plants, minimal loss from cultivated plots and overall savings in the consumption of fertilizers;

    - in fish pond husbandry it will be necessary to categorize ponds with regard to their production, water management, recreational and stabilization functions in the Trebon landscape; the aim is to attain a further modest increase in fish production, to maintain duck breeding at the current level, and to secure the utilization of pond mud for improving the balance of organic matter in agricultural soil;

    - peat exploitation should be preserved at the current level; increasing demands should be met by discontinuing the use of peat for compost production (50 per cent of the total amount of peat exploited) and replacing it with suitable waste products, such as tree bark and pond mud; the selection of deposits for exploitation should respect the water management and ecological function of the landscape; the choice between fish pond husbandry and forest management should always be made with due ecological considerations;

    - the area of the Trebon basin should be divided into zones of intensive exploitation, zones of exploitation conditioned by water management interests and zones of strict control.

Appendix III

Accords and Conflicts of Interest

Variants of Economic Development of the Region — Impacts of individual variants on the possibilities of land-use and of the exploitation of natural resources

a = minimal variant
b = optimal variant
c = maximal variant

+ = accord of interests
− = conflict of interests
o = indifferent relation

Columns:
1. use of water resources
2. gravel sand mining
3. forest management
4. agricultural production
5. pond husbandry
6. utilization of past fields
7. spas
8. development of settlements
9. hygiene
10. recreation
11. nature protection
12. character of landscape (aesthetics)

Variant	1	2	3	4	5	6	7	8	9	10	11	12
1. Use of water resources												
1(a) protection of determined take-off areas of ground water resources		−	o	o	o	o	+	+	+	+	+	+
1(b) protection of used and prospective groundwater resources including optimal management techniques		−	o	o	o	−	+	+	+	+	+	+
1(c) establishment of protected groundwater accumulation area		−	−	−	−	−	+	+	+	o	+	+
2. Gravel and mining												
2(a) closing down of currently mined deposits and orientation of further development of mining outside the Trebon area	o		o	o	o	o	o	o	o	+	o	−
2(b) development of mining in the region (outside the Luznice catchment), the closing down of all currently mined deposits after their rational exhaustion		−	−	o	o	−		o	o	o	−	−
2(c) gradual development of mining in all considered localities	−	−	−	−	o			o			−	−
3. Forest management												
3(a) the classification of all forests into the category of forests for water management purposes, i.e. excluding the application of chemicals and the use of heavy machinery	+	o		+	+	o	+	o	+	+	+	+
3(b) the use of heavy machinery on 10 – 20 per cent of the total area, land improvement and the application of chemicals is only allowed outside the area of water management interests	o	o		+	o	o	o	o	+	−	o	−
3(c) intensive forest management preferring the productive function of the forest	−	o		o		o	−	o	−		−	−
4. Agricultural production												
4(a) agriculture with a protection regime throughout the area	+	o	+		+	o	+	o	+	+	+	+
4(b) optimal structure of the agricultural soil stock, land improvement and chemicalization outside the area of water management and nature conservation	+	o	+		+	o	+	o	+	+	+	
4(c) intensive agriculture, maximum land improvement, drainage of all pasturelands and meadows and their conversion into arable land, the application of chemicals without any special restriction	−	o	o		o		o		o	−	−	−
5. Pond husbandry												
5(a) priority is given to the water management, recreational and soil conservation function before the production function	+	o	+	o		o	+	+	+	+	+	+
5(b) optimal ratio between production and non-productive functions (stagnation of duck breeding)	+	o	+	+		o	+	+	o	o	+	+
5(c) absolute priority is given to the productive function of the fish ponds (fish and duck breeding are developed and enhanced)	−	o	o	−		o	−	−	−	−	−	−
6. Utilization of peat fields												
6(a) closing down of mined deposits and opening of deposits in Bransky forest, Hrdlorezy and Pribraz for mining	o	o	o	o	o		o	o	o	o	o	−
6(b) gradual development of mining also in the area of the former Hradecek pond	−	o	−	o	o		o	o	o	o	o	o
6(c) gradual development of mining also in the Zablati area	−	o	o	−	−		−	o	−	−	−	−

Models for Impact Assessment for Important Public Works: Case Study of a Linear Infrastructure 2 × 400 kV High-tension Electric Power Line from Chinon to Distre

M. Giacobino

(France)

The purpose of the high-tension line referred to in the study is to transport power produced by the Chinon power station to the major interconnexion station at Distre, near Saumur. The region concerned, namely the Loire valley, fairly near Paris, is famous for the beauty of its landscapes and historical monuments (castles, abbeys), the quality of its vineyards and its forests. When the first technical surveys were made, it seemed that the existence of so many restrictions in so small a geographical area would make it particularly difficult to plot an alignment.

This paper should be regarded as a first-generation study, because the technical surveys had started when impact assessments became compulsory. The need to show how the final choice was made from among the various alignments considered obliged technicians to delve deeper into the initial state of the environment and the comparison between the value and advantage of each alternative. Incidentally, the final alternative will be the first example of a new type of solution which Electricité de France is trying to develop for its new projects: namely, that of placing new lines parallel to existing ones where possible new alignments offer the same number of environmental problems. The solution was discovered by examining closely the role of each part of the network within the framework of the impact assessment, which showed that the creation of a new 400kV line would make it possible to replace a 225kV line if the two transformer posts on the regional grind were strengthened. In this instance, the impact assessment was simplified by the fact that the existing line to be replaced could be used as a visual datum line and that the impacts on farming and afforestation could be extrapolated from impact studies that had been examined on the spot.

Another innovation, so far as France is concerned, was the obligation to publicize the impact assessment: the public thus learned the content of the impact assessment, whereas previously power lines had been the only public works for which the authorization procedure had not required the public to be informed (formerly only mayors and owners of plots of land directly affected were consulted).

The first-generation impact assessment showed that research programmes should be launched to improve existing knowledge about the initial state, impact assessment techniques and protective measures. The knowledge gained is gradually serving to improve the second-generation assessments, which are being designed in precisely the same spirit as the present impact assessments.

Another highly interesting side effect, however, has been the preparation of a plan for the future interconnexion network between the places of production and of consumption. Accordingly, it has been possible to take environment considerations into account at the planning level. In France this is one of the best examples of the fact that impact assessments, far from replacing physical planning, are both supplementing and developing it by enabling environmental considerations to be incorporated in the usual planning mechanisms.

Les Methodes d'Etudes d'Impact pour les Grands Ouvrages: Etude de Cas d'une Infrastructure Lineaire la Ligne de Transport d'Energie Electrique a Haute Tension 2 × 400 kV Chinon-Distre

M. Giacobino

(France)

En France, la réglementation concernant les lignes électriques à haute tension présente des caractéristiques différentes de celles des autres ouvrages d'infrastructures linéaires comme les routes et les canaux. Pour ces dernières, en effet, la réglementation utilisée est basée sur le code de l'expropriation qui définit des règles précises en matière de conduite de consultation du public par l'intermédiaire de l'enquête publique. Or la possibilité de réalisation d'une ligne électrique n'est pas liée à l'expropriation des terrains mais à l'établissement de servitudes. Le propriétaire du terrain n'est donc pas exproprié mais l'usage de son terrain est obéré par la ligne, ceci moyennant le versement d'indemnités dont le montant est fonction de la valeur du terrain et des éléments risquant d'être directement concernés (arbres abattus, etc.).

Le principe d'établissement de servitudes a permis à l'Electricité de France (SEDES) organisme public qui réalise les lignes, de construire très rapidement et sans problèmes particuliers les liaisons électriques vitales pendant les phases de reconstruction de l'après-guerre jusqu'au début des années 1970 où les notions de développement et de croissance commençaient à évoluer et où les idées de prise en compte de l'environnement ont commencé à être connues du grand public.

Mais les particularités de procédures qui avaient permis de réaliser rapidement les lignes allaient être très critiquées en particulier par les principales associations de protection de l'environnement. En effet pour les routes par exemple, le code de l'expropriation demande qu'une enquête publique permette au public de s'informer et d'exprimer son avis sur la réalisation projetée. Pour les lignes électriques, la procédure de demande de déclaration d'utilité publique est limitée en matière de consultation aux seuls services de l'administration et au maire (et non à l'ensemble du conseil municipal) de chaque commune concernée par le projet de tracé. Il n'y a donc pas d'enquête publique.

L'abondance des projets de lignes, la sensibilisation croissante du public aux impacts des lignes électriques, notamment en terme de paysage, et les défauts de la procédure en ce qui concerne l'information du public ont conduit le législateur à exiger que tout projet de ligne électrique aérienne de tension égale ou supérieure à 225 kV fasse l'objet d'une étude d'impact afin d'illustrer la façon dont l'environnement avait été pris en compte dans la conception du projet.

Les deux études de cas suivantes illustrent bien comment les idées et les comporte-
ments ont pu évoluer depuis le 1er janvier 1978 dans le contexte des études d'impact.

La ligne de transport d'énergie électrique à haute tension Chinon-Distre

L'étude de la conception de cette ligne illustre parfaitement le contexte dans le-
quel un tracé de ligne pouvait être élaboré au moment où l'article 2 de la loi sur
la protection sur la nature devenait applicable. Cette étude d'impact peut être con-
sidérée comme une étude de première génération; en effet, les études techniques du
projet et les études de paysages étaient commencées au 1er janvier 1978. L'obligation de présentation de l'étude d'impact allait obliger les techniciens de l'Electricité de France (EDF) et les membres des différentes administrations concernées
de réfléchir sur les transformations qu'il fallait apporter aux anciennes pratiques
afin de cristalliser sous la forme d'un dossier particulier la façon dont l'environnement avait été pris en compte. Nous considérons comme études de deuxième génération celles qui ont commencé alors que la réalisation d'une étude d'impact était
obligatoire : les études de deuxième génération ont donc pu être entièrement con-
çues dans l'esprit de la prise en compte de l'environnement qui résulte du respect
du décret du 12 octobre 1977.

L'exemple d'étude de première génération que nous avons choisi d'examiner présente
l'avantage d'être de dimension suffisamment réduite pour que les éléments déterminants puissent être facilement appréciés dans le cadre d'un rapport de synthèse.

Les caractéristiques essentielles du projet

Il est prévu de créer deux nouvelles tranches de production d'énergie électrique en
1981 et 1982 à la centrale de Chinon. Pour évacuer l'énergie produite, il est nécessaire de créer une ligne de 2 x 400 kV entre les postes d'Avoine, avoisinant la centrale de Chinon et Distre (à proximité de la ville de Saumur).

Cette ligne de 2 x 400 kV est du même type que toutes celles qui sont prévues dans
le cadre du futur réseau d'interconnexion reliant les centres de consommation (principales villes, industries) et les centres de production (centrales nucléaires, hy-
droélectriques, turbines à gaz, etc.).

Le régime administratif

En 1975, au moment où commencent les premières études techniques pour incorporer au
réseau l'alimentation générale en énergie électrique, concédée à l'Electricité de
France par la convention du 27 novembre 1958, cet organisme devait déposer une demande de déclaration d'utilité publique conformément aux dispositions de l'article
6 du décret N° 70-492 du 11 juin 1970, qui ne demandait pas alors de réaliser une
étude d'impact. Or, la loi sur la protection de la nature, approuvée le 10 juillet
1976, et son décret d'application du 12 octobre 1977, ont introduit la notion d'é-
tude d'impact et demandé l'organisation de la publicité de celle-ci, dispositions
nouvelles pour les techniciens du centre régional de l'EDF. Il faut reconnaître que
ceux-ci avaient, dans le cas de cette ligne, commencé à prendre en compte les préoccupations d'environnement, mais la nécessité de réaliser concrètement l'étude d'impact allait leur permettre d'approfondir leurs réflexions sur la prise en compte de
l'environnement tout au long de la réalisation de l'étude d'impact. C'est pour des
raisons de facilité de présentation que nous suivrons l'ordre des différents chapitres de l'étude d'impact que le décret a imposé, mais il est bien évident que, dans
la réalité, les réalisateurs de l'étude sont constamment obligés de faire de nombreu
allers et retours entre les différents chapitres.

La réalisation de l'état initial de l'environnement

Les premières études et surtout les expériences antérieures de l'EDF en matière d'implantation de lignes électriques, dans le secteur concerné, avaient dès 1975 attiré l'attention des responsables sur la grande sensibilité de la région.

Description des éléments principaux de la région

La zone traversée est située au sud de la Loire, entre Chinon et Saumur, à environ 150 km au sud-ouest de Paris. On rencontre successivement d'est en ouest la vallée de la Vienne au sud de Candes-Saint-Martin, la forêt de Fontevrault et la vallée du Thouet. Le paysage est à dominante agricole. En particulier, les vignes sont situées entre la forêt de Fontevrault et la Loire, au flanc de petits vallons, et dans la vallée du Thouet. Comme toute la vallée de la Loire, c'est une région riche en châteaux et en monuments religieux (château de Chinon, Saumur, Montsoreau, abbaye de Fontevrault, etc.). Elle est, de plus, bien équipée du point de vue accueil et exerce un fort attrait sur la région parisienne dont elle est relativement proche.

Les contraintes d'environnement

Pour situer un tracé, les techniciens ont tout d'abord recherché toutes les contraintes d'environnement existantes, qu'elles soient réglementaires (monuments historiques), ou plus qualitatives comme la qualité des paysages ou l'équilibre des milieux naturels.

Ont été ainsi repérés :

- la forêt de Fontevrault, déjà traversée par plusieurs lignes à haute tension, qui constitue à priori une zone écologiquement sensible et dans laquelle il est souhaitable de ne pas créer de nouvelle tranchée. La Commission d'enquête qui a instruit la demande de déclaration d'utilité publique des deux nouvelles tranches de la centrale nucléaire de Chinon a d'ailleurs demandé que les lignes électriques soient concentrées au maximum et n'entraînent pas de saignées dans les forêts avoisinant le site;

- les vignobles qui s'étendent entre la Loire et la forêt de Fontevrault, et dans la vallée du Thouet. Le passage d'une nouvelle ligne dans les cépages des grands crus de l'Anjou devrait autant que possible être évité;

- toute la zone du bord de Loire, au riche passé historique, qui constitue une zone d'habitat relativement dense. Une ligne ne pourrait la traverser sans éviter de nombreux surplombs d'habitations.

En outre, des sites classés tels que ceux de l'abbaye de Fontevrault, de Candes-Saint-Martin et de Montsoreau, devraient voir leur intégrité conservée; toute confrontation entre l'objet industriel que représente la ligne et le signifiant culturel attaché à ces sites devrait être évitée. Enfin, la zone entourant le poste de Distre est essentiellement à vocation céréalière, et l'arrivée d'une ligne supplémentaire ne pouvait que constituer un obstacle supplémentaire à la mécanisation de la culture.

L'étude d'impact a permis de mieux formaliser la recherche des contraintes et d'approfondir certains points de l'état initial qui allaient s'avérer déterminants au niveau du choix du tracé.

La réalisation du choix du tracé parmi les partis envisagés

Ce chapitre de l'étude d'impact est probablement le plus important, car il permet effectivement de s'assurer que l'environnement a été pris en compte. En effet, seul un examen comparatif des avantages et des inconvénients des différentes solutions permet de mettre en évidence les éléments qui ont déterminé le choix final. Dans le cas des lignes électriques, les diverses solutions sont soit des variantes de

localisation soit des alternatives techniques. Le cas de la ligne Chinon-Distre présente la double particularité d'être une des premières études d'impact que l'EDF a
dû réaliser, et d'être à l'origine d'un changement des habitudes de conception des
tracés qui tend à se généraliser dans des cas semblables sur l'ensemble du terri-
toire.

Jusqu'alors les spécialistes de l'EDF et les administrations consultées limitaient
la recherche des variantes à deux types de possibilité, implantation de la nouvelle
ligne en parallèle et à proximité immédiate avec un ouvrage existant ou la création
d'un nouveau tracé. L'intérêt du regroupement de nuisance était toutefois contreba-
lancé par un effet de coupure accentué dans les massifs boisés; en outre, le couloir élargi trouve parfois difficilement sa trace dans les régions où l'occupation
des sols est particulièrement dense.

La recherche d'un tracé résolument nouveau est elle-même difficile dans les régions
où la densité des lignes existantes est grande et où les habitants, non encore concernés par un passage de ligne, souhaitent évidemment que leur région encore vierge
ne soit pas traversée par un éventuel projet.

Dans la région de la vallée de la Loire, la mise en parallèle avec une ligne existante pouvait être réalisée sur une partie de deux lignes existantes (variante 2 :
ligne Distre-Arnage, variante 3 Distre-Eguzon), mais pour la première de celles-ci
réalisée quelques années auparavant, les techniciens de l'EDF avaient encore en mé-
moire les protestations des administrations et des élus. La création d'une nouvelle
ligne, parallèle à la ligne Distre-Arnage, dans une région où la densité des points
sensibles rend particulièrement difficile le passage d'un couloir très large, paraissait utopique. Ce tracé imposait en outre que le segment de ligne se raccordant
à Chinon traverse une nouvelle fois la Loire.

Quant à elle, la variante N° 3 impose la traversée d'un bois important, et surtout
les vignobles de la vallée du Thouet. L'examen des possibilités d'un nouveau tracé
direct entraînait automatiquement la traversée du massif forestier renommé de Fontevrault, ce qui paraissait impossible.

Aucune solution ne paraissant satisfaisante, les techniciens durent repenser entièrement l'organisation de leur réseau. En effet, jusqu'alors la création de cette
nouvelle ligne était étudiée de la même façon que d'habitude, c'est-à-dire en ajou-
tant un élément supplémentaire au réseau. Or, dans ce cas, il leur apparut que la
création d'une ligne très importante allait peut-être pouvoir permettre de déposer
une ancienne ligne aux possibilités de transport plus réduites.

Cette opportunité se révéla intéressante pour les anciennes lignes de 225 kV Distre-
Chinon (variante 1' et 1). La mise en parallèle avec ses lignes aurait entraîné la
réalisation d'une tranchée très importante dans la forêt de Fontevrault, mais la dé-
pose de l'ancienne et son remplacement par la ligne de 400 kV paraissaient possibles
La variante 1' passant à proximité de monuments historiques, le tracé 1 semblait don
celui qui offrait le plus de garantie sur le plan de l'environnement.

Ce tracé présentait donc les avantages suivants :

- la longueur totale des lignes établies dans la zone d'étude ne change pas;

- le tracé reste éloigné des zones touristiques du bord de la Loire où l'habitat se
  trouve concentré, et où est établi le vignoble. Il évite aussi au maximum la proximité d'habitations;

- le tracé ne crée pas de nouvelle percée dans la forêt de Fontevrault; un simple
  réaménagement de la tranchée existante suffit.

- cette solution minimise le nombre de croisements avec les ouvrages existants et n'entraîne pas de suggestion d'exploitation particulières.

En outre, et cela n'avait sûrement pas échappé aux techniciens de l'EDF, ce tracé est un des plus courts qui soit envisageable. Mais il faut pourtant préciser qu'il n'est pourtant pas le moins cher. En effet, il faut d'abord déposer la ligne de 225 kV existante avant de commencer à établir la nouvelle ligne. Ensuite les techniciens s'aperçurent qu'il fallait rééquilibrer les charges du réseau en renforçant la puissance des deux postes de Marmagnec(Bourges) et de Chanceaux (Tours).

Avant le choix définitif de cette variante, les techniciens durent vérifier que la création de la nouvelle ligne, aux dimensions plus importantes que la précédente, n'allait pas rendre un impact existant beaucoup plus néfaste pour l'environnement.

L'évaluation des impacts de l'ouvrage sur l'environnement

Cet examen a été réalisé sur des secteurs aux caractéristiques homogènes. L'examen a essentiellement porté sur les problèmes d'occupation du sol (surplomb éventuel de construction, tranchée dans les forêts, gêne de pratiques agricoles) et sur les problèmes d'insertion visuelle dans les paysages. Dans ce cas particulier, une ligne existante est un point de repère idéal pour évaluer la plupart des impacts.

Pour le tronçon où la nouvelle ligne doit être édifiée en parallèle avec la ligne de 225 kV conservée, il est important de choisir des supports de 2 x 400 kV d'aspect plastique compatible avec les pylônes "chat".

Un examen détaillé des secteurs les plus sensibles, l'utilisation de croquis sur lesquels figure une simulation dessinée de la future ligne permirent d'évaluer les impacts et de rechercher des solutions. La difficulté essentielle à examiner était le passage dans la forêt de Fontevrault.

La tranchée existante pouvait être réutilisée par la ligne de 2 x 400 kV mais devait pouvoir être réaménagée. Toutefois, au stade actuel des études techniques, il est difficile de prévoir quelle sera l'étendue exacte des déboisements supplémentaires nécessaires par rapport à la tranchée existante.

Les taillis existants bordant la tranchée de déroulage pourront, lorsqu'ils sont bas, être conservés au voisinage des supports de manière à éviter l'effet visuel de couloir créé par une tranchée large totalement déboisée; mais en milieu de portée, il sera nécessaire de déboiser pour conserver les distances de sécurité.

Les mesures permettant de réduire les impacts

Celles-ci peuvent être réduites si le tracé ne présente pas d'impacts majeurs. Dans le cas de la ligne Chinon-Distre, ces mesures ont surtout consisté à essayer d'obtenir une cohérence visuelle acceptable entre la nouvelle ligne de 2 x 400 kV et les autres lignes avec lesquelles elle est amenée à voisiner. L'emploi de postes au rythme identique, l'utilisation de pylônes d'apparence voisine devraient permettre d'apporter en grande partie une solution à ce problème.

Les techniciens ayant, à leur avis, déterminé le meilleur tracé possible conciliant technique, coût et environnement, le tracé 1 fut retenu définitivement par l'EDF et présenté aux administrations de contrôle et à tous ceux qui sont consultés dans le cadre de la procédure d'instruction.

Organisation de la publicité de l'étude d'impact

L'obligation de rendre publique l'étude d'impact était donc une nouveauté tant pour l'administration de contrôle (Ministère de l'industrie) que pour l'EDF. L'annonce du dépôt dans les mairies des chefs-lieux de cantons concernés et des préfectures, de l'étude d'impact fut faite dans des journaux nationaux et régionaux.

Pour rendre les documents techniques habituels plus facilement compréhensibles pour le grand public, l'EDF a réalisé une brochure illustrée reprenant les caractéristiques essentielles de la démarche de réalisation du projet.

Bilan et insuffisances de l'étude d'impact de la ligne Chinon-Distre

Bien que les études techniques aient été engagées avant l'obligation de réalisation de l'étude d'impact, celle-ci a pu apporter des éléments intéressants : l'amélioration de la connaissance de l'état initial et la nécessité de montrer les différentes solutions ont permis d'introduire une réflexion plus complète sur le fonctionnement du réseau et de trouver une meilleure solution.

Dans ce cas, l'apport le plus intéressant a concerné les administrations consultées dans le cadre de la procédure, les élus, et surtout le public, qui ont enfin pu apprécier les méthodes de travail et les raisons du choix des techniciens.

Pour le moment, l'instruction continue et la déclaration d'utilité publique (DUP) n'est pas encore prononcée. Il faudra peut-être attendre la phase de réalisation de l'ouvrage pour voir les réactions du public et si celui-ci a été informé et a admis le choix fait par l'EDF.

Les insuffisances

Pour l'Atelier central de l'environnement, ce dossier présente les faiblesses caractéristiques des études de première génération : les contraintes essentielles prises en compte concernent surtout le paysage, les monuments historiques et l'occupation du sol. Dans ce cas, l'étude a été complétée par une approche simplifiée de l'agriculture et des masses boisées. On peut regretter que les équilibres écologiques n'aient pas pu être étudiés, par manque de références existant en France dans ce domaine.

Même avec ses insuffisances de forme et de fond, l'étude d'impact a participé à la mise au point d'un tracé qui a paru au Délégué régional à l'environnement être très acceptable dans le contexte donné.

Les enseignements tirés de cette expérience par les services centraux des ministères et de l'EDF

La mise en évidence des problèmes communs à toutes ces études de première génération a obligé les principaux intéressés, Ministères de l'industrie, de l'environnement et de l'EDF, à faire progresser les idées et les méthodes au sein des groupes de travail.

La première difficulté est le manque d'informations de base, en particulier dans les domaines de l'écologie et du paysage. En effet, seule une bonne connaissance des milieux permettra aux techniciens de réaliser en amont, avant même qu'ils commencent les études techniques proprement dites, des cartes de contraintes qui aident à rechercher le meilleur tracé possible. On trouvera par la suite dans ce rapport un exemple de traitement d'information de l'état initial dans le cas d'une étude de deuxième génération.

Pour essayer de dégager le plus vite possible les éléments essentiels à des tracés d'infrastructures linéaires, l'Atelier central de l'environnement a lancé un programme de recueil de données au niveau départemental sous la forme de fichiers d'études d'environnement existantes accompagnant une cartographie montrant les zones les plus sensibles du point de vue de l'environnement. Ce système permettra progressivement de récupérer les informations mises en évidence par les différents maîtres d'ouvrage à l'occasion d'études d'impact et à les rendre accessibles à tous les maîtres d'oeuvre, aux associations et au public souhaitant vérifier au cours des enquêtes publiques que ces données ont bien été utilisées.

La recherche sur l'évaluation des impacts

Les premières études d'impact ont bien montré le manque de connaissances que nous avions en matière d'évaluation des impacts. Les études d'environnement réalisées avant les études d'impact accordaient une importance maximale au paysage et à l'occupation des sols. Chinon-Distre a montré l'importance de l'évaluation des impacts dans les masses boisées et dans les régions possédant une agriculture spécialisée comme les vignobles. D'autres lignes ont amené les techniciens à se poser le problème des impacts sur les milieux naturels et la faune. Chaque nouvelle étude d'impact permet de progresser, mais il s'est avéré urgent de lancer des programmes de recherche.

Un des sujets les plus délicats, qui a été souvent évoqué par la presse française, est l'éventualité d'effets biologiques sur l'homme. Jusqu'à maintenant, il n'a pas été possible d'enregistrer des faits significatifs, mais cela peut être dû à des méthodes et des moyens inadaptés. Il semblerait toutefois que l'utilisation de la tension de 400 kV - l'EDF ayant renoncé à l'emploi du 730 kV - corresponde dans une certaine mesure à une limitation des risques éventuels qui paraissent beaucoup plus probables vers les tensions approchant les 1.000 kV. Il est bien évident que toutes les recherches effectuées sur le plan mondial sont suivies attentivement.

L'EDF et l'Atelier central de l'environnement ont lancé des recherches dans un autre domaine encore mal connu : les impacts sur l'avifaune. Ces études devraient permettre d'améliorer les connaissances sur les voies de migrations des oiseaux, sur leurs habitudes de vol, afin d'éviter par exemple les risques de percussion directe par les oiseaux de grande envergure (rapaces diurnes et nocturnes) des câbles sous tension ou de garde (parafoudres).

La nature de ces données exclut toute recherche théorique. Aussi a-t-il été décidé de lancer des opérations de "suivi écologique" afin de comparer l'état initial à l'état constaté après réalisation de l'ouvrage. Ceci permettra d'essayer de déterminer la nature des impacts et d'évaluer leur importance relative par rapport au contexte. Des laboratoires d'observations sur le terrain seront ainsi disposés sur des voies de migration de l'avifaune bien connues dans le nord de la France (vallée de la Somme, etc.).

Un autre groupe de travail réunissant l'EDF et les responsables du Ministère de l'agriculture et du Service des forêts, est en train d'approfondir les connaissances sur l'évaluation des impacts du passage des lignes dans les milieux forestiers. Des méthodes de passage par pylônes géants ont ainsi permis le surplomb de forêts particulièrement intéressantes (sapinières des Vosges, etc.).

Le financement de ces recherches est parfois assuré par l'EDF au titre de mesure de compensation (quatrième chapitre d'une étude d'impact) quand les connaissances précises permettant d'apprécier les impacts sont insuffisantes et que le milieu traversé semble avoir à priori des caractéristiques intéressantes : exemple de la traversée des Marais de Guines dans le nord de la France.

L'amélioration de l'information du public
_____

L'obligation d'organiser la publicité de l'étude d'impact a obligé le Ministère de
l'industrie à compléter sa procédure. Un groupe de travail entre Ministère de l'environnement et Ministère de l'industrie a ainsi défini dans une circulaire
le contenu type d'une étude d'impact et l'organisation pratique
de la consultation de l'étude par le public.

Ces instructions ont été suivies pour le dossier de la ligne Chinon-Distre : elles
ont consisté à annoncer dans des journaux locaux et régionaux l'existence de l'étude
d'impact et de préciser les lieux où l'étude pouvait être examinée : chefs-lieux
d'arrondissements, sous-préfectures, préfectures.

Ce public était convié à exprimer son avis sur un registre. Il faut toutefois noter
que cette première expérience n'a pas eu l'effet escompté, très peu de personnes
ayant saisi l'opportunité d'exprimer leur point de vue. Plusieurs raisons semblent
avoir joué, mais il semble surtout que le public était mal informé des nouvelles
possibilités d'expression qui lui étaient offertes.

C'est à la demande du Ministère de l'environnement et du cadre de vie que le Ministère de l'industrie étudie une amélioration du décret du 11 juin 1970 qui réglemente
l'instruction des dossiers afin d'introduire expressément l'existence d'une enquête
dans des conditions se rapprochant le plus possible de celle prévue par le code de
l'expropriation. Cette disposition devrait en outre permettre de régler des difficultés pour l'inscription des couloirs de lignes dans le Plan d'occupation des sols,
les enquêtes pouvant alors être menées conjointement si nécessaire.

Ainsi, l'obligation de réaliser une étude d'impact a entraîné l'amélioration du
point de vue environnement d'une procédure peu adaptée, et cela bien que l'étude
d'impact n'ait été conçue dans le cadre du décret du 12 octobre 1977 que pour s'in-
sérer dans les procédures sans les transformer.

L'Atelier central de l'environnement étudie même la possibilité dans l'avenir d'organiser à titre expérimental une audience publique en s'inspirant de l'expérience
du port de Carry-le-Rouet.

Une expérience à suivre : l'étude d'impact de deuxième génération Tourbe-Rougemon-
tier (Caen-Rouen en Normandie dans l'ouest de la France).

A la suite de la réalisation du dossier Chinon-Distre, l'EDF a cherché à améliorer
la prise en compte de l'environnement dans le cadre de l'étude d'impact en réalisant
une étude pilote confiée à un nouvel organisme : la cellule environnement du centre
de transport à Paris, créée pour définir une doctrine et mettre au point avec l'Atelier central de l'environnement une méthodologie adaptée.

A l'heure actuelle, seule la première partie de cette étude, l'état initial sur l'environnement, a été réalisée. Par comparaison entre les cartes, on est parfaitement à
même d'apprécier le chemin parcouru. Dès le départ de l'étude, il a été décidé de
réaliser la démarche dans l'esprit d'une étude d'impact. Les thèmes d'étude sont
maintenant plus complets et l'analyse des contraintes permet maintenant beaucoup
plus facilement de trouver un tracé qui soit le moins dommageable possible pour
l'environnement.

L'étude Chinon-Distre n'avait présenté que deux cartes d'état initial; Tourbe-Rouge-
montier présente successivement :

- les grandes unités de paysage régional,
- sensibilité des paysages,
- milieux naturels,

- sensibilité des milieux naturels,
- agriculture,
- habitat : zone de meilleure insertion,
- tourisme : loisirs,
- dynamique régionale,
- synthèse des données.

C'est à partir de ce dernier document, mais avec la possibilité de revenir sur les données de base, que les techniciens recherchent actuellement un tracé qui intègre préoccupations techniques, financières et d'environnement. Mais il faut bien insister sur ce point, les études d'état initial de l'environnement ont été faites avant le commencement des études de tracé.

Il est d'ores et déjà possible de faire un bilan portant sur les améliorations que l'on peut constater sur l'ensemble des études d'impact. Pour les études de génération, le tracé n'a quelquefois pas été conçu selon la démarche d'une étude d'impact. Celle-ci a au moins permis d'améliorer sensiblement les tracés dans les zones sensibles :

- un important effort de recherche méthodologique comportant des opérations de suivi écologique a été lancé;

- des équipes de spécialistes ad hoc ont été constituées au sein de l'EDF. Une de leurs missions essentielles est la sensibilisation et la formation des ingénieurs chargés des études de tracé au cours de stages consacrés aux problèmes d'environnement;

- nette amélioration de l'information du public grâce à l'organisation obligatoire de l'étude d'impact, mais des progrès sensibles restent à faire dans ce domaine;

- amélioration de la procédure d'autorisation prévisible à court terme;

- négociations amont le plus tôt possible engagées entre les différents ministères concernés et l'EDF pour la mise au point d'un schéma de réseau d'interconnexion prévoyant les liaisons de principe entre les centres de production et les lieux de consommation. Ce schéma permettra ainsi de prendre en compte l'environnement pour le choix des emplacements des postes de transformation et d'interconnexions qui formeront ultérieurement les extrémités des tronçons de lignes qui feront l'objet par la suite d'étude d'impact. On sera ainsi assuré qu'entre deux points retenus il apparaît possible de réaliser un tracé qui respecte au maximum les préoccupations d'environnement.

Dans ce cas, les études d'impact ont donc provoqué une amélioration du système de planification du réseau des lignes électriques à haute tension, contrairement aux craintes exprimées par certains spécialistes de la planification qui pensaient que les études d'impact allaient provoquer un abandon progressif des systèmes de planification existants. L'étude d'impact constitue donc bien un complément à la planification; elle ne peut se substituer à elle.

On peut affirmer que, sans la loi sur la protection de la nature et son décret d'application, ces résultats n'auraient jamais pu être obtenus dans un délai aussi court et cela sans que l'obligation de réaliser des études d'impact n'ait créé auprès de l'EDF des difficultés majeures, celle-ci ayant bien compris l'intérêt des études d'impact pour éviter de nombreuses difficultés au moment de la réalisation des ouvrages.

Environmental Impact Assessment (EIA) Based on the Example of Federal Highway Planning

S. Summerer

(Federal Republic of Germany)

AREA OF APPLICATION OF EIA

Environmental impact assessment (EIA) of actions taken by public authorities in the Federal Republic of Germany was introduced in August 1975 on the basis of a Federal Government decision. It applies to drafts of legal regulations, general administrative regulations, administrative acts, agreements and other acts of public authorities which affect the environment as well as to programmes and plans pertaining to public tasks. The purpose of such assessment is to protect man, animals, plants and valuable property against any action by the Federal Government which would affect the environment and to try to avoid damage to the environment by means of preventive and protective measures.

CONTENTS OF EIA

The Federal Government has established a formal procedure for environmental impact assessment which is intended to:

(a) clarify conflicting environmental issues;

(b) promote expert assessment and discussion of environmental matters;

(c) improve the basis of decision-making.

As it is a multi-dimensional plan of action, environmental impact assessment is designed to assure that environmental concerns are considered in an integrated way in various specialized planning procedures. It is intended to provide the basis for a systematic assessment of the effects of legal and planning measures on the environment and has been conceived as a kind of "institutional self-control" for public administration. At the same time, such assessment is intended to demonstrate the effectiveness of preventive measures, prevention of damage being one of the three fundamental principles of environmental policy.

EIA studies are required for federal highway construction, regional and state (Land) planning, specialized planning by Federal and State Governments, development planning and planning of airports, waste disposal areas, etc. In substance, the EIA requirements correspond to the prescriptions in the revised versions of paragraphs 41 and 50 of the Federal Emission Protection Act, according to which the construction or alteration of highways, railways, etc., must not lead to harmful environmental effects such as traffic noise, if available technology permits avoidance. In addition, for plans of regional significance, individual areas have to be evaluated in terms of their respective utilization in order to prevent harmful effects on residential areas and other areas needing protection.

According to the revised version of paragraph 17, sub-paragraph 4, of the Federal Highways Act, the authority that is financially responsible for highway construction must also assume responsibility for the building and maintenance of equipment necessary for protection against emissions, such as walls to protect against noise. Comparable regulations are included in the Land Consolidation Act and the Federal Protection of Nature Act.

SCOPE AND LIMITS OF EIA

The basic idea behind the requirements of an environmental impact assessment (EIA) and the related procedure is to establish a system for a methodical assessment and rational evaluation of planned measures. It requires, in particular, that all planning should give careful consideration to alternatives. Although precise instruments are uncertain, the procedure should help to ensure that:

- EIA is institutionalized as an obligation on planners.
- the tasks of the agencies involved are clearly defined.
- the environment-related agencies can give expert advice to the responsible, specialized agency.
- EIA is integrated into all relevant planning as soon as possible.

The plan described is, so far, largely an outline: its substance still remains to be determined. The individual steps of the procedure are not yet linked to specific stages in the planning process, or to the instruments of the technically competent agencies which would enable them to comply effectively with the requirements of EIA. As the present requirements for impact assessment do not contain any indication of the methods for assessing environmental impact in planning, expert advice must be sought from agencies concerned with the environment, especially the Federal Environmental Agency, to ensure effective implementation of legal regulations.

In its present form, environmental impact assessment has not established priorities among the requirements for environmental protection. The requirements listed in the procedure for EIA (prevention of dangers, protection of resources, elimination of damages, anticipatory environmental policy) have not been ranked and the only legally binding requirement is therefore that they receive due consideration. Without a catalogue of undesirable conditions or a precisely-defined check list, there can be no guarantee that ecological or socio-political considerations will be adequately taken into account in the planning stage. At present, EIA may provide only a choice among two or three predetermined options depending on the extent of negative environmental effects; this represents a procedure which conflicts with the fundamental idea of environmental impact assessment. In contrast to its American counterpart-environmental impact statements (EIS)-environmental assessments in the Federal Republic of Germany remain matters for the public administration, somewhat inappropriate for their intended purpose, which is to clarify procedural questions and conflicting aims. In addition, the observance of environmental impact assessment procedures by other authorities, including those dealing with environmental matters, is not obligatory, even for the ministry with central responsibility for environmental questions, i.e., the Federal Ministry of the Interior.

The following are major weaknesses of environmental impact assessment practice
in the Federal Republic of Germany:

- EIA remains an internal matter of government administration and thus is
  not subject to public control;

- Legal investigation by the parties concerned as a group is not possible;

- first-hand, immediate participation by related agencies concerned with
  environmental matters is not established;

- EIA still lacks systematic implementation.

However, it should be noted that, as a positive step forward, the Conference of
Environment Ministers (January 1975 and October 1977) made a commitment by which
the federal states will adopt the procedure of EIA for all measures taken by
public authorities, as was suggested by the Federal Government. EIA can become
fully effective only if accepted by the "Länder", i.e. the federal states, because
in the federal system, concrete measures can be taken almost exclusively only by
the "Länder" on the basis of uniform federal laws and decrees; there is often
only framework legislative authority at the federal level.

In the Federal Republic of Germany, citizens have traditionally had an opportunity
to voice their objections to virtually all planning measures relating to the
environment (cf. opportunities for civil action in procedures of plan
determination and plan development, as well as procedures for the approval of plans
under the Federal Emissions Act). In such processes, specialized agencies may
introduce environmental aspects into planning even without the new instruments
of EIA. The present lack of effectiveness of EIA does not imply that such assessment is the only means through which environmental aspects can be taken into
account in planning.

PLANNING DEVICES OF THE FEDERAL ENVIRONMENTAL AGENCY WHICH WOULD
MAKE EIA OPERATIONAL

Because of the above-mentioned weaknesses, the Federal Environmental Agency began
to elaborate planning devices for the agencies responsible for EIA. For this
purpose, the Agency was asked to prepare a handbook for federal highway planning
that would offer concrete planning aids on the procedure to be followed and the
choice of methods for the relevant types of specialized planning. This handbook
would provide planning authorities, for the first time, with an instrument in
the form of a comprehensive check list for reviewing all stages of planning,
including assessing requirements involved in determining routes, choosing among
alternative routes, optimizing main alternative routes, examining the plans for
possible negative impacts, ranking such impacts and summing up a total picture
of negative impacts.

The Environmental Agency was involved in the planning of the federal highway
No. B 202 in Schleswig-Holstein. This was undertaken in the Agency's capacity
as an advisory authority on environmental concerns. The work involved a very
detailed comparison of two motorway routes in terms of their ecological impact.
As a result of environmental impact assessment, the Federal Motorway Authority
opted for the ecologically - preferable but much more expensive route.

POSSIBLE EIA PROCEDURE FOR FEDERAL HIGHWAY PLANNING

Procedures for planning may be outlined as follows:

(a)   Assessment of requirements:

- determination of alternate connexions — location of very sensitive areas between the points to be connected

- examination of the impact on the neighbouring regions — determination of environmental consequences in these areas

- assessment of feasibility — comparisons of the resultant relief with the negative environmental effects

(b)   Determination of approximate alternative routes:

- determination of approximate alternative routes — avoidance of fragmenting, dividing or passing near environmentally sensitive areas

- determination of variations — carrying-out rough analyses and evaluation of all variants; criteria: noise, disjunctive effects on ecologically important areas

(c)   Finding alternative routes and subvariants:

- choice of alternative routes — analysis and evaluation of all alternatives; review of the choice of different options

- determination of subvariants — avoidance of disturbance to the specific character of the topography; consideration of anti-noise measures

- optimization of alternative routes — exact analysis of the evaluation of all subvariants; review of the choice of subvariants

(d)   Consideration, together with other relevant matters:

(e)   Decision.

The procedures set out above and the methods for implementing them should be noted. Implementation of environmental impact assessment procedures, as described below, followed the handbook prepared (in October 1976) for the Federal Environmental Agency. The handbook was recently issued as a first draft and provides a viable basis for future environmental impact assessments in federal highway planning.

A.   PLANNING TO MEET THE NEEDS

In the highway construction sector, the stage of assessing requirements in the planning process is eminently relevant to environmental concerns. For this reason, the feasibility study on the technical possibilities for the improvement of the traffic capacity between two defined points should include, together with the determination of the approximate route of all variants, and the examination of the possibility of improving and widening present highways, an analysis of whether the planned, new construction is really necessary or if additional transport capacity could be provided by an improvement of public transport.

After the traffic requirement has been established, it is imperative to draw
up an over-all picture of the environmental impact expected from a new construction
measure. Particularly sensitive areas (e.g. densely populated areas, recreation
areas in the vicinity of nature reserves, areas important for maintaining an
ecological balance and protected watershed areas) which could disintegrate as a
consequence of the planned measures must be defined first. Negative environmental
effects which may be brought about by placing traffic have then to be studied;
this is especially true of effects which entail increased noise or pollution by
toxic substances. Along with the potential positive results of the projected
construction measure, an over-all picture of the concomitant changes in environmental quality has to be drawn up. On this basis a decision can be reached on
whether the planned measure is acceptable from an environmental point of view.

B.   ENVIRONMENTAL CONSIDERATIONS DURING PRELIMINARY STUDY TO DETERMINE
            THE ROUTE

Once the basic decision to extend a motorway network has been taken, the question
arises regarding which areas are suitable to lay out the highway, in order to
connect two given points. The criteria are:

(a) topography,

(b) technical traffic facilities,

(c) regional planning

In determining approximate and alternate routes, it should be ensured that
settlements, recreation and established ecologically important areas, as well as
watersheds, are not fragmented, adversely divided or closely infringed upon.
The definition of route variants, apart from reference to technical traffic
facilities, should also include initial studies of noise levels and fragmenting
effect for the projected route. The present handbook suggests that a track 1 km
wide on either side of the highway route should be considered as an affected area.
Methods for grading noise pollution and the fragmenting effects an various kinds
of topography are also covered. While it can be assumed that methods for
measuring emissions (CO, Pb, noise etc.) are known, the authors suggest the
following methods for the grading of noise or fragmentation effects in different
topographical areas:

(a) Noise pollution

     Distance zones in metres

     zone 1   up to 150 m

     zone 2   150 to 300m

     zone 3   300 to 1 km

     Weighting

Degree of interference $d = \frac{P}{10} \times NZF$

P = number of people living in the affected zones

NZF = noise zone factor with the values

noise zone	NZF
1	2.5
2	2
3	1

(b) Grading of separation effects

Degrees of interference (d) are suggested for the different topographies. They
vary according to the type of topography, for instance:

topography	degree of interference (d)
Settlement area	0.6
nature reserve	2
national park	1.5
protected landscape	0.6
recreational forest	0.6
watershed area	1.5

By reviewing the preliminary studies, those routes may be excluded which have
been indentified solely for reasons of construction cost or technical traffic
requirements and which are clearly poor choices in terms of negative
environmental impact.

C.   DETERMINATION OF AN OVERALL BALANCE OF ALL ALTERNATIVE ROUTES AS A
          PRECONDITION FOR SELECTING THE ROUTE

In the process of selecting or examining alternative routes, economic, traffic-
related and environmental factors have to be regarded as being on an equal
footing. The authors of the handbook indicated an overall balance of negative
effects for each of the alternative routes and the total of negative impacts on
all affected sections of the area under consideration. On the basis of this
aggregate value, one of the alternative routes can be suggested as the option
which offers the most favourable choice in terms of least environmental impact.
Having determined the optimum route, with respect to minimizing environmental
interference, a comparison can be made between the forecast of the development
entailed by the planned measure and the forecast of the development if that
measure were not carried out.

D.   EXACT ANALYSIS AND EVALUATION OF SUBVARIANTS ON THE BASIS OF A
          DIVISION OF THE PLANNING REGION INTO REFERENCE AREAS

Before choosing subvariants, all parts of the planning area have to be
considered from the view point of environmentally relevant effects. Indirect
effects (dislocation of traffic, changed use of land because of disintegration,
etc.) have also to be included. In addition, all subareas under consideration
should be examined for possible environmental effects related to their utilization
or function (e.g. mainly residential areas, industrial areas, recreational areas,
forests, areas of critical ecological balance, watershed areas). The change in
impact on each of these reference areas has to be determined and graded according
to an evaluation procedure which would be specific in every individual case.

Two examples of this type of grading are given below:

(a) the expected impact on a watershed area can be quantified in the following manner:

$$D \times GWP \ (m^3/ \ sec) \times WQ \times DH$$

where D = drainage area in hectares

GWP = ground water presence or potential deposit

WQ = water quality

DH = distance from the highway in metres

and the weighting

GWP under

$$0.2 \ m^3/sec = 1$$
$$0.2 - 1.0 \ m^3/sec = 2$$
$$1.0 - 5.0 \ m^3/sec = 3$$
$$5.0 - 10.0 \ m^3/sec = 4$$
$$10.0 - 50.0 \ m^3/sec = 5$$
$$over \ 50.0 \ m^3/sec = 6$$

WQ according to water-soil-air determination procedure

(b) the loss of the land surface of a recreational area can be assessed in terms of a benefit value analysis:

$$NSR \times DS \ or \ ASV$$

where NSRL = naturally suited recreational land (hectares)

DS   = degree of suitability

ASV = aggregate suitability value

weighting

ASV

1 = barely suitable   x 0.2

2 = little suitable   x 0.5

3 = suitable   x 1.0

4 = very suitable   x 2.0

5 = highly suitable   x 4.0

By combining the individual environment impacts on all reference areas, the total impact of each subvariant can be obtained. The planner is then in a position to eliminate those subvariants which are comparable in terms of construction cost and technical traffic requirements but which have an unfavourable total impact on the environment. If the various impacts are considered as separate items, the planner also has the opportunity to improve considerably the total impact of a subvariant by means of corrections to individual reference areas.

E.   DECISION

Of course, the value obtained in this way is not objective; it is dependent on the relative grading factors selected. Nevertheless, reaching a decision on a certain route and assessing the related variants based on this method reaches a higher degree of rationality than the usual cost-benefit analysis.

THE PLANNING OF HIGHWAY NO. 202 IN SCHLESWIG-HOLSTEIN AS A CONCRETE
EXAMPLE FOR FUTURE EIA IN FEDERAL HIGHWAY CONSTRUCTION

A.   INITIAL SITUATION

At the request of the Federal Government, the Government of the State of
Schleswig-Holstein planned the construction of a motorway between Kiel and
Rendsburg in the period 1975 to 1977. Heavily travelled and passing through
several small towns, the need to improve B 202 had never been questioned, but the
location of the new highway was. The arguments against the southern route put
forward by the highway construction administration (cheapest variant) centred on:

- division of communities;

- impact of emissions on residential areas;

- encroachments on protected landscapes and parks;

- negative effects on water supply and water ecology;

- impairment of recreational opportunities.

The administration for highway construction proposed a northern variant which
was, however, much more expensive. The Federal Government first favoured the
southern route, but then postponed its decision to allow time for a closer
examination of the impact of both routes on the ecology and on settlement
structures .

The expert report on the improvement of highway B 202 is a model for further
highway construction measures. It is applicable to other planning measures in
terms of both (a) methods (benefit-value analysis) and (b) devices for
implementing them. The expert report incorporated an overall ecological evaluation
of the given situation for the decision between two alternative highway routes.
This report represents an important contribution to the establishment of
environmental impact assessment.

B.   GENERAL PREREQUISITES

The expert report was requested by federal agencies to assist them in defining
their attitude to the two alternative routes. Its purpose was not to question
the necessity of building the motorwy, or to prejudge the choice of the two
proposed routes. This is why predictable effects of the alternative routes
were examined, in keeping with the terms of reference of the respective agencies
involved, from the point of view of landscape ecology, environmental protection
and settlement structures.

C.   DEVELOPMENT OF A TARGET SYSTEM

Owing to the nature of the task, time constraints, and the variable measurability
of ecological, environmental and structural criteria, the authors of the report
had to develop a system which took into consideration:

(a) scientific knowledge of the interacting forces in the natural environment,
and

(b) objectives set by government and local planning with respect to the
various aspects of structural development of the area under discussion.

D.   METHOD

As selection of one of the two alternative routes, on the basis of ecological
criteria, did not allow for an evaluation in terms of money, the authors of the
report decided to employ a benefit value approach. This made it possible to rank,
subdivide and evaluate the elements and characteristics of complex alternative
actions corresponding to the wishes of the competent authorities with regard to a
multi-dimensional objective. By this means, the authors arrived at a much more
complex, although more subjective, result than they would have achieved if, for
example, the classical cost-benefit analysis approach had been used.

E.   QUANTIFICATION OF INDICATIONS

To make the evaluations more easily understandable for the decision-making
authorities, the presentation of criteria, indicators and grades had to be
systematized and consistent. Thus, for each criterion, a list of indicators was
devised on a form which contained the following information:

- name of criterion;
- short description;
- calculation method, including explanation of abbreviations;
- measurement regulation, including description of grading;
- method of obtaining the necessary data;
- evaluation method with references to the corresponding computer map;
- explanations of the detailed description of the gradings carried out
  by the authors.

F.   RESULT OF THE ROUTE COMPARISON

After the evaluations of all 41 criteria were considered, it became evident that
the southern route would impose a greater impact on natural resources and have
greater conflicts with respect to land use than the northern route. This impact
especially concerned residential uses and recreational functions of the natural
environment. It was considered so serious by the authors of the report that they
opted for the northern route even though this implied an additional cost of 17 per
cent. The Federal Ministry for Transport followed this option.

Complex Development Programme for the Balaton Region

K. Lóránt

(Hungary)

Lake Balaton is one of the natural treasures of Hungary. The beauty of the lake and the landscape, and its cultural traditions, make it an attractive area for recreation not only for Hungarians but for foreigners as well. The popularity of the region is illustrated by the fast-growing domestic and foreign tourism, which surpassed 15 million nights in 1978. During hot weather, the weekend population simultaneously present at Lake Balaton reaches 600,000 people, a figure which had been considered earlier to represent an upper limit. This presents a serious challenge for the institutions and experts engaged in the development of the region. Problems related to the development of the Balaton region also occupy a significant place in economy-wide planning.

Planning for the development of the Balaton region started relatively early in the history of Hungarian planned economy, and had already begun in the early 1950s. In the course of this work various regional analyses were made and in 1957 the Balaton Regional Plan was drawn up, in which the limits of the area for recreation and tourism were drawn and land use was regulated. The plan was approved by a resolution of the Council of Ministers. The same resolution created the Balaton Executive Commission, composed of deputy ministers, to co-ordinate the complex development tasks of the Balaton region.

In the Balaton Regional Plan provisions were made for environmental protection, for the regulation of the water level, for the reduction of siltation and for the prevention of industrial waste waters from entering the lake. In the plan, measures aimed at protecting the beauty of the natural landscape also found a place; in order to protect the recreational area and the landscape, the quarrying of basalt in the Badacsony mountain was stopped and several other quarries were also closed down.

Relying on the Balaton Regional Plan, in 1969 the "Central Development Programme (CDP) of the Balaton" was drawn up, mainly covering development projects up to 1975, but also outlining development to 1985. The programme began with forecasts of the growth of the resident and tourist population and assessments of the service institutions necessary for the expected population on this basis. The programme covered the building of hotels and camping sites to accommodate the expected tourists, the development of recreation homes for trade unions and enterprises, and the expected increase of available private accommodation. It determined the necessary consequential development of public utilities (drinking

EIA p

205

water, sewage, energy) as well as the development of other services needed by the
tourist population (beaches, restaurants, shops, cultural, health and sports
establishments, etc.).

The CDP encompassed a wider range of environmental protection problems than the
preceding regional plan. This was justified by the fast increase of the tourist
population in the preceding ten years, the growing burden on the environment in
consequence of industrial and agricultural development in the region, as well as
the advent of new problems or the increased importance of problems earlier
considered negligible.

The central problem of environmental protection remained the control of the water
level of the lake. The agricultural and industrial use of water in the catchment
area of the lake exhausted the permissible use of the Balaton for such a purpose.
In view of this, the National Water Control Board prohibited further agricultural
and major industrial use of the lake water. It was suggested that, in order to
improve the water level of the lake, the water should be complemented from the
river Drava or from other copious sources whose water quality is adequate. At
that time a through examination of the problem from technical and economic
aspects was suggested, but later investigations and considerations of environmental protection prompted experts to discard this solution - independently of
technical and economic feasibility - merely on grounds of water quality.

An important environmental protection problem is the siltation of the lake. In
the catchemnt area of the lake siltation has been accelerated during the last
200 years by deforestation and by agricultural growth. This siltation is
particularly strong at the mouth of the river Zala, in the Keszthely bay; after
river control works in the 1920s   it even increased because of the elimination
of the Little Balaton reeds. The CDP intended to mitigate siltation first by
means of land protection measures in the catchment area of the lake and recommended that the Ministry for Agriculture and Food as well as the National Water
Control Board should work out rules of land protection.

The spread of seaweed also caused much concern. An attempt was made to prevent
its spreading by means of mechanical devices, but without success. The idea was
then raised to prevent the spread of seaweed by letting herbivorous fish into the
lake, but further analyses and experiments were stipulated. Time has justified
this caution, since after a few years, in possession of results of experiments,
experts took a unanimous stand against the grass-eating fish.

The programme also covers the problems of air pollution and noise. Regarding air
pollution, the only industry in the Balaton area causing major air pollution is
a chemical plant. The programme prescribes that, through modernization measures,
air pollution should be reduced to a minimum.

Noise appears for the first time among environmental protection problems. Much
of the problem is caused by railways around the lake, and this is difficult to
eliminate. The case is different with motorboats: their noise can be reduced
by reducing their number. The programme provided for relevant measures and, with
the exception of boats for public use (e.g. for emergencies), motorboats were
banished from the lake. This also reduced the water pollution.

The programme also comprises protection of the natural environment. As quarrying
had already been stopped earlier, the regulations concerning land use came to
the fore. The Government passed a resolution which asked the local executive
councils to prevent, through their construction authorities, undesirable uses
of land and unauthorized constructions.

The CDP of the Balaton region was approved by a Government resolution. In the resolution the Government created an interdepartmental commission for the control and co-ordination of implementation. The chairman of the commission is the head of the ministry for construction and urban development: members are the ministers directly interested (home trade, agriculture and food) as well as heads of functional bodies and ministries (Minister of Finance, President of the National Planning Office), the chairmen of the local councils and the chairman and the secretary general of the Balaton Executive Committee.

The Government resolved that, in order to promote the implementation of the CDP, the interdepartmental commission should be given a definite budgetary allocation and that a certian part of the fund for tourism should be ceded to the commission. Further, the Government resolved that the investment and budgetary means serving the implementation of the programme should be secured by the fourth five-year plan, the annual plans and the relevant annual budgets. The co-ordinated use of these sums is supervised by the interdepartmental commission.

The first stage of the programme was implemented during the fourth five-year plan and ended in 1975. This meant the end of an almost 20-year development period in the region and provided a good opportunity for the competent bodies to analyse and evaluate results, against the original concepts. The critical evaluation stated that, though the targets set in the regional development plan of the Balaton region had been correct, even as seen retrospectively, and had been mostly attained, the growth of tourism exceeded all expectations and the greater intensity of agricultural activity around the lake increased the problems identified earlier.

The analysis dealt in detail with environmental protection in the region, since this could be judged more reliably with the control measurements that had been introduced in the meantime. Environmental protection now covers not only the assessment of the main sources of pollution but, in a complex manner, almost every factor influencing the ecosystem of the whole region. In the course of the analysis, economic development projects were more closely linked with environmental protection (recreational areas, industrial and agricultural activities, transportation).

One of the greatest problems is the agricultural activity in the catchment area of Lake Balaton. Most of the polluting materials reach the lake through eroded soil. In order to reduce soil erosion, proposals were developed for changes in the proportions of different land uses (arable land has to be reduced in favour of grass and forests), for the mode of cultivation (slopes, contour ploughing), and, in general, for using the land everywhere with a view to the inclination of the slopes. Several rules were issued with a view to reducing and preventing pollution from the use of fertilizers and plant protective agents, as well as from animal breeding farms.

Industrial production is still unimportant in the Balaton region. Adequate measures were taken to reduce the pollution caused by the only chemical plant.

The five-fold increase in automobile traffic in the last ten years has led to grave air pollution problems in a few places. No feasible ideas have been developed as yet for their reduction.

Development of the recreational area itself does not cause much concern. Development plans were implemented for the creation of sewage networks and related cleaning works.

The second stage of the CDP of the Balaton region for 1976–1980 was implemented through a wide range of environmental protection tasks, affecting the whole ecosystem. The tasks related to protecting the quality of water in Lake Balaton are summed up in a separate Development Programme of Water Management. This includes a comprehensive plan for the control of the river Zala, which carries almost half of the pollution, and for the protection of the coasts to prevent erosion. Also a concept is being developed for the channelling of sewage into other catchment areas.

The national economic plan for 1976–1980 allocates more than ten billion forints for the implementation of the second stage of the CDP of the Balaton region. One quarter of this sum is allocated directly for environmental protection purposes; the rest is spent on increasing the availability of accommodation and improving the transport and the commercial network. Because of the nature of environmental protection, a part of the latter sum will be spent, indirectly, on projects serving protection.

The programme is complemented by a complex research programme aimed at the environmental protection problems of Lake Balaton and its catchment area. It includes:

- investigation of the factors characterizing, harming or improving the quality of water in the lake;

- economic, legal and other social science research to prepare decisions on the environmental protection of the region;

- examination of the environmental factors affecting tourism and recreation in the recreational area.

Co-ordination of the research programme, carried out in about thirty different research institutes, is the duty of the Hungarian Academy of Sciences. The second stage of the CDP is being implemented now. Its evaluation may be undertaken only after the end of the five-year plan covering 1976–1980, that is, in the early 1980s.

The history of the CDP of the Balaton region shows how the viewpoints of environmental protection have gradually gained ground in national economic planning. The gradually increasing weight of the environmental questions was determined partly by the growing problems themselves, but partly also because the environmental effects had to be better understood before discussion took place on the merits of the problem. This was made possible by the wider research and by the creation of a monitoring network for environmental pollution.

The CDP of the Balaton region clearly shows that the recognition of environmental protection needs is a many-sided task of national economic planning.

(a) Above all, the national economic plan secures the assets and funds for the implementation of an accepted programme for environmental protection and instructs the competent institutions to carry out the programme.

(b) In cases which require a close intertwining of economic development and environmental problems, the Government creates adequate bodies for the co-ordinated implementation of the economic and the environmental protection tasks. (E.g., in the case of the CDP of the Balaton region, the Government created the intergovernmental commission already mentioned, composed of ministers and chiefs of other bodies with national authority.)

(c) Relying on the environmental analyses, the competent authorities work out recommendations or issue instructions regarding the development of individual sectors of the national economy. (E.g., the recommendations regarding the proportions of land use or the mode of cultivation in the catchment area of Lake Balaton.)

(d) The legal rules for environmental protection are also an important part of integrating the protection of the environment into the national economic plan. Legal rules prescribe either the reduction of emission from sources of pollution in conformity with local relations, or prohibit certain activities in general or in certain given areas.

(e) To check on the planned development of the economy, in the field of environmental protection,an adequate information system is also needed. This objective is served by the monitoring network for environmental protection.

Development of the Balaton region also shows how particular disciplines gradually join in the planning process. The first Balaton Regional Plan had only recognized aspects of water management, while the CDP drawn up later already made use of the results of several scientific disciplines, among which biology carried the greatest weight.

Public opinion and the media (writers, journalists, experts) played a particular role in working out the ideas on the development of the Balaton region. As Lake Balaton is perhaps the most characteristic natural treasure of Hungary, ideas about its development have been always accompanied by wide interest. It was public opinion which directed the attention of planners - waning sometimes among the many tasks - again and again to the growing problems of the lake. Public opinion has maintained that the development of the region should be considered a central task for some time longer.

In the course of working out the ideas of development several, often sharp, discussions - attentively followed by the public - took place among experts with greatly diverse opinions. One of the more lively discussions was about the introduction of herbivorous fish. In such cases the official bodies decided on a further investigation of the problem and generally the passage of time and accumulating knowledge has finished the discussion. (In the case mentioned no herbivorous fish were let into the lake.)

To sum up, in Hungary it was the development of the Balaton region where environmental aspects received due regard very early, and where the harmony between economic and environmental protection targets could be relatively well secured by the means available to planning. Thus the drawing up of the CDP of Balaton region also helped to develop a methodology for other fields of economy-wide planning, where the determination of aspects of environmental protection has begun only in recent years.

Development of Impact Studies on Infrastructures for Authorities and Railways in Switzerland: Procedures, Institutions, Methods and Planning

M. Börlin

*(Switzerland)**

1.   POINT OF DEPARTURE

At present administrative procedures for authorizing highway and railway projects in Switzerland usually do not include provisions for impact studies. In its work, the Federal Commission for a comprehensive Swiss transport plan (CGST) ** which deals with all modes of transport, has now included consideration of environmental indicators; the new proposal for an environmental protection law (October 1979) (1) introduces assessment of environmental impact. This paper examines existing administrative procedures, the 1979 legislative proposal and various methods for studying the impact of national highway and railway projects.+

A. National Highways

At the end of 1977, investment costs for the network of national highways - which represents approximately 3 per cent of the total road network - were estimated at 30 to 35 thousand million Swiss francs, of which 55 per cent was for highways already in use, 19 per cent for those under construction, 12 per cent for highways in the planning stage and the remaining 13 per cent for future projects. The main responsibility is borne by the federal road agency (OFR). Recently, opposition has developed to challenge the basic principle of whether certain sections of autoroute should be constructed.

B. Railways

The federal law on railways (2) includes railways of standard gauge and also those of narrow gauge, rack railways, tramways and funicular railways. The present paper, however, considers only standard gauge railways (existing at the end of 1957). These represented a total length of 4,000 km, of which 2,000 km were operated by the federal railways (CFF), plus narrow gauge railways (1,400 km).

* Translated into English by the ECE secretariat with the help of the author.

** Abbreviations used are given at the end of the paper.

+ Comments concerning the implementation of the law are the personal views of the author.

For CFF projects, the paper is concerned only with those involving more than
5,000,000 Swiss francs and which are thereby fairly complex operations.

According to law, the federal permission necessary to construct and operate
a railway is given provided that it is in accordance with the national public
interest, in particular in regard to land-use planning and the protection of
nature and landscape. A more important instrument in this connexion is, however,
the authorization procedures for general projects, and it is with these procedures
that this paper is primarily concerned.

The law on railways deals also with the substitution of other methods of transport.
The substitution of three "little trains" by bus services will therefore also be
discussed.

At present, such a substitution escapes any impact study, either in connexion
with the discontinuation of regional train service or through the licencing of
new road service. The rapid link from St. Gall to Lausanne, a new link from
Basle to Olten through a long tunnel, the rail link to the Geneva airport, the
main line of St. Gotthard and a new railway in the eastern Alps (Coire) are
examples of possible future projects.

C. Evaluation methods in the comprehensive Swiss transport plan

To take account of the inter-relationship that exists among the different
methods of transport, a federal commission was created in 1972 to develop a
comprehensive Swiss transport plan (3). Its mandate requires it to make proposals
to the political institutions on ways that would enable individual and public
transport to contribute to economic and social development.

To assist in this task, a very disaggregated inter-regional transport model was
developed, containing origin and destination analyses at a very detailed scale.
It distinguishes between passenger traffic and various categories of freight.
It includes all modes of transport, and internal, export, import and transit
traffic. From this can be obtained very disaggregated forecasts of transport
in terms of policy instruments (such as infrastructure, investment, prices
and costs) and of such independent variables as population and domestic and
international economies. It is thus possible to simulate an effect, in terms of
traffic projections of specific sections of an autoroute and sections of the rail
system. The simulation model is being used, for example, to obtain significant
information during the official review of the six sections of autoroute referred
to later in this paper.

These transport forecasts are then evaluated in terms of a system of objectives
and indicators (4, 5). It is assumed that the contribution of the transport
network to the quality of life depends on the satisfaction of transport needs, on
network efficiency, the use of energy and indirect benefits such as the balance
between different regions, personal safety and the absence of effects on the
environment, as measured through seven indicators: five air pollutants plus noise
and the protection of landscape values. For air pollutants, concentrations are
compared with permissable values; noise is measured in terms of the population
per hectare; landscape protection is considered through critical areas affected by
the transport network in terms of their fragility (including the significance of
ground-water sources), their agricultural value and their importance from a
nature conservation viewpoint. These indicators are transformed into comparable
units (on scales from 0 to 100) by means of weightings defined by the transport
commission.

The number of environmental aspects that are taken into account is necessarily limited. However, the model does enable account to be taken of the effects of a particular project on the whole of the transport system; the impacts considered are not limited to the segment studies, as is usually the case in traditional impact studies. Rather, one can at the same time compare the impact in the region – where the new link is to be created – with the reduction on impacts due to the diversion of traffic that it causes. This example of impact assessment at the programme level (rather than in terms of one specific project) deserves to be followed with interest.

D. <u>The legislative proposal of October 1979: compatibility of new public projects with environmental protection requirements</u>

According to this proposal, the competent authority will authorize the construction of alternations of installations with potential to pollute the environment, only after having determined whether the development is compatible with the requirements of environmental protection. What is envisaged is neither a special form of authority nor a procedure that seeks to impose supplementary requirements on development. Great importance is, however, given to a comprehensive review of all environmental aspects. New private and public developments, such as autoroutes and railways, will require appropriate reports containing a section on protection measures that are proposed and on acceptable pollution levels. An opportunity would also be provided to justify the project in its own terms, taking account of all relevant interests. Annexes II and III provide a summary of the procedure proposed. This legislative proposal will be discussed by the federal parliament in 1981 or later.

II   NATIONAL HIGHWAYS

The present administrative procedure

In the administrative procedure of the Federal Government relating to national highways, a distinction is made between the overall plan (1:25,000), the general project (1:5,000), the final project (1:1,000) and the project blueprints, as indicated in Annex I (6,7).

The different stages of procedure

The overall plan of national highways has been adopted by a federal decree. In it is determined the overall pattern and the type of national highway to be constructed. Essentially, this task was completed in 1960. These decisions, though final, can be reconsidered by the federal Assembly, as noted below.

The general project plan for a national highway indicates in a fairly precise way the line of the route and the junctions and interchanges. The procedure for this is summarized in Annex II.

The final project provides information on the type, scale and location of the necessary works as well as the details of the technical structure and alignment. Projects prepared by the cantons are put forward for public review for a period of 30 days; the cantonal government takes into account any objections. The final revised projects are then submitted for approval by the federal Department of the Interior. Its approval can be taken to the Federal Council of Ministers for reconsideration.

Details of the construction or detailed project are developed with the competent cantonal authorities, e.g. insofar as they involve the protection of water resources, protection against nuisances (noise, exhaust fumes) and safeguarding of

fisheries. When the project is submitted to the OFR it must be accompanied by
reports from the cantonal services affected. Construction projects must be
approved by the OFR before commencement of construction work and an appeal to
the federal Department of the Interior is possible.

Ecological aspects

In the planning of national highways, ecological aspects enter, in principle,
during the development of projects or through objections raised. Thus, reactions
are invited from the cantonal services affected, the commune governments,
landowners, federal services and the general public, throughout the administrative
procedure (see Annex I). Further, the bodies responsible for the development of
projects are required to take into account ecological considerations. This involves a comparison of the present situation, as compared with various autoroute
alternatives from the points of view of noise, air pollution, landscape and
nature protection, highway safety, and regional development. (8, 9, 10)

Similarly, the Division for the Protection of Nature and Landscape of the federal
Inspectorate of Forests has undertaken a study concerning the alteration of the
Ticino river, made necessary by the construction of the Gotthard national highway. This has given support to standards for vegetation stabilization along a
water course, published in 1973 by OFR (11). However, the relatively strong
initial emphasis given to technical and economic aspects (by comparison with
ecological viewpoints), and the real disadvantages of the protectors of "other
important interests" in terms of the time allowed and the financial resources
required, limit in practice the consideration of ecological elements.

An official re-examination of six particularly controversial sections

Beyond the appeal procedures already described, there are other possibilities
related to public rights: petitions, cantonal initiatives, federal constitutional
initiatives and the activities of members of parliament. One important example is
the decision of the Swiss parliament in 1977 to subject six controversial sections
of highways to an official re-examination. It concerned, inter alia, the urban
sections of the autoroutes of Zurich and Lausanne, the Rawil autoroute linking
the Bernese Oberland to the Rhône valley (70 km) and the connexion between Berne
and Neuchâtel (50 km) via the Zurich-Berne-Lausanne axis. From this examination,
modifications could be made in the autoroute network approved in 1960 by the
Federal Assembly. The controlling agency remains the OFR , in principle, but ecological aspects could be taken into account more vigorously and in the light
of the actual preferences of the people.

Introduction of the impact study

A. Basic arguments

Experience teaches us the information regarding the total effects on the
environment must be combined within a single document when the definition of the
project leaves open a choice between actual alternatives, and when the effects
can already be estimated accurately. The general project mostly meets this condition
At the level of the overall plan, the studies of the comprehensive Swiss transport plan must allow for consideration of requirements for the protection of the
environment while options are still open. At the level of the final project, by
contrast, some indications can still be taken into account regarding aspects
which affect environmental protection (for example: the location of tunnel
entrances, bridges and ventilation works, important with regard to air pollution).
In such cases it would be necessary to provide for a related impact study if the
final project had undergone considerable modification by comparison with the

general project.

Therefore, it seems evident that the impact study foreseen in the proposed legislation should be applied to general projects; Annex II considerations therefore expand on those of Annex I for such projects. Distinctions would be made among main characteristics: (a) the substantive content, (b) the formal procedure and (c) follow-up or monitoring.

The legislator has to choose between a procedure for determining effects on the environment independent of the land-use planning system (c.f. United States) and a syntheses of the two procedures under a single responsible agency (c.f. United Kingdom, Scandinavia). The Swiss legislation makes it clear that it is not concerned with a special authorization. The proposal requires that the administrative structures which already exist, both federal and cantonal, must be utilized to the maximum extent possible and applied to the implementation of the law for the protection of the environment. New authorization procedures are to be kept to a minimum. Thus clearly a unified procedure for both land-use planning and the protection of the environment is applied.

B. Substantive content

(a) Criteria for examination

The present procedure provides for consideration of the following aspects: protection of water and fisheries, control of noise and air pollution and protection of the soil and biosphere. The Inspectorate of Forests is required to comment on these aspects, among others.

The 1979 environmental impact assessment is mainly concerned with the impacts covered by the legislation of October 1979, that is, air, noise, vibrations, radiation, ecologically harmful products and waste. However, impacts dealt with in other laws, that is those affecting water, nature, landscape, fisheries and forests are also taken into account.

(b) Alternatives

Each segment of the autoroute capable of being considered a separate entity must be the object of a separate evaluation so that the choice is not limited by unrealistic constraints. Imbedded in the planning system developed by the CGST which operates at successive scales (1:25,000, 1:5,000 and 1:1,000) the general projects may still leave open a choice, for example, between the use of a tunnel or a bridge (Brugg), between a long tunnel and a shorter one at a higher altitude (Rawil), between different places for motorway access points in the urban area (St. Gall), etc.

At present, the elimination of such variants at the stage of the general project must, in principle, lead to the proposal of only a single solution. Two, or at the very most three, variants can on rare occasions survive to the next stage. In the new procedure, however, the elimination of variants must be done explicitly and for clear reasons. The legislative proposal requires indications of the environmental protection measures that would be required. In principle, these can only be given if one compares an alternative without such measures with an alternative that includes protection measures.

(c) Analysis of anticipated impacts

For each alternative that is related, forecasts are needed of the impact on the categories mentioned in (a) above, if the general project affects these criterea. In this context, the scientific problems arising are numerous and the approach

must be pragmatic. However, standardized diffusion models exist to forecast levels
of noise and air and water pollution. It should be remembered of course that the
impact may have a positive character.

(d) Normative analysis by criteria

Are the probable future impacts of the project identified by the descriptive analysis acceptable or not? In certain cases a response to this question can be given
by making a comparison with existing immission standards.* The impact study,
however, can only be justified as an instrument that goes beyond impacts and
enables account to be taken of a much wider range of effects. Acceptance or rejection
of the impacts should, however, be made explicitly.

(e) Integrated normative analysis

At this stage, if the preceding steps have been followed, there should be available,
for each alternative considered, forecasts of the impacts and their evaluation.
In order to decide on the relative merits of different alternatives, which offer
advantages and disadvantages according to different evaluation criteria, the
criteria themselves must be weighted. In practice, this takes place through
negotiation among the various agencies concerned. The legislative project requires
that, if both the authorities representing the development proposal and those
concerned with the protection of the environment reach a compromise, the case should
go to a higher authority which, without itself taking a decision, should give
instructions on how various interests should be reconciled.

According to the law it is not essential to express environmental impact – and
the lack of damaging effects due to protection measures – in monetary terms.
One might ask whether the legislator should not utilize the opportunity to seek
more compatibility between methods for evaluating negative effects on the environment in terms of the economic importance of projects, and the methods of the
tribunals which are confronted frequently with the task of defining compensations,
for example, for autoroute noise, etc. The opportunity exists also to benefit from
welfare economics theories developed during the last few decades. Such a strategy
would make more practical the principle, set out in the proposed legislation, of
proportionality between the expenses for certain protection measures and the desired
result.

Implicitly, the proposed legislation recognizes the validity of the arguments
presented when it requires that the objectives justifying the desirability of a
project take into account environmental protection interests.

C. Formal procedure and follow-up

Starting with a given situation, and taking into account the proposed legislation
of October 1979, the formal considerations lead to suggestions for implementation.
These steps are summarized synoptically in Annex II. It introduces the concept of
an impact study report. This is an analysis which would be more systematic than
that which could be obtained from the separate statements of the affected agencies.
Presentation in a single document would provide an overview of problems and solutions
A "flexible model" would facilitate the enquiry and the environmental impact assessment to be undertaken by the cantonal highway bureau, which is the regional organ.
One could, however, postulate a "strict model", in which the cantonal bureau would
request the work to be undertaken by an independent party, for example, specialists

---

*   The legislation proposed envisages thresholds applying to air, noise, vibration
and radiation for emissions and to air, noise and vibrations for immission.

from the private sector, accompanied by experts from the federal office for the protection of the environment (OPE).

According to the 1979 legislation proposal, OPE and the cantonal services affected* would work together on the research from the beginning, thus guaranteeing a certain "unity of approach" of the different competent cantonal agencies. Further, the environment would be protected at least cost if impacts were taken into account from the beginning. The different agencies required to collaborate should have the right to propose alternatives to the project as foreseen by the proponent agency.

The participation of interested parties at the level of impact analysis is also achieved through public notices and hearings based on the initial version of an impact study. At present, the reports are sent to the affected federal services, notably to OPE, the Federal Commission for the Protection of Nature and Landscape, the federal Inspectorate of Forests and to the agency for land-use planning, so as to get their opinions. The proposed legislation further envisages that everyone, and particularly the affected organizations, should have access to the results of the environmental impact assessment.

In a more strict approach, however, it would be necessary to supplement this right with the right to express an opinion on the final version of the impact study. This can be achieved as collective interventions are possible. However, the burden of obligatory public hearings should be avoided.

For environmental protection, the difficulties owing to time constraints are well known. These could be avoided by requiring that the public agency responsible for the proposal issue a declaration of intent to undertake an impact study of a particular project. This procedure could be made mandatory, as a preventative ecological policy.

The 1979 proposed legislation does not explicitly envisage scientific appraisal of the impact studies. However, taking into account the fact that the scientific problems in the impact studies can be resolved only in part, such a review should be introduced at the level of implementation. It appears particularly important for the definitive impact study, since anyone can place decisions of the Federal Council, and final proposals of the proponent agency, before another tribunal. Either OPE, a specialized institute or possibly the Swiss Association for Research on the Environment (SAGUF) could take responsibility for this scientific review. The conclusion of the scientific experts would take the form of a report available to everyone. At this stage, there would be available the initial impact study and several sets of commentary and advice. Next would come the development of the definitive version of the impact study which synthesizes the various documents. The legislation proposed would require that this report provide indications on:

(a) the status quo;

(b) the project, including protective measures for safeguarding the environment;

(c) anticipated pollutant loads which would harm the environment;

(d) possibilities for further reducing the pollution load;

(e) objectives justifying the execution of the public project, taking into account environmental protection interests.

---

* In the present procedure the affected services are those for water protection, noise and nuisance protection, landscape and nature protection, forests, land-use planning, fisheries, water management, land-management, water supply, etc.

In a "strict model", it would be necessary to add to this list the following elements

(f) discussion of the definition and choice of alternatives;

(g) significant conflicts, notably for point (e) above, between the anticipated
     effects by individual criteria and the integrated normaltive analysis.

These elements are important in that the final versions of the impact studies and
proposals are prepared by the agency responsible for autoroute construction (OFR)
which is an interested party.

The final version of the impact study must be made available to everyone. At the
present time, the final decision is taken by the Federal Council of Ministers, but
with the option of reviewing a decision already taken. It must, however, be
recognized that the opportunities for intervention at this stage are limited. The
scientific review of the final version of the impact study thus would have considerable weight in terms of overall protection of the environment. The present directiv
envisage that, after the opening of a highway, the cantonal authorities will monitor
the effectiveness of measures taken in critical areas to ensure environmental
protection.* The new law should include this requirement.

III.   RAILWAYS

Present administrative procedure for construction projects

Following the present procedure, described in annex III, the railway company submits
a project to the federal office of transport (OFT) which is the monitoring agency.
The federal Commission for the Protection of Nature and Landscape may collaborate
in the development of the project or express its preliminary opinion, as may the
federal and cantonal services and the communes affected. Finally, OFT accepts
or rejects the project; however, interested parties may of course appeal. One
example of such an appeal was the Swiss League for the Protection of Nature and the
commune of Oberwald which appealed without success to the DFTCE(14). The commune o
Oberwald then appealed again to the Federal Council. The latter declared the appeal
admissible because the section in question, i.e. the access ramp leading from
Oberwald to the Furka tunnel would require a level crossing in a region liable to
avalanches. It would also impact on rivers and forests and sharply divide a
populated zone. The alternative finally accepted required further costs of about
7.5 million Swiss francs.

Plans for the general project of the sorting yard of Zurich-Limmattal were approved
by OFT in 1969. The DFTCE decided to appeal in 1971 and a second appeal to the
federal Council was withdrawn in 1976 following an acceptable compromise. To avoid
destroying a forest that was a recreation area - in order to construct an access
line to this sorting yard - a tunnel was built and the cost divided between the CFF
(250 million) and the canton, the commune and environmental protection interests
(150 million).

These few examples seem to suggest that, at present, no impact study is required bu
that some direct effects on the environment are taken into consideration. In
practice, there is a requirement to negotiate with the various interested parties
at an early stage of planning.

_____

* C.f. the pilot study on the effects of the Geneva-Lausanne motorway (12).

Introduction of the impact study

Impact study must be introduced for general projects, possibly taking account of the environmental analyses of CGST, in a unified procedure linking land-use planning and environmental protection.

As for the substantive content of an impact study, i.e. the criteria to be considered, the alternatives and the descriptive and normative analysis are applicable, mutatis mutandis, as for autoroutes.

The formal procedure is analysed in annex III, based on the considerations for autoroutes. The project requires an impact study to be undertaken by an independent party.

It lets OPE be involved with the research from the beginning. The affected cantonal services must also be able to request studies of alternatives. According to the 1979 proposed law everyone has the right to know the results of the impact study. It is necessary also to provide for public opinion being taken into account in the final version of the declaration of impact. The canton must bring together the opinions of the affected communes. A declaration of intent published at the beginning of the impact study would enable interested groups to review the plans. Scientific review of the impact study would guarantee the comprehensiveness of the approach and would assist research in environmental disciplines. The OFT will synthesize the initial impact study and the positions taken in a final version of the impact study as discussed above (c.f. under autoroutes). It would then be published. The right to appeal is satisfactory at present and should be retained. In following up a project, the effectiveness of environmental protection measures must be monitored.

IV.   CONCLUSIONS

1.   Early objections to the precise line of autoroutes have been overshadowed today by a more basic opposition to the construction of certain sections. Growing preoccupation with environmental protection also requires proponents of railway development projects to take better account of ecological factors than in the past. This reinforces the role of environmental protection in planning infrastructure for highways and railways.

2.   Generally, the CGST, which is responsible for both highways and railways, takes explicit account of environmental protection. Impact studies for sectoral programmes complement the impact studies on projects foreseen in the 1979 proposed legislation.

3.   The impact studies should be introduced at the general project level using a procedure as economical and efficient as possible which covers both land-use planning and environmental protection. The cost of the procedure, however, should be weighed against costs and delays caused when projects do not proceed because of opposition. Certain sections of autoroutes must be re-examined. In this regard, it would be useful to undertake appropriate impact studies to serve as pilot projects for a more general introduction of this technique for the protection of the environment.

4.   A similar requirement for an impact study should be envisaged if the final project has undergone considerable change in terms of the general project plan.

5.   The importance of specifying the evaluation criteria, the explicit distinction between descriptive and normative analyses, and the consideration of alternatives to the original project, all follow from an analysis of the substantive content of impact studies.

6.   Annexes II and III deal with the formal procedures and suggest ways to strengthen the 1979 proposed legislation.

7.   Some of these conclusions could lead to reformulation of the article concerning impact studies in the 1979 proposed legislation. Others affect the implementation. Finally, one could conceive a third level of action, which would involve the preparation of guidelines or general methodological models for carrying out an impact study (criteria to be considered, etc.). These could be based on experience gained during the re-examination of the six controversial sections of motorways.

Abbreviations

B. Cant.AR	Bureau cantonal des autoroutes
CFF	Chemins de fer fédéraux
CGST	Conception globale suisse des transports
EIA	Etudes d'impact
OCPE	Office cantonal de protection de l'environnement
OFR	Office fédéral des routes
OFT	Office fédéral des transports
OPE	Office fédéral de la protection de l'environnement
SFRD	Service fédéral des routes et des digues
DFTCE	Département fédéral des transports et communications et de l'energie

Annexe I

Routes nationales - Procédure actuelle ordinaire a/

	Plan directeur 1 : 25,000	Projet général 1 : 5,000	Projet définitif 1 : 1,000	Projet de constr. (Projet détaillé) 1 : 1,000
21 Agence directrice (Commettant)	OFR			
22 Agence mandatée	OFR	B.Cant.AR	B.Cant.AR	B.Cant.AR
24 Collaborations	Services féd. intéressés: Services canton. intéressés	Services canton. intéressés		Services canton. intéressés
26 Préavis		Services canton. intéressés Communes Propriétaires fonciers Services féd. intéressés	Enquêtes publiques	Services canton. intéressés
28 Propositions	Conseil féd.	OFR	OFR	B.Cant.AR
29 Approbation	Assemblée féd.	Conseil féd. b/	Dept. féd. Intérieur	OFR
2.12 Appel	Assemblée féd.	Conseil féd., Tribunal féd.	Conseil féd.	Dept. féd. Intérieur

a/ Numérotation: D'après l'annexe 2

b/ Une initiative populaire rejettée en 1978 déléguait ce pouvoir décisionnel à l'Assemblée fédérale avec possibilité de référendum populaire.

EIA q

Routes nationales – Procédure pour projet général 1 : 5,000   Annexe II

	Situation actuelle a/	Projet octobre 1979	Propositions d'exécution du Rapporteur
2 Procédure formelle			
21 Agence directrice (commettant)	OFR	OFR	OFR
22 Agence mandatée	B.Cant.AR	B.Cant.AR	B.Cant.AR
23 Déclaration d'intention	Non	Non	Oui
24 Ei Version initiale, collaborations	Services canton. intéressés	Services canton. intéressés	Services canton. intéressés
25 Ei Version initiale, enquête et rédaction	Pas de Ei	Ei préparée par B.Cant.AR	Ei préparée par partie indépendante
26 Ei Version initiale, préavis, auditions	Commune: Cant., Services canton. intéressés. Services féd. intéressés	Commune, Cant., Services canton. intéressés, Services féd. intéressés. Legitimation de chaque privé et association nationale intéressée	Commune, Cant., Services canton. intéressés, Services féd. intéressés Légitimation comme dans le projet
27 Ei Version initiale, contrôle scientifique	Non	Non	Oui, par établ. de recherche
28 Ei procédure de révision: finalisation et contenu de la version définitive: Propositions	OFR	OFR: Contenu Ei spécifié	OFR: Contenu Ei spécifié
29 Approbation	Conseil fédéral	Conseil fédéral	Conseil fédéral
2.10 Ei version finale: Contrôl scientifique	Non	Non	Oui, par établ. de recherche
2.11 Ei version finale: possibilité d'appel b/	Communes: chaque privé et association intéressée	Communes: chaque privé et association intéressée	Communes: chaque privé et association intéressée
2.12 Ei version finale: décision d'appel: Instance	Conseil fédéral	Conseil fédéral	Conseil fédéral
3 Suivi, monitoring	Efficacité des mesures de protection	Non	OCPE

a/ Voir annexe I;   b/ Possibilité de lancer une petition, etc.

Chemins de fer – Procédure pour projet de construction[a]   Annexe III

	Situation actuelle	Projet octobre 1979	Propositions d'exécution du Rapporteur
21 Autorité de surveillance	OFT	OFT	OFT
22 Initiateur: rédacteur du projet général	Société concessionnaire	Société concessionnaire	Société concessionnaire
23 Déclaration d'intention	Non	Non	Oui
24 Ei version initiale, collaborations	Services fédéraux intéressés[b]	Services fédéraux intéressés[b]; OPE	Services fédéraux intéressés[b]; OPE; Services canton. intéressés
25 Ei version initiale; enquête et rédaction	Pas de Ei	Ei préparée par Société concessionnaire	Ei préparée par partie indépendante
26 Ei version initiale, préavis, auditions	* Service féd. intéressés[b], OPE, Dél. à l'aménagement du territoire, * Services canton. intéressés * Communes	Services Fédéraux et cantonaux et communes comme actuellement; légitimation comme dans le projet; privé et association intéressée	Services fédéraux et cantonaux et communes comme actuellement; légitimation de chaque privé et association nationale intéressée
27 Ei version initiale, contrôle scientifique	Non	Non	Oui, par établ. de recherche
28 Ei procédure de révision: finalisation et contenu de la version définitive; Propositions	OFT	OFT: Contenu Ei spécifié	OFT: Contenu Ei spécifié
29 Approbation	OFT	OFT	OFT
2.10 Ei version finale: Contrôle scientifique	Non	Non	Oui, par établ. de recherche
2.11 Ei version finale: droit d'appel	Cantons, communes et société concessionnaire. Les assoc, privées de protection de l'environnement[c]	Comme actuellement	Comme actuellement
2.12 Ei version finale: Décision d'appel: Instance	1.e instance: DFTCE 2.e instance: Conseil féd.	Comme actuellement	Comme actuellement
3 Suivi, monitoring	Non	Non	OCPE

a/ Voir les positions de l'annexe II; b/ Comm. féd. pour la protection de la nature et du paysage; Inspection féd. des forêts.

c/ Ces dernières uniquement concernant la protection de la nature et du paysage. Les recours de privés ne sont pas admis.

Environmental Aspects of the Installation of a Pulp Mill

P. von Boqushawsky

(Finland)

INTRODUCTION

Environmental impact assessment procedures in Finland are generally incorporated into the physical planning process (Planning and Building Act of 1958). Water management and planning processes are based upon the Water Act of 1962; health protection management is based on the Public Health Act of 1965. Comprehensive legislation concerning environmental impact assessment has, so far, not been developed in Finland. However, the revision of the Planning and Building Act is under way and will probably lead to a thorough integration of regulations concerning environmental impact assessment in planning and building legislation.

In this report on the environmental aspects of the installation of a pulp mill, the problems owing to inadequate environmental legislation will be analysed. However, the case study describes a way of dealing with the difficulties arising from heterogenous environmental legislation as well as the difficulties in linking the planning and decision-making process of a private enterprise to supervisory actions and decision-making at various levels of public administration. The report, therefore, focuses on the process-related, more or less voluntary, environmental impact assessment actions taken by a pulp company; it also examines government-induced assessments and monitoring systems.

For the sake of clarity and readability, the report proceeds chronologically with few exceptions. For the same reasons, the report is, of course, schematic and does not cover all details in the planning, assessment and monitoring process. As a case study, it is primarily a qualitative evaluation of the procedures used in the assessment process. Quantitative data are provided only to illustrate the magnitude of the project described.

THE PULP MILL

A. General Description of the Pulp Mill and the Construction Project

The planning of the chemical pulp mill was begun in the early 1970s. It was designed to be one of the biggest sulphate cellulose plants in Finland, with an annual output of 250,000 tons of bleached pulp. The production units of the plant were designed to form a single production line, so that the size of the separate units would be considerable. From an environmental point of view, this would provide some advantages, as emission cleaning systems could be designed to operate more effectively.

The production units of the pulp mill may be summerised as follows:

(a) Wood handling department

- incoming logs;
- hardwood debarking unit;
- chipping, chip screening and storage.

(b) Pulp Mill proper

- cellulose cooking;
- washing;
- screening;
- bleaching;
- stock cleaning;
- drying;
- baling lines.

(c) Power Plant

- evaporation plant;
- soda recovery boiler;
- steam boiler;
- production of tall oil;
- extraction back pressure and condensing turbine.

(d) Chemical Plant

- preparation of cooking and bleaching chemicals;
- lime recovery;
- reception and storage of new industrial chemicals;
- mechanical and chemical treatment of fresh water.

(e) Waste Water Plant

- clarification;
- handling of fibre sludge;
- aeration of waste water;
- treatment of malodorous condensates.

In addition to the pulp mill itself, accommodation in 280 new flats was to be built in the vicinity of the plant together with roads, railroads, tunnels and public service buildings.

B. Environmental Requirements of the Pulp Mill and Main Environmental Impact Sources

The operation of the pulp mill requires that the physical environment should fulfil certain technical conditions. On the other hand, the construction impact and emissions from the plant into the environment had to be evaluated at an early stage of planning to make a proper siting decision possible.

In this case study, the main requirements of the pulp mill, affecting the siting decision, were as follows:

(a) manpower reserves;

(b) good harbour facilities;

(c) economical and continuous supply of logs;

(d) developed transport network and other infrastructure;

(e) abundant fresh water supply;

(f) flexible energy supply.

The fresh water supply (1.3 m^3 a second), raw material supplies and harbour facilities were considered to be especially crucial factors influencing the siting-decision.

The main environmental impacts resulting from construction activity and emissions from the operating plant were estimated as follows:

(a) excavation and transport of earth, blasting of rocks;

(b) impact from road and railroad construction on nature; traffic impact;

(c) general impact on landscape;

(d) effects on ground-water level and fresh water demand;

(e) effects on water quality and fisheries from waste water discharge;

(f) impact from estimated quantities of air pollutants;

(g) socio-economic impact on existing social structure.

The impacts of fresh water requirements, waste water discharges and air pollutants as well as impact from transport were considered to cause most environmental concern.

ENVIRONMENTAL CONSIDERATIONS AFFECTING THE CHOICE OF LOCATION FOR THE PULP MILL

The pulp company conducted the investigations and search for an environmentally, technically and economically convenient site with emphasis on, inter alia, the critical criteria in terms of efficient operation: since fresh water, raw material supply and harbour facilities were dominating aspects from the company's point of view, the very small town of Kaskinen (Swedish name: Kaskö), with 1,800 inhabitants on the west coast of Finland, was tentatively chosen as the site for the planned pulp mill. According to this study, the following circumstances, among others, favoured Kaskinen compared with other alternatives:

(a) raw material supply from the southern province of Vaasa;

(b) infrastructure (road and railroad network);

(c) year-round deep harbour facilities in Kaskinen;

(d) manpower reserves in the predominantly agrarian region.

Even though the environmental considerations affecting the preliminary decision-making regarding the siting of the mill were brief in scope and the technical and ecnomic aspects dominated, the procedure could be regarded as appropriate at this stage of the planning process. A demand for a detailed environmental impact assessment procedure for every siting alternative would hardly be necessary. The natural conditions in Finland usually provide several environmentally-equal siting alternatives for industrial projects. Environmental impact assessment procedures thus seldom have a specific effect on the location decision.

Due to the environmental legislation, however, the company's decision on the preferable site was followed by a complex concession and permission process based on the main environmental acts: the Planning and Building Act, the Water Act and the Public Health Act. In this process, detailed environmental impact studies were required as a basis for decision-making by administrative and governmental bodies. It should be pointed out that this process could have led to a decision rejecting the company's request for siting permission, forcing the company to choose another siting alternative.

After the tentative location decision in this specific case, the pulp company started the necessary investigations and research work on the environmental impact studies, in co-operation with and under the supervision of the public authorities concerned. The scope and content of the assessment procedures and their integration in the general planning and decision-making process are described in the following section.

ENVIRONMENTAL STUDIES ON THE IMPACT FROM THE CONSTRUCTION AND OPERATION OF THE PULP MILL

A. The Legal Framework

According to the Planning and Building Act, land-use planning and building activities in a municipality are directed by the municipal board. Building is today controlled by separate bodies, by magistrates in cities and boroughs and by municipal building boards in rural municipalities.

The municipality draws up and approves the land-use plans at municipal level. These are the master plan, the town plan and the building plan. It also approves shore plans which generally are drawn up by land owners. Depending on the size of the municipality, planning is performed either by municipal officials or commissioned from consultants. Municipal planning can be directed by a special planning board, or it can be directly controlled by the municipal board. The final approval of plans lies with the municipal council.

At different stages of planning, landowners have the opportunity to express their wishes concerning the planning. To ensure that all requirements are taken into consideration they can also use a two-stage system for application of amendments. This system is established by law. The possibilities to influence decisions open to those other than land owners are more restricted. Any member of the municipality can, however, have an indirect influence on planning via representative democracy. Furthermore, a member of the municipality can make an appeal and thus open the decision of the municipal council to examination by State authorities with regard to both its legality and its expediency. The existing opportunities available to members of the municipality have been felt to be insufficient and many proposals have been made in order to expand them. Special exphasis has been given to the fact that members of the municipality should have the possibility to influence both planning at an earlier stage and also decisions affecting the immediate living environment at the implementation stage.

There are good basic premises for the integration of land-use planning at the municipal level with environmental and socio-economic planning, since the municipality itself is the executive unit using independent economic power. Decisions on approval of plans at municipal level have to be submitted, with some exceptions, to ratification by a State authority. The Ministry of the Interior can also order that a plan be drawn up. Responsibility for building permissions, building controls, and also for controls on the existing building stock, lies with the building inspection authorities at the municipal level. The building inspection receives considerable financial assistance from the State and its administration is connected to State administration. Directions are given in the building permissions on whether special drawings such as drawings on structure or ventilation should be inspected while the work is done. It is also made known which surveys have to be made before the building can be used.

According to the Water Act and Water Decree certain conditions, concerning both public and private interests and both benefits and damage, must be met before a permit can be granted for the projects. A permit cannot be granted when the action to be taken is detrimental to public health, causes detrimental changes in the natural conditions of the environment which are considerable and far-reaching, or substantially impairs local habitations or occupations. If the conditions set out in the reports are met, the water court grants a permit for implementation of the project which includes the related rights, and may also require the applicant to observe certain obligations in the form of permit terms. The latter facilitates the adoption of the measures to be taken prior to use of the water course, with both public and private interests in mind. Waste water discharge permits are generally issued for a set period of time; they can later be revoked or the terms themselves can be changed. Compensation to be paid is generally determined at the same time the permit is granted. In principle, compensation for damage which can not be prevented by specifications in the permit terms must be paid to the party in question.

Legal proceedings for a project involving the use of water may be started with an application made to a water court. This does not apply to less important projects which come under the jurisdiction of water boards or casual inspection boards for ditching activities. There are detailed regulations in the Water Decree on the specifications which must be appended to the application and on the plan for the project. The water courts have various means of informing those whose rights or interest are involved in an application, depending on the type and extent of the matter; these means are based on public notification and special announcements.

In matters of sufficient importance, the water court sets in motion a special inspection procedure to deal with the application. The purpose is to prepare the water court's decision in the matter. An inspection board is created composed of an engineer appointed by the National Board of Waters and two trustworthy persons from the municipality in question. At the request of the engineer, the National Board of Waters may assign one of its civil servants with special knowledge, e.g. of fish biology, limnology, process technology or landscape planning, to assist in the inspection. The water court may assign its own legal secretary or other expert to assist in the inspection. The inspection board examines project plans and clarifies the nature and extent of the damage which may be caused by the project. Both the legal conditions of the permit and the permit terms are clarified.

According to the Public Health Act of 1965, a communal body, the Public Health Board, is responsible for, among other things, the quality and hygiene of the environment. The lack of a comprehensive air protection act in Finland has made it necessary to utilize the Public Health Act as a legal base for air quality and noise abatement objectives at the communal level. The Ministry of the Interior co-operates regularly with the Public Health Boards in questions concerning air protection measures, noise abatement and impact assessments.

According to the Public Health Act, the communal Public Health Board has the right to demand an assessment of the impact of an action on the air quality and noise level as well as related environmental damage in the commune. The Public Health Board can also demand technical measures for the prevention of air pollution in the area as well as monitoring of the air quality. These demands are expressed in the so-called siting permission, which is required when an action is taken that may be damaging to air quality. In case, however, the action is taken in an area allocated for this kind of activity in the detailed land-use plan, the Public Health Board has the right only to express its opinion in the planning process. In every case, the Public Health Board has the right to close down a plant which apparently is causing damage to the human environment.

B.   Preliminary Study of the Impact on the Environment at the Construction Stage

The pulp company assigned a firm of consultants to investigate the scope and the impact of the construction work in the planned pulp mill site at Kaskinen. The investigation, primarily technical in character but of course interesting from an environmental point of view, was needed for the handling of the company's application for a concession from the Ministry of Commerce and Industry.

The study gave an impression of the scope of the construction project and the expected changes in the environment:

(a)   earth excavations: 180,000 m^3;

(b)   rock blastings: 210,000 m^2;

(c)   construction of 4.7 km of new roads;

(d)   construction of 6.0 km of new railroads;

(e)   clearing and cementing of a 90,000 m^2 storage area;

(f)   enlargement of an existing fresh water regulation basin to 19 million m^3 and the building of a new reservoir in the estuary of Närpiönjoki River; and

(g)   construction of approximately 600,000 m^3 of factory buildings.

A project of this magnitude is likely to have profound environmental and socio-economic impact on a predominantly agrarian community with a small population, as well as on the region as a whole. Therefore the company, in co-operation with the authorities, initiated base-line research concerning the state of the vegetation, water areas and air quality. These investigations were conducted by, inter alia, Oulu University, the Finnish Pulp and Paper Research Institute, the Central Office of Meteorology, the National Board of Waters as well as private consulting companies. The Public Health Board, common to the two neighbouring municipalities of Kaskinen and Närpiö (Swedish name, Närpes), furthermore initiated a study, inter alia, on the mercury content of pike in the waters outside the planned pulp mill. The contents and scope of these studies will be elaborated in the following sections.

C.   Specific Environmental Studies

The environmental studies and investigations conducted during the planning and construction of the pulp mill may be divided into two categories:

(a) base-line studies on the natural or prevailing state of the environment, also providing background data for the impact monitoring programme, and

(b) analyses and assessment concerning the impact on the environment from estimated pulp mill emissions, and waste water loadings, _inter alia_, serving the planning of the emission control technology.

1. Studies on the water quality and fisheries

The following studies were conducted to provide basic knowledge for the planning and decision-making process.

(a) Hydrographic surveys of the waters outside the planned plant. These surveys included investigation of the structure of the sea bottom, and the direction, temperature and fluctuations in the bottom streams as well as the surface water streams under different weather conditions and times of the year. The results of these basic investigations were used to estimate the effluent discharged and the transport and dilution rate of the waste water coming from the waste water treatment plant via the aeration lagoon in the Tallvarpen bay as well as for the design of the waste water treatment plant. The investigations were of importance for the planning and design of the waste water plant and the water quality monitoring programme.

(b) Surveys of the waterways and fish population in the vicinity of the planned pulp mill. These surveys included studies on the sea bottom flora and fauna as well as on the age distribution of fish as a result of fishery in the area. These surveys were of importance mainly to obtain basic knowledge of the aquatic ecosystems for long-term monitoring studies.

(c) The Public Health Board of Kaskinen and Närpiö initiated a survey of the mercury content of pike in the waters outside Kaskinen. The survey was conducted in 1976-1977 immediately before the plant was to be started. This survey was also intended to serve long-term monitoring needs.

(d) On the basis of these preliminary results and estimates concerning the amounts and contents of waste waters, the company conducted an assessment of the waste water impact on the aquatic environment in several alternative waste water discharge situations.

The integration of the results of these investigations into the planning and decision-making process is described later in this case study.

2. Studies on vegetation and landscape

The following studies were conducted:

(a) General survey of the impact on the landscape from the construction of the plant, roads, railroads, storage areas, etc., as well as on the ground-water level. The impact was considered to be substantial but bearable. The area affected has, previously, been a popular recreational area for the local population. The loss could, however, be compensated quite easily elsewhere in the vicinity of the community. Impact on groundwater level was considered to be minute due to the rock foundation. The fresh water basins planned were considered not to affect the landscape as they could be naturally integrated in the existing milieu.

(b) The company ordered a comprehensive base-line study programme on the vegetation from the Botanical Institution of Oulu University, with fieldwork in 1975 and 1976. The vegetation study programme included the following investigations and stages:

- a qualitative inventory of the plant species in the possible impact
  area;

- selection of eleven representative test plots for monitoring
  investigations;

- detailed inventory and description of the eleven test plots,
  especially the lichen populations used as bio-indicators;

- laboratory tests on lichen chlorophyll content, appearance, electric
  conductivity, pH and sulphur dioxide content;

- sulphur dioxide content of pine needles;

- transplantation of lichens from one plot to another;

- tests on transplanted lichens: size, appearance, chemical tests and
  fluorescence microscope analyses.

The objectives in these investigations were to provide data on the conditions
of the terrestrial ecosystems before the operation of the pulp mill. The results,
therefore, serve the needs of the monitoring programme described later in this
paper. In addition, the results can be used as a reference for the technical
emission and dust downfall measuring system created around the plant.

3. Studies on air quality

The annual energy consumption of the planned pulp mill was estimated at 25,000 to
40,000 tons of heavy fuel oil. In addition, the plant was designed for an
alternative use of about 50,000 tons of bark residues and up to 130,000 tons of
dried peat. The amount of oil used was to depend on the supply of usable peat.
Thus, the energy production was estimated to produce quite large quantities of
sulphur oxides as well as dustfall. In addition to the emissions from the energy
producing unit, the pulp mill proper and the chemical plant were expected to
produce hydrogen sulphide (H_2S) and other foul-smelling sulphur compounds. These
emissions presuppose, of course, adequate emission control systems as well as
an emission monitoring programme.

The company initiated a series of base-line investigations of the air quality
level in the Kaskinen-Närpiö area. In co-operation with the Ministry of the
Interior, the Finnish Central Office of Meteorology and the Public Health Board
in Kaskinen and Närpiö, the company ordered an air quality survey from the
Finnish Pulp and Paper Research Institute. The survey was of particular
importance as it seemed likely that emissions from a power plant in the town
of Kristiinankaupunki as well as from Swedish industrial plants at the west
coast of the Gulf of Botnia already had an impact on the ambient air quality.

(a) The air quality measurements were conducted at seven different points
between 1 and 10 kilometres from the planned pulp mill. The measuring points
were located on the basis of a diffusion model for the area, developed by the
Finnish Central Office of Meteorology. The survey was carried out over a six-
month period. The survey covered sulphur oxides as well as suspended particulates.
The results from the emission measurements were to be used as references for an
elaborate air pollution prevention programme, including control technology,
emission measurements and continuous emission measurements as well as
possibilities to alter the technical processes.

(b) In addition to the sulphur oxides and suspended particulates surveys, the
company initiated a hydrogen sulphide emission control measurement programme,
intended to test the control technology of the pulp mill.

4. Studies on noise level and traffic impact

The expected noise level in the vicinity of the plant as well as along the roads and railroads was estimated on the basis of experience from comparable plants and the expected traffic intensity. As the plant was to be situated at a distance of approximately two kilometres from the nearest residential area and the heavy traffic to and from the plant was to be guided around the community centre, the expected noise level was regarded as moderate or low.

5. Socio-economic studies

The socio-economic studies conducted in the planning process of the pulp mill were of the following kinds:

(a) Supply of raw material (timber) in the southern Vasa region. The income of the forest owners in the region, as well as their interest in efficient timber production, was expected to rise.

(b) The impact on employment in the region as well as the impact on manpower structure and training was regarded as positive.

(c) The impact on the important agrarian trades and fisheries in the region (for instance, tomato and cucumber cultivation) was not considered harmful, as most of the sensitive crops were cultivated in greenhouses and not directly exposed to dust downfall or odours.

(d) The overall impact on the social structure was considered positive; the percentage rise in population in the town of Kaskinen (approximately 25 per cent) was considered to strenthen the public service supply of the region.

The socio-economic studies were not comprehensive or exhaustive. However, the planning and decision-making system in Finland - as well as in the other Nordic countries - gives the local, elected government bodies sufficient authority to decide on matters concerning the economic or social development of their area. Therefore, extensive social or socio-economic studies in connexion with the siting and planning of isolated industrial projects are seldom necessary, unless the project is obviously contradictory to the development objectives of the community.

INTEGRATION OF THE ENVIRONMENTAL IMPACT ASSESSMENT INTO THE PLANNING
AND DECISION-MAKING PROCESS

According to legislation in Finland, a company which wants to build a new plant should, inter alia, apply for a concession from the Ministry of Commerce and Industry, siting permission from the Public Health Board of the municipality, a permit decision from the Water Court and building permission from the Building Board of the municipality.

If there is a detailed plan (town plan, building plan) for the area in question, the siting permission is not needed; the Public Health Board must, however, be given the opportunity to express its opinion on the matter to the Building Board before the building permission is granted. The claims of the Public Health Board may also be considered in the conditions of the building permission. As there is no comprehensive air protection legislation in Finland so far, the Public Health Act and the local Public Health Board are of great importance in air pollution and noise abatement questions. An Air Protection Act is under preparation in the Ministry of the Interior.

The legal proceedings concerning a project involving the use of water - such as a pulp mill- start with an application directed to the Water Court. In the Water

Act and the Water Decree there are detailed regulations on the specification
which must be appended to the application and the project plan. Projects with a
profound impact on the environment lead the Water Court to demand the special
inspection procedure already described.

The inspection procedure proceeds as follows:

Initiation: - application;

             - Water Court orders an inspection to be made and requests the
                National Board of Waters to assign a member to the Board.

Inspection: - assignment of the other members of the Inspection Board;

             - examination and completion of the plan and drafting the
                inspection document;

             - displaying the plan and the inspection documents; public
                announcement;

             - drafting a statement by the Inspection Board; public
                announcement.

Permit   - by the Water Court
decision

It should be pointed out however, that the National Board of Waters may – at the
request of the member – assign a specialist on, for example, fish biology,
limnology, process technology or landscape planning to assist in the inspection.

In this case study, the pulp company applied to the Ministry of Commerce and
Industry for a concession in 1973. The application contained, in addition to
detailed economic and technical specifications, a statement of the objectives and
principles of the planned pulp mill and also a brief assessment of the socio-
economic and environmental impact of the enterprise, described above. Due to the
scope and nature of the planned pulp mill, the application was discussed in the
State Council.

The company applied to the Water Court for a permit in 1974. In the Court's
decision, the principal conditions concerning discharge of waste waters from the
pulp mill were as follows:

    - the company was required to keep the discharge of suspended solids and
       the BOD_7-load under a certain fixed limit in 1977 and 1978;

    - in 1979 and following years discharges must be even lower,
       approximately half the initial level of 1977 and 1978;

    - the waste water treatment plant should be maintained to operate as
       effectively as possible;

    - the company must carry out the above-mentioned plans and measures to
       further reduce the waste water load on the eco-systems; and

    - monitor and investigate the amount and quality of the waste water and
       its impact on the aquatic environment. The monitoring programme should
       be accepted by the National Board of Waters.

With regard to air protection conditions, as there was no detailed physical plan
(town plan) for the siting area in question, the company applied for siting
permission from the Public Health Board of Kaskinen and Närpiö. The Public Health
Board, with assistance of the Department of Environmental Protection in the

Ministry of the Interior and the Central Office of Meteorology, as well as the
National Health Board, issued a series of conditions for the granting of the
siting permission. The conditions included the demands for environmental surveys
to be made, mentioned above, as well as a number of technical control measures
to be implemented at the plant before operation.

The conditions issued by the Public Health Board included, inter alia, that the
company should:

- prepare a programme for the continous monitoring of emissions into the
  air (sulphur oxides, hydrogen sulphide and particulates);

- make periodical surveys concerning the state of the vegetation in the
  area with lichens as a bio-indicator;

- prepare, in accordance with guidelines given by the Finnish Institute
  of Meteorology and the Ministry of the Interior, a programme for air
  quality monitoring (the air quality monitoring programme included the
  seven control stations in the vicinity of the plant);

- initiate a monitoring programme for periodic noise measurements; and

- bear the expenses for the monitoring and survey programmes.

The company accepted these conditions and siting permission was granted by the
Public Health Board in 1975.

The size of the pulp mill project gave the Ministry of the Interior reasons to
demand a detailed physical plan for the planned industrial area before the
building permission was granted. The City Council of Kaskinen decided on the
subject in 1974 and the planning proceeded simultaneously with the environmental
surveys. The physical plan covered the industrial area proper as well as the
related infrastructure network. Alternative solutions were discussed between
the company and planning and building authorities. Possible delays in the
company's building schedule were averted by an intermediate building permission
for the central parts of the plant. The decision to make a physical plan for
the area did not eliminate the need for a special siting permission by the
Public Health Board, as the physical plan merely served to organize the industrial
area proper. The building permission, however, was granted after consultations
with the Public Health Board.

The construction of the pulp mill was completed in 1977, when it began to operate.
First results from the various monitoring systems indicate an environmental
impact lower than expected in the assessment. The long-term and secondary effects,
however, can be evaluated only after many years of operation. Reaction among
the local population has been predominantly positive during the first months of
operation.

The Search for Optimum Coastal Locations for Oil Refineries

G. A. Walker

(Ireland)

INTRODUCTION

Unlike many other European countries Ireland suffers from a deficiency in refining capacity and the Irish Government has adopted a policy which aims at the development of additional capacity to the extent that this can be done competitively (1). The search for suitable locations, which is the theme of the present paper, and the testing of the feasibility of such developments are current problems even though the probability of similar developments elsewhere in Europe may be quite remote.

In the first part of this paper there is a brief introduction to the Irish economy and likely growth patterns. The legal and administrative structures are also outlined in this section. This is followed by an analysis of the demand for energy with particular reference to petroleum. The last section outlines the approach to the site selection process including descriptions of refinery characteristics, site identification and site assessment.

The analysis which is summarised in this paper was undertaken as research project - "A Study of Suitable Coastal Locations for Oil Refineries" (2) by An Foras Forbartha, the National Institute for Physical Planning & Construction Research. The study is not an environmental impact study as generally understood but is an essential first step in the total planning process. The preparation of an environmental study for the most likely sites would normally follow the completion of the present analysis.

BACKGROUND

A. Population Trends

In 1841 the population of the State exceeded 6 million persons; by 1961 it had fallen to 2.8 million. In addition to this national trend, there were two marked redistributions within the state: from rural to urban areas and from the West to the East. In 1936, the aggregate urban population (i.e. persons living in settlements of over 1,500 persons) represented only 37.0% of the total; by 1971 this proportion had increased to 52.1%. Similarly in 1936 the East Region (centred on Dublin) contained 25.8% of the total population while the West accommodated 11.1%. By 1971 the West's share had declined to 8.7% while the East's had increased to 35.7%.

---

* This seminar paper was abridged for publication.

EIA r

237

More recently the decline in the national population has been halted and the
estimated population in 1977 is 3.2 million which is about the 1901 level.
This abrupt change in the long-term trend is due primarily to the elimination of
migration, combined with improved economic conditions which permit younger
marriages and a more rapid rate of family formation. The net result is that the
population is now one of the youngest and fastest growing in Europe: 16% of the
male population is under 16 years of age (U.K. 11.9%). As a result of these
factors the population is expected to be between 3,486,000 and 3,514,000 in
1986 with consequent impacts on the demand for employment opportunities, housing,
social and physical infrastructure, etc. A further consequence of migration
in earlier periods is that Ireland now has a population weighted at both ends,
yielding a dependency ratio of 73.7% (U.K. 59.7%, France 60.3%).

B.   Employment Structure

In 1926 53.5% of the total persons at work were engaged in agriculture, 12.9%
in manufacturing industry and 33.6% in the service sector. By 1971 this
distribution had changed to 25.9%, 30.6% and 43.5% respectively. Of course it
will be noted that these proportions relate to a declining labour force because
of the reduction in the population to 1961 and because of a change in the age
structure thereafter. These factors combined with the relatively low female
participation rate result in an activity rate which at 35.7% in 1976 is also
low by European standards (U.K. 46.0%, France 41.3%). While the decline in the
proportion engaged in agriculture is continuing (23.8% in 1976) this is still
a very high figure (U.K. 2.7%, France 10.9%) and reflects the accepted picture
of Ireland as a predominantly agricultural country.

The post 1973 recession has had a major impact on the Irish industrial sector -
unemployment has increased from 6.0% in 1973 to 9.7% in 1977. Most of this
increase in unemployment was caused by redundancies in traditional industries,
many of which had been established in an economic environment sheltered by
tariff barriers erected shortly after the foundation of the State. The
competition created by freeing trade, initially with Britain, and later as
full members of the E.E.C., together with the impact of the very rapid increase
in fuel prices after 1973 combined to seriously affect employment in areas
such as textiles, footwear and leather, brewing/distilling, etc.

Programmes currently being implemented by the Government are expected to result
in a decline of 4,000 per annum in agriculture and annual increases of 3,300,
13,500 and 11,800 in Building/Construction, Manufacturing and Services industries
respectively on the basis of an annual growth of 7% in G.N.P.

C.   Economic Indicators

As a result of the evolving socio-economic structure the economic trends of
the third quarter of the 20th century stand in stark relief to the pattern in
the first half. In 1938 for example the United Kingdom supplied over 50% of
Irish imports and purchased a massive 93% of her exports. By 1976 imports from
the U.K. were still high (49%) but exports had fallen to 47% with a high
proportion going to other members of the European Community and to the rest of
the world. Similarly, Gross National Product which had grown by only 1% for the
forty years after the foundation of the State has (apart from the post 1973
recession) grown much more rapidly since the economic revival in 1958-63 and
exceeded 6% in 1978. Indeed, the annual growth in GNP over the period 1966-76
(4.5% per head of occupied population) has only been equalled by the Netherlands
among the members of the E.E.C. However there are still significant disparities
between Ireland and her partners in the European Economic Community: Gross
Domestic Product per head population in 1973 was only £882 in comparison with

£1,277 in the U.K., £1,026 in Italy and £1,716 in the Netherlands; in 1976 the ownership of television receivers, telephones and cars are the lowest in the Community as is the consumption of steel, electricity and total energy.

In general, therefore, the picture is one of a country which is going through a very rapid transition and, although it is making significant progress, Ireland still lags behind her colleagues in many areas.

D. Social Structure

As the economy develops there are also forces for change on the social fabric: from a strongly rural community which was insular in every sense of the term, Irish society is emerging to a more liberal and cosmopolitan structure. Increasing incomes combined with increasing mobility, the influence of emigrants, the penetration of mass media and also the prevailing economic conditions have led to a questioning of traditional values. As a consequence, Irish society is now almost schizophrenic in that it is torn between deeply held beliefs and the more liberal attitudes of Europe generally. The fact that a large and growing proportion of the population is under 25 years of age, together with improved economic conditions and changed educational opportunities, suggest that the rate of change may even accelerate in the short term. There are many mainfestations of these changes in attitudes and structures.

E. Administrative Structure

Ireland, with a population in April 1977 of 3,192,300 is divided into the following units:

    27   mainly rural counties

     4   county boroughs (the cities of Dublin, Cork,
                          Limerick and Waterford)

     7   boroughs or smaller cities

    47   urban districts or towns

    28   towns with Town Commissioners.

The functions of the various units are illustrated in Fig. 1.

F. Management System

Under the management system, the functions of local authorities are divided into reserved functions and executive functions. The reserved functions are performed directly by the elected members of the local authority. They comprise mainly decisions on major matters of policy and principle, and include the making of rates, borrowing of money, making, amending or revoking of by - laws, bringing enactments into force and nominating persons to act on other public bodies. Every function which is not a reserved function is an executive function, performable directly by the manager. The executive functions include the employment of staff, acceptance of tenders, management of the local authority's property, the collection of rates and rents and, generally, the day-to-day administration of the affairs of the authority. The county manager, as well as being manager for the county council, is manager for every borough corporation, urban district council, board of town commissioners, and every joint body whose functional area is wholly within the county. It is the duty of the county manager to advise and assist the county council and every other local authority for which he is manager in regard to the exercise by them of their reserved functions and in regard to any particular matter on which the local authority requests his advice or assistance.

G.   Physical Planning & Development

Under the Local Government (Planning and Development) Act, 1963, each of the main
local authorities is charged with two main functions (4):

(a) the preparation of a development plan and its review at five-yearly
intervals (at least) for the area within its jurisdiction (Sections 19-23 of the Act)
County councils prepare development plans both for the rural parts of the county
and any urban area specified in the legislation which is not a planning authority
in its own right. Thus all settlements greater than about 1,000 persons are
included.

(b) the control of all development (other than exempted development) proposed
within its area of jurisdiction (Sections 24-41).

In county boroughs, boroughs, urban districts and scheduled towns the
development plan must provide for:

1. Zoning;

2. Traffic and pedestrian movement;

3. Renewal of obsolete areas;

4. Preserving, extending, improving amenities.

Similarly in rural areas the development plan must provide for:

1. Development and renewal of obsolete areas;

2. Preserving, improving and extending amenities;

3. Provision of new water supplies and sewerage services and the extension of
    existing supplies and services.

Further objectives may be included in development plans. These embrace topics
such as zoning in rural areas, and objectives relating to structures, community
planning and amenities.

The procedure by which the development plan is made involves the following stages:

(a) preparation of a draft;

(b) provision of copies to the bodies prescribed in Regulations made under
     the Act;

(c) publication in Iris Oifigiuil of a notice to the effect that the draft has
     been prepared, and in at least one newspaper circulating in the area;

(d) public display of the draft for a period of at least three months;

(e) consideration of objections and representations;

(f) adoption of the draft (amended if necessary) by the elected representatives.

The second major function which is statutorily required of the local planning
authority under the Local Government (Planning and Development) Act, 1963 is the
control of development in the best interests of the 'proper planning and
development' of the area of the planning authority's jurisdiction. In general
all development, other than certain classes of exempted development, requires
permission from the local planning authority.

The method by which an application is processed is illustrated in Fig. 2. In summary, the developer submits an application (possibly following initial consultations with the local authority) which is assessed by the local authority who advise the developer and other interested parties of its decision. Assuming a positive outcome, the developer then undertakes the proposed development according to the terms of the local authority decision.

Alternative paths through the process involve the local authority seeking additional information on the nature of the proposed development, the local authority requesting the preparation of a study specifying the environmental impacts of the proposed development, objections by third parties to the local planning authority and appeals by the developer or third parties to An Bord Pleanala (The Planning Appeals Board) against the decision of the local planning authority.

The decision to grant or withhold permission rests exclusively with the manager. The manager indicates his decision in a notice of intent which is sent to the applicant and to any third parties who have objected to the proposed development. The developer then has twenty-eight days (third parties have twenty-one days) in which to appeal against the manager's decision. If there is no appeal within the specified time period then the manager formally notifies the developer and other interested parties of his decision by way of a manager's order.

In the event of an appeal against the decision which the manager has indicated he intends to take, recourse is to An Bord Pleanala which is an independent, statutory planning appeals board. Members of the Board are appointed by the Minister for the Environment and the Board is chaired by a judge of the High Court. The Board hears the appeal de novo and may use the mechanism of an oral hearing if requested to do so. It is significant that neither a local planning authority nor the Minister for the Environment can issue directives to the Board in specific cases. The Minister may, however, indicate general policy guidelines which the Board will then pursue in its decision-making: the Minister must advise the Oireachtas (Parliament) of these guidelines.

The legal basis for the Environmental Impact Study rests in the first instance on Section 25(2) (C) of the Local Government (Planning and Development) Act, 1963.

> "Regulations . .. may make provision for requiring any applicant to
> furnish to the Minister (Board) and to any other specified persons
> any specified information with respect to their applications" (4).

Article 28 of the Local Government (Planning & Development) Regulations, 1977 states, inter alia, that:

An application to a planning authority for permission for any development to which this article applies shall ... be accompanied by two copies of a written study of what, if any, effect the proposed development, if carried out, would have on the environment relative to the place where the development is to take place....

This Article applies to any development:

(a) for the purposes of any trade or industry (including mining) comprising any works, apparatus or plant used for any process which would result in the emission of noise, vibration, smell, fumes, smoke, soot, ash, dust or grit, or the discharge of any liquid or other effluent (whether treated or untreated) either with or without particles of matter in suspension therein,

<u>and</u>

(b) the cost of which, including all fixed assets... may reasonably be expected to be five million pounds or more. (5)

It should be noted that:

(a) In the event of a proposed development meeting both criteria then the planning application must be accompanied by an environmental study.

(b) If there is some doubt about whether the development meets the criteria, then the planning authority has discretion in deciding whether or not to request such a study.

(c) There is no provision for an environmental study of development which is exempted development, e.g. developments by the local authority such as major roads, housing schemes, etc.

(d) The criteria employed imply that the concept of the environmental study applies only to industrial proposals.

(e) There is no provision for inflation.

(f) There is no provision for studies of smaller plants even though they may have serious environmental impacts.

(g) Neither the Act nor the Regulations define the 'Environment' although the emphasis is clearly on pollutants. This is in contrast with definitions adopted by the World Bank, the Council of Europe, the European Economic Community and others.

THE GROWTH IN THE DEMAND FOR ENERGY

It seems likely that Ireland's total energy requirements will rise from 7.5 million tons of oil equivalent (mtoe) in 1977 to the region of 18 mtoe by 1990. The associated oil requirement is expected to be in the region of 11.0 mtoe, assuming the planned construction of nuclear and coal fired electricity generating stations.

"... At present about 40 per cent of the normal market demand in Ireland for oil products is refined in Ireland at Whitegate. The balance of the demand is met by importing oil in product form. By 1985 oil consumption is likely to reach 10 million tonnes per annum. If no additional refining capacity is located in this country by that time total refinery capacity would account for about 20 per cent of market demand and we would have to import almost 8 million tonnes of oil products. The added value content of these products would also be lost to this country"(6)

There is clearly a need for a new refinery in the 1980s to meet the increased demand for refined products. On the basis of the above considerations, the minimum size of refinery likely to be developed in the 1980s would be in the region of 5 million tonnes capacity. Such a refinery would fill the gap between current domestic refining capacity and the additional level of imports of refined products required by 1990. If the domestic refinery ceased operation in the 1980s (for technical or other reasons), and the level of existing imports of refined products were replaced by a new Irish refinery, then its capacity would need to be in the region of 10 mtoe.

Economies of scale favour the larger development, having regard also to the fact that refineries frequently do not operate at full capacity, while the additional throughput and product mix requirements which an associated petrochemical industry would generate would also favour a 10 million tonne development. If a large refinery of 10 million tonnes came on stream in the mid-1980s it would have to sell its output on both the export and domestic markets with the exporting function gradually being replaced by the expansion of the Irish market after 1990.

Accordingly, a 10 million tonne refinery was taken as the selected scale of development for the purpose of this study.

THE SEARCH FOR AN OPTIMAL COASTAL LOCATION

Having identified the likely scale of development, typical characteristics of a plant of the appropriate size were listed and where possible quantified. The study then examined 112 possible sites, comparing the characteristics of a 10 million tonnes per annum refinery with the operational and community/environmental characteristics of the site. The performance of each site under each criterion was assessed and its performance recorded. On this basis it was possible to classify sites into those:

- likely to be acceptable,
- likely to be acceptable but only with modification,
- unacceptable.

A.   Characteristics of a 10 million tonne per annum Oil Refinery

The design and construction of an oil refinery is clearly extremely complex and depends on the souce of the crude (particularly sulphur content which can range from 0.1 to 3% or more, by weight), the mix of products (e.g. fuel oil or gasoline orientated), the degree of environmental control imposed, and so on. It is therefore very difficult to identify and quantify the characteristics of oil refineries in general: the design of a unique plant could cause marked variations from average conditions.

This paper considers a refinery designed on the basis of the following parameters:

(a) Throughput of 10 million tonnes of crude per annum;

(b) Crude arriving in 300,000 d.w.t. vessels involving jetty or single buoy mooring;

(c) Marine conditions:

Wind:	less than Force 8
Visibility:	over 1.5 km
Depth:	20-25 metres
Sea State:	less than 7 (mean wave height 5.5 metres approximately)
Current:	less than 3 knots;

(d) Products to be transported in 60-100,000 d.w.t. vessels;

(e) 14 days storage;

(f) 2.5% sulphur content involving hydro-treating facilities;

(g) Refinery to be water cooled;

(h) 60 megawatts of power required, involving a back-up supply from the national grid;

(i) Cooling water (possibly saline): 1.8 million tonnes per day;

(j) Process water: 9,000 tonnes per day;

(k) Slope not to exceed 1:12;

(l) Area approximately 200 hectares minimum; 400 ha preferred;

(m) Employment (operational) 760 persons;

(n) Employment (construction maximum) 4,000 persons;

(o) Construction period 3 years;

(p) Liquid effluent disposal;

   1. Sanitary water to public sewage plant;

   2. Rainwater runoff (unpaved areas) to ditches and thence the estuary;

   3. Surface water (paved areas) to oily water sewer system to oil separator
       and skimming system. Slop tank to return recovered oil to the process.
       Flocculation and biological treatment plants to be provided;

   4. Process Water: to be handled in conjunction with surface water system;

   5. Cooling Water: returned to sea via a settling pond and API interceptor;

(q) Solid waste disposal;

   1. 365 tonnes of trash and garbage per annum;

   2. 547 tons of spent catalyst;

   3. 2737 tons of incinerator ash from the combustion of oiled and biological
       sludges. After treatment these wastes may be transported to a landfill
       for burial;

(r) Gaseous effluents;

   1. Use of three stage reactors ensuring 97-99% sulphur conversion leaving
       about 10 tonnes of unconverted H_2S to be burnt to SO_2 daily;

   2. Use of high and/or low level flames to burn off excess gases and
       (on occasion) hydrocarbons. This will create an odour nuisance;

(s) Load bearing capacity 22-24 tonnes/m^2;

(t) Tank farm area approximately 100 ha including roads and pipetracks.
     Floating roof tanks.

B. Method of Site Selection and Assessment

A major problem in this area is the standpoint from which the assessment is made.
Thus the entrepreneur will view the site selection process from the standpoints
of cost and operational factors while the community will be concerned about
maximizing economic benefits while minimizing negative social and environmental
impacts. In each case, consideration is given to much the same range of locational
factors but priorities (and therefore the importance or weighting assigned to
each) will differ.

From the developers viewpoint the significant factors may be grouped under
three main headings:

1. Material Considerations - availability and suitability of certain physical,
infrastructural and service components;

2. Economic Considerations - relative cost of developing any one site over
another, security of plant and investment and ease of general operation;

3. Social Considerations - compatibility with local authorities, the local
and extra-local communities.

In contrast, the community will consider the following factors important:

1. Economic considerations – return to the community in economic terms, including possible direct and indirect costs;

2. Environmental considerations – effect of the development on the environment;

3. Social considerations – overall effect of the development on the community in social and cultural terms and its role in the overall structure of the community.

Clearly there are considerable overlaps: the provision of fresh water will be considered under both the material and economic headings by the operator and under all three headings by the community. All the factors listed (in a non-hierarchical structure) are non-modifiable components in the form of minimal requirements and modifiable where it is possible to negotiate or alter conditions.

ASSESSMENT FACTORS A – OPERATIONAL

1.   Material Considerations

1.01   Physical

          1.011 Availability of flat land in quantity

          1.012 Sites of regular shape

          1.013 Adequate bearing capacity and drainage of the soils

          1.014 Ease of land assembly

          1.015 Environmental suitability (climate)

          1.016 Existing land use

1.02   Infrastructural

          1.021 Access to terminal facility/cooling water

          1.022 Availability of fresh water

          1.023 Adequate communications

          1.024 Adequate power supply

          1.025 Adequate transport facilities

          1.026 Existence of industrial infrastructure

1.03   Service

          1.031 Availability of commercial and professional services

          1.032 Social and community services

2.   Economic Considerations

2.01   Development costs

          2.011 Site character

          2.012 Infrastructures

2.02   Operational

          2.021 Transport (supply)

          2.022 Transport (distribution)

2.023 Labour supply (availability, training, etc.)

2.024 Security

2.025 Safety

2.026 Potential for the supply of local raw materials

3.   Social Considerations

3.01   Compatibility with local community

3.011 Density of settlement

3.012 Local environment

ASSESSMENT FACTORS B - COMMUNITY

1.   Economic Considerations

1.01   Sectoral

1.011 Agriculture and Forestry

1.012 Tourism

1.013 Fishing (commercial)

2.   Environmental Considerations

2.01   Landscape and amenity

2.011 Natural Beauty

2.012 Scenic views and prospects

2.013 Recreational Amenity

2.02   Scientific Interests

3.   Special Considerations

ASSESSMENT FACTORS C - FACTORS WHICH COULD ONLY BE ASSESSED IN THE
COURSE OF DETAILED IMPACT STUDIES

1.   Site drainage, waste disposal/dispersal

2.   Developers contribution, infrastructure

2.01   Water supply

2.02   Roads

2.03   Power

2.04   Communications

2.05   Pollution levels/control/monitoring

2.06   Housing and social services

3.   Compatibility/Attitudes

3.01   with Local Authority

3.02   with Local Community

4.   Impact on Social Environment

4.01   Noise

4.02   Odour

4.03   Health

4.04   Safety

5.   Impact on Marine Environment

6.   Operational Costs

It is impossible to weight or even order the factors listed above - the developer and community will look at all appropriate factors and attribute to them weighting factors which are unique to the scale of values of a particular individual, community or location.

The quantification of each of the factors is beyond the scope of the present paper. However, a wide range of agencies was involved, including the Agricultural Research Institute, the Institute for Industrial Research and Standards, the Meteorological Service and others. The potential impact of sulphur dioxide on agricultural incomes, the availability of labour (and of course, housing), the consequence of a cordon sanitaire and the possible conflict with tourism were among the detailed considerations embodied in the more general statement of assessment factors listed earlier.

Three stages were involved in the site selection and assessment process:

1. the identification of potential sites or areas,

2. a general assessment in which all of the factors listed above were considered to be of equal weight,

3. an assessment involving key factors only - the availability of land, deep water, process water and environmental considerations.

1. Arising from previous studies undertaken by An Foras Forbartha (The National Institute for Physical Planning and Construction Research) (7,8) and from field studies, a total of 112 possible sites and areas (groups of sites) was identified. These were selected solely on the basis of the existence of flat land. Further considerations, involving site size, access, the suitability of soils and physiographic characteristics generally, reduced the total number of possible sites to 59, plus 13 areas within which sites might be found.

2. In regard to this general assessment it should be emphasized that all factors were considered equally important in the first instance. No attempt was made to weight individual factors; consequently the summing of the factors tends to cloak the importance of certain key factors. For example a site which performs badly under the heading "availability of fresh water" might, when its total performance is considered and assuming it had no other major shortcomings, emerge as having distinct potential. Bearing in mind the reservation expressed above, thirteen sites and six areas were considered as possessing real potential. When the Operational or Community sections of the General Assessment are separated and the performance of the individual sites is studied under these two headings, 18 and 13 sites respectively emerge with distinct potential. From Table 1 it can be seen that only six sites have equal potential under both the operational and community headings. Many sites have high potential in the general assessment because of their attractiveness in community/environmental terms.

This brief and limited analysis of the findings of the general assessment and its elementary breakdown under operational and community headings illustrates the dangers of generalization at this stage in the study of refinery location and the need to refer continually to the detail of the assessment. However, it does allow identification of extremes – those sites or areas which are consistently good or consistently poor in terms of potential – but the selection of sites can only be undertaken through a weighting of the individual factors and consequent recasting of shortlisted sites.

3. In employing the concept of key factors the findings of the general assessment are re-examined by extracting the selected factors and studying the performance of sites in terms of these. However, there are difficulties in selecting an agreed listing of key factors. Analysis of the interaction between the various factors is extremely complex and does little to assist in the identification of key factors. The simplest classification of factors is that which distinguishes between those concerned with the intrinsic characteristics of the site and its environs (i.e. its natural features) and those which relate to human intervention or the human condition (provision of services, social facilities etc.). All the factors are modifiable in some degree, but it was concluded that those which related to the intrinsic characteristics of the site are most likely to influence locational decisions in the first instance. The following factors were selected as being of prime importance in the analysis of site suitability.

- availability of land in quantity;

- access to deep water/terminal facilities;

- availability of fresh water;

- environmental considerations.

It will be noted from Table 1 that only ten of the sites or areas shortlisted in the general assessment as having distinct potential are listed under key factors: of these ten sites, three are listed here as having potential, i.e. slight problems are associated with their development. Several sites which did not emerge at all in the general assessment are listed under key factors. Conversely, eight sites, which were listed as having distinct potential in the general assessment do not emerge from this assessment based on key factors. The following sites however, are listed in both the general and key factor assessments:

SLIGO	SS12
	SA 2
MAYO	MS15
	MA 3
CLARE	CA 5
LIMERICK	LS36
	LS37
KERRY	KA 6
CORK	CS52
	CS53

In the final stage, the findings of the overall assessment, its breakdown into operational and community sections and the key factor assessment were compared. Sites and areas which performed consistently well, or badly, were determined, and from this the following classification of sites, according to the likelihood of their being acceptable or otherwise, was made.

Group 1.   These are likely to be acceptable in economic and environmental
                  terms and would require only slight modification. They performed
                  consistently well in the assessments described earlier (6 sites,
                  4 areas).

Group 2. (a)   These could be acceptable, but only with some modification. (11
                  sites, 4 areas).

         (b)   These could be acceptable, but only with major modifications i.e.
                  they are marginal in terms of the assessments described in this
                  Section (13 sites, 4 areas).

Group 3.   These are considered to be unacceptable in either economic or
                  environmental terms. They performed consistently poorly in the
                  assessments. (29 sites).

It must be stressed that there are many ways of using the assessment, depending
on the weighting assigned to the individual factors or the range of factors
selected for analysis. If, for example, it was decided that the question of
safety should dominate all other considerations, the final classification of
sites would be quite different to that demonstrated above. This is an extreme
and unlikely example, but it does amphasize the need to maintain the flexibility
of the assessment at this stage in the analysis of location. The weighting of
factors remains the prerogative of the decision maker.

It is essential that impact analyses should be carried out when applications
concerning oil refineries and related industries are being considered by the
appropriate authorities. In addition, it is recommended that baseline studies
should be carried out as soon as possible on the ten Group 1 sites or areas
in the expectation that some of these may be developed. The detailed information
and understanding which these analyses can yield will greatly assist the
satisfactory integration of major new development - socially, economically,
and environmentally - within the country.

REFERENCES

1. Energy - Ireland, Stationery Office, Dublin, 1978.

2. A Study of Suitable Coastal Locations for Oil Refineries in Ireland,
An Foras Forbartha, Dublin 1975.

3. Strengthening the Local Government Service, McKinsey & Co., Stationery
Office, Dublin 1971.

4. Local Government (Planning & Development) Act, 1963.

5. Local Government (Planning & Development) Regulations, 1977. Stationery
Office, Dublin.

6. Programme for National Development 1978-1981, Stationery Office Dublin 1979.

7. National Coastline Study, An Foras Forbartha, Dublin 1973.

8. National Ports Study, An Foras Forbartha, Dublin 1975. (Unpublished
confidential report to the Minister for Tourism & Transport).

Table 1: Assessment Summary

	General Assessment	Operational Factors	Community Factors	Key Factors Distinct Potential	Potential
DONEGAL		DS3			DS3
	DS4		DS4		
	DS9		DS9		DS11
SLIGO	SS12.	SS1 2	SS12		SS12
					SS13
					SS14
	SA 2	SA 2	SA 2	SA 2	SA 2
MAYO	MS15	MS15			
	MS16	MS16			
	MS17		MS17		
			MS18		
			MS20		
	MA 3		MA 3		MA3
CLARE			CS33		CS33
	CS34	CS34			
					CS35
	CA 5	CA 5			CA 5
CORK			CS48		
	CS52	CS52	CS52	CS52	
	CS53	CS53	CS53	CS53	
				CA10	
	CA11	CA11			
LIMERICK	LS36	LS36	LS36	LS36	LS36
	LS37	LS37	LS37	LS37	LS37
	LA13	LA13			
KERRY	KA 6	KA 6	KA 6	KA 6	
					KA 7
				KA8	KA 8
					KS38
WATERFORD	WS54	WS54			
	WS54 a	WS54 a	WS54 a		
WEXFORD		WA12			
GALWAY			GS27		GS27
					GS30
		GA4			

| Function | County borough corporations | County councils | | Urban district councils/ borough councils |
| | | Rural areas | | |
		Direct	Town commissioners	
Roads -Construction and maintenance. -Traffic -Road safety -Public lighting	✓	✓	✓ Lighting in some town	✓ Local roads
Housing - Standards -Council housing -Loans/grants	✓	✓	✓ Not construc- tion	✓
Sanitary services - Water -Sewerage -Refuse -Burial grounds	✓	✓		✓
Planning and development -Development plans -Development control -Amenity improvement	✓ To coordinate with other development programmes	✓		✓
Miscellaneous -Fire brigade -Library -Etc.	✓	✓	✓ e.g.,fairs, school meals, allotments	✓ e.g.,fairs, school meals allotments
Agency services -Motor tax -Special employ- ment - Etc.	✓	✓		

Fig. 1. Functions of Local Authority Units

Source: (3)

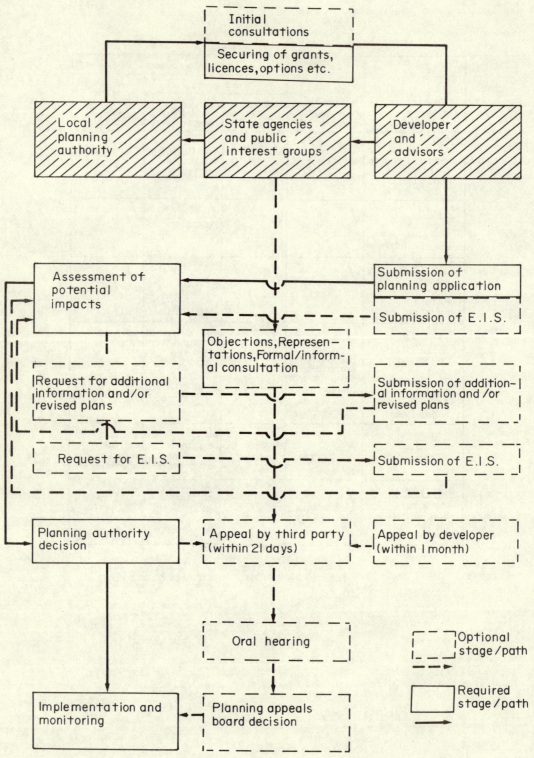

Fig. 2.   The Planning Process

The Decision to Develop Petro-chemical Industry in Bamble Municipality, County of Telemark (South-Norway)

H. P. Johansen

(Norway)

INTRODUCTION: THE PROJECT, AND ITS BACKGROUND

The petro-chemical complex in the municipality of Bamble in the County of Telemark is the largest single industrial complex built in Norway up to the present time: 1979. The final decision concerning this development was taken in June 1974, when the Storting (parliament) approved a proposal put forward by the Government. A significant minority, however, voted for a proposal whereby the complex would be divided geographically between two locations, of which one was Bamble.

Construction of plants was begun immediately, and these were to be ready to start production in the period 1977-79. A peak employment of somewhat over 3,000 persons was reached during the construction phase, and a total of about 1,000 employees will be needed to run the project. Only minor extensions are likely. About 5,000 million Norwegian kroner have been invested in the project.

The background for the Bamble complex was the discovery of oil and gas in the Ekofisk field in the North Sea in 1969-70. These Ekofisk finds were the first exploitable deposits found on the Norwegian continental shelf. As soon as it became evident that these deposits were exploitable, it immediately became relevant to consider the question of landing. The solutions chosen for landing oil or gas would require the approval of the public authorities, and a committee was appointed – the Ekofisk Committee – to evaluate these questions in more detail. The Committee included representatives of both the central authorities and the licensees in the Ekofisk field (the Phillips Group). The Committee made its report in February 1972 and recommended that oil and wet gas from the field should be transported by pipeline to Teeside in England, and gas by pipeline to Emden in the Federal Republic of Germany. The landing of oil and gas by pipeline to Norway was not recommended, primarily because of the technical problems which, at the time, were thought to be related to laying and maintaining a pipeline at great depths.

It was of interest to both the central authorities and Norwegian industry that the oil and gas deposits should provide the basis for the development of a processing industry in Norway. It was therefore considered important that the recommended solutions for landing oil and gas from the Ekofisk field should contain conditions which ensured that this objective was attained. This matter was solved through an agreement between the Ministry of Industry and the

EIA s

253

Phillips Group whereby the Norwegian State was given an option on up to 250,000 tons of wet gas per year delivered to Norway from the Teeside plants at very favourable terms. This was approved by the Storting in June 1973, when the question of landing oil and gas from the Ekofisk field was dealt with.

At that time, however, no concrete plans had been formulated as to how this wet gas should be utilized in industrial production, where the necessary plants should be located, or what agencies should be made responsible for planning and operations. Nor had any consideration been given to the possible consequences to society of the different development alternatives. Most of the work on these matters was done in the period from June 1973 to June 1974, when the Storting made its final decision concerning the industrial development. This case study draws attention to the various studies and planning processes which took place during this phase of operations.

SUMMARY OF CURRENT NORWEGIAN LEGISLATION AND REGULATIONS RELATING TO ROUTINE PROCEDURES CONNECTED WITH THE ESTABLISHMENT OF NEW INDUSTRY

Particularly relevant legislation in such cases included:

(a) The Establishment Control Act, aimed at encouraging and spreading industrial activity in accordance with national resource and regional planning policies and in such a way as to benefit society as a whole. Decisions pursuant to this Act shall be made by the central authorities after a collective evaluation from the point of view of society, including consideration of developments in different parts of the country and in the local community, as well as assessment of economic balance, the labour market and protection of the environment. The Act became effective on 1 January 1977, and the provisions apply to all large industrial undertakings, irrespective of the planned locality. The plans for developments at Bamble were considered prior to this date and were consequently not dealt with in accordance with the provisions of the Establishment Control Act.

(b) The Building Act, which includes regulations requiring the municipal and county authorities to prepare master plans for land use and development policies for the districts in question. It is assumed that approved master plans will serve as guidelines for administrative procedures connected with the handling of cases in accordance with the Establishment Control Act. When the Bamble project was being assessed by the authorities, no master plan had been prepared either for the Bamble municipality or the Telemark county. Land areas had, however, been set aside in Bamble with a view to the development of large-scale industry.

A new Planning Act which is being prepared at present will cover, among other things, regulations now included in the present Building Act. This new act will also include regulations relating to environmental impact assessments of plans and enterprises which may have important effects on nature and the environment.

(c) The Water Pollution Act is aimed at protecting groundwater, water courses and sea areas against pollution. Activities causing pollution are usually prohibited unless special permission to discharge has been granted. Such permission may include conditions relating to the treatment of discharges and to other efforts necessary to reduce the effects of pollution. The Act also includes regulations concerning the handling of applications for permission to discharge. It is required, among other things, that the application must include information on what effects the discharge may have upon the receiving waters and on what interests may be adversely affected. The act also provides the authority to demand that the applicant carry out or pay for expert studies to clarify discharge circumstances. The County Governor gives permission for municipal discharge, while the State Pollution Control Authority gives permssion for industrial discharges. In particularly important cases, or when a matter of principle is involved, permission is granted either by the Ministry or by Royal Decree.

(d) The Neighbour's Act states that a licence is required for all industry, or similar activity, which may result in air pollution or noise. This licence may include conditions concerning cleansing treatment or other measures required to reduce the effects of pollution. The Neighbour's Act also includes provisions requiring the applicant to provide information about the expected injurious effects of the emissions. As a rule, licences are granted pursuant to the Neighbour's Act by the specially appointed Smoke Control Council. In important cases, or when a matter of principle is involved, the licence may be granted by the Ministry or by Royal Decree.

In addition to the above there are a number of acts and regulations relating, among other things, to licences and to safety and work conditions.

THE BAMBLE PROJECT

This case affects a number of different interests and considerations and implies both short-term and long-term consequences of various kinds. Thus a study of the procedure for dealing with the question of the development of the petro-chemical industry in Bamble will help to clarify complex causal relations and reveal points of conflict. It will also supply a great deal of information on the extent to which the different fields of interest are drawn into the evaluation process and to what degree their opinions and demands are actually taken into account.

This report draws attention to the more complex and problematical aspects of administrative procedure relating to the development at Bamble. A short, critical study of this kind does not pretend to give a comprehensive picture of all aspects of the issue in question.

The Bamble project is particularly relevant for Norway. As an oil-producing nation, Norway may be faced with new development situations of a similar nature in the course of the next few years. The lessons drawn from the study and planning process in the case of the development at Bamble may therefore provide valuable information for future dealings with other projects of a similar size and nature.

Other factors which were significant in selecting this project as a case-study are the following.

(a) The petro-chemical plants at Bamble are Norway's largest industrial establishment so far. Planning operations preceding the decision to build were followed with great interest - by both local and central authorities, political parties, trade unions, Norwegian industry, the mass media and by the general public. It is rather extraordinary that a project of this character became the subject of a relatively wide public debate outside the realm of the public authorities.

(b) The preparatory phase was particularly short, considering the size, complexity and importance of the project. The main work relating to the technical/economic aspects of the project, analyses of consequences for society and final processing of development plans by the local and central authorities all took place in the course of about one year.

(c) When assessing the project, emphasis was placed on environmental aspects, because the planned facility would be a new and polluting industry in the district, which already suffered the greatest load of air and water pollution in the country. This made it particularly relevant to consider other locations for the project, or for parts of it, and also to evaluate polluting emissions from the project in relation to the demands made on other polluting industry in the area regarding abatement measures and the schedule for these measures to be put into effect.

(d) It was obvious that implementation of the project would have significant consequences for the Bamble municipality and for the surrounding locality, in terms of population growth, settlement, employment, development of infrastructure, and social conditions. Therefore, it is of great interest to find out to what extent an attempt was made to obtain relevant data on the consequences and preventive measures related to these factors.

Further details of these, and other important matters relating to the routine administrative procedures are discussed in more detail below.

MAIN FEATURES OF THE DECISION-MAKING PROCESSES

A. The Principal Decision-making Arenas

In reality, this case was considered in a number of decision-making arenas characterized by the participants involved, fields of interest, planning resources and degree of organization. Furthermore, the administrative procedure can be divided into two or three time-phases, though these overlap to some extent.

The decision-making arenas were as follows:

(a) The national political arena, composed mainly of central authorities and relevant industrial companies. It was here that the basic assumptions for the project were formulated and discussed, and it was here that insight into the problem, and planning resources, was greatest.

The parties in this arena held a dominant position in the first phase of the decision-making process. It was only after about six months had passed that the main alternatives which formed the basis for further consideration became recognized.

(b) The local arena, composed mainly of representatives of local authorities. These representatives did not consider it a priority task to gather information related to the various possible consequences of the project for the affected districts. Their efforts consisted mainly of giving support to the development plans, both vis à vis the central authorities and vis à vis the local population. The already existing load of pollution in the area formed the basis for the local authorities' concern as to what requirements would be laid down for the industry in this connexion, but the actual evaluation of this matter took place elsewhere. The parties in this arena had rather limited planning resources, and little was done to improve them.

(c) The third arena was related to other local elements and was composed of trade union organizations in existing industrial enterpriese in the area, interest groups concerned with nature and the environment, and the local population at large. Insight into the problem varied in the different groups, as did their resources and political influence. They also held different views on what solution should be chosen. On the whole, their planning resources were small, but in spite of this the trade union organizations in particular exerted a strong political influence.

B.   Consideration of the different alternatives from the point of view of
      location, organization of production and emission

The primary location proposal was the Bamble municipality. This choice was
related to the fact that Norsk Hydro, the leading company in the project
assessment and Norway's largest industrial company, already had extensive
industrial installations in the area and previously had acquired areas of land
in the Bamble municipality suitable for extensive industrial development. In
addition, siting the petro-chemical industry in Bamble would provide possibilities
for co-ordinating production techniques at the new plant with Hydro's other
industrial enterprises. Bamble was, furthermore, the location recommended in
November 1973 by an inter-Ministry committee under the Ministry of Industry:
the Negotiating Committee for New Industrial Enterprises. However, other
alternative localities were also evaluated. This was partly as a result of
pressure from various districts interested in large industrial development, and
partly to ensure that the recommendation to locate the project in Bamble was
comparable to a reasonable extent with other locations – technically, economically and from the points of view of the environment and of district policy.

C.   How the different alternatives were generated: the sources of the various
      proposals

The industrial companies showed a distinct preference for Bamble as the location
of the project. This standpoint was based on technical-economic assessments. In
particular, a proposal to divide the plant between two different locations
(seriously considered in the final stages) was thought to be undesirable. For the
most part, proposals for other alternative locations originated with the
municipal or county-municipal authorities, but these alternatives were not based
on any systematic assessment of possibilities and limitations. The Negotiating
Committee also considered siting the project at Mongstad (in West Norway) as an
interesting alternative from an industrial-economic standpoint. Construction of
a petroleum refinery had already started at Mongstad, and extensive areas of land
had been set aside for the development of large-scale industry.

D.   Selection of impacts subjected to further analysis

A number of decisions and other measures were necessary before the authorities
were in a position to adopt a final position on the implementation of a large-
scale industrial project and its resulting impact. What is required in this
connexion will vary in each individual case, depending on the technology of the
different kinds of industry, current legislation, and the demands of various
social organizations. We may call these issues, which must be classified either
wholly or in part during the decision-making process, questions directly relating
to establishment. Such matters include technical, economic and marketing
conditions, the secure supply of raw materials both now and in the future,
finance and credit considerations, energy and water supply, acquisition of a
suitable site, communications (including waterways), the labour market,
contingency measures against fire and emission of gas and a number of other
environmental aspects.

It is beyond the scope of this report to study in detail the planning and
preparatory work carried out in connexion with all these different factors. It is
possible to state, however, that in this case the time factor itself set a limit
on what data could be obtained. Furthermore, there were only limited public funds
available for comprehensive impact assessments. At that time there was no legal
authority whereby the industrial companies were required to cover the entire

costs of preparatory studies.

The limited time available explains to a large extent why a complete picture of
the various emissions in the area (the pre-situation) was not obtained. There
was also some uncertainty about how great the emissions from the new plants
would be, taking into consideration the production technology, probable production
volume and cleaning requirements. It was even more difficult to assess the
consequences for the environment of the total emissions in the area, as it was
not until the final phase of the decision-making process that it became clear
what requirements would be imposed on other polluting industry in the district
to ensure a reduction of the total pollution in the area.

In spite of a certain lack of background material, it is correct to maintain
that the issues directly related to siting, which were given priority in the
administrative procedures, were reasonably well clarified and assessed by the
time the decision was taken to proceed with the project in Bamble.

The establishment of large-scale industry, particularly in relation to small
municipalities, will in most cases result in drastic changes in the living
conditions of the population in the area. The work opportunities provided by
the new industry and by other associated industrial and service activities
usually leads to significant net immigration to the district. In such a
situation, the municipality receiving the new industry is faced with extensive
planning and development tasks connected with infrastructure and social services.
It is not always necessary to deal with these questions in order to take a
position on the industrial development itself. But it is precisely the solutions
to these problems which determine to a great extent whether the community will
function in the best possible way. Planning activities relating to these matters
are therefore of definite importance from the point of view of preparedness.
Experience shows, for example, that there is a greater chance of preventing
social problems if, at an early stage in the decision-making process, a
systematic assessment is made of how this can be done. Relevant questions
include: What may be done to increase the recruitment of women to the new
industrial work places? What groups in the community will be particularly
affected by the new situation? How can they be helped? What measures should be
given attention to ensure better integration between the new and the old
populations?

In the case of Bamble, the central authorities considered that the main
responsibility for providing data and views on these questions lay with the local
authorities. But, as noted above, the latter did not give sufficiently high
priority to planning work and preparatory studies of this type. The Bamble
municipality did try to some extent, but limited municipal planning resources,
little expert assistance from other public authorities, and limited insight
into what the new situation would require of the municipality made it difficult
to obtain a comprehensive picture of the situation. Nor did the county
authorities consider it a priority task to assess the local and regional
consequences and the need for preventive measures. In their opinion, the primary
concern was to secure the project, leaving questions of this kind to be
considered afterwards.

E. The organizations and expertise responsible for the environmental impact
    assessments

The foregoing has shown that planning and assessment was mainly concerned with
questions directly related to siting. This is due to the fact that the central
authorities and the industrial companies carried out most of the assessments.
The industrial companies were given primary responsibility for handling the

technical and economic aspects of the projects, while the central authorities
made an assessment of questions relating to the structure of industry, energy
supply, credit and finance, matters of safety and emergency preparedness and
various environmental aspects, on the basis of material prepared by the companies.

Discussion of questions of interest to the central authorities, as well as
negotiations and contact with the industrial companies, were carried out through
the Negotiating Committee for New Industrial Enterprises – a permanent committee
contributing to the authorities' assessment of larger industrial projects. Both
the industrial companies and the authorities made some use of independent
expertise. This applied in particular to the evaluation of environmental aspects,
where information was sought from technical and scientific experts both in
Norway and abroad. However, it became apparent that there was a certian difference
of opinion among the experts, both with regard to the magnitude of the emissions
and their possible consequences. To some degree, this was due to the fact that
the companies were able to state definitively what processes would be used in
production only at a late stage in the proceedings. During the final consideration
of the development plans the various attitudes to the development question
were influenced by what expertise each party considered to be most reliable.

F. Co-ordination of the partial assessments: how the different impacts were
    assessed and ranked

In the case under consideration, the need for administration and co-ordination
of the preparatory studies was particularly great as a result of the time factor.
The Ministry of Industry and the Negotiating Committee for New Industrial
Enterprises played a central role in this connexion. It was the Negotiating
Committee which was to make recommendations to the Minister of Industry as to how
the wet gas option should be utilized and where the plants should be located. The
Ministry of Industry, in turn, was responsible for preparing the case for final
consideration by the Government and in the Storting (parliament). However, it
turned out to be difficult to co-ordinate all the studies in time. The survey
and evaluation of pollution aspects was not completed until the final phase of
the administrative proceedings. The main reason for this was that the industrial
companies and the environmental authorities had for a long time regarded the
danger of photo-chemical smog as relatively small. A more detailed evaluation
showed that the problem was much more serious than first anticipated. However,
this information was not available until January–February 1974, with the
result that it was absolutely necessary to continue analyses of pollution
problems. Thus, a situation arose where recommendations for development at
Bamble, which were put to the Government in 1974, became dependent on whether
further analyses of pollution questions showed that this location was acceptable
from the point of view of the environment. Had environmental authorities arrived
at the opposite conclusion, the Government's primary position would have been
invalidated.

The assessment techniques used in the Bamble case cannot be described as particularly advanced. There was a reasonable attempt to obtain a comprehensive picture
of the advantages and disadvantages, but little effort was made to use collective
cost-benefit analyses which took into account the necessity of making priority
rankings of qualitative aspects. So the general evaluation became based largely
upon quantitative factors, with the major emphasis on industrial economics, and
a rough, non-structured assessment of both short-term and long-term qualitative
aspects. It seems reasonable to assume that, in the final evaluation of alternatives, this type of analysis results in great emphasis being placed on
economically quantifiable conditions.

G. The role of the general public in the decision-making process

The participation of the general public in the decision-making process was
mainly through active debate in the relevant community - particularly in the local
press, and through different forms of information meetings. Most active in this
connexion were those individuals or groups of individuals who were most negative
towards the proposed plans. Much of the opposition was channelled through the
Telemark Nature and Environment Conservation Society.

Importance was attached to the following three arguments:

(a) What the area needed first and foremost was lighter industry providing better
employment possibilities for women, not large-scale processing industry of which
there was already enough.

(b) The pollution load in the area was already very great, and people were
concerned that new processing industry in the area might make the situation
worse through interaction between old and new emissions (smog).

(c) Industrial development of such large dimensions as formulated in the plans
would result in unacceptable strain on the region, from the points of view of
the population and of industry. This might result in significant long-term
social consequences.

The Telemark Nature and Environment Conservation Society did not oppose the
location of parts of the planned project in Bamble, but the Society could not
accept the entire project, as the smog problem was not adequately clarified.

It is worth noting that the Telemark Nature and Environment Conservation Society
gradually built up, through voluntary efforts, a capacity and competence which
was soon recognized. This is illustrated by the fact that the members of the
society were asked to attend a meeting of the parliamentary committee dealing
with development projects, so that they could express their points of view. This
was not the usual practice and must have meant that the parliamentary committee
expected to hear significant arguments.

H. The time factor in the different phases

It has been mentioned earlier that the entire process took about one year and
so the time factor, in itself, distinctly limited the possibility of obtaining a
well-founded basis for decision. We have pointed out the factors which became
the primary objects for evaluation, but even in these cases much was lacking to
meet even relatively modest information requirements. Furthermore, not all the
impact assessments were co-ordinated in time.

Particularly in connexion with the assessment of pollution aspects, time became
very short in the final stages of the administrative procedures. Evaluations
of these factors continued right up to the time the proposed development was
discussed in the Stroting (parliament). As regards the feed-back of results to
the planning and decision-making process, the conditions necessary to achieve
this were not the best. In addition to the time factor, importance was also
attached to the contributions to the decision-making process from the three
arenas described earlier, as well as the lack of systematic contact or guidelines
for distribution of work between the different levels.

I. The effect of the impact assessments on the original plans for the project

The result of the analyses primarily affected the requirements for polluting
emissions established by the authorities.

Both the Government and the local authorities had made it quite clear that the total air and water pollution in the district must be reduced. So in addition to strict requirements with regard to emissions from the new activities, it was also necessary to implement measures which would result in a significant reduction of emissions from other industry in the area. Technical and economic analyses showed that this was possible. Consequently, specific conditions were laid down in accordance with the results of the analyses. If this had not been the case, it is improbable that the entire petro-chemical complex would have been sited in Bamble.

The companies were also required to ensure that construction of all the plants was not started simultaneously. In this way it was hoped that pressure on the local labour market would be reduced. This was acceptable to the companies, both technically and economically, since the internal relationship between the plants allowed staggered construction of the complex.

WHAT MAY BE LEARNED FROM THE ADMINISTRATIVE HANDLING OF THE BAMBLE CASE

We have pointed out above that the time constraints had important consequences for the arrangement and scope of the administrative procedures. The time was short because the State, in accordance with the agreement with the Phillips Group on the wet gas option, was obliged to give a reply by May-June 1974 on whether they would utilize the option. The question whether the State, through negotiations with the Phillips Group might have achieved a postponement of that date lies outside the scope of this discussion.

In the Bamble case, the decision-making process was divided between a national arena and one or two local arenas. While the national authorities dealt with matters of national political interest and administrative procedures, those aspects which may be referred to as "subsidiary effects of industrial develop-ments in the localization district" were studied and dealt with by the local authorities. As already pointed out, no comprehensive evaluation was actually made of these aspects.

To work under strict time limits requires particularly good administration and co-ordination of preparatory studies. This was achieved in the central decision-making arena, where there was a proper organizational structure, a relatively clear distribution of work, and in most cases co-ordinated progress. The local level represents a complete contrast. Co-operation between the parties at this level was not very well organized, and there was little discussion as to how these authorities could best contribute towards a proper clarification of the situation, based on the tasks and requirements of the local community.

During the debate on the Bamble project in the Storting in June 1974, the Minister of Environment noted that the environmental authorities had learned that it was necessary to emphasize the importance of starting evaluations of environmental consequences as early as possible in the administrative procedures. The Minister also stated that any collective evaluation made by the Government must be based on complete background data, taking into account the pollution effects.

NEW LEGISLATION ON ENVIRONMENTAL IMPACT ASSESSMENTS

Some of the problems experienced in the Bamble case are now of historical interest only, as new legislation has been passed or is proposed which gives clearer guidelines for dealing with such cases. (See earlier references to the Establishment Control Act and to other legislation). In addition, measures have

been taken to ensure a greater degree of co-ordination between central and local
authorities. A few of these measures are outlined below.

Preparatory studies were published in 1977 relating to a new Planning Act and a
comprehensive Pollution Act, which proposed the inclusion of regulations
requiring environmental impact assessments of measures and enterprises with
potential effects on the environment. The new proposals imply better updating
of information and improved co-ordination of legislation. The obligation to
carry out the analyses will rest on those responsible for preparing plans which
are affected by the regulations in these acts. The objective of an impact
assessment is to provide a sound basis for evaluating long-term considerations
on the management of resources against other considerations connected with a
balanced development of settlement and the employment and living conditions of
the local community.

The requirement to carry out environmental impact assessments will place new
demands on preparatory administrative procedures, with regard to qualified
manpower and to time. Those responsible for planning and preparing an enterprise
will be required to cover the costs of carrying out the analyses and publishing
the results. It is emphasized that the responsible planning authorities at the
central, county and municipal levels will have prime responsibility for putting
the arrangement into practice. Furthermore, it is important that the general
public and all interested parties be briefed as early as possible and be given
the opportunity to express an opinion before the case is decided.

According to the legislation proposals, the environmental impact assessments shall
be performed in a sound professional manner. They shall not go into more detail
than necessary to clarify the most important anticipated effects of the
enterprise on the environment. The authorities responsible for granting
permission for the enterprise will decide the breadth and depth of the studies
to be performed.

Proposals for legislation relating to environmental impact assessments to be
included in the Planning Act and the Pollution Act are now being evaluated by the
central authorities. There seems to be wide political agreement on the necessity
for improved legislation on these matters. It is also apparent that a number of
larger enterprises presently under preparation and evaluation are being dealt
with largely in accordance with the proposed legislation relating to
environmental impact assessments.

As for the question of improved co-ordination of studies and planning to clarify
the effects of a large enterprise on the local community, special investigating
committees have in recent cases been appointed with representatives from the
central, regional and municipal authorities and from industry. These committees
are intended to administer, initiate and co-ordinate the relevant studies at
this level, and to act as a forum for the exchange of information between the
different parties. The work of these committees is financed mainly by the
industrial companies and by public funds.

Environmental Appraisal for Future Petro-Chemical Developments at National and Regional Levels in Scotland

R. G. H. Turnbull

(United Kingdom)

INTRODUCTION

Within the past two decades there has been growing concern in the United Kingdom about the effects of new development on the quality of the environment and the ability of the planning system to take these effects into account at the project submission stage and in the context of forward planning. Encroachment on the countryside by new and expanded towns, motorways and industry has been a significant factor in increasing public anxiety regarding the implications of development for the environment. The concern is by no means new, but until recently the projects which have aroused opposition have been intermittent and geographically dispersed. Since the discovery of dry gas in the southern part of the North Sea in 1965, and the discovery of oil and gas beneath the North Sea off the Scottish coast in 1970, this has no longer been the case.

The onshore requirements for the exploitation of North Sea oil and gas resulted in the concentration of many unfamiliar and controversial proposals within a few areas; these have had a profound effect on the social, economic and physical environment. The industrial developments gave rise to a range of environmental problems because of the different degrees of scale and urgency and, due to their diverse and changing nature, presented difficulties in obtaining reliable estimates of land requirements at any given point in time. The main types of development ranged from service bases, landfall for pipelines, tank farms, gas and oil separation plants, module and platform construction, pipecoating and storage yards,. refinery and petrochemical processing plants, to a very large number of old-established and new firms providing commercial and professional products and services as a partial activity.

The transport of oil, gas, men and materials has also given rise to massive investments in infrastructure, including marine and port facilities, onshore pipeline routes and improved road, rail and air facilities for fixed wing aircraft and helicopters. In addition, the provision of housing and accommodation camps for the immigrant labour force attracted by the upsurge in development resulted in the need to extend and develop the social services including schools and community facilities.

Against this backgound, this paper reviews the historical and evolving situation regarding the preparation of National Planning Guidelines and the effort made to

apply environmental impact assessment to determine the land potential for petrochemical development in Scotland. It discusses some of the procedural and
institutional questions in the use of environmental impact assessment in the
forward planning process at national and regional levels, and the development
in public awareness and concern for the protection of the environment. Attention
is drawn to the problems and many inherent difficulties of ensuring adequate
examination and analysis of complex proposals without undue delay in reaching
a decision. A description of the approach being attempted in Scotland is given
together with an outline summary of the studies being undertaken by the Scottish
Office to facilitate the application of environmental considerations.

BACKGROUND TO THE NATIONAL PLANNING GUIDELINES

A. New planning legislation and re-organization of local government

The issue of the National Planning Guidelines in Scotland followed the introduction of new planning legislation (1) and the reorganization of local government.
Among the aims of the new legislation, which came into operation in May 1975,
was the desire to separate strategic from local planning issues, and to leave the
latter to be dealt with at the local level (2). In this way it was hoped that
some of the criticisms of the old development planning system could be overcome.
Formerly all proposed amendments to approved plans had to be referred to the
Secretary of State for approval, but the new system made provision for local plans
to be amended and adopted by the new district authorities. The system also made
provision for the new regional authorities to prepare structure plans containing
strategic and policy guidance rather than the precise land-use allocations which
had characterized the old style plans.

B. Disengagement

One move towards greater local responsibility for development planning was a
redefinition of the role of the Secretary of State in planning matters. This new
stance can be summed up in the word "disengagement". A circular issued in May
1977 stated that "... the Secretary of State intends to authorise planning
authorities to grant planning permission for a wide range of developments not in
accord with development plans, without prior reference to him. In future he will
wish to be notified only about proposals which raise national issues, or which
would not be in accordance with an approved structure plan or with a local plan
called-in and approved by him ... As a corollary, guidelines on national planning
issues will be issued from time to time in order to indicate the broad policies
which planning authorities should have in mind in preparing development plans
and in exercising their development control functions".

The circular was accompanied by a series of guidelines covering sites for large-
scale industry, petrochemicals, agricultural land, nature conservation, landscape
and recreation and aggregates. Reference was also made to the coastal planning
guidelines issued in 1974, which divided the coast of Scotland into preferred
development and conservation zones. These would continue to form a basis for
policy, and the existing arrangements for notification of oil-related developments
would continue to apply. It was noted that any developments of a significant
scale within a preferred conservation zone would raise a national issue.

C. Evolving situation on national planning guidelines

The circular on guidelines described their function in terms of defining the level
at which there was a 'national interest' in development control matters, but it
also made clear again that development control could not be considered independently of development planning. As it is through development control that the

provisions of the development plan takes shape, guidelines which offer principles
for development control must inevitably be taken into account at the development
planning stage. Planning authorities were simply encouraged to "have in mind"
the broad policies indicated in the guidelines when preparing their development
plans.

The guidelines themselves, however, contained suggestions for more positive
action. In the guidelines on "Sites for Large-Scale Industry", site selection
criteria were set out, together with an indication of the areas most likely to
meet the criteria. Planning authorities were encouraged to examine the potential
for large-scale industry in these areas, and to frame their plans and development
control policies accordingly. Similarly, the guidelines for petrochemical
developments stated that "it would be prudent for planning authorities to establish
the potential for petrochemical developments in their area and to frame their
structure plans, local plans and development control policies so that sites can
be readily identified if and when required". In practice, working partnerships
have been established between central and local Government to consider and
develop the best means of implementing the recommendations contained in the
guidelines.

D. Issues raised by the guidelines

The guidelines'emphasis on establishing the potential for different types of
industrial sites have raised a number of interesting issues and questions to which
the working partnerships between central and local government are addressing
themselves. For example:

(a) How is 'potential' to be defined? Can a potential in an area be identified
which does not include some consideration of individual sites within the area
and of the type of industry which may become established on the sites? Recent
developments suggest probably not. The days are past when sites could be earmar-
ked as 'suitable for industry' - and so zoned in the development plan - simply
because they met the physical criteria for industrial land, i.e. were suitable
from a developer's viewpoint. The growth in concern for the environment and the
increase in public awareness of the health and hazards associated with some types
of industry mean that effectively, sites defined as "suitable" for industry would
have to meet any environmental and safety criteria as well as having a basic
physical capability of being developed for industry. It follows, then, in defining
the potential of an area for industry, that at any but the most superficial level
some consideration must be given to the availability of "suitable" sites.

(b) Notwithstanding concern over the environmental effects of industry, there
are certain types of industrial activity with locational requirements so
stringent that only one or two physically-suitable sites exist in the whole of
Scotland. For example, a petrochemical complex requiring deepwater marine access
on the east coast may well find itself very short of alternatives. Should such
rare sites be safeguarded, even if no firm proposal exists to use them? And if
there is a firm proposal to use such a site, at what point should environmental
and safety criteria override outstanding - even unique - physical suitability?
If such a dilemma occurs over site selection, is it possible that closer scrutiny
of industrial policy could identify such potential difficulties before they arise
in relation to actual sites?

(c) If sites are to be defined as "suitable" on environmental and safety grounds
as well as in terms of physical suitability, what level of detail can be attained
and usefully applied when it is not known precisely what industry will use a
site? Some progress has been made in helping to fill this gap by the preparation
and issue to planning authorities of Planning Information Notes dealing with

various types of petrochemical developments.

(d) Finally, a question which exists at national level; if several "suitable"
sites are identified by Regional and District Authorities, how many should be
given development plan status?

ENVIRONMENTAL IMPACT ASSESSMENT

A. Background in the United States

Impact assessments were largely the outcome of the National Environmental Policy
Act (NEPA) of the United States which came into effect in January 1970. This Act,
which required the production of Environmental Impact Statements for major federal
projects, stimulated research into ways of identifying and measuring such impacts.
This happened more or less simultaneously with the first effects of offshore
exploitation of oil in Scotland, and it was against this background that the
American ideas about environmental impact analysis first found their way to the
United Kingdom.

B. Background in Scotland

Offshore oil and gas activity resulted in a series of proposals for major onshore
developments from 1970 onwards. Some of these proposals posed unusually difficult
problems for the planning authorities for some or all of the following reasons:

- large size of project   - scenic significance of area

- unusual activity or process   - temporary project

- small resident population in area - national interest in the project

- insufficient infrastructure in area - changing site requirements.

Many of the earliest applications were made in rural areas where planning
authorities were not accustomed to handling projects of this complexity. It was
clear therefore that a special effort would be needed to ensure that the proposals
were adequately understood and that planning staff were not overloaded in dealing
with them. To this end the Scottish Office issued a technical advice note in 1974
which provided outline guidance on how to approach the appraisal of the impact of
oil-related development. The essential steps in asking the right questions about
a proposal were set out, and the possibility of carrying out an impact analysis
was discussed.

To overcome the twin problems of staff and project complexity, consultants were
appointed to carry out the necessary work. In the early cases, the Scottish Office
called-in* the planning applications and commissioned the consultants. In
subsequent cases, the planning authorities appointed consultants or were able
to emulate the consultants' studies themselves. From 1973 to the present some
thirteen major oil related proposals have been the subject of impact or similar
studies (excluding various development plan studies). These impact studies are
listed in annex I.

From the experience gained in these studies two main conclusions were drawn.

(a) It was apparent from the variety of these studies that there were many different situations where this kind of analysis was relevant. The scope, organization,
and emphasis of the analysis varied according to the importance and size of the

_____
*i.e. assumed responsibility for decision-making

project, whether it was a remote possibility or a highly probable development, and whether one developer or several were likely to be involved. This applied, even more, to linked proposals extending over a large geographical area. The common element was the attempt to predict the effect of a proposed project on the physical, social and economic environments of the host areas.

(b) It became clear that there are four critical factors in compiling a satisfactory report of this kind within a reasonable time:

1. adequate information about the project(s) and area(s);

2. adequate expertise to identify and predict potential impacts;

3. a methodical approach to date collection, analysis and consultations;

4. sufficient awareness of the external context of national, regional and local attitudes, and of administrative procedures to make judgements based on the study results.

C. Commissioning of research

What these conclusions added up to was a need for guidance on how to carry out an adequate assessment of a complex project efficiently. Central Government commissioned the preparation of a manual of guidance which could be used by planning authorities and others in the United Kingdom when dealing with this type of application. A two-year study included consideration of procedures and techniques of impact assessment used in the United States and other countries, and a review of the practices adopted by planning authorities in the United Kingdom when dealing with major proposals. The research team, under the guidance of a steering committee of central and local government officers and other representatives, then produced an interim manual "The Assessment of Major Industrial Developments", published in December 1976 as Research Report 13 of the U.K. Department of the Environment.

D. Evolving use of the research manual

The interim manual was designed for flexible use within the framework of the present United Kingdom planning system. Its use does not require any alteration in statute, and the structured method of appraisal which it recommends for major projects is largely based on planning authority experience gained from a number of sources. It is perhaps for this reason that, in addition to being used on single projects, the manual has proved adaptable to other planning tasks. It has become clear that a number of planning authorities have made use of it in trying to resolve the issues raised earlier in this paper on industrial site selection. In Scotland, the manual procedure has been adapted to assess alternative sites for petrochemical developments, new gas terminals related to the government-sponsored gas-gathering pipeline study, and it may be used in a comparative assessment of harbour sites and other such comparative site assessments.

E. Use of the Manual Procedure

Examples of the use of the manual procedure both in the way it was designed to be used and in the new ways which may be found of applying it will help to demonstrate the difficulties and advantages of project appraisal in both old and new applications.

The first major project to be the subject of an assessment using the approach advocated in the manual was a proposal to build a natural gas liquids separation plant near Peterhead. The intention was to ship the separated liquids out by tanker from a new jetty in Peterhead Harbour, but this aspect did not form part

of the planning application as it was permitted development. There was some
uncertainty about the harbour but it was not until a full investigation was
arranged that it became clear that even if the chosen processing site proved
acceptable, export of liquified petroleum gas from Peterhead Harbour would present
major difficulties. It was also found, in a separate study, that venting of gasoline vapor from ships during loading could under certain weather conditions cause
tainting of foodstuffs at a processing factory across the harbour. Neither of
these points arose directly out of the planning application, nor was there an
obvious way to investigate them in the existing system. The resultant need for
close co-operation between all the authorities concerned with approval or
licensing of new developments is clear. For example in some recent projects the
planning authorities concerned have commissioned work from private consultants
on safety questions, in order to have information on hazard available at the
same time as information on other planning issues.

F. Problems of assessment

Further problems arise in the assessment itself. In project appraisal, impacts
of development must be considered in three distinct stages. They must be identified; then measured; and then the significance of the impacts singly and in total
must be assessed. Each of these stages has its difficulties.

(a) Since our knowledge of the environment and of the effects of activities is
incomplete, impacts may fail to be identified; effects on human health for
example may not become apparent for many years.

(b) There may be no acceptable means of measuring impacts which are believed
to exist; for example, subtle changes in values, attitudes, and culture may
prove impossible to predict or describe.

(c) The most difficult area of all is concerned with assessing the comparative
significance of the impacts identified and measured (even if they can be
measured).

G. Value of EIA in relation to time spent on assessment

In these circumstances one may ask, whether the trend in the last few years
towards making explicit the basis of decision-making by means of project
appraisal and similar methods has been worthwhile. Or has the result simply been
to complicate and lengthen the process of consideration? The answer must be that
the growth of environmental pressure groups and the extent of public concern for
the environment is such that it has become a political necessity to ensure that
major issues are clearly seen to have been identified and adequately examined by
authorities concerned. The complexity of such decisions is real, and if the public
is made aware of this complexity, the level of debate can only be improved. The
proper scrutiny of major proposals is bound to take time, but if it is carried
out methodically, the time taken will have been well spent. In the last five
years impact assessment has become an integral part of the planning system, even
if an unofficial one, and it is difficult to imagine that it will be abandoned.

FORWARD PLANNING FOR PETROCHEMICAL DEVELOPMENTS

A. Need for contingency planning

The development of North Sea offshore petroleum reserves has already led to
demands for land, labour and infrastructure, with consequent social, economic
and physical impacts. As development moves into the production stage the
opportunities created by these resources are of increasing significance in areas
of Scotland which are not present major centres of oil and gas activity.

Experience suggests that the ability of central and local government to influence development in these areas is dependent on many factors, but not least upon a continuous information flow and forward assessments of changing capacity, capability, and desirability for development in particular areas.

Since the publication of the Coastal Planning Guidelines in 1974, the Scottish Office has maintained a close working relationship with planning authorities, the purpose of which has been to exchange information and to identify the potential of the areas involved to accommodate oil and gas related developments. The formal background to this work was reinforced by the National Planning Guideline for Petrochemical Developments, issued in 1977; the seven mainland regions most concerned with contingency planning for petrochemicals now have a fairly well developed appreciation of the potential and environmental capacity in their respective areas. This part of the paper reviews the work to date and the contribution made at the national level.

B. Regional initiatives

The terms of reference, approach and methods adopted by the regional working groups have differed according to local conditions, attitudes and the availability of information. In some cases, the initial approach has been made purely from a technical standpoint whereas other approaches have been tempered by political considerations. However, this has in no way diminished the value of the work done. Again, depending on geographical location and local interests, the composition of the working groups has varied.

The working groups have carried out or have been associated with studies aimed at establishing the physical and environmental capacity for petrochemical development within their areas and, to date forty-six site search areas have been examined. Some of the regional authorities concerned have commissioned consultants to undertake special studies, ranging from the economics of feedstock and product transport to site selection criteria, environmental capacity and safety aspects.

Through the application of a blend of site suitability, constraints to development and local authority policy, the original list of forty-six sites has been reduced to thirteen which are thought to have the requisite potential to support petrochemical development. On present evidence, most of the thirteen sites will be presented in structure plan submissions. It should be noted that the establishment of these thirteen preferred petrochemical sites does not mean that the remaining thirty-three sites have no industrial potential. On the contrary, several of the residual sites were identified as being suitable for large-scale non-petro-chemical development.

From the work done under the guideline initiative the Scottish Office has taken the opportunity to enhance the national site register and to establish a better understanding of the industrial site potential in Scotland. Schedules of available information for each of the sites examined have been prepared and compared with a summary list of the information that prospective developers have asked for in the past. In this way, it is hoped to identify deficiencies in the information and what further investigations should be undertaken.

C. Approach to contingency planning

The Regional Working Groups quickly identified the main direction and the purpose of the work to be done, but a number of important difficulties arose out of the uncertainty regarding the availability of feedstock and where it might come ashore. Similarly, because the requirements for different types of petrochemical development vary so considerably, it is difficult to identify a specific piece of

EIA t

land for development until more is known about its precise use. In the event, it was agreed that assumptions would have to be made about the availability of feedstock and that it would be unlikely that planning approval for petrochemical developments would be obtained until a public inquiry had been held.

Against this background, the working groups proceeded to undertake considerable research into indentifying typical sites which might be considered suitable for petrochemical plants through the use of standard 'sieve' techniques and to assess the kinds of impact which may result. None of the sites reached perfection in satisfying all criteria, but the initial selection had been a matter of identifying sites which would meet a prospective developers' needs as economically as possible, which would cause the least disruption to the rest of the community, and which could be released from existing land use.

D. Environmental considerations

(a) Safety: Consultants were commissioned by a number of regional authorities to define the dimensions and layout of petrochemical plants, to draw up general guidelines concerning community safety zones, and to apply these hazard guidelines to the sites identified. Consideration was also given to the potential impact on existing neighbouring industry of hazardous events occurring on the potential petrochemical site.

(b) Pollution: Studies were also commissioned into marine, airborne, visual and aural aspects of pollution. Evidence obtained so far indicates that in some areas there are no difficulties which cannot be overcome at acceptable levels of cost. As existing pollution is very low in some of the areas identified, the capacity to accept new industry without risk is accordingly large. Standards of pollution control in these areas however would not be below those in other parts of the United Kingdom.

(c) Land acquisition: While no formal approaches were made to landowners of the sites identified, an effort was made to establish ownership patterns and to form some view about the problems that might arise over the purchase of land, if required.

(d) Utilities and communications: Through the co-operation of the service departments of the various regional authorities and others, assessments were made to establish the existing pattern and availability of water, electricity, effluent disposal facilities and road, rail and air services. In a general way, attempts were made to identify the engineering cost and environmental implications to extend these utilities should this prove necessary.

(e) Industrial infrastructure: Assessments were also made of the ancillary industrial requirements of a petrochemical complex, including such services as civil engineering, metal fabrication, plant cleaning, mechanical and electrical engineering, pipe insulation painting and stockholding. Where these facilities did not exist in a fully developed form, particularly in relatively remote locations, it was recognised that the expansion and diversification required to undertake these ancillary activities could give rise to secondary environmental problems. Similarly, assessments and estimates were made of the probable labour supply and demand, and the concomitant need for housing, education and community facilities.

(f) Environmental impact appraisal: One regional authority commissioned consultants to carry out an examination of the engineering and other physical factors which would be involved in developing industrial plant on the sites identified. Analysis of environmental problems and environmental costs of possible development was undertaken within the Physical Planning Department. The general conclusion reached was that none of the sites examined was considered suitable for petrochemical development in terms of the environmental consequences. Development on almost all of the sites would cause serious damage to landscape, ecology, the tourist industry, agricultural and recreational use. This, combined with the potential hazard to existing development and existing population, was considered to be an unacceptably high price for the region to pay.

It is perhaps of interest that the conclusions drawn from this initial environmental assessment led to a more comprehensive review of alternative sites, appropriate in environmental terms for petrochemical development. In this and approaches by other regions, the preliminary application of environmental assessments was clearly of value, in that at a very early stage it was possible to identify the main environmental impediments to the use of the identified sites for petrochemical development.

E. Operational factors

From the studies so far undertaken, it would appear that there is a number of operational factors which limit the range of potential sites. These factors include the need for relatively flat land of adequate size with good load-bearing characteristics, proximity to both suitable pipeline landfall conditions and sheltered deep water for marine facilities, the availability of adequate infrastructure and in particular the desirability and feasibility of providing an adequate safety zone around the plant or complex.

The process of selection is:

(a) elimination of land on steep slopes or too high above sea level to meet the needs of the industry;

(b) elimination of land already intensively used for urban development or for other uses which cannot be interfered with;

(c) elimination of land within 1 mile (1.5km) of the built-up area where the erection of a hazardous plant is unlikely to be acceptable without imposing drastic restrictions on other development and high cost on the developer;

(d) elimination of land where heavy liquid gases are likely to flow into dangerous pockets;

(e) elimination of sites within airport safety zones;

(f) acknowledgement of best quality agricultural land, mature woodland and the best grades of nature conservation sites;

(g) acknowledgement of sites where foundation or reclamation cost would be very high;

(h) acknowledgement of sites where servicing and road and rail cost would be very high;

(i) acknowledgement of the number of houses which have to be avoided within the community safety zone;

(j) acknowledgement of pipeline landfalls and possibilities for laying effluent pipes;

(k) acknowledgement of other environmental factors which may be significant in particular areas, and the need to inform the public at the appropriate time.

F. Contribution at the national level

In issuing the guidelines for larger-scale industry, and in particular for petrochemical development, it was appreciated that major chemical developments

inevitably raise pollution and other environmental issues and that it was important
that these should be evaluated by planning authorities at an early stage,
preferably in advance of receiving a planning application. From past experience,
it was recognized that environmental resistance to certain types of industrial
developments is likely to grow, not only in the United Kingdom but throughout
Europe. The causes of this resistance deserve to be treated with respect, and no
Government can be expected to ignore objectors. Great care is necessary in the
preparation and presentation of counter arguments, which are persuasive to the
public at large and may reduce the general antagonism towards industrial
development. The case for proposals must cover economic and environmental issues,
putting the safety risks into a general perspective.

The need to safeguard specific areas of land with special characteristics, a
matter of major importance for industry, was made known at the national level
through the issue of guidelines covering agriculture, forestry, nature conservation, landscape, recreation and the coast. These guidelines on national planning
issues indicated broad policies which planning authorities should have in mind
in preparing development plans and in exercising their development control
functions. They also provided a broad backcloth which was of assistance in the
search area identification for suitable industrial sites.

G. Supporting initiatives

In addition to the issue of national planning guidelines the Scottish Office has
been responsible for a number of initiatives designed to assist planning
authorities and others with forward planning work for oil, gas and petrochemical
developments. Some of these are listed below.

(a) Pipeline Landfalls Discussion Paper: Identified areas in which sites
suitable for both landfalls and associated development might be required and
discussed the steps that might be taken to encourage concentration of development at specific locations.

(b) Oil Terminals Discussion Paper: Described the principal characteristics and
major land use implications of oil terminals and provided a schedule of the
various bodies which have a statutory interest in such developments.

(c) Planning Advice Note on High Pressure Methane Gas Pipelines: Provided
information on the statutory procedures, technical requirements and planning
considerations involved in the routing of high pressure natural gas pipelines
and the siting of surface installations.

(d) Project Appraisal for Development Control: A manual published in 1976
containing a method of appraising major projects, including those related to oil
and gas, for development control purposes. The method of assessment was
supplemented by a series of technical appendices giving detailed advice on the
analysis of particular types of impact and, where appropriate, suggested means
of measuring their effects. Research is continuing.

(e) Landscape Assessment Code for Petrochemical Developments: A commissioned
research project, to carry out a landscape assessment of selected sites for
petrochemical development and to investigate the ways in which different plants
could best be located in terms of layout, safety factors and landscaping
requirements. The second part of the exercise was the preparation of a landscape
design code that could be applied to petrochemical sites generally, based on the
information gleaned from the earlier site investigations and the characteristics
of plants and process provided in the Planning Information Notes issued by
the Scottish Office.

(f) Planning Information Notes (PINs): Series A deals with the specific interest
in petrochemicals of certain central government departments and other agencies,

the legislation under which they operate, and the kind of advice that is available from them to planning authorities. Series B provides information on the main
plants and processes that characterize the basic hydrocarbon processing, primary
petrochemical processing, and downstream petrochemical processing sections of the
oil, gas and petrochemical industry.

(g) Environmental Monitoring by Remote Sensing: A commissioned experimental
project to test the usefulness of using false colour aerial photographs to
provide a basis from which the environmental effects of any new oil and gas
related developments within the areas covered can be progressively monitored.

(h) Instiute of Geological Sciences: Close liaison has been established between
the Scottish Office and representatives of IGS so that technical expertise can
be focused on those matters arising out of oil and gas related activity in which
there is a geological interest. Some examples of the work covered to date are
the determination of the suitability of certain areas for the storage of oil
in underground caverns, the identification of those areas of the North Sea bed
where the regime is suitable for pipelaying, assessments of ground stability on
potential major petrochemical sites, and the identification of geological hazards
to overland pipeline construction such as hard rock.

H. Consultations

The main purpose of consultation, whether with official bodies or with the public,
is to ensure that those with an interest in an area have the opportunity to present information and voice opinions before decisions are taken. Statutes require
planning authorities to consult with a number of authorities in the preparation
of structure plans and local plans and in exercising their development control
functions. For this reason, and because petrochemical developments inevitably
raise pollution and safety issues, the regional working groups sought early
advice from the control bodies on the requirements of prospective sites and
plants. Discussions were facilitated by the availability of preliminary
environmental assessments and other studies prepared by the working groups. It
is a matter of judgement for the planning authority to decide when this preliminary investigation and analysis work should be publicized. Similarly, statutory
provision is made for consultations with the public at various stages of the plan-
making process. A table of the possible stages for publicity and public consultation is in annexII. It is to this extent that consultees participate in plan-making
although the responsibility for what is included in a submitted plan rests with
the planning authority in the light of the information and advice it receives.

REFERENCES

1. Town and Country Planning (Scotland) Act 1972, 1977.

2. Local Government (Scotland) Act 1973.

Annex I

LIST OF IMPACT STUDIES

1. Oil Platform Construction at Loch Carron (Drumbuie)
2. Oil Platform Construction at Loch Broom
3. Oil Related Developments - Stornoway
4. Oil Terminal at Flotta
5. Concrete Platform Yards in Firth of Clyde
6. Oil Refinery at Nigg
7. Comparative Analysis of Platform Sites in Loch Carron Area
8. Loch Eribol Feasibility Study for Oil Related Developments
9. Buchan Impact Study for Petrochemicals
10. NGL Plant Safety Study at Peterhead
11. British Gas Terminal Retrospective Environmental Audit - St Fergus
12. NGL Plant Safety Study at Mossmorran
13. Development of Beatrice Field

Annex II

PUBLICITY AND PUBLIC CONSULTATION IN DEVELOPMENT PLANNING:
TABLE OF POSSIBLE STAGES

Recommended in the 'Skeffington Report'	Required by the Act	Suggestions
Publicity at outset, giving details of how and when the public will be informed and consulted as plan preparation proceeds. (representations should be considered continuously while plan is being prepared but there should also be set pauses for public consultation, particularly at the following stages:)	Publicity concerning opportunity for making representations (public consultation)	FIRST STAGE: Publicity at outset giving details of how and when the public will be informed and consulted as plan preparation proceeds, with outline of plan purpose and opportunity for initial public comment
Public consultation after surveys on the choices open to the authority in deciding the main planning issues.	Publicity for survey findings.	SECOND STAGE: Publicity for survey findings with opportunity for public comment
Public consultation on a statement of proposals including any remaining alternatives with preferences and reasoning.	Publicity and public consultation on matters proposed to be included in the plan.	THIRD AND MAIN STAGE: Publicity and public consultation on tentative package of draft policies proposals, with reasoning. (At this stage the public should have access to all relevant survey material).
Plan finalised, taking account of representations	Plan finalised, taking account of representations	PLAN FINALISED, TAKING ACCOUNT OF REPRESENTATIONS
Opportunity for formal objection.	Opportunity for formal objection	OPPORTUNITY FOR FORMAL OBJECTION

PART III

Public Information and Participation

Public Participation in the Canadian Environmental Assessment and Review Process

F. G. Hurtubise and R. G. Connelly

(Canada)

INTRODUCTION

This paper illustrates, by means of four case studies, public participation in
the Canadian Environmental Assessment and Review Process. The case studies,
involving different development proposals in geographically distinct areas of
Canada include a uranium hexafluoride refinery in southern Ontario, hydrocarbon
exploration in the Artic, port expansion on the Pacific coast and a highway
project in the Yukon. In each instance, the public played a significant role in
influencing the development proposal.

The examples illustrate how the public has influenced project site selection,
effectively questioned the need for development action, and required the
investigation of a particular proposal to be extended to include consideration
of resource use in a much broader geographical area. The case studies also
illustrate the flexibility of the Canadian Environmental Assessment and Review
Process in allowing for wide citizen participation in different geographical
regions and in adjusting to accommodate changing needs.

THE ENVIRONMENTAL ASSESSMENT AND REVIEW PROCESS AND THE PUBLIC

The Canadian Environmental Assessment and Review Process is based on a firm
agreement by ministers of the Federal Government that they will be responsible
for the environmental consequences of activities proposed by their departments,
including the incorporation of suitable mitigating measures. The mechanism is
not a legal instrument and consequently the public does not have the option of
recourse to the courts.

The process is essentially based on a self-assessment approach, in which departments and agencies are responsible for determining the environmental consequences
of their own programmes, projects and activities and deciding upon the environmental significance of the anticipated effects. In order to ensure early public
input in the process, the Federal Cabinet has directed that information be
provided and public response sought early in the planning stage, before vital
decisions are taken that may be difficult to alter. When an activity is deemed
by the federal initiator or sponsor to have a potentially significant
environmental impact, it is referred to the Federal Environmental Assessment
Review Office for a formal review by an Environmental Assessment Panel. The

Federal Environmental Assessment Review Office is responsible for the establishment of Environmental Assessment Panels to review referred projects and for provision of secretariat support to the panels.

Each panel is an independent group of experts (usually four to six) having a
mandate to review the environmental consequences of a specific project or activity
and to report its findings to the Minister. The case studies presented in section
III illustrate projects that were reviewed by various panels.

Provision of information to the public and public participation is central to
the panel phase of the Environmental Assessment and Review Process. It is
recognized that the public has an important role in determining the environmental
significance of a development action. After a panel is formed, one of its first
tasks is to issue guidelines to the proponent for the preparation of an
Environmental Impact Statement. Public input on the guidelines may be solicited
at this point by inviting written and oral comments or by convening public
meetings. Guidelines are made public at the same time as they are forwarded to the
proponent. Once the Environmental Impact Statement is completed, and after allowing sufficient time for public and government review, the panel holds public
meetings to receive comments on the Environmental Impact Statement and on the
project. These are normally held in the immediate area of the project.

Very early in the review process, panel staff undertake an information programme
to inform the public of the nature of the review and to ensure that the public
has adequate opportunity to review and comment on the project. Once the
Environmental Impact Statement is available, it is sent to interested parties
and government agencies well in advance of public meetings. Written comments on
the project are solicited and these also receive wide distribution prior to the
hearings. Advertisements are placed periodically in the media advising the public
of progress of and procedures for the review, location of viewing centres
(libaries, government offices) that contain information on the project, and
finally, the time and location of public meetings. Public meetings may be
conducted at various stages in the process. They may be held to receive comment
on the guidelines, to review and determine any major deficiencies in the
Environmental Impact Statement and, when it is considered that sufficient
information is available to allow the panel to reach its conslusion, to receive
final comment on the project. The proponent is also encouraged to conduct an
information programme in order to acquaint the public with the implications of
the proposal.

Environmental Assessment Panel meetings are not legal proceedings. Rules of
evidence normally followed by commissions of enquiry or other tribunals do not
apply, although each panel establishes procedures for the conduct of its meetings.
Panel meetings are normally structured so as to provide the greatest opportunity
for an individual or group to express opinions or provide information on the
potential impact of the proposal. Panel staff are available before and during
meetings to assist anyone wishing to participate in such reviews. Thus at public
meetings, both facts and opinions from technical experts and individual members
of the public are heard by the panel.

After completing its deliberations, the panel prepares its report to the Minister
of the Environment with recommendations on whether a project should proceed. The
report of the panel is normally released to the public shortly after it is
submitted to the Minister. Decisions on the panel's recommendations are made
by the Minister of the Environment and the Minister of the initiating or
sponsoring department.

CASE STUDIES

A.   PROPOSAL FOR A URANIUM HEXAFLUORIDE REFINERY

This provides an illustration of the ability of the public to influence a
development proposal and be involved in site selection. In 1975, Eldorado Nuclear
Limited, a Canadian Crown Corporation, proposed to construct a uranium
hexafluoride refinery in the Province of Ontario. The Environmental Assessment
Panel's mandate was to review potential environmental, socio-economic and
community impacts of the project.

1. The Port Granby Review

In June 1976, guidelines for the preparation of an Environmental Impact Statement
were issued to Eldorado and made public. The Company examined fourteen potential
sites over a two-year period and announced in January 1977 that Port Granby
(near Port Hope, Ontario) was the most attractive location. In June 1977, the
Environmental Impact Statement for the Port Granby site was presented to the Panel
and made public.

When the Environmental Impact Statement was received, an information and
participation programme was organized to provide the public with adequate
opportunity to review and comment on the project. Reviews were also carried out
by federal and provincial government agencies. In the immediate project area,
Eldorado undertook, of its own volition, a public communications programme to
acquaint area residents with the project and its implications. Independent of
Eldorado's programme, panel staff attempted to ensure that the views to be
presented to the Panel at the planned meetings would adequately reflect the range
of interests and concerns of all interested parties.

Public meetings were conducted in two phases. The first phase of meetings, held
in September and October 1977, was designed to identify data deficiencies in the
Environmental Impact Statement. After considering all the submissions made by
the public and government agencies during the phase 1. meetings, the Panel
forwarded to Eldorado a list of clarifications required and deficiencies observed
in the Environmental Impact Statement. The list was also made public and sent to
all the participants at the meetings. Eldorado's response, in December 1977,
was also made public by the Panel and forwarded to meeting participants together
with a list of issues to be discussed in the second phase. The final meetings
were held one month later.

During the course of the two phases of meetings, discussion centred on a number of
issues. Eldorado planned to locate the new refinery on prime farm land, in a
highly-productive agricultural area which supported a small local population
through market gardening. There was concern expressed as to the effects of the
proposed development on the local lifestyle. The proposed management of low-level
radioactive wastes was found to be contentious by the government review agencies
and the public. Eldorado proposed a method of on-site disposal that had undergone
only limited trial in the United States. Another issue of concern was the potential
effects of hydrogen fluoride emissions on community health and on agriculture. In
addition, concern was also expressed about the effectiveness of current
regulatory control and the adequacy of current monitoring programmes.

Following the public meetings, the Panel prepared a report on its findings. The
Panel concluded that the refinery and the refining processes could be
environmentally acceptable on an appropriate site if several conditions were
met. The Port Granby site, however, was found to be unacceptable. The Panel was
concerned about the potential environmental effects of the project as well as its

social impact on the Port Granby community. It was particularly concerned about
the intrusion of the refinery, as an industrial use, into an area where the
present and long-term character is rural and favours agriculture. The Panel also
rejected Port Granby as the site for the proposed waste management facility.

It was clear that public participation had played an important role in the decision
not to locate the proposed Eldorado refinery in Port Granby. The public presentations to the Panel were able to demonstrate effectively the impact the refinery
might have on local agricultural patterns and community lifestyle. Information
that was lacking in the Environment Impact Statement on potential social and
community impacts on the local area had been provided by the public. This led
the Panel in its final analysis to make a further recommendation that any new
proposal should include a more comprehensive analysis of the anticipated impacts
on the local community and evidence that its concerns had been taken into account.

2. <u>The Hope Township (Port Hope), Dill Township (Sudbury), and Blind River
    Review</u>

Following the rejection of the Port Granby proposal, Eldorado identified potential
sites in the Port Hope, Sudbury and Blind River regions of Ontario and requested
that they be reviewed. The Federal Cabinet agreed in June 1978 that it would make
the final choice of location for the new refinery following completion of the
Environmental Assessment Panel's report on these new sites. Eldorado prepared
separate Environmental Impact Statements for each location based on the guidelines
issued for the Port Granby review and on the results of the public meetings
conducted in that area. These were distributed to the public and government
agencies for review approximately two months prior to public meetings which were
held in each of the three areas. Eldorado's new proposal contained more information on the plant processes and operations than the previous Port Granby proposal.
In addition, the proposal for management of low-level radioactive wastes was
altered considerably.

A public information and participation programme similar to the one used in the
Port Granby review was re-established by the Panel. A considerable effort was
made in the three regions to create an awareness of the Environmental Review
Process and to ensure that all persons and organizations having an interest in the
project were informed of the hearings, and of the opportunities to make their
views known to the Panel.

In keeping with the Panel's recommendation regarding a more comprehensive
analysis of the anticipated impacts on the local community, Eldorado undertook
a much more intensive public communications programme. Eldorado made a greater
effort to contact various citizens' committees, formed either in support of or
opposed to the proposed project. Information offices were established in each
area and numerous neighbourhood meetings were held to acquaint the public with
the project implications. The result of this intensive public information
programme was evident during the Panel meetings. In all three areas, the public
was more aware of the nature of the project than had been the case in Port
Granby. During the Port Granby review, most people who participated in the meetings
were opposed to the project. As a result of Eldorado's revamped information programme, participation was more evenly-balanced between those who supported and
those who opposed the project.

Many of the issues discussed during the Hope Township, Dill Township and Blind
River review had been raised at the Port Granby meetings. There were, however,
a number of specific issues peculiar to each of the three sites. In the case
of the Hope Township site, as it was within 5km of the Port Granby site, there
was again concern that the refinery would constitute a major industrial intrusion

into an area substantially committed to agriculture. The Panel, however, found
the combination of circumstances to be considerably different and concluded that
the proposed refinery would not add to the "development wedge" while other
industries that might locate on the site could do so. During the Dill Township
meetings many of the citizens living adjacent to the proposed site voiced their
objection to this location. Their major concern was that the proposed refinery
would increase developmental pressures in the area, thereby altering the rural
character of the area which consists of scattered residential development and a
number of small farms. The Panel felt, however, that any adverse impacts of the
refinery would be less than that feared by the residents. In Blind River, there
was considerable discussion of the socio-economic effects of the refinery on
the small community. Local citizens presented information to augment that
provided in the Environmental Impact Statement and to show the positive socio-
economic benefits of the refinery locating in that area.

In conclusion, the Panel's recommendations, which were subsequently endorsed by
the Minister of Environment, were that all three sites were acceptable for the
refinery if certain conditions were met. One of the conditions, which would
ensure continuing participation in both construction and operation of the
proposed refinery, was the formation of a Citizens' Monitoring Committee. Regardless of the refinery location, the Panel gave strong support to the creation of
such a committee, whose purposes would be to provide for information dissemination
of the monitoring results of the industry and regulatory agencies, to increase
industry/regulatory agency accountability and to facilitate ready access to
Eldorado management by members of the local community. This committee, which
would be unique in Canada, would be composed of the main interest groups in the
local community; government agencies would participate only as observers.

Not only had the public played a role in selecting a site for the refinery,
public participation had resulted in substantial changes to the original development proposal and had ensured that there would be continuing public involvement
in the plant operations by means of a Citizen's Monitoring Committee. In the
process, both the company and government agencies had learned a lot about the
value of public participation.

B.   PROPOSAL FOR HYDROCARBON EXPLORATION IN LANCASTER SOUND

This project illustrates how a very specific proposal led to the consideration of
resource use in a much broader geographical area. The procedures for environmental
impact assessment review were influenced by wide citizen participation in
geographical terms and by cultural diversity among the participants. Considerable
emphasis was placed on the socio-economic impact of the project.

In 1977, the Federal Department of Indian and Northern Affairs, the initiating
department, requested that an environmental impact assessment review be
undertaken on a proposal by Norlands Petroleum Limited to drill one exploratory
well in Lancaster Sound. It also requested that consideration be given
at the same time to regional clearance for other exploratory drilling proposals.

Lancaster Sound is located in the Canadian Arctic, north of Baffin Island. It is
the entrance to the Northwest Passage and hence is a migratory path and living
area for marine mammals and birds as well as a transportation artery. It is also
a very important nesting area for significant colonies of many species of birds.

Guidelines for the preparation of an Environmental Impact Statement were issued
to Norlands in March, 1978 and made public. The Environmental Impact Statement
was submitted to the panel in July 1978 for public and government agency review.
Prior to the receipt of the Environmental Impact Statement, Panel staff visited

the four potentially affected Inuit settlements in the area to meet the public
and explain the review process. It became apparent that socio-economic matters
were closely linked to environmental issues. The Inuit live in harmony with
their environment and, in spite of developmental pressures, have maintained close
cultural ties to the land. The harvest from hunting and fishing provides an
important nutritional balance to their diet and is significant to the local
economy. The scope of the review was expanded, therefore, to consider both
socio-economic and environmental matters.

Norlands' public information programme was limited to a few community visits.
In general, residents felt that Norlands had not discussed the proposal with them
to the extent they considered necessary. In order to hear the views of the
residents of the potentially affected communities, the Panel visited each
settlement in October 1978. To further the Panel's understanding of northern
conditions and with the active support of the community councils, arrangements
were made for the Panel members to live with Inuit families in two of the
settlements, and to participate in local activities. By means of this direct
contact between the Inuit and Panel members many local people, who might have
been reluctant to address the panel in a more formal setting, made their views
known. General and more structured meetings were held at the end of October in
Pond Inlet to receive input from government agencies, public interest groups as
well as from local residents. Due to great concern among the local people that
they had insufficient time to adequately prepare for and make presentations at
the meetings, it was agreed to hold a second phase a month later. The second
phase was intended to permit a more detailed examination of issues raised at
the October meetings.

During the course of the community visits and structured meetings many issues of
a very broad nature were raised. It was pointed out that the secondary effects of
oil and gas production, in the event of a hydrocarbon discovery, would be far
greater than the initial exploratory well. The lack of co-ordination of
government policies relating to the area was of conern; potentially conflicting
uses of Lancaster Sound were identified which varied from hydrocarbon exploration
to preservation of the area as a national park. Canada's international treaty
obligations to protect polar bears and migratory birds were also cited. In
addition, there was considerable discussion on the potential socio-economic
impact of the project on the Inuit people. There was concern that the proposed
drilling project could affect traditional uses of Lancaster Sound for transportation and as source of food supply. Inuit spokeman also emphasized the importance
of settling the issue of land claims. They felt that a premature decision on
drilling would stall negotiations which were underway.

Given the importance of these issues, it was evident that the Panel could not
restrict its review to one exploratory well. In fact, acceptance of the Panel by
the local people as an effective vehicle for consultation was predicated on the
expectation that the Panel would take into account the whole spectrum of public
concerns in its deliberations.

During the course of its review, the Panel listened to the concerns of the Inuit
and considered potential physical, biological and socio-economic impacts of the
project. It concluded that Norlands was not sufficiently prepared to undertake
the proposed drilling in 1979 in a safe manner and with minimum risk to the
environment. It also recommended that the whole resource-use question of Lancaster
Sound should be examined before determining whether any drilling should be
allowed in that area. In this regard, the Panel further recommended that any
future request for regional clearance should be supported by a comprehensive
regional assessment. These conclusions and recommendations were accepted by the
Minister of the Environment.

C.   PROPOSAL FOR A PORT EXPANSION

This case study provides an example of how the public was able to influence the Panel's recommendations concerning the magnitude of a proposed development. In 1975, the National Harbours Board proposed to expand the existing Roberts Bank port facility near Vancouver, by adding up to 110 hectares through the addition of four new terminal areas and an administrative area. There would also be a widening of the causeway and an increase in the size of the ship berthing channel, including the addition of a ship turning basin. The expansion was proposed to meet future west coast terminal requirements to handle sulphur, potash, grain, bulk liquids and increased coal exports.

The existing facility consists of a 20 hectare terminal located within the ecologically important Fraser River estuary. The Roberts Bank ecosystem is characterized by a variety of important habitat types. Notable among these are extensive beds of eelgrass which support populations of varied estuarine life forms including fish, crabs and birds.

Guidelines for the preparation of an Environmental Impact Statement were published in March 1976 and made public. The Environmental Impact Statement was prepared by the proponent in October 1977 and submitted to public and government agency review. On the basis of written submissions received from the public and government agencies on the adequacy of the Environmental Impact Statement, the Panel issued a statement of deficiencies to the proponent. In June 1978, supplementary information was recieved in response to the deficiency statement. This information was given wide public distribution and, along with the Environmental Impact Statement, served as the basis for a further public review of the major aspects of the project. The final review consisted of public meetings, held in late October and early November 1978.

Throughout the public review of the port expansion proposal, especially at the meetings, the Panel heard concerns expressed by many individuals, groups and agencies on a wide variety of issues. The main ecological concerns were the impacts of port expansion on salmonoid, crab and waterfowl habitat. The major social/community issues raised were the effects of train noise and the possible use of adjacent lands for port-related industrial development.

The Panel was critical of the lack of information in the Environmental Impact Statement concerning the probable social impact. Public input during the meetings allowed the Panel to develop a better understanding of the local concerns in this regard. There was also considerable discussion on the question of project justification. The main support for the proposal originated from industry; however, not all industrial sectors were in favour of the port expansion and some agreed there was no demonstrated need for expansion at Roberts Bank other than for the shipment of coal.

Following the public meetings, the Panel concluded that proposed expansion of Roberts Bank port should not be permitted to proceed. It felt that extensive development of the kind proposed by National Harbours Board would have too great an impact on the Fraser River estuary. While its conclusion was largely based on environmental grounds, other issues were considered as well. The Panel was not satisfied that a need had been adequately demonstrated for an additional facility to export commodities such as sulphur, potash, grain and bulk liquids. The Panel also felt that information on social impacts, while generally inadequate and inconclusive, gave rise to concerns related to a number of potentially affected groups if the full expansion were to proceed.

At the same time, however, the Panel did not recommend that further development

EIA u

should be stopped. It recognized that the area of the proposed expansion was not
of uniform ecological value or sensitivity and therefore it recommended that,
instead of a 110-hectare expansion to handle various commodities, limited
expansion of 40 hectares could be tolerated for coal export facilities. This was
not a case of making trade-offs between development and environmental damage, but
of restricting development to an area, and under conditions, where environmental
impacts were at their least. The Panel felt that adverse environmental impacts
associated with reduced expansion could be kept to tolerable levels if a number
of mitigating measures were implemented. A number of the measures recommended by
the Panel were related to social and community concerns raised by the public in
the course of the review process.

Public participation played an important role in influencing the Panel's decision
and hence in shaping possible future development at the Roberts Bank port. In
addition, as a direct result of the public review process, certain deficiencies
relating to the operation of the existing port were identified and recommendations
were made for corrective action. Furthermore, as a result of the extensive
discussion by the public on the basic need for the project, the Panel made a
general recommendation that it should be incumbent upon the proponent to
demonstrate publicly the need for a development, prior to the submission of
an Environmental Impact Statement.

D.   SHAKWAK HIGHWAY PROJECT

This case study provides an illustration of public participation in a project
covering a wide geographical area. It also provides an example of a flexible
environmental assessment review process, capable of dealing with a project
subject to an international agreement between Canada and the United States.

The project proposal involved the paving and upgrading of the Haines Road from
the Alaska/British Columbia border to Haines Junction, and of the Alaska Highway
from Haines Junction to the Yukon/Alaska border, a total distance of approximately
520 km. An internationl agreement between Canada and the United States provides
that, pending appropriate environmental clearances, the United States will pay
for the construction of the project and will direct construction efforts. Since
United States funds are involved, the United States Federal Highway Administration
was also required by United States law to conduct an environmental assessment
of the project.

The highway would involve construction in one of Canada's most beautiful regions.
It is an area in which wildlife abounds and is relatively undisturbed. There
are also specific physical characteristics in the region, such as continuous and
discontinuous permafrost, that if disturbed could lead to significant environmental damage. The lifestyle of the people living in four communties along the
proposed route is unique. The infrastructure of the area is presently undeveloped
and the main economic support of the communities is derived from tourism. There
is also a substantial native population along the route. Another factor
requiring consideration in the review was the planned building of the Alaska
Highway Gas Pipeline which would create a substantial cumulative impact along the
portion of the route from Haines Junction to the Alaska border.

As in the case studies already described, the Panel made the Environmental Impact
Statement widely available to the public and sought reviews of the project from
government agencies. Guidelines for the preparation of an Environmental Impact
Statement were issued by the panel in March 1976. Due to the non-site specific
nature of the project, a different approach to public participation was required.
Each Environmental Assessment Panel attempts to structure hearings to suit the
expectations and level of awareness of the public in the area. In the case of the

Shakwak project, therefore, it was considered that two different kinds of meetings were required. Formal, relatively structured meetings were held in March in Whitehorse, the capital of Yukon Territory, where people have experienced similar enquiries of various kinds and have had previous experience with the Environmental Assessment and Review Process. In the communities along the actual route, however, informal discussions were held on issues defined by those living in the area. The Panel felt that a highly structured format could discourage these people from making their views known.

United States officials participated in the Canadian review. In accordance with United States requirements, a final Environmental Impact Statement was issued by United States authorities which contained, among other things, a summary of mitigative measures and a response to the major questions raised during the hearings in Canada. During the course of the review, the Panel recognized that the potential for adverse social impact was great during the construction period. During that period the population of the highway corridor would more than double. It was obvious that, given the prevailing socio-economic infrastructure, there was a need to minimize adverse impact to the greatest extent possible.

In its report, the Panel concluded that there were no over-riding environmental or social concerns preventing the project from proceeding as scheduled. While the potential for adverse ecological and social impact from the project was considered to be significant, the Panel concluded that these impacts could be mitigated if certain procedures were followed and specific conditions were met. Specific recommendations were made dealing with co-ordination of the Shakwak project and the construction of the Alaska Highway Gas Pipeline, with physical and engineering issues, and with ecological issues.

Of major concern to the Panel, however, was the potential social impact of the project. The Panel, therefore, recommended a number of measures to mitigate these adverse impacts. Furthermore, the Panel felt there was no single government agency in place to effectively monitor the implementation of these recommendations. It therefore recommended the establishment of a Shakwak Review Committee, composed of representatives from federal and territorial government agencies, to carry out this function.

EXPERIENCES GAINED FROM THE CASE STUDIES

The case studies presented in this paper have demonstrated how public participation in the Canadian Environmental Assessment and Review Process has influenced various development proposals. Public involvement in the decision-making process has affected and will continue to affect development action in Canada. Some of the main experiences gained from the case studies are summarized below.

A.   FORMATION OF THE ENVIRONMENTAL ASSESSMENT PANEL

During the Eldorado public meetings in Port Granby it became evident that, in order for the review process to be credible, the Environmental Assessment Panel must be perceived as an independent body, free from "conflict of interest" situations. Specific recommendations on this subject were made by the Panel. In February 1977, the Environmental Assessment and Review Process was adjusted by the Federal Cabinet to permit individuals from outside the public service to act as Panel members. Furthermore, public servants serving as Panel members agree to dissociate themselves from any position taken by their departments or agencies on the project under review.

B.   ASSISTANCE TO PUBLIC GROUPS

Experience has shown that a proponent is able to provide opportunities to involve
and inform people who support a project. It is doubtful whether opponents enjoy
similar opportunities. As a result, various Panels have recommended that funding
and other mechanisms be developed by the Federal Environmental Assessment
Review Office to ensure that the public participation element of the process
provides an opportunity for all points of view to be adequately expressed.
Although a funding mechanism has not been approved, Panels have recognized the
difficulties experienced by some concerned parties in obtaining expert advice
and have arranged for technical witnesses or independent experts to be present
at public meetings.

C.   PUBLIC ACCOUNTABILITY

Public review of development proposals has resulted in a requirement for greater
accountability on the part of government agencies and proponents. Regardless of
the Panel mandate, the public generally adopts a broad definition of the
environment. When confronted with, for example, demands for increased access to
monitoring information, questions related to the efficiency of government
regulatory and planning agencies, and questions related to the need for a specific
project in the first instance, the developer and government agencies find they
have little choice but to respond.

D.   FLEXIBILITY OF THE ENVIRONMENTAL ASSESSMENT AND REVIEW PROCESS

As the Environmental Assessment and Review Process is based on Cabinet Directives
rather than an Act of Parliament, it is flexible and can be readily adjusted to
accommodate changing needs. In the two northern projects (Shakwak Highway and
Lancaster Sound), for example, the Panels held informal community meetings in
which the public defined the issues of importance, as well as more formal,
structured meetings where discussion of a more technical nature occurred in
accordance with an established agenda. In all projects, public meetings are
held to review the Environmental Impact Statements; however the nature of public
consultation prior to the meetings may vary according to the specific project.
In the Eldorado case study, for example, public meetings were also held to
determine deficiencies in the Environmental Impact Statement; in the case of
Roberts Bank the public and government agencies were invited to submit
deficiencies in writing; in the Lancaster Sound and Shakwak Highway projects,
deficiencies were not sought prior to the final public review. The convening of
informal public meetings, together with more formal public reviews, is becoming
accepted as an effective means of gaining public input, especially for northern
projects.

Early public involvement in the review process is considered essential. A
combination of soliciting written comments from the public and government agencies, together with one or more phases of public meetings, is becoming standard
practice in the review of development proposals.

The case studies have shown that, in spite of the advantages of relatively
informal meetings in encouraging public participation in small communities, there
is neverthelss, an advantage to developing a methodology for structuring such
meetings.

While the main purpose of public meetings is to allow the Environmental
Assessment Panel to gather as much information as possible so as to be able to
make recommendations to the Minister, it is also in many cases, a learning
experience for the participants. Procedures are being developed to ensure that

interested parties have sufficient time to prepare briefs and intervenors are
given a reasonable opportunity to present their case at the meetings.

E.   SOCIO-ECONOMIC CONCERNS

The case studies have show that, in a public review, socio-economic issues are
preceived as important and inseparable from issues related to the physical
environment. This close relationship is particularly evident in northern projects
where the livelihood of people is dependent on the natural environment.

F.   PUBLIC INFORMATION PROGRAMMES

The Eldorado and Lancaster Sound case studies, in particular, demonstrated the
importance of the developers' public information programmes. The lack of effective
programmes created public suspicion, and resulted in a general misunderstanding
of the nature of the project.

G.   MONITORING ACTIVITIES

For any project for which approval to proceed is recommended and which may have
a social and environmental impact, there is a public demand for co-ordinated
follow-up studies involving the public, the proponent and all levels of government,
in order to assess actual impacts and to recommend additional mitigatory
measures, as well as to serve as a guide for future projects.

Public Information and Participation in The Netherlands

A. A. M. F. Staatsen

(The Netherlands)

INTRODUCTION

The increased involvement of the public in the work of the authorities in the last few decades and a growing awareness of environmental problems have resulted in an increase of provisions relating to public information and participation in many Dutch laws, including legislation on environmental matters. In this paper, reference will first be made to education and information on environmental matters; then, with the help of a description of a number of statutory and non-statutory procedures some of which relate directly to environmental protection, an idea will be given of the role of public information and participation in relation to decisions which are important to the environment.

It should be mentioned that environmental policy in the Netherlands is by no means the concern of a single ministry. Authority in this field is exercised not only by the Ministry of Health and Environmental Protection (Ministerie van Volksgezondheid en Milieuhygiene, V & M) but also by the Ministry of Cultural Affairs, Recreation and Social Work (Ministerie van Culturr, Recreatie van Maatschappelijk Werk, CRM), the Ministry of Housing and Physical Planning (Ministerie van Volkshuisvesting en Ruitelijke Ordening, VRO), the Ministry of Transport and Public Works (Ministerie van Verkeer en Waterstaat, V & W) and others. For example, the Nature Conservancy Act which will be discussed below falls within the competence of CRM, physical planning legislation within that of VRO and the procedure of the Council of the Public Works Department within that of V & W.

An account will also be given of some experiences with public information and participation in connexion with experiments on environmental impact assessment which were recently conducted in preparing for the introduction of environmental impact assessment in the Netherlands. Finally environmental pressure groups and the relationship between these groups and the authorities will be discussed.

EDUCATION AND INFORMATION

If proper use is to be made of the opportunities for participation provided to members of the public by the various statutory and non-statutory procedures, it is essential that attention be paid to environmental education and information. This is now being done in one form or another at various educational institutions. The central government also subsidized such activities as World Environment Day and a

variety of information campaigns on noise nuisance, sensible use of energy, etc.
The private environmental organizations, of which more will be said below, also
contribute by organizing conferences, demonstrations and exibitions and by
publishing pamphlets.

PUBLIC INFORMATION AND PARTICIPATION IN LAWS RELATING DIRECTLY TO
ENVIRONMENTAL PROTECTION

The laws governing environmental matters can be loosely divided into those which
relate directly to environmental protection and those which do not but which
are nonetheless of importance for the environment. In the following, the role
of public information and participation provisions in two laws in the first of
these categories will be discussed, viz. the Environmental Protection (general
provisions) Bill and the Nature Conservancy Act.

A.   PROVISIONS IN THE ENVIRONMENTAL PROTECTION (GENERAL PROVISIONS) BILL
              RELATING TO PUBLIC INFORMATION AND PARTICIPATION

For a number of years environmental legislation in the Netherlands was developed
separately for each sector. Separate acts were passed to combat pollution of
water, air, etc. As the sector-by-sector programme neared completion, there was a
growing need for general legislation on environmental matters, in order to remove
unnecessary discrepancies between the individual environmental laws and to include
aspects not covered by these; this applied to public information and participation
as well as to other aspects.

In December 1976, therefore, the Environmental Protection (general provisions)
Bill was presented to Parliament. In March 1979 the Bill passed the Lower House
of the States General. (1) This Bill contains provisions on a number of general
environmental protection matters. Some of these are matters which the individual
laws share in common, while others go beyond the scope of the individual laws and
therefore cannot be included in them. It was decided to adopt the form of an
"extensible" act, which means that the Bill would later be extended to cover other
general matters in the field of environmental protection. What the Bill already
contains are general provisions on participation and appeal in connexion with
administrative decisions, and provisions on co-ordination of the preparation and
processing of applications for a decision (in particular relating to licences).
It should be borne in mind that the Bill as it now stands does not yet apply to
regulations and plans. With regard to an extension of the Environmental Protection
(general provisions) Bill, further investigation and discussions are necessary.
(2) In order to achieve a coherent policy on environmental protection this Bill
will be extended in phases to form an outline law on the environment. It will be
necessary to work along the following lines:

      - broadening the scope of the law and its sphere of applications;

      - extending the law to cover subjects which are of importance in harmoniz-
        ing and co-ordinating the policies of the central government with those
        of the local authorities.

One extension proposal has already been put before the Lower House of the States
General. This concerns the establishment by law of a Central Council for
Environmental Protection, with the task of advising the Minister for Health and
Environmental Protection on environmental protection matters. Representatives of
various social groups will sit on this Council, which will take the place of the
existing Provisional Central Council for Environmental Protection. In this way a
framework will be created for the people outside governmental organizations who
are most involved in developments in environmental protection to contribute to
policy making in this field. This will supplement the existing knowledge and

insight of the official bodies.

Most of the other subjects that could possibly be considered for inclusion in the Environmental Protection (general provisions) Bill are still under discussion. Priorities have been established with regard to these subjects. The next topic to be regulated in the act will be the system of licences. It has been decided that legislation on environmental impact assessment will also be included in the act. A third subject is the setting of standards and the fourth subject to be regulated in the act will be levies. (3)

As stated before, the Environmental Protection (general Provisions) Bill now accepted by the Lower House of the States General contains uniform provisions for consultation with the relevant agencies, public participation and administrative review of licensing procedure pursuant to a large number of environmental protection laws. (4)

A cornerstone of this Bill is the principle that no prerequisite is needed for any person to be entitled to make objections, although these should be made at an early stage in the planning and decision making process. The application for a license must be made public as soon as possible and not later than six weeks after the day of receipt, through, _inter alia_, the newspapers, by deposition for the public, and by notification to the administrative authorities involved, including the advisers whcih are to be consulted according to the law. If the application concerns factories or works, the application must also be made public by the posting of notices and by notifying those entitled to the use of buildings in the neighbourhood. The application, together with the reports and recommendations which are sent to the competent authority during the processing of the application, is deposited for the public scrutiny until the expiration of the term fixed for appeal against the decision. Any person is entitled to make written objections until one month after the beginning of such deposition. At the public hearing that regularly follows, any person present may make objections. On that occasion an exchange of views on the application is possible between the competent authority, the applicant and the public. A report of the public hearing is added to the application and sent to the applicant, the advisors and those who were present at the hearing.

After the expiration of the term for objections, the competent authority makes a draft decision as soon as possible. The draft decision must be sent to the applicant and the administrative authorities involved. Next, it is made public and added to the deposited documents. In addition, a copy is sent to those who have already made objections. For a period of 14 days after the deposition of the draft decision, the applicant, those who have made objections against the application, and those who were prevented from making objections in the preceding stage are entitled to make written objections to the draft decision.

The decision is made as soon as possible after the expiration of this period. If this decision has not been taken within seven months of the date of receipt of the application, an appeal may be submitted as if the licence had been refused. When the application concerns a very complicated subject the competent authority may extend this term. This may only be done after consulting the applicant, and with just cause. A copy of the decision is sent to the applicant and the administrative authorities involved, and to those who have made objections. The purpose of the decision has to be published and a copy of the decision has to be deposited for one month with the annexed documents.

Appeal to the Crown is open during this same month to the applicant, the advisors involved, those who have made objections and those who are affected by the decision but who have not been able to object during the preceding preparatory procedure.

The decision does not enter into force until the term for appeal has expired. In the meantime it is possible to apply to the chairman of the Administrative Disputes Department of the Council of State for suspension of enforcement of the decision or for an interim provision. Such an application is granted if the execution of the decision of the competent authority can have a major influence on the decision in appeal, as a consequence of the costs involved or a change in the actual circumstances. In this case the decision does not enter into force until judgement has been passed on such application. The aim of this arrangement is to ensure that submission of an appeal leads to suspension of the decision only in cases where this is necessary.

In view of the extensive publication of documents which the bill prescribes, it was also necessary to make provision for the applicant to request that information be treated as confidential. At the applicant's request, the competent authority may authorize submission for publication of a second text, approved by the authority, which does not contain any information which in the view of the competent authority may justifiably be kept secret and from which text such information cannot be deduced. In the above cases the competent authority may require the submission of further information which is deemed useful for a proper judment of the application. Such a text is also submitted if information is contained in or can be deduced from a document which, in the view of the Minister concerned, should be kept secret in the interests of State security or in compliance with international agreements.

PROVISIONS IN THE NATURE CONSERVANCY ACT RELATING TO PUBLIC INFORMATION AND PARTICIPATION

Although the Nature Conservancy Act relates directly to environmental protection, it does not fall within the scope of the Environmental Protection (general provisions) Bill. The purpose of the Nature Conservancy Act is to safeguard and preserve, in the public interest, areas of the countryside for their natural beauty or scientific significance. After departmental preparation, the Minister for Cultural Affairs, Recreation and Social Work publishes a statement of intent to designate an area as protected. This is sent to the appropriate landowners and local government authorities, the Nature Conservation Council (an advisory body of the Ministry of Cultural Affairs, Recreation and Social Work which consists of representatives of nature conservation organizations and experts) and the National Physical Planning Committee (a body of various central government officials). The burgomaster and aldermen of the municipality or municipalities concerned publish the statement and hold it for a month for public inspection. Those whose interests are affected and those to whom copies of the decision were sent may submit objections within 14 days of expiry of this term.

The Minister decides on the final designation within one year. In this connexion the following points are worth noting:

- it is only after the Minister for Cultural Affairs, Recreation and Social Work has taken a provisional decision with regard to a designation (which can already have all the legal consequences of final designation) that the statement of intent to designate an area as protected is published;

- this statement is sent only to those who are directly affected by it;

- only those who are directly affected are permitted to voice objections to the statement;

- these objections can be made only in writing;

- the actual decision, in principle, is arrived at without any participation
  at all, and only those whose interests are affected by it can participate
  thereafter; there is therefore no opportunity for people who have a
  general interest to participate in the proceeding.

PUBLIC INFORMATION AND PARTICIPATION IN LAWS NOT DIRECTLY RELATING TO ENVIRONMENTAL PROTECTION

In the following, a brief description will be given of the provisions relating
to public information and participation in the Physical Planning Act, the purpose
of which is not primarily environmental protection, but land-use planning.

There are two main aspects to the relationship between physical planning law
and environmental law. On the one hand, environmental protection and nature
management must, in the context of the physical planning process, be balanced
against other factors; for instance, economic considerations. On the other hand,
physical planning is an important weapon in the fight against environmental
pollution and the destruction of nature.

Under the Physical Planning Act the desired physical development of an area must
be laid down in plans. At the national level there is the "crucial physical
planning decisions" procedure, which is not yet decreed by law. This will be
discussed below. At provincial level there are the regional plans, which do not
contain any provisions directly binding on the public. At municipal level there
is the structure plan, which has the character of a programme, and the allocation
plan, which contains provisions directly binding on the public.

Draft regional plans are deposited for two months with the provincial secretariat
for public inspection. This is announced in the Government Gazette and in one or
more provincial newspapers. During the deposition period anybody may submit
written objections to the draft. Draft structure plans and draft allocation plans
are deposited for one month with the municipal secretariat for public inspection,
and this is announced in the Government Gazette and in one or more local newspapers. During this month anybody may submit written objections to the Municipal
Council. Next the draft plans become definite. Again there is a possibility to
submit objections. Then the provincial government approves the plan. Appeal to the
Crown is open to a limited number of persons and official bodies. (5)

PUBLIC INFORMATION AND PARTICIPATION IN PROCEDURES NOT LAID DOWN BY LAW

In the following a description will be given of the role of public information
and participation in two procedures which are not laid down by law.

PROCEDURE FOR CRUCIAL DECISIONS ON PHYSICAL PLANNING

As has already been mentioned, the Physical Planning Act provides no opportunities
for participation in decision-making relating to physical planning at the national
level. Since there appeared to be a great need for this, an attempt was made to
fill the gap by creating such a procedure for crucial decisions on physical
planning. The Government intends to incorporate provisions on the crucial physical
planning decisions procedure into the Physical Planning Act, which is to be amended.

After proposals and recommendations had been made from various quarters, the
Government of the Netherlands published, in 1972, the "Report on publicity in the
preparation of physical planning policy". The "crucial physical planning decisions"
procedure was introduced in this report. The report, however, covers a much wider
field. It elaborates on the following fundamental principle which is defined at

the beginning of the report:

> "The Government considers it of great significance that decisions
> affecting the physical structure and the quality of the human environment
> are not made without anyone whose personal environment is involved having
> had the opportunity to contribute to the underlying philosophy."

On the basis of this principle the Government states that, for all decisions
relating to physical planning and thus, more specifically, also for the numerous
decisions that cannot be regarded as crucial, physical planning and decision-
making procedures with the following features should apply:

(a) interdepartmental consulations on physical planning, for the purpose of
checking the decisions to be made against the objectives of physical planning
policy, should take place in appropriate consultative physical planning bodies in
which the various ministries are represented;

(b) consultation on physical planning should take place between the provinces
and the municipalities for the purpose of making adjustments, on the one hand,
to decisions at central government level, and, on the other, to the relevant
regional, structural and allocation plans;

(c) for publication and public participation, the making of the decision will
invariably have to be preceded by the publication of a policy resolution in order
to give the community the opportunity to influence that decision through public
participation and public discussion.

Futhermore, the report announces measures to improve publicity and public
participation when regional plans, structure plans and allocation plans are being
drawn up by provinces and municipalities.

By crucial decisions on physical planning is meant:

(a) decisions and formulation of standpoints concerning main outlines and
principles which are of general significance for national physical planning policy;

(b) decisions concerning specific policy plans which are of significance for
national physical planning policy and deviate from the establishments main outlines and principles;

(c) decisions concerning specific policy plans which are of significance for
national physical planning policy and anticipate the formulation of main outlines
and principles.

One of the most essential elements in this procedure is that no decision is taken
without prior publication of a policy decision, about which anyone can have his
or her say. With the municipalities and provinces this has already been the case
for some time. As stated before, the Physical Planning Act specifies that
allocation plans, structure plans and regional plans must be published in draft
form and that anyone should be given the opportunity to express an opinion on such
plans. This procedure, however, was not yet in use at the national level. The
majority of decisions, reports, etc., were simply published as final. At most,
the public could turn to members of parliament.

The crucial physical planning decision procedure has changed all this. The
publication of a policy decision initiates a phase of public participation,
recommendation and consultation which presents every opportunity to examine the
Government decisions, to bring them up for discussion and amendment, or to arrive
at their acceptance. Naturally, the actual effects of the public participation, the
recommendations of the Advisory Physical Planning Council and the administrative

consultations with local government bodies will vary from one case to another; the desiderata presented from various quarters will usually also vary. The Orientation Report and the Structure Scheme for Drinking Water and Industrial Water Supply were hardly amended at all. The Urbanization Report on the other hand was amended and supplemented on a number of points.

Practical experience with the first two crucial physical planning decisions, i.e. the Orientation Report and the Structure Scheme for Drinking Water and Industrial Water Supply, revealed that it is hardly possible to bring any influence to bear on detailed Government reports (the documents mentioned numbered 118 and 85 pages respectively), because it is difficult for the public, the advisory bodies and the consultation partners, and at a later stage for parliament, to indicate clearly what they want changed. To meet this difficulty it has now become customary to list the "points of decision" in a final chapter. This final chapter is now also referred to as the "crucial physical planning decision" so as to indicate that the actual decisions are formulated in this chapter and that the remainder of the text serves only an explanatory function. This final chapter is concisely formulated (in the Urbanization Report, 28 paragraphs in 5 pages; in the Report on the Rural Areas, 24 paragraphs in 8 pages).

The policy statements given here constitute a sound basis for the public participation procedure, the recommendations and the consultations as well as for parliamentary debate. This has turned out to work well in practice. Quite a number of people have used this opportunity to propose amendments to crucial physical planning decisions.

Experiments are still going on with respect to the manner in which public involvement is organized and stimulated. The following measures can be mentioned (figures and examples relating to the Urbanization Report are in parenthesis):

- the policy resolution is widely distributed and sold at a subsidized price (27,000 copies);

- a popular edition is drawn up, indicating, among other things, a number of points of discussion (123,000 copies);

- the policy resolution is deposited for public inspection in many places (all townhalls, provincial council buildings, public libraries and reading rooms, and chambers of commerce);

- an information campaign is arranged on television and in the newspapers;

- information evenings are organized throughout the country;

- a subsidy is made available for the assistance of discussion groups among the population (about f. 1 million);

- public hearing are organized throughout the country; reactions may be submitted in writing in advance, but anyone who so wishes may also express his or her views;

- the reactions to the policy resolution presented in writing are collected and made available to advisory and political bodies;

- an analytical survey is drawn up of the written and verbal responses and is made generally available.

The extent to which all these activities succeed in arousing the interest of the public or in forming public opinion naturally varies from one case to another. In the case of the Urbanization Report, the information sessions were attended by more than 3,000 people. In all, 412 written responses were received. Considering that

most of these had been prepared by organizations and discussion groups, the number
of people actually taking part in this public procedure can be put at a much
higher figure. For example, in all, more than 1,300 people took part in public
discussion groups. Reaction such as those from the trade union movement, the
house-building association and the organizations concerned with the protection of
the environment must also have involved the collaboration of many people.

In the last five years, experience has been gained with about 10 of the procedures
which are discussed here. During this time, the organizations and methods of the
publicity and participation procedures have been greatly improved. One consequence
of this has been an increase in the number of participating groups and responses
from the public. For example, more than twice as many people entered into
participation over the Rural Areas Report as participated in the Urbanization
Report. There has been much scientific research into all aspects of participation
during the last few years.

PROCEDURE OF THE COUNCIL OF THE PUBLIC WORKS DEPARTMENT

In order to show how decisions are arrived at with regard to the works for which
the Minister of Transport and Public Works is responsible, and what role public
information and participation play in this, a description will be given of how
proposed routes are decided for national highways. This procedure, which has been
followed since the beginning of the 1970s, but which is not laid down by law, is
known as the "procedure of the Council of the Public Works Department".

The Public Works Department, which is under the authority of the Minister, conducts
a proposed route investigation during which consultations are held with the
appropriate provincial and municipal authorities, other official bodies and
groups representing various interests. Consideration is given not only to the
transport engineering and planning aspects, but also to the consequences for
nature and the environment, agriculture, recreation, etc. A number of variants,
including the option of not building a road at all, are examined and compared
aspect by aspect. The results of this study are recorded in a proposed route
memorandum with drawings and presented by the Public Works Department to the
Minister, who passes it on to the Council of the Public Works Department for
an opinion.

The function of this Council is to advise the Minister for Transport and Public
Works on matters of policy relating to the Public Works Department. The Council
consists of representatives of different Ministries, interest groups and experts.
A number of permanent committees are attached to the Council which, whether
at the request of the Council or on their own initiative, advise the Council on
matters with which it is the Council's task to deal. The Council and its function
are laid down by law.

In cases where a decision on the route has to be taken, the Council passes the
proposed route memorandum to the Roads Consultative Committee. This Committee
is composed of independent experts and representatives of various ministries and
interest groups, who discuss the various proposed routes in detail. In order to
discover the views of all interested parties the memorandum is deposited for a
period of one to two months for public inspection at the townhalls of all the
municipalities concerned and at the offices of the Public Works Department.
Anybody who is interested can also obtain copies of the documents. This procedure
is announced in local newspapers and on municipal notice-boards. After the
deposition period, the Public Works Department holds an information meeting at
which further explanations are given and questions are answered. Those who have
objections to the plans, or to part of them, then have 14 days in which to submit
their objections to the Council of the Public Works Department in writing.

At the end of 14 days the Roads Consultative Committee holds a public hearing at which everybody who has submitted objections or so wishes is given the opportunity to speak about them. After the opinions of the provincial and municipal authorities and of such bodies as the Chamber of Commerce and nature conservation and agricultural organizations have also been heard, the Roads Consultative Committee draws up a report in which it gives its opinion on the objections and wishes which have been submitted and states whether changes should be made in the plans. This report is passed to the Council of the Public Works Department which draws up a recommendation and submits it, together with an analysis of the objections which have been received, to the Minister for Transport and Public Works, who then decides on the proposed route.

The Minister's decision is sent to both houses of the States General and is published in the press; it is also directly communicated to the organizations and individuals who have taken part in the planning. Thus, those who have submitted objections are also informed. Reasons are given in support of the decision, and both the report of the Roads Consultative Committee and the recommendation of the Council of the Public Works Department are sent with it. The route decided upon is also published in the Government Gazette with an indication of how to obtain information on the content of the documents.

The same procedure can be followed for other public works such as canal building, river improvement and the construction of new rail links. As mentioned earlier, before the procedure is initiated a study is made of the various possible alternatives and their consequences for the various relevant aspects under consideration. In particular, the consequences for nature and the environment constitute an important part of such a study, from which a complete picture is obtained of all the relevent aspects, compared for each alternative.

There is no provision for appeals in this procedure, but there is an opportunity to appeal at a later stage when the proposed route which has been decided upon comes to be incorporated into municipal allocation plans. Under the procedure as laid down by the Physical Planning Act (see Section A above),   the new or revised allocation plan, now incorporating the proposed route, is made available for public inspection. The Public Works Department provides information and anybody who wishes to submit objections may do so. After this there are the normal appeal procedures, pursuant to the Physical Planning Act.

EXPERIENCE OF PUBLIC INFORMATION AND PARTICIPATION IN TRIAL RUNS ON ENVIRONMENTAL IMPACT ASSESSMENT (EIA) IN THE NETHERLANDS

In preparation for the introduction of environmental impact assessment in the Netherlands, nine trial runs are being conducted for the Ministry of Health and Environmental Protection. In these trial runs, experience is sought of various procedures for drawing up and processing environmental impact statements. The point of departure for this is that the environmental impact statement is a public document and that public participation is therefore an essential element in the procedure to be selected. As much use as possible will be made of existing decision-making procedures to which the relevant proposed activity is subject. A short description follows of general experience of public participation in these trial runs.

EIA can be a valuable instrument for the planning and decision-making process. One of the reasons for this is improved public participation. Not only is relevant information on the pending decision published at an early stage, but public participation is also one of the major features of the EIA process itself, as the public has the opportunity to comment on the contents of a provisional (draft) environmental impact statement(EIS) before it is finalized and used for making the decision. In theory, a distinction can be made between public participation with respect to the EIS and to the pending decision. However, the trial runs show that the public will not restrict its comments to the contents of the statement. It will also express its opinion about the decision itself.

Up to the present the trial runs provided experience of public participation regarding EIS mainly in   informal planning and decision-making procedures resulting in decisions which would normally be made behind closed doors. Adoption of this type of public participation, however, means that the public gets the opportunity to express its views on the pending decision. In general this was appreciated by all parties concerned.

As was mentioned earlier, in practice it seems impossible to separate the two types of public participation. Though this means that when participation is already provided for in the original planning and decision-making procedure no separate (time-consuming) participation procedure regarding the EIS is needed, there is the disadvantage that the public will comment on the pending decision on the basis of a provisional EIS. A finalized EIS is, in that case, not available to the public until the appeal stage.

Though there is little disagreement that public participation should be a major feature of the EIA process, the question as to when it should take place remains unanswered. Assuming that there is a review of the provisional EIS by independent experts, as has been the case with the trial runs in the Netherlands, there are three possibilities, namely before, after or simultaneously with the review. The third possibility has the advantage that no time is lost. It also enables public participation to take place in the presence of the independent experts, who simultaneously review the quality and adequacy of the EIS and public comments. Comments by the public on the contents of the statement can be addressed to the reviewing experts, while comments on the pending decision are referred to the competent authority. This was tried out in one of the experiments. (6) However, it seemed to be difficult to keep separate the roles of the competent authority (in this case also the proponent and author of the provisional EIS) and reviewers. This in fact means that there was less opportunity for the public to comment on the decision. Though the public was not conscious of this at the time, it may find itself over-optimistic about influencing the decision-makers directly.

As far as a choice between public participation before or after the review is concerned, experience in the trial runs seems to indicate that the former is to be preferred; otherwise the public feels superfluous. Which participation will over-rule a reviewing expert? This contradicts the common belief that the public should be presented with a reviewed statement, with technical errors uncovered.

So far, the trial runs have confirmed that sufficiently long terms of publication of the provisional EIS (e.g. four weeks before the hearing) and of notification of the hearing (e.g. three weeks in advance) are a prerequisite for successful public participation. Equally important is the ample availability of copies of statements, at a low price, including good summaries in straight-forward language. It is sometimes suggested that, in order not to overload the public, part of the information should be released before the provisional EIS is completed. Generally speaking this does not seem advisable. Partial information could give a distorted view of the expected impact of a proposed action. However, experience in the trial runs indicates that unnecessary protests after completion of the provisional EIS could be avoided by immediately releasing the results of the process which has defined the scope and focus at the start of the EIA. They could also be avoided by interviewing key persons or even by co-operating with private environmental protection groups when defining the scope and focus.

In some of the trial runs the proponent and the competent authority organizing the public hearing were the same. This appeared to carry the danger that the competent authority tries to "sell" the EIS to the public by, for example, showing biased slides or by playing down possible environmental consequences, thus irritating the public. Even an open and objective approach by the competent authority did not seem likely to result in the trust and commitment of the public concerning the final decision. Possibly this is because of a basic mistrust in government. This is an argument for introducing in those cases a panel of independent experts to review the quality of the provisional EIS.

The information supplied in the trial runs did not seem to increase the environmental awareness of the general public. The average citizen appeared to participate only where his or her own individual interests were concerned; often information from the (provisional) EIS was used selectively to make a point and other information disregarded, even though such information might be much more important from an environmental point of view. It should be noted that one cannot speak of public participation in general. However, the same is – to a lesser extent – also true for local interest groups, even though these do provide generally valuable information on the local situation. Only the national environmental protection groups make a more fundamental contribution to the EIA, provided that this does not interfere too much with their local members' interests, which generally will not occur when the EIA concerns policy plans instead of projects. With respect to the general public and to local interest groups, participation in the trial runs was often successful, giving participants a chance to raise objections as well as to let off steam.
Nevertheless, in a few cases the public was frustrated for several reasons. One was that the public did not want to be tied to participation with regard to environmental aspects alone; it also wanted to consider social, economic and other aspects. Moreover it wished to address itself to people with direct influence on the decision. When this was not possible participation was perceived as useless. Another cause of frustration was that the role of the different parties involved and the procedure followed were sometimes not clear to the public.

THE ROLE OF PRIVATE ENVIRONMENTAL ORGANIZATIONS

A phenomenon which has grown up in response to environmental problems and has become an integral part of our society is the multiplicity of action groups and unofficial environmental organizations. Private individuals have played an important part in nature conservation in the Netherlands since the beginning of this century. At first this took the form of small groups with specific aims only. Now a process of "socialization" of nature conservation and environmental protection is occurring, as we can see from the increasingly large membership of national nature conservation and environmental protection organizations, as well as the appearance on the scene of many regional and local action groups. In recent years, these groups have also begun to take an interest in the social background of the causes of environmental damage.

Campaigns are conducted and organizations spring up when people have the impression that proper justice is not being done to the environment. In decision-making which affects the environment – which is mostly in the hands of the authorities – either through lack of information or because interests other than those of the environment have gained the upper hand this feature is marked. A number of associations active in this field took the initiative of establishing a joint working organization, the Foundation for Nature Conservation and Environmental Protection, which serves as an umbrella organization for a great many regionally active groups. This structure enables the environmental organizations to make their opinions known at every level of policy formation; they contribute to it by such means as submitting written objections, publishing scientific reports and mobilizing the public. Through their work they alert and inform both the authorities and the public. They also suggest alternatives for policy measures, for example in connexion with the planning of road routes.

The Government sees the work of environmental organizations and action groups as an essential element in the policy-forming process, and has long since recognized environmental organizations as partners for consultation on national environmental policy. Of the provisions relating to participation in environmental protection legislation and in procedures not (yet) subject to legislation, of which a few have been discussed above, one important aim is to enable private environmental organizations to participate in reaching various decisions as organized and interested members of the public.

In addition, the work of these environmental organizations is subsidized by the authorities. The central Government's policy, for instance, is to subsidize those organizations whose activities are of more than regional importance. In general there is a subsidy for the staffing and administration costs of these organizations and a separate one for their activities. The subsidy of the national Government totals about 3 million guilders of which approximately 1.3 million comes from the Ministry of Health and Envrionmental Protection and 1.7 million from the Ministry of Cultural Affairs, Recreation and Social Work. The subsides enable the organizations to keep a critical eye on the Government's policies.

REFERENCES

1. See Tweede Kamer zitting 1976-1977, 14311, nr. 2 (parliamentary document).

2. See Tweede Kamer zitting 1976-1977, 14311, nr. 3, page 15 (parliamentary document).

3. See Tweede Kamer zitting 1977-1978, 14311, nr. 6, page 9 (parliamentary document).

4. 1903 Mining Act, Nuisance Act, Dry Rendering Act, Nuclear Energy Act, Pollution of Surface Waters Act, Air Pollution Act, Seawater Pollution Act, Chemical Waste Act, Waste Substance Act. Planned additions to this list are the Earth Removal Act, the Groundwater Act and the Noise Nuisance Act. It should be observed that even when these have been added, not all of the laws directly relating to environmental protection will fall within the scope of this law.

5. See also the paper in this volume prepared by J. Witsen (Netherlands).

6. The choice of a location for a sanitary landfill at Ede.

Public Participation in Conservation and Sustainable Development of Nature Resources

D.-R. Vinogradov

(USSR)

In our country the solution of some problems cannot be restricted to a one-country scale; they have to be tackled on an international level. Such is the problem of humanity's relationship with Nature. Nature conservation and sustainable utilization of living resources have acquired great economic and social significance for all countries under the present scientific and technological revolution. At the same time, together with the deep concern for ecological problems expressed by various strata of society, great importance is attached to public participation in development planning and decision making. The latter cannot be achieved without maintenance and sustainability of an adequate quality of human environment and nature resources.

The obligation of Soviet citizens "to defend nature and to conserve its riches" is now explicity incorporated in Article 67 of the Soviet Constitution. It has become a law. But it is not only an obligation; it is also simultaneously a right. Public involvement in nature conservation is frequently carried out through control over conservation legislation fulfilment, public discussions of an individual's or organization's treatment of protection and utilization of nature resources, and the preparation of recommendations for various conservation measures. These represent powerful means of realization of the Soviet citizen's right to participate in state and social management. The means to enjoy this right and to satisfy this obligation is provided by the Society for Nature Conservation which is obliged, by the law on nature conservation, to lead all public activities dealing with nature protection.

The foundation of the All Russia Society for Nature Conservation was initiated by Lenin's associated as far back as 1924. Over the years the Society has initiated conservation measures of great national significance. Thus a number of zapovedniks ("reserves") were organized, and strict restrictions or total bans on the taking of endangered animals were laid down following its recommendations. The Law of Forests was expanded by total banning of logging along river banks not only in upper streams but at river mouths as well. Some other pro-conservation measures were also implemented.

The Russian Soviet Federal Socialist Republic's Law on Nature Protection, adopted by the Supreme Soviet of the Republic in 1960, was a major step to further development of public nature conservation activities; similar laws were adopted by all 15 fraternal republics.

The decisions taken at the 24th and 25th Congresses of the Communist Party of the Soviet Union were also of great importance to the implementation of the nature conservation strategies.

Nowadays the All Russia Society for Nature Conservation has 30 million members, 22% of the entire population of the Republic. Its basis is laid by the 200,000 primary organizations established in practically all industrial enterprises, collective and state farms, in forestry, at institutes and schools as well as at house maintenance offices.

Under the Charter passed by the Government of the Republic, the principal nature conservation objectives are as follows:

(a) promotion of the main principles laid down in the programme and rules of the Communist Party of the Soviet Union, party and governmental regulation acts on nature protection, the Law on Nature Protection in the RSFSR; promotion of conservation knowledge, specific objectives and goals of the All Russia Society for Nature Conservation;

(b) establishment of an effective public environmental education system;

(c) maintenance of close collaboration and cooperation with state, public and management bodies in implementing nature conservation policies and programmes;

(d) consolidation of public participation in nature conservation activities, sustainable utilization and reproduction of living resources;

(e) organization and realization of control of public organizations over rational use of nature resources and their conservation status.

In practice these objectives are mutually interwoven. Thus public involvement in various campaigns, such as those for "Protection and sustainable utilization of soils", "Full flowing and cleanliness to small rivers", "Operation "Ant"", organization of campaigns in each republic to maintain control of public organizations over implementation of the conservation legislation, are indispensable means of public environmental education.

Considerable work to spreading environmental knowledge and conservation techniques is carried out by "public universities dealing with nature conservat- ion". They were founded 15 years ago by the All Russia Society for Nature Conservation, in cooperation with the "Znaniye" Society. Now there are 925 such universities in the RSFSR. They are financed from public organizations' funds. Conservation engineers and technicians of various enterprises, experts in agriculture, building-trade workers, scientists and other specialists improve their environmental knowledge in these public universities. Lectures at the universities are delivered by competent specialists from universities and other centres of higher education and research institutes, specialists in various branches and fields of national economy, leading workers and production innovators.

Environmental education programmes are carried out by special lecturing groups, i.e. creative teams consisting of experienced conservationists, scientists, teachers, writers and journalists. There are 2,500 groups of this kind now. By 1978 they had delivered more than 500 public lectures and held 2 million discussions and consultations.

In planning their activities, district, regional, autonomous and republican councils of the All Russia Society for Nature Conservation take into account suggestions made by the users and consumers of living resources (enterprises and institutes based on living resources). Hence their subject programmes are tightly coordinated with the principal objectives of conservation of living resources.

Houses for Natural History and Nature Conservation have become one of the new forms of environmental education. They also act as methodology centres. Their activities (lectures, discussions, exhibitions, subject discussions, meetings with scientists, writers and artists, evenings of questions and answers, consultations, film festivals excursions to <u>zapovedniks</u> and so on) deal with current urgent problems of conservation, sustainable utilization and reproduction of natural resources that are faced by different district, regional and republic authorities.

In the process of environmental education the mass media (radio, television, newspapers and periodicals) are fully used. Non-staff editorial boards have been organized by local sections of the All Russia Society for Nature Conservation at nearly all mass media agencies. The 1977 All Russia Competition of autonomous and republican as well as of regional public editorial boards, organized by the Central Council of the Society, gave a new impetus to the development of public conservation activities.

Although much attention is focused on the environmental education of adults, environmental education of children and consolidation of their involvement in the protection of Nature are matters of still greater concern. Groups of the Young Friends of Nature are encouraged at every primary organization of the All Russia Society. Their activity is directed by "Methodics Boards" for work with the youth, consisting of teachers, experts in national economy, members of the Young Communist League (Komsomol) and Young Pioneer Organizations.

Scientific and technical committees attached to the central and local councils of the All Russia Society and responsible for elaboration of environmental problems, together with the special sections for protection of waters, soils, forests, wild life, and so on, and sections and clubs of gardeners, flower-growers and bee-keepers – are valuable means to develop the creative abilities of the members of the All Russia Society for Nature Conservation. There are 16 thousand sections of that kind in the Russian Soviet Federal Socialist Republic now. They unite half a million scientists, experts in national economy and production innovators.

The activities mentioned above makes it possible to prepare adequate recommendations on nature protection and rational use of the living resources for planning bodies.

Thus, for example, the Krasnoyarsk Society's Scientific and Technical Council has submitted scientifically well-founded proposals for the thorough examination and consideration of conservation aspects in the planning of the Kansk-Achinsk power station complex. This played a major role in the local development programme, and it has been appreciated. The same Council has considered a problem of deer grazing-grounds conservation in the process of its economic development; its recommendations have been submitted to the organizations concerned. The Council's pro-conservation proposal concerning long-term (1980-1990) economic planning of the area was also of great importance.

The scientific and technical councils usually deal with integrated conservation problems. Questions of rational use allocation of individual living resources are considered by the appropriate sections attached to the central and local councils of the Society. Much work is done by its numerous sections on land protection, in the framework of the All Russia campaign for protection and rational use of lands. They contribute to the adoption of recommendations on conservation measures against soil erosion and weed introduction, and for soil reclamation. As a result of the campaign, more than 300 thousand hectares of earlier unused lands were brought back into the economy in the period 1976-1977.

Following the instructions of the Mordovian Society's Council its section on
land protection has prepared and submitted to the Commission of Agriculture of
the Council of Ministers of the Mordovia Republic a report dealing with the
accomplishment of land protection and its sustainable utilization.

The Chechen and Ingush Republican Council has initiated the development of
grazing-lands on sands. Its section of land protection has participated in
working out a recommendation on the development of the Tersk desert area.

In some areas, following pro-conservation recommendations prepared by a number
of sections on water protection of the local councils of the Society, the
executive committees of Soviets of Working People's Deputies have passed
resolutions banning motor boat use.

Members of the section on water conservation of the Orenburg regional council
of the Society have taken an active part in planning actions on improvement of
water use through increasing water supply rotation systems, on river bed
cleaning, improvement and safeguarding of protected areas in river basins, and
on promotion of rational use of water resources.

The Yaroslavl regional executive committee has passed a regulation on measures
concerning integrated use and conservation of water resources. Information has
been collected by the section, following recommendations of the Society's
regional council. Similar actions are performed by nemerous district, regional,
autonomous and republic Councils and their sections.

Enormous opportunities for creative work by the general public in the field of
nature conservation and improvement of the environmental quality are provided
through public participation in the social and technical Councils established
in the framework of primary organizations on nature conservation at various
enterprises within many industries. Their members are responsible for preparing
measures on technology improvement, and for the invention and improvement of
technical appliances directed at reducing impacts on the environment in the
course of production. There are now 8,700 councils of this kind.

Among the top priorities faced by the All Russia Society for Nature Conservation
is the establishment of control over implementation of the Law on Nature
Protection in the Russian Soviet Federal Socialist Republic, and other
governmental acts to ensure conservation of individual living resources at
different enterprises, factories, in collective and state farms, forestry,
municipal offices and other bodies. The most experienced members of the
scientifical and technical councils and the sections participate in discussions
of various conservation and development projects, including control over their
implementation. There are 200,000 public inspectors whose powers are confirmed
by the local Soviet authorities.

Different forms of public participation in planning, decision making and
realization of control are valuable means of testing and integrating economic,
social and ecological objectives. This participation tends to build public
(and especially young peoples') confidence and to improve the understanding of
conservation objectives.

All conservation activities are financed from annual fees of members (collective
and individual) as well as through income from manufacture and sale of
environmental goods.

PART IV

Environmental Impact Assessment as an Instrument for Handling Transboundary Problems

Principles of International Law Concerning Information and Consultation in Regard to Questions of Transnational Pollution

C. A. Fleischer

(Norway)

<u>The need for international rules on information and consultation</u>

Although the need for international rules may seem obvious, information on activities leading to transnational pollution may be a prior need, to enable an exposed country to take steps to eliminate or mitigate as much as possible the consequences of pollution. Information is also a prerequisite to consultations and must be supplied to enable the authorities of the country of origin as well as the exposed country to consider whether consultations should be held and on what basis, to assess the situation and to consider steps to avoid, prevent, eliminate or mitigate foreseeable pollution and its consequences. Information may further lay the basis for other action which a State may wish to take at the international level; for instance, by international litigation in cases where it is alleged that the State of origin has transgressed the limits set by international law.

Consultations are evidently a means which, in many cases, permit the parties involved to eliminate or mitigate the consequences of transnational pollution; e.g. where alternative methods of production or of waste disposal can be found which do not affect the country which otherwise would habe been exposed to pollution.

<u>General observations on the obligation to respect the environment of other States, and to take account of possible damage to such environment before permitting an activity or undertaking an activity on behalf of the State</u>

Briefly, two fundamental legal considerations are involved, both of which are substantiated by sufficient legal material, and cannot by themselves be denied validity in any court of law, be it domestic or international:

(a) Every State has the right to act within its own recognized sphere of activity.

(b) Every State has the right to claim that other parties should respect its own recognized sphere of activity, and the right to decide by itself which acts shall be performed or permitted.

Both (a) and (b) may be regarded as expressions of the fundamental principle of State sovereignty. It seems evident however, that this principle, by its very nature, cannot be pursued to an extreme end; an uncurtailed exercise of State

sovereignty, if permitting acts which lead to pollution in other States, would by
itself infringe on the principle of sovereignty for such other States.

Special considerations concerning areas which lie beyond the limits of State sovereignty (high seas, etc.)

Environmental law cannot be considered in terms of State sovereignty alone. In
addition, one must take account of those activities which lie beyond the limits
of State sovereignty, in particular such areas as the high seas.

The obligation to restrict one's own activities and to take account of the
corresponding rights of others has, in particular, been set out in Article 2,
paragraph 2, of the Geneva Convention on the High Seas of 29 April 1958:

> "These freedoms, and others which are recognized by general principles
> of international law, shall be exercised by all States with reasonable
> regard to the interests of other States in their exercise of the freedom
> of the high seas."

It may be noted that article 2, paragraph 2, does not lay down mandatory and
general rules regarding the form in which the principle of "reasonable regard"
shall be implemented. One method might be consultations between the parties
involved but there is no obligation regarding consultations as such. It may be
relevant in this context to observe that the need for consultations and concerted
action has increased as a result of technical developments and more extensive
utilization of the resouces of the sea in recent years. The establishment of
regional fisheries commissions, the delegation of State powers to such bodies,
and the attempts of the Third United Nations Law of the Sea Conference (1973)
to establish a new, complete, legal framework for the use of the sea are evidence
of this increasing need.

Possible sources of obligation to respect the environment of other States and to enter into consultations with such States before an activity is undertaken or permitted

In the following, attention will be given to several possible bases for obligations
which may be considered as incumbent upon States according to contemporary
international law. As the body of law to be considered is of fairly recent date,
and in a state of progressive evolution, final conclusions cannot easily be drawn.

It would seem appropriate to start with the question of general principles of
law – principles which may be applied to all States on the basis of the general
rules of international law – and then to consider some examples of treaty law
which is binding only upon States that have expressed their consent to be bound
by the treaty in question.

The question of a general international environmental law: the 1972 Stockholm Conference and the Declaration on the Human Environment

Principle No. 1 may be regarded as the basic provision. This principal sets out
the right of man to adequate conditions of life and to environmental quality.
In other words, here is the provision of a basic human right, linking modern
environmental law to the law of human rights. Reference should further be made,
inter alia, to Principles Nos. 2, 6, 7, 13-18, 20, 21 and 22.

The important aspect of co-operation between States, and the obligations which
must be deemed to exist in this regard, are considered in Principles Nos. 24 and
25. They stipulate, among other concerns, that "international matters concerning

the protection and movement of the environment should be handled in a co-operative
spirit by all countries, big or small, on an equal footing. Co-operation through
multilateral or bilateral arrangements, or other appropriate means is essential
to prevent, eliminate or reduce and effectively control adverse environmental
effects". Due account should be taken of "the sovereignty and the interests of all
States" and international organizations should play "a co-ordinative, efficient
and dynamic role for the protection and improvement of the environment".

Status of the Stockholm Declaration in contemporary international law

The Stockholm Declaration on the Human Environment is not binding upon States.
It is generally accepted in principle, however, that such a solemn declaration,
expressing rules of conduct which are fundamental both for the life of human
beings and for relationships between States, may be regarded as expressing
generally binding principles of law. One may point here to the interesting discussion in the 1969 Judgement of the International Court of Justice (ICJ) in the
North Sea Continental Shelf Cases concerning the possible application of article
6 of the 1958 General Convention on the Continental Shelf and the principle of
equidistance to a State not party to the Convention (e.g. ICJ Reports 1969, pp. 1
and 5).

The principle of the Stockholm Declaration on the Human Environment were referred
to as part of the legal basis for the contention of Australia and New Zealand
regarding general rules of international law. However, as is well known, the
cases of Australia and New Zealand against France were left undecided in regard
to substance, because France had meanwhile undertaken not to perform further tests
of the same nature (see Nuclear Tests Cases Judgement in ICJ Reports 1974, pp. 253
and 457).

An interesting contribution to the theory on the formation of general international
law through international instruments which may not be adhered to formally through
ratification, etc. by the parties, was made by the International Court in its
two judgements of the same year in the Fisheries Jurisdiction Cases (see Judgements
in ICJ Report 1974, pp. 26 and 195). The Court considered that Iceland had a
certian priority right in regard to the exploitation of the resources of the area
adjacent to its territorial sea. This was based on the view that the principle
of so-called "preferential rights" for coastal States in a situation of "special
dependence upon fisheries", expressed in a resolution at the 1958 United Nations
Conference on the Law of the Sea, had entered into the body of general international law.

The question of general environmental law - the Trail Smelter Case

In the much-quoted arbitral award in the Trail Smelter Case between Canada and
the United States it was found that:

> "under the principles of international law, as well as of the law of
> the United States, no State has the right to use or permit the use of
> its territory in such a manner as to cause injury by fumes in or to
> the territory of another or the properties or persons therein, when
> the case is of serious consequence and the injury is established by
> clear and convincing evidence" (U.N.R.I.A.A. vol. 3 p. 1965).

The Judgement by the International Court of Justice in the 1949 Corfu Channel Case

In the 1949 Corfu Channel Case, regarding Albania's obligations to prevent the use
of its territory in such a way as to infringe upon the right of other States to
navigate through the Corfu Channel, the International Court of Justice stated that:

> "Such obligations are based . . . on certain general and well-recognized
> principles, namely: elementary considerations of humanity, even more
> exacting in peace than in war; the principle of the freedom of maritime
> communication; and every State's obligation not to allow knowingly its
> territory to be used for acts contrary to the rights of other States"
> (ICJ Reports 1949, p.22).

The Court's reasoning is founded upon two fundamental elements. First, it presumes
the existence of the right or rights of other States. Second, and in this there
is similarity to the Trail Smelter decision, the existence of a right of one
party entails the obligation of another party to prevent acts which are contrary
to the rights of the first-mentioned party.

Violation of Sovereignty

The sovereignty of States is a fundamental concept of international law and one
of the corner-stones of the Charter of the United Nations (cf. in particular,
article 2, paragraphs 1 and 7). Paragraph 7 states the following principle:

> "Nothing contained in the present Charter shall authorize the
> United Nations to intervene in matters which are essentially within the
> domestic jurisdiction of any State or shall require the Members to
> submit such matters to settlement under the present Charter; but this
> principle shall not prejudice the application of enforcement measures
> under Chapter VII".

What may be termed "matters essentially within domestic jurisdiction" depends
on the evolution of international law, and on whether or not a certain matter is
at a given time subject to regulation by treaties or by other rules of international law. In particular, it cannot be argued that matters concerning fundamental
human rights are beyond the scope of international law and the Charter of the
United Nations. This was clearly stated by the International Court of Justice in
its advisory opinion of 1971 concerning the situation in Namibia (South-West
Africa) (ICJ Reports 1971, p. 16).

Nor can it be claimed that transnational pollution is a matter exclusively or
essentially within domestic jurisdiction. Transnational pollution involves both
the country of origin and any other State affected. Damage caused by transnational
pollution may be a violation of the sovereignty of the State affected. Such
pollution implies the introduction by the State of origin, or by persons under its
jurisdiction, of substance or energy into the environment of the State affected,
in principle without its consent and to the detriment of the State itself or
persons within its jurisdiction. No State can have a general right to pollute the
environment of any other State.

This was the line of argument invoked by Australia and New Zealand in their
actions to prevent further nuclear testing by France in the Pacific. For instance,
it was stated in the Australian application instituting proceeding (filed 9 May
by the Registrar of the Court, p. 28) that:

> " The deposit of radio-active fall-out on the territory of Australia
>   and its dispersion in Australia's air space without Australia's consent:

(a) violates Australian sovereignty over its territory; . . ."

We shall not try to deal here with how far-reaching, according to present law,
may be the right of one State to undertake activities which may have consequences
in the environment of another State. It must, however, be emphasized that whatever

distinction may be drawn between nuclear tests, on the one hand, and industrial and similar activities, on the other hand, does not imply the existence of a general, uncurtailed right of any State to commit acts which may damage the environment of any other State.

Right to decide

In the Australian application for proceeding against France in the Nuclear Test Case it was set out as a separate basis for the claim, that the test:

> "impairs Australia's independent right to determine what acts shall take place within its territory and in particular whether Australia and its people shall be exposed to radiation from artificial sources" (application instituting proceeding filed 9 May 1973 by the Registrar of the Court, p. 28).

This line of argument is, of course, closely related to violation of sovereignty.

Abuse of rights

Another relevant principle of international law (originally built, it is suggested, on analogies to systems of municipal law) is the principle of abuse of rights. This principle may be particularly pertinent in relation to the problems under review.

Even if it is granted that the State of origin might have a certain "right", within its jurisdiction, to commit or permit activities having certain adverse consequences on the environment of other States, the exercise of such a "right" might be unlawful because of the manner in which it is exercised.

In so far as the State of origin of pollution claims it is acting within its rights, and if this claim is accepted for the sake of argument, it would still be a valid contention that the State acts contrary to its obligations under international law if it does not pay due regard to the interests of the State affected. In particular, this would seem to be the case when the State of origin refuses to take part in a system of information and consultation.

State responsibility

An important legal foundation for restrictions on the freedom to cause trans-national pollution may also be found in the traditional principles of State responsibility. The 1961 Draft Convention on the International Responsibility of States for Injuries to Aliens, worked out by the Harvard Law School, proposes a definition of an "internationally wrongful act", including an act which:

> ". . . without sufficient justification . . . creates an unreasonable risk of injury through a failure to exercise due care."

Other relevant bases of general international law; "voisinage", shared resources, "sic utero tuo", etc.

There is, as will be seen, necessarily some overlapping of the different legal bases for restrictions on transnational pollution and for a requirement regarding information and consultations.

We may also point to the following legal grounds, which, to some extent, are related to the foregoing:

(a)   concepts of "voisinage", or neighbourly relations;

(b)   the concept of "shared resources"; (Here, reference may be made to the traditional principles concerning the use of the sea, and in particular the high seas beyond territorial limits; as evidenced <u>inter alia</u> by the 1958 Geneva Convention on the High Seas, particularly in article 2, paragraph 2, regarding the obligation to take account of the rights of other States and of mutual interests in utilizing the same resource) and;

(c)   the obligation to avoid damage, or unreasonable damage, to other parties in the form of transnational pollution. It may be argued that this obligation has itself become a specific rule of international law. In legal theory one often refers to the maxim <u>sic utere tuo ut alienum non laedas</u> (i.e., use one's own property in such a way that one does not damage others). General principles accepted by nations in their own domestic systems can form a valid source of international law, as set out in article 38, paragraph 1.c, of the Statute of the International Court of Justice.

The obligation to co-operate

As has been seen, the obligation upon States to co-operate is one of the fundamental elements of the Stockholm Declaration.

An even more primary basis is found in the Charter of the United Nations. The principle of human rights and the aim to "promote social progress and better standards of life" and to "employ international machinery for the promotion of economic and social advancement of all peoples"is mentioned in the Preamble. The Charter of the United Nations, article 1, paragraph 3, lists among the purposes "To achieve international co-operation in solving international problems of an economic, social, cultural or humanitarian character ..." According to paragraph 4, the United Nations Organization shall be "a centre for harmonizing the actions of nations in the attainment of these common ends". Attention should also be drawn to articles 55 and 56, regarding international economic and social co-operation. In article 56, all members "pledge themselves to take joint and separate action in co-operation with the Organization for the achievement of the purposes set forth in article 55".

There can be no doubt that the protection of the environment plays an important part in the achievement of social progress and a better standard of living for all persons. This involves especially co-operation to avoid or mitigate environmental consequences in a State affected by the activities of another State.

Provisions which are more limited in scope, but which may nevertheless tend to support a general obligation between nations to co-operate in order to avoid detrimental effects on people and areas exposed to pollution, are found in articles 24 and 25 of the 1958 Geneva Convention on the High Seas.

Suggested approaches for the implementation of a system of information and consultation

The arguments submitted above do not lead to any conclusions regarding the exact manner in which an affected State may take part in consultations. Exception must, obviously, be made for cases where co-operation takes place according to a certain agreed organizational framework, as in the 1972 Dumping Conventions or in regional economic organizations such as the European Economic Community, where such organizations have competence which relates to matters of transnational pollution.

It seems evident that a satisfactory system of international control regarding transnational pollution must be based on sufficient control at the domestic level.

In other words, each State must be under an obligation to take those measures within its own national legislative system which are necessary to prevent any activity which cause pollution beyond certain acceptable levels, or without sufficient justification.

A general prohibition against "unjustified pollution" will contribute to the improvement of the environment, but will not in itself be sufficient. The obligation to establish and enforce such a general standard must necessarily be combined with obligations to establish more specific standards for types of acts which are likely to lead to pollution. This will include standards concerning various industrial activities, modes of transport, the design, construction and operation of industrial machinery, disposal of waste, etc. It is, obviously, of importance that the legal framework should be designed to cover those areas where the risks and extent of transnational pollution are greatest, and that the system should not be made unreasonably cumbersome by trying to regulate details of minor importance.

The rules should secure the obligation to maintain a concession system at the domestic level; i.e., an obligation upon States to regulate in national law that certain activities cannot be undertaken without the prior permission of a governmental authority. That this type of control is necessary has been borne out in the experience of individual States through their efforts to legislate against pollution. In particular, the consession system would enable authorities to obtain information from an industry, etc. on the risk of pollution, and on the methods of production, upon which decisions could be based regarding the manner in which an activity should be performed. Furthermore, it should provide that the necessary information be conveyed to other States that might be affected. A concession system, however, must allow for a certain degree of flexibility, to avoid overburdening the administrations with the consideration and issuing of concessions in cases where such a procedure is not necessary.

Such a system of domestic control is both a necessary prerequisite and a supplement to the principles of equal access and non-discrimination. Per se equal access to the systems of environmental control in the State of origin, and non-discrimination in relation to the subjects of that State, are not sufficient to guarantee to the State affected and its subjects that unreasonable environmental damage does not occur. As such, the principles of equal access and of non-discrimination depend upon the rules which are in effect in the State of origin, in relation to its own subjects. If these interests are not sufficiently considered in the domestic system of the State of origin, then pollution to whatever extent is permissible may be caused and affect persons in other States.

If the principles of equal access and of non-discrimination are given a place in a conventional framework of a universal nature, they would thereby form an additional base for the establishment of a sufficient system of prohibition and control in the municipal law of the State of origin.

Further, the authorities of the State affected must themselves have the right and opportunity to take up matters and consult with the State of origin before damage occurs. There must, therefore, be an obligation to provide and disseminate information so that both the authorities of the State affected and the persons and the organizations interested are informed in due time.

In regard to activities which may lead to pollution, another corner-stone in the legal framework should be international rules governing maximum levels. This would imply the establishment of substantive rules whereby both the State of origin and the State affected could take action to prevent or to claim the cessation of activities undertaken contrary to the limitations established. Mechanisms should be established for the elaboration of such rules.

The system of joint or international commissions should also be considered, in order to review the continuous flow of information and to recommend new rules which might seem appropriate from time to time.

The Environmental Impact Statement

A workable system of environmental control in relation to transnational pollution must have provisions whereby those who undertake activities which may have substantial impact on the environment must assess such impact and provide a statement which can be evaluated by the competent authorities, in the State of origin as well as in any State affected. A well-known precedent here is Section 102 (2) (c) of the 1970 National Envrionmental Policy Act (NEPA) of the United States of America (42 (SC 4321-4347)).

In practice it has been held that the American legislation requiring an impact statement applies also in relation to environmental consequences beyond the limits of United State's jurisdiction. In the case of Wilderness Society v. Morton 463 G.2d 1261 (D.C.Cir. 1972) the court granted standing to Canadian intervenors in a case concerning the Trans-Alaska Pipeline. According to the court, the interest of the intervenors were within the area protected by Section 102 (2) (c) of NEPA.

In the decision in Sierra Club, et al. v. Coleman, 405 F. Supp. 53 (D.D.C. 1975, also reported in International Legal Materials, 1975 p.1425, cf. also I.L.M. 1976 p.1417), it was found that an environmental impact statement was not sufficient in relation to possible damage caused to certain Indian tribes living in Panama and in Colombia, who would be affected by a highway project. Consequently, the defendants, their agent, etc. and "any persons in active concert or participation with them", were by the Court's order:

> "enjoined from entering into any contract, obligating any funds, expending any funds, etc. ..., unless and until defendants have fully and adequately supplemented their Final Environmental Impact Statement, in the manner prescribed by law for the initial preparation of such statements, to remedy the deficiencies outlined in this memorandum".

Reference may be made also the proposal for a general planning act in Norwegian domestic law (see NOU 1977:1; in particular, the proposed 5.6 considering irreversible changes of use of land or other natural resources).

Participation by individuals and groups of individuals

One of the most remarkable developments in practice concerning the National Environmental Policy Act (NEPA) of the United States has been the active participation of individuals and groups of individuals in the decision-making process. This development was not explicitly foreseen in the provisions of the Act, but has come into being as a result of the court's interpretation of the Act, with specific reference to the fact that the Act as such was intended to protect the interests of individuals and not only the State.

Participation by individuals and companies in disputes - including, but not specifically related to, disputes concerning environmental problems - has also been provided for to some extent in the European Communities, cf. in particular the Treaty establishing the European Economic Community, articles 173, 175, 177 and 184. The EEC Treaty provides for an interesting combination of competences concerning individuals, member States and community bodies.

Some examples of Treaty Law

The following list, which does not pretend to be exhaustive, contains examples
of co-operation, information and consultation provided for by treaty:

(a)   the so called <u>Bonn Convention of 9 June 1969</u>, which is a regional arrangement
between the North Sea countries on co-operation in dealing with pollution of the
North Sea by oil;

(b)   the <u>Oslo Convention of 15 February 1972 for the Prevention of Marine Pollution
by Dumping from Ships and Aircraft</u>, also a regional arrangement;

(c)   the <u>London Convention of 29 December 1972 on the Prevention of Marine
Pollution by Dumping of Wastes and Other Matter</u>, which is a world-wide, multilateral convention based on the same principles as the Oslo Convention;

(d)   the <u>International Convention for the Prevention of Pollution from Ships,of
2 November 1973</u>, which, according to its preamble, aims rather ambitiously to
"achieve the complete elimination of intentional pollution of the marine
environment by oil and other harmful substances and the minimization of accidental
discharge of such substances"; it consists of a rather short convention combined
with two protocols and five annexes giving more specific provisions concerning
different pollutants and other aspects;

(e)   the <u>Paris Convention of 4 June 1974</u>, on the Prevention of Marine Pollution
from Land-Based Sources; and

(f)   the <u>Nordic Convention on Environment Protection, of 19 February 1974</u>,
between Denmark, Finland, Norway and Sweden.

As the basic provision of the last-mentioned Convention, one may note article 2,
which has the following wording (translated into English):

> "When an authority in any Contracting State is considering the permissibility
> of environmentally harmful activity, the nuisance such activity entails or
> may entail in another Contracting State shall be regarded as equivalent to
> a nuisance caused in the former State."

The Nordic Convention further gives competence for the authority designated by the
State affected (Article 4) to take up questions with the authorities of the State
of origin, and to demand further information regarding projects which may lead
to environmental damage (article 6). The concession authorities in the State of
origin have the obligation to convey the necessary material to the competent
authority of the State affected (article 5).

Conclusions

The above material drawn from various sources of international law gives firm
support for the conclusion that an affected State has a claim <u>vis-à-vis</u> the
State of origin of transboundary pollution on the latter to provide information
and to allow for consultations between it and the State affected in cases where
an activity undertaken in the State of origin may be the cause of transnational
pollution. However, there seems to be no general rule of contemporary international
law which lays down exactly in what manner the obligations of consultations and
information are to be performed.

It seems desirable to try to achieve a further development of international
and national or supporting law on information and consultation through international co-operation and possibly the establishment of one or more international
conventions on the subject. Important elements of such a further development
would seem to be the following:

(a) a sufficient system of prohibition and control in domestic laws in the State of origin;

(b) equal accesss and non-discrimination in relation to interests in the State affected, before the courts and the administrative organs of the State of origin;

(c) rules on information and the dissemination thereof;

(d) rules on the participation of the State affected, to enable it to influence the decision-making process;

(e) the establishment of joint or international commissions or bodies, as may be appropriate;

(f) to the extent possible, rules defining the levels of transnational pollution acceptable under international law;

(g) rules on the obligation to provide environmental impact statements, in cases where the environment of other States may be substantially affected.

Shaping Environmental Assessment for Use in International Activities

W. H. Mansfield

(United States)

USING ENVIRONMENTAL ASSESSMENTS INTERNATIONALLY

Successful experience with environmental assessment techniques and procedures for
evaluating domestic environmental effects of governmental activities and projects
has raised the possibility of using similar assessment measures in international
activities. From the effective use of environmental assessments for identifying,
evaluating and communicating information on environmental effects of activities
at home, it is a natural step to look for possible benefits of the assessment
process in international affairs. Several countries are now assessing the domestic
environmental effects of certain activities; others are considering the possible
development of assessment procedures. Several international organizations are
seeking to develop methodology and guidelines for environmental assessments and
are assisting Governments in the use of assessment techniques.

Governments undertake several different kinds of activity for which international
environmental assessments can prove valuable. In the field of development
assistance planning, environmental assessments can furnish direct benefits to
aid donor and recipient countries. They can identify potential environmental
problems and enable planners to avoid the need to take costly corrective measures
later. Through early evaluation they can prevent irreparable damage to valuable
resources. At the same time, the assessment process permits the integration of
environmental considerations and values into the development process.

Environmental assessment procedures provide also a valuable tool for governmental
decision-makers to detect and analyse the potential environmental impacts of
their actions on neighbouring countries and the global commons. In the future,
environmental assessment may provide a mechanism for neighbouring countries
to work together to identify and solve transboundary environmental problems that
involve effects on nearby countries and the global commons.

DIFFERENCES BETWEEN DOMESTIC AND INTERNATIONAL SITUATIONS

In considering the assessment of foreign environmental impacts, Governments must
weigh the significant differences between the approaches to assessing domestic
and foreign environmental effects. There are important jurisdictional, practical
and procedural differences between reviewing environmental effects at home, where
domestic governmental authority exists, and abroad, where another nation has

jurisdiction. States are jealous sovereigns within their own boundaries. They
regard themselves as custodians of their own environment. Actions occurring within
a State are subject to its laws and control, and most nations will resist any
outside efforts which even appear to impose upon them foreign values or provisions
of foreign jurisdiction. Governments will reject any environmental review procedure which they believe will infringe upon important foreign policy, security
or export activities.

There are, as well, practical difficulties in trying to evaluate environmental
effects in another country. The information required for an adequate environmental
assessment may simply not be available. The affected country may not have the
information, or, if it does, may not wish to make it available to another
Government. Also, the difficulties of assessing foreign environmental impacts may
cause delays in decision-making and lead to increased costs. Some international
activities (e.g. commodity negotiations) may not lend themselves to environmental
study with present assessment techniques. In other cases, a Government's
investigation of environmental effects might prove to have little or no bearing
on the final decision on an activity because the individual Government's role
(e.g. in multilateral activities) might not be subject to prior analysis or
conclusive in the ultimate decision to implement the activity. There are, as well
the usual problems of value judgements about what constitutes "significant"
damage to another country, particularly where development and environmental
priorities may differ as between nations.

Because of these complexities, conducting studies on foreign environmental effects
is likely to be more difficult than assessing domestic environmental impacts. The
activities that nations undertake are many and varied. Consequently, activities
selected for environmental study must be those where substantial environmental
impact is anticipated. Examples are prime candidates for review for transnational
impacts might be large industrial complexes located along national boundaries,
such as power plants, chemical and steel factories, smelters, dams and refineries.
Large mining and extractive industrial developments and major transportation
developments, such as airports, roads and harbours, projects for water supplies,
waste and sewage treatment plants and pesticide spraying may be appropriate for
review for effects on the global commons (e.g. the high seas and atmosphere),
for example, activities creating or designed to control ocean pollution and to
promote deep sea mining. Similar review would be appropriate for actions affecting
marine mammals and wildlife or impacting on the global atmosphere.

Documentation evaluating international environmental impacts should be concise
and analytical rather than simply descriptive. It should alert decision-makers
to the significant foreign environmental impacts and key environmental issues
and discuss possible measures for preventing or mitigating environmental
problems. Streamlining the evaluation process and documents will prevent the
environmental assessment from becoming a source of excess delay and cost for
Governments.

ENVIRONMENTAL ASSESSMENT IN INTERNATIONAL DEVELOPMENT ASSISTANCE
PLANNING

Development assistance planning already appears to be one field where
environmental assessment yields useful results. In recent years it has become
apparent that environmental objectives are complementary to, and not in
competition with, development goals and objectives. Environmental objectives
should be integrated early into development planning. The environmental assessment
process provides both host and assisting nations with an evaluation of the
potential environmental effects of a proposed project at a cost much lower than
the potential expense of remedial measures that a poorly designed project might

require. Additionally, the assessment process furnishes a systematic procedure for integrating environmental considerations into project planning. This procedure is greatly facilitated in development project planning because both the assisting and the host countries have responsibility and influence in project planning.

Recognition of the benefits of environmental assessment has led the United Nations Environment Programme (UNEP) to develop environmental impact assessment guidelines for use in development planning at the national level. UNEP is also assisting Governments in the use of assessment techniques.

Since 1970, the World Bank has reviewed projects it finances for environmental implications and has designed safeguards when needed to avoid adverse environmental side effects. At the national level the United States Agency for International Development (AID) has prepared environmental assessments for certain development programmes and projects since 1976 (1). The assessment process is used as a vehicle to integrate environmental considerations into the early phases of project planning. Among the projects AID has assessed for environmental considerations are land developments in Sri Lanka, tsetse fly control in Tanzania, integrated rural development in Liberia, water and sewer development in Yemen, and the Macarin Dam in Jordan. As a contribution to a multinational development assistance project on the Senegal River, AID will finance the environmental effects studies for construction of the two dams which will be built in the project.

These uses of environmental assessment in development planning have proved to be valuable. Many developing nations recognize the benefits of incorporating environmental considerations into the development process. The assessment procedures are, however, still relatively new and they are evolving as more experience is gained. A study of nine multilateral agencies undertaken by the International Institute for Environment and Development (IIED) (2) indicated that other multilateral banks and institutions are less advanced in the use of environmental assessment techniques than the World Bank and US/AID. The IIED is now preparing a study of the environmental assessment interests and capabilities of selected national development assistance organizations.

ASSESSMENT TECHNIQUES IDENTIFY TRANSBOUNDARY ENVIRONMENTAL IMPACTS

By extending domestic environmental evaluation procedures to the analysis of foreign impacts, environmental assessment can also become a valuable tool for indentifying significant environmental effects of actions upon a neighbouring State or States or upon the global commons. The assessment helps decision-makers to identify and possibly to avoid potential boundary problems that might become foreign relations problems.

It is evident from the earlier discussion that assessing transboundary environmental impacts can be more difficult than evaluating development projects where the donor and recipient countries are working together. Transboundary environmental problems most often arise from activities in which one country is acting independently and the affected nation has little influence in shaping the planning of the project. The information needed to prepare an environmental study may be in the affected country and may not be available to the country preparing the assessment. Additionally, because of the potential implications of transboundary environmental effects for relations between the acting and affected countries, the environmental assessment may become sensitive from the standpoint of international relations.

Nevertheless, interest in environmental assessment in the cases of transboundary pollution is growing. The Organization for Economic Co-operation and Development has provided information and made recommendations on the administrative and technical aspects of environmental impact assessment procedures involving transboundary effects in coastal management and frontier regions (3). The Council of Europe, the Economic Commission for Europe, the European Communities and the United Nations Environment Programme have expressed interest in the possible international uses of environmental assessment (4). In boundary activities between the United States and Canada and Mexico, modified approaches to environmental assessment have been used for transboundary environmental studies for a number of years (5).

PRESIDENTIAL EXECUTIVE ORDER ON ENVIRONMENTAL ASSESSMENT

Growing concern in the United States that the Government should undertake its major actions with an awareness of their potential significant environmental consequences led to a consideration of the need to assess the environmental effects of the Government's activities outside the United States. On 4 January 1979, President Carter signed (Presidential) Executive Order No. 12114 establishing a US Government-wide framework for developing Federal Government agency procedures to review environmental effects of agency actions outside the United States (6).

The actions to be reviewed will include treaties, agreements, programmes and projects having significant potential environmental effects outside the United States. The reviews will be prepared by the US agency conducting the action. Usually the review will take the form of a report which accompanies, or is included in, the agency's other internal decision documents on the activity.

Because it is clearly recognized that consideration of foreign environmental impacts can bear upon important foreign, economic and national security goals and interests, the Executive Order seeks to reconcile the legitimate, but possibly competing, considerations of concern for the environment outside the United States with these other national policy concerns. The Order calls for environmental reviews of the most serious potential environmental problems and seeks to minimize unnecessary undesirable effects of the assessment process upon foreign and security objectives and upon exports.

A. Affected Actions and Types of Review

The Order specifies certain major governmental actions which may have potential environmental effects abroad. It indicates which of these actions must be reviewed under the Order and it sets out alternative types of environmental review documents that may be prepared, as follows:

(a) When impacts occur in the global commons areas Environmental Impact Statements (EISs) will be prepared when actions may have significant environmental effects. Such actions might include ocean pollution control, conservation, wildlife protection, fisheries and weather modification activities.

(b) When impacts occur in foreign countries, where the environment may be significantly affected concise reviews or bilateral or multilateral studies (as distinct from the more detailed environmental impact statements) of the environmental impacts will be prepared in the following situations:

1. where the foreign nation affected is not participating with the United States in the project (an "innocent bystander" situation, such as US-financed dam in one foreign country that cuts off water to another);

2. where the US Government's action involves a product or a facility whose principal products or whose emissions or effluents are prohibited or strictly regulated by law because their toxic effects on the environment create a serious public health risk (such as certain kinds of governmentally financed or approved industrial facilities or other governmental actions involving pollution from toxic chemicals);

3. where the US Government's action involves a facility which is strictly regulated or prohibited in the United States in order to protect against radioactive hazards (such as the export of nuclear reactors); and

4. where the US Government's action affects natural or ecological resources of global inportance that may in the future be designated by the President or, in the case of resources protected by binding international agreement, by the Secretary of State.

B. Exemptions and Modifications

The Order provides for certain exemptions and modifications of the procedures where necessary to ensure that the assessment process does not impair effective conduct of foreign affairs, national defence and export or other commercial activities.

(a) The Order exempts a number of activities, including:

1. actions taken directly by the President involving national security considerations, disaster and emergency relief, circumstances involving exceptional foreign policy and national sensitivity, or occuring in the course of armed conflicts;

2. export licences, permits or export approvals, and actions relating to nuclear activities except actions providing to a foreign nation a nuclear production or utilization facility or a nuclear waste management facility;

3. votes and other actions in international conferences and organizations; and

4. intelligence activities and arms transfers.

(b) Agencies are authorized to modify the content, availability and timing of the required environmental analyses to:

1. enable the agency to decide and act promptly;

2. avoid adverse impacts on foreign relations or infringe on the sovereignty of other nations; and

3. ensure appropriate reflection of diplomatic factors, export promotion, governmental and commercial confidentiality, national security, lack of information and the level of agency involvement in the action.

Effects on US Agencies

It is anticipated that only a limited proportion of governmental activities will need to be reviewed under the Order. Most private export business is not affected because most exports do not require specific federal agency permits or licences. In cases where such permits or licences are required, the Order exempts most of them from mandatory environmental review because they would not have significant environmental effects.

Nuclear reactor exports will be evaluated, while nuclear fuel exports are exempted from review. An inter-agency work group is developing nuclear export environmental review procedures which are consistent with US nonproliferation objectives and the US intention to remain a reliable nuclear supplier. Agencies would normally review actions involving toxic substances, such as asbestos, vinyl chloride, isocyanates, polychlorinated biphenals (PCBs), pesticides, mercury, beryllium, arsenic, cadium and benzene. Such substances as chlorine, caustic soda, ammonia, sulphuric acid, phosphoric acid, nitric acid, sulphur dioxide, nitrogen oxides and sulphate and sulphite liquors would not ordinarily be reviewed for environmental effects under the Order.

Major loans under the Export-Import Bank's direct lending programme will fall under the Order's provisions. The existing procedures of the US Agency for International Development for assessing the environmental effects of development projects will not be affected by the Order.

Effects on Other Countries

Since the procedures call for preparation of environmental documents to enable the US action agency to inform itself of the potential consequeces of its own action, the assessment procedures should not directly affect other nations. But other Governments should benefit from the assessment studies. The Order does permit agencies to use bilaterally - or multilaterally - prepared studies as one form of environmental documentation, so other nations may be invited at times to take part in such studies to assist the US agency to prepare the necessary analysis and information.

US agency procedures will provide for informing foreign Governments when environmental documents prepared under the Order are available to host countries for their information and use in their planning.

ENVIRONMENTAL ASSESSMENT AS AN AID IN TRANSBOUNDARY PROBLEMS

Experience with environmental assessment in international situations points to additional uses of environmental analysis techniques. If environmental studies can help to identify, evaluate and consider environmental factors in domestic, foreign and global commons areas, they might also serve as an aid in dealing with transfrontier environmental impacts. The United Nations Environment Programme has incorporated environmental assessment considerations into draft principles of conduct in the field of the environment, for guiding States when using and conserving shared natural resources; it is pioneering with steps to consider environment in weather modification (7).

Last year the United States Senate passed a resolution, introduced by Senator Claiborne Pell, (8) which urged the United States Government to promote an international treaty which would use "international environmental assessments" as a means to identify and deal with potential transboundary environmental problems.

Under the proposal, States would:

(a) prepare international environmental assessments for any major actions taken within their own territory or in the global commons, such as the high seas, that could be expected to have a significant harmful effect on the environment of another nation or a global commons area;

(b) send the environmental assessment to the affected country or, in the case of the global commons, to the United Nations Environment Programme (UNEP) before initiating the action; and

(c) refrain temporarily from an action to consult, if requested, with affected States or with   UNEP to prevent or minimize potential adverse effects of planned actions.

Such an arrangement would provide new, valuable uses of environmental assessment techniques and procedures. Such assessments would indentify potential transnational environmental problems and provide scientific and technical background information and data on effects; this would provide a basis for Governments to consult and work together to evaluate and solve or minimize undesirable environmental impacts and any conflicts they may cause.

There are questions to be answered before the international community can develop and accept an international arrangement like this. But the potential benefits of using environmental assessment techniques for dealing with transnational environmental problems are worth the effort. The United States announced its intention to work with other nations to develop an international environmental assessment arrangement for this purpose during the seventh session of the UNEP Governing Council at Nairobi in April-May 1979. The United States is taking steps to consult with a number of other Governments about such an arrangement for dealing with transnational environmental effects. If the consultations show there is interest, the United States plans to make a specific proposal on the matter.

The possible uses and the values of environmental assessment are opening to us. We are still learning and adopting assessment techniques, procedures and documentation. We are coming to appreciate the values of assessing environmental effects and integrating environmental considerations into our domestic activities. At the same time we can already see expanded uses for environmental assessment in international affairs for evaluating development assistant projects and assessing effects of our actions on other countries and the global commons. Even more exciting is the possibility of applying these analytical measures as an aid in resolving transnational environmental problems. A great deal of knowledge and experience is needed and many hurdles will have to be overcome before environmental assessment can be fully and easily used in international affairs. But the possible applications are already evident and our first experiments in the international uses are underway. Flexibility, ingenuity and, above all, experience may make it possible for us to make environmental assessment as valuable a tool in international affairs as it has been in domestic activities.

REFERENCES

1.   The US Agency for International Development's Environmental Procedures are published in 22 C.F.R. Part 216. Pesticide and other Procedures are published in the Federal Register Vol. 42, No. 245, 21 December 1977. Revised procedures are expected to be published in 1979.

2.   Johnson, Brian and Stein, Robert E., Banking on the Biosphere, Environmental Procedures and Practices on Nine Development Financing Agencies, Lexington Books, Lexington, Massachusetts, 1979.

3.   See "OECD and the Environment", Organization for Economic Co-operation and Development, Paris 1976.

4.   Within the Council of Europe, Ministers supported in 1976 a wider introduction of Environmental Impact Assessments. The Economic Commission for Europe collected information on environmental impact assessment in its member countries in 1978 and scheduled the present Seminar on Environmental Impact Assessment. The United Nations Environment Programme has prepared a variety of documents dealing with the use of environmental assessment in transboundary pollution, e.g.

"Draft Principles of Conduct in the Field of the Environment for the Guidance
of States in the Conservation and Harmonious Utilization of Natural Resources
shared by Two or More States," 23 January - 7 February 1978 (UNEP/GC.6/17, 10
March 1978); "Draft Principles of Conduct for the Guidance of States Concerning
Weather Modification", Report of the WMO/UNEP Informal Meeting on Legal Aspects
of Weather Modification (Na.78-2195).

5.   Canada, Mexico and the United States have had some experience with modified
approaches to environmental assessment within the context of Joint Commissions
established by treaties to deal with boundary waters, sanitation and other
environmentally-related problems along their borders. Within these organizations,
the technical aspects of transboundary environmental problems were periodically
identified, analysed and resolved. More often than not, however, the Commissions
were asked to evaluate an existing environmental problem rather than to assess
activities to identify problems in the planning process. In recent years, US
agencies have transmitted environmental documents to Canada and Mexico on
selected projects having potential transboundary impacts.

6.   US Executive Order No. 12114 of 4 January 1979 concerning Environmental
Effects abroad of Major Federal Actions, Federal Register, Vol. 44, No. 6,
9 January 1979.

7.   See reference 4.

8.   US Senate Resolution 49, 21 July 1978, Description contained in the 95th
Congress, 2nd Session, Senate Calendar No. 919, Report No. 95-990, International
Environmental Assessment.

Methodology of Investigations of Long-Range Transport of Sulphur Compounds

Yu. A. Izrael, I. M. Nazarov and A. G. Ryaboshapko

(USSR)

Sulphur compounds are now considered the most important atmospheric pollutants, and rightly so. The global man-made emission of sulphur dioxide is about 130 million tons per year (1). The energy programmes now under development in many countries lead one to expect a further increase of the global sulphur emission from coal used as fuel, at least up to the year 2000, because of technological difficulties and the high cost of coal desulphurization before combustion and difficulties of cleaning the stack gas. At the same time one is certainly aware of a possible negative impact of sulphur compounds on the environment both in the vicinity of sources and even at a rather long distance from them. Such circumstances necessitate serious study of geophysical, ecological and other aspects of the transport of sulphur compounds in the atmosphere. The techniques to study long-range transport of sulphur compounds should include the determination of the following elements:

(a) the field of the emission sources;

(b) typical height of emission above ground level;

(c) parameters of vertical dispersion during transport;

(d) the wind;

(e) parameters of removal and transformation of sulphur compounds in the atmosphere;

(f) the nature of the impact of sulphur compounds on the biosphere and detection of critical links in the biosphere.

Each of these aspects and the problem of transboundary pollution will be considered below. Also outlined will be a possible way to establish standards for flows of sulphur compounds across a boundary between States.

Sulphur emissions are not homogeneous in space but are more concentrated in the regions of intensive consumption of sulphur-bearing fuels and non-ferrous metal production. There are several techniques to estimate the spatial dispersion of manufactured sulphur. The simplest, and rather frequently-used, technique has been an estimation based on population density data and values of specific sulphur dioxide emission per inhabitant. This method may lead to significant errors in some regions that amount to 100 per cent or more. For example, in the study by B. Ottar, (1976) (2) the emission in Moscow and its suburbs was estimated

327

from population statistics as having a value of about 1.5 million tons of SO_2 per year. Actually this figure would be several times lower because, in principle, natural gas with low sulphur content is used as fuel; for regionas where coal is consumed the value of emission may be underestimated.

The approach based on data for separate types of products (for instance non-ferrous metals) and consumption of fuels with different sulphur content is more correct. In this case many more factors should be taken into account compared with the first approach. For example, both the calculations of different types of fuels and the sulphur content for each different type of fuel should be considered. The estimated errors of emission while using this approach are 30 to 50 per cent.

More accurate data could have been obtained by direct measurement of SO_2 emitted from each separate industry and power plant. However, at present no country has such a detailed network for emissions control. Therefore, while solving practical problems of inventory one should combine different approaches and be aware of the possibility of errors.

The allowance for temporal variability of emission intensity is very important in determining the emission field. The variability occurs, first of all, owing to an emission increase in winter because of higher energy consumption for heating. According to Barnes' data (1976) (3) winter emission in England and Wales is 1.6 times higher compared to summer emission. One should take into account, however, that this relation is also determined by geophysical characteristics of the region. In addition it can be significantly higher for northern regions and lower for southern ones.

At present, the principal means to control dangerous local levels of sulphur compounds concentrations in human settlements is to increase the height of the emission. This involves decreasing the surface concentrations but it promotes dispersion and long-range sulphur transport. The height of the emission is consequently an important parameter that is characteristic of long-range sulphur transport. The mean height of sulphur emissions in developed countries is about 80 metres (4) but the value will be constantly increased.

The character of sulphur compounds distribution in the atmosphere together with their height both over their sources and while being transported to "clean" regions is closely connected to emission parameters. Only average characteristics may be described because the type of distribution as well as the height depend primarily on such variable conditions as the presence or absence of inversions, degree of atmosphere stability, and formation of the underlying surface.

Data obtained during the investigations carried out under the auspices of OECD in 1977 (5) have indicated that for west and central Europe the mean height of the sulphur dioxide distribution layer was equal to 1,200m; that of sulphates was 1,235m. Similar, although higher, values were obtained by Soviet scientists, V.A. Ionov and co-workers, from an aircraft study made over the territory of the European part of the USSR. Data on vertical distribution of sulphur compounds in the atmosphere has been very important for estimating flows across the boundaries of countries. The Soviet Union has developed its programme of monitoring transboundary flows using both ground-based networks of stations and regular flights of aircraft labs. Further, more intensive investigations have been aimed at the possible application of laser techniques for remote measuring of total sulphur dioxide in the air column as well as characteristics of its height distribution. This direction of work seems extremely promising as it may in future circumvent expensive aircraft methods.

The horizontal transport of sulphur compounds is determined by wind currents and can be estimated on the basis of available information on the structure of pressure fields at different levels. A network of meteorologic stations and upper-air sensing stations in Europe has been sufficient to obtain such inform-ation. In the USSR, the transport of polluted masses is followed at three barome-tric levels: 1,000, 925 and 850 mbar. We would like to emphasize the importance of the 925 mbar level as it has been shown that this is the level at which the principal mass of pollutants is transported. The introduction into the routine meteorologic services of central and western Europe of processing and broadcas-ting information on the 925 mbar surface would make it possible to establish a unified technique to estimate polluted air massess for the whole of Europe.

For a better understanding of particularities of long-range sulphur transport in the atmosphere one should trace the transformation of the emitted SO_2. Sulphur dioxide readily dissolves in water and so when in contact with cloud and fog vapour, as well as with falling rain, it is transformed into a water phase producing a solution of sulphurous acid. Under actual conditions the sulphur in the liquid phase oxidizes quickly to a valence state of plus six. The oxidation is promoted by salts of some metals (Mn, Fe and others) dissolved in cloud vapour which serve as catalysts of oxidation. Therefore, when SO_2 precipitates from the atmosphere, the sulphuric acid falls on the underlying surface. The speed of the process depends mainly on physiochemical characteristics of the absorbing surface, the height of the SO_2 distribution layer in the atmosphere and the extent of turbulence in the layer. The third mechanism of SO_2 removal is its oxidation to sulphuric acid directly in the atmosphere. Oxidation reactions can take place both in the gas phase and at the surface of aerosol particles. These reactions are most probable in polluted atmosphere. Atomic oxygen, ozone, hydroperoxide radical, etc., are oxidizing agents. In any case, sulphuric acid is a result of a reaction as sulphuric anhydride combines instantly with water molecules that are permanently present in the atmosphere.

The sulphuric acid produced in the atmosphere mainly takes the form of semi-liquid particles of submicron size. These particles are so small that, for the most part, they are not subject to sedimentation but, as in the case with SO_2, they can be washed out with precipitation or be absorbed by the underlying surface. While being transported in the atmosphere, the sulphuric acid can be more or less completely neutralized; ammonia is the principal neutralizing agent. Consequently, 70 to 80 per cent of man-made sulphates are in the form of ammonium sulphate. Sulphate particles range in size from 0.1 to 1 um so that the principal mechanisms for their removal from the atmosphere are washing out with cloud vapour and rain and absorption by the underlying surface;

A summary of what has been stated above regarding the behaviour pattern of sulphur compounds in the atmosphere is shown in Fig. 1. As a first approximation, one can suppose that the amount of substance entering the block and leaving it is proportional to the amount of substance in the block and that these processes are described with a kinetic equation of the first order.

$$\frac{dN^{SO_2}}{dt} = (K_1 + K_2 + K_3) \, N^{SO_2}$$

$$\frac{dN^{H_2SO_4}}{dt} = K_3 N^{SO_2} - (K_4 + K_5 + K_6) \, N^{H_2SO_4}$$

$$\frac{dN^{MeSO_4}}{dt} = K_6 N^{H_2SO_4} - (K_7 + K_8) \, N^{MeSO_4}$$

In this set N is the amount of the corresponding substance in each block, $K_1 \div K_8$ are coefficients characteristic of the speed of processes given in the block.

diagram.

Values of the $K_1 \div K_8$ coefficients depend on a number of factors: type of
underlying surface; presence and height of the inversion layer; precipitation
intensity and frequency; presence of other pollutants in the atmosphere, etc.
In estimating the absorption speed of sulphur dioxide or sulphates, one usually
determines linear vertical velocities of sedimentation $V^{SO_2}_a$ and $V^{SO_4^=}_a$ rather
than values of the K_1; K_4; K_7; coefficients. In this case the coefficients' values
can be determined from the relation $K_i = V_a/H$, where H is the mean height of the
distribution layer. The washing out speed of sulphur compounds is determined by
the relation between between dry and wet periods for a year. For Europe, the time
fraction with precipitation can be considered equal to 6 to 10 per cent. The
estimates for sulphur dioxide oxidation and sulphuric acid neutralization
directly in the atmosphere are rather indefinite. The author's estimates, as well
as those of others indicate that sulphur dioxide oxidizes rather quickly in the
atmosphere, especially in polluted atmosphere and this is promoted by aerosol
particles, ammonia, and by some types of metals, such as manganese, etc.
Practically nothing is known about the speed with which sulphuric acid is neutralized to sulphates. Roughly, its value can be estimated on the assumption that
50 to 80 per cent of sulphur in precipitation in central Europe which falls out
in Norway is in the form of sulphuric acid (Ministry of Environment, Norway,
1974 (6). When the time duration for transport is about 20 hours, the constant
of the neutralization velocity can be within 0.02 to 0.04 hr^{-1}. On the basis of
data obtained by many authors, as well as the authors' own investigations, an
estimate has been made of the possible intervals of values for all coefficients
that are characteristic of velocity both of transformation and removal of sulphur
compounds from the atmosphere for European conditions:

SO_2 absorption by the underlying surface

$$K_1 = 0.15 \div 0.030 \ hr^{-1}$$

SO_2, H_2SO_4, $MeSO_4$ wash-out

$$K_2 = K_5 = K_8 = 0.22 \div 0.036 \ hr^{-1}$$

Oxidation of SO_2 to H_2SO_4

$$K_3 = 0.07 \div 0.15 \ hr^{-1}$$

H_2SO_4, $MeSO_4$ absorption

$$K_4 = K_7 = 0.01 \ hr^{-1}$$

H_2SO_4 neutralization

$$K_6 = 0.02 \div 0.04 \ hr^{-1}$$

The graphic solution of a set of differential equations that describes the block
diagram is given in Fig. 2, expressed as a relation between amounts of SO_2, H_2SO_4
and sulphates and time duration of their transport in the atmosphere. Figure 2
also shows the additional distance scale that allows an estimate to be made of
possible spatial scales of transport. A value of 30 km/hr is taken as an average
transport speed. On the basis of the information plotted in Fig. 2, it follows
that directly over the area of emission there are practically no H_2SO_4 or sulphates in the atmosphere but with the disappearance of SO_2 their concentration in
the atmosphere increases and reaches the maximum for H_2SO_4 in approximately 10
hours; the maximum for sulphates is reached in 30 to 40 hours. During such
periods of time, air masses can be transported for hundreds of kilometres from
the emission point.

It is worth noting that initial sulphur dioxide content falls quickly and that
ten hours later or at a distance of about 300 km its content is five times less.
It follows that the products of SO_2 transformation, that is, sulphuric acid and
sulphates, are of primary importance for the long-range atmospheric transport
of sulphur compounds.

Theoretical calculations and field observations performed during our investigation of a long-range transport of sulphur compounds from such powerful sources
as the Danbass industrial region (7) show that, at a distance of 100 km, SO_2
concentrations in the transport jet do not exceed 10 g/m^3, but sulphate
concentrations and precipitation acidity remain high at a distance of several
hundreds of kilometres. It, therefore, follows that while estimating the impact
of sulphur compounds on the environment at a distance removed from the emission
sources, one should first of all look at effects produced by sulphuric acid and
sulphates.

The following types of sulphuric acid and sulphates' effects can be emphasized:
increased number of respiratory diseases in man and animals; destruction of
vegetation and suppression of its growth; increase of corrosion damage in metals;
destruction of limestone and marble constructions; acidification of soils and
closed water bodies; change of optical characteristics of the atmosphere.

The impact of suspended sulphates on man may be observed beginning with concentrations of 6 to 10 g/m^3 (8). At an average level of concentrations of 10 to
12 g/m^3 there is observed an increase of respiratory diseases by 6 per cent when
the ambient air temperature is around 1 to $10^{\circ}C$ and by 32 per cent when the
temperature exceeds $10^{\circ}C$ (9).

In principle, acid sulphur-bearing substances, sulphuric acid and acidic
sulphates do impact on vegetation. The impact is of an indirect nature: nutrient
soil characteristic deteriorate. It was estimated that because of deterioration
of nutrient properties of forest soils in case of acid precipitation fall-out,
the velocity of forest increment in Sweden has decreased by 4 per cent in 1965
compared with that of 1950 (10). A negative impact of acid precipitation at
mean pH values (4.0 to 4.2) has been noted on the growth of fir trees and
deterioration of nutrient soil properties at a mean pH value of 4.7 (11). On the
basis of a statical analysis of the thickness of tree rings there has been noted
a retarded growth of trees in industrial regions of the middle west since 1930;
the authors attribute this to the fact that precipitation was acidified for this
period of time to mean values of pH = 4.2 to 4.5 (12).

A serious problem in a number of regions is the acidification of fresh water.
The acidification is strongly pronounced during snow-melting when a large amount
of the acids accumulated in snow during winter reach water bodies. For most kinds
of fish, the period concides with the spawning period; as a result of the
acidification of surface waters, many lakes and rivers of Norway and Sweden lost
their fish (6; 13).

If account is taken of the prevailing movement of air masses in moderate
latitudes from west to east, the problem of the long-range transboundary flow of
sulphur compounds is very real for the Soviet Union. The authors have shown that
owing to the impact of acid precipitation transported across the western boundary,
the annual agricultural damage in the north-west zone of the USSR is 100
million roubles (14).

On the basis of data on dynamics of transformation and removal of sulphur
compounds from the atmosphere and their effects on separate elements of the
environment an idea on spatial characteristics of the impact may be derived.
Figure 3 shows the extent of zones affected by the long-range transport of
atmospheric concentrations of SO_2 and sulphates as well as precipitation
acidification. The effects of pollutant dilutions in the atmosphere indicate that
the most far-reaching effects (to 200 km) result from precipitation acidification.
Zones of SO_2 (50 to 100 km) and sulphate (300 to 500 km) impacts are of a more
local character.

Practically all countries recognize the need to prevent the harmful impact of pollutants exported from one country affecting the environment of another country. Moreover, a pollutant flux which has been transported from a neighbouring country should not reach the maximum permissible concentrations as this would limit the development of a country's own industry in the boundary region. Indeed, any emission whatsoever originating in such a region might add to the concentration and result in an excess of the maximum permissible concentrations already present.

Let us consider a situation at the boundary of two countries A and B. The pollutant flow from country A to country B should constitute only a fraction of the maximum permissible concentration (MPC) established in country B. The same condition of not exceeding the permissible standards should be assured in boundary regions of country A regarding pollutants from country B. It follows naturally from this that in adjacent boundary regions the quantity of "imported" pollutants should amount to concentrations not exceeding, for example, $0.2 \div 0.5$ of MPC. However, the fraction of a possible transport across the boundary should be carefully discussed on an international scale. For example, if one were to assume that a sulphur dioxide concentration equal to 20 ug/m^3 is not dangerous at the regional level, then in the case of transboundary transport,

$$C \text{ permissible import} = (0.2 \div 0.5) \ C_{MPC} = (4 \div 10) \text{ ug SO}_2/\text{m}^3$$

where C permissible import is permissible "import" SO_2 concentration; C_{MPC} is maximum permissible concentration at the regional level.

From the viewpoint of control of adopted transport standards, it is convenient to operate the notion of an integral flux of a pollutant across the boundary or its area with great space and time averages. The value of such maximum permissible flux (MPF) from country A to country B on the boundary area with the length of L, in the case where mean value of C permissible import was observed for a long period of time, can be calculated according to the formula

$$MPF = \frac{Lh\acute{u}}{P} \cdot C \text{ per import}$$

where L is boundary area length which can be equal to 100 km, h is distribution layer altitude, ú is mean velocity of air mass transport in the o-h layer along the L area, and P is possible air mass transport from country A to country B.

In considering sulphur compound transport, it is reasonable to have a differential approach to the estimation of the value of h depending on the type of impact of some sulphur compounds on the environment. As sulphur dioxide has a direct impact only on the objects located directly on the underlying surface, h value in relation to sulphur dioxide can be limited to the altitude of the layer of "direct impact", for example, 200 metres. In case of sulphuric acid another approach is needed to assess h. Sulphuric acid impact is revealed in acidification of precipitation and further impact of acid precipitations on ecosystems and construction materials. In this case the height of the distribution layer should be limited by the height of the undercloud layer or not limited at all as, under real conditions, the major part of sulphur compounds lies within the undercloud layer. Thus, MPF for sulphuric acid can be determined from the expression:

$$MPF = \frac{L\acute{u}}{p} \int_{b}^{\infty} C(h) \ dh$$

It is worth noting that a solution to limit transboundary transport is within the competence of international law. Attention need only be drawn to geophysical aspects which may be taken into account in future while developing approaches for setting out standards for transboundary transport.

A consideration of the principal techniques of long-range sulphur transport investigation would indicate that certain progress has been made recently although the extent of resolving some aspects of the problem still remain insufficient. This situtation emphasizes the necessity for further broadening the corresponding investigations both at the national level and within the framework of ECE.

REFERENCES

(1)   Granat L., Rodhe H., Hallberg R.O., "The global sulphur cycle", SCOPE Report 7. The Swedish SCOPE Committee of the Royal Swedish Academy of Sciences, Orsundsbro, Sweden, 1975.

(2)   Ottar B., The long-range transport of air pollutants in Europe. International Conference on the Effects of Acid Precipitation, Telemark, Norway, June 14-15, 1976.

(3)   Barnes R.A., Long-term mean concentrations of atmospheric smoke and sulphur dioxide in country areas of England and Wales. Atmosph. Env., Vol. 10, No. 8, 1976, p. 619-631.

(4)   Bolin B., Ch. Persson, Regional dispersion and deposition of atmospheric pollutants with particular application to sulphur pollution over western Europe. Tellus, vol. 27, No. 3, 1975, p. 281.310.

(5)   The OECD programme on long-range transport of air pollutants. Measurements and findings. OECD, 1977, Paris.

(6)   Acid precipitation and its effects in Norway, Ministry of Environment, Oslo, Norway, 1974, pp. 1-19.

(7)   Bovykin Yu. B., P.A. Bryukhanov, A.V. Lyssak, A.G. Ryaboshapko, Estimation of sulphur life-time in the atmosphere of a large industrial region. Report on the technical meeting of ECE Programme on Long-range Transmissions of Air Pollutants, Bilthoven. the Netherlands, May 23-25, 1978.

(8)   EPA USA, Position paper on regulation of atmospheric sulphates. US EPA-450/2-75-007, 1975, p. 1-88.

(9)   Franch J.G., Effects of suspended sulphates on human health, Environmental Health Perspective, vol. 10, No. 1, 1975. p. 35-37.

(10) Dochinger L.S., Th.A. Seliga, Acid precipitation and the forest ecosystem. BioScience, vol. 26, No. 9, 1976, p. 564-565.

(11) Abrahamsen G., Tveite B., Horntvedt R., Impacts of acid precipitation on coniferous forest ecosystems. Water, Air and Soil Pollution, Vol. 8, No.1, 1977, p. 57-73.

(12) Ashby W., H. Fritts, Tree growth, air pollution and climate near la Porte. Bulletin of the America Meteorological Society, No. 3, 1972, p. 246-251.

(13) Schofield C.L., Effects of acid precipitation on fish. International Conference on the Effects of Acid Precipitation, Telemark, Norway, June 14-19

1976.

(14) Lysak A.W., I.M. Nazarov, A.G. Rjaboshapko, Problems dalnego atmosfernogo perenossa zagrjaznenii. Journal ECHO, 1979 (in press).

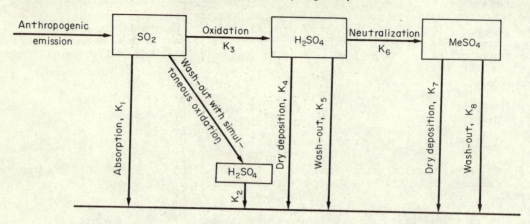

Fig. 1. Block model of sulphur behaviour in the atmosphere

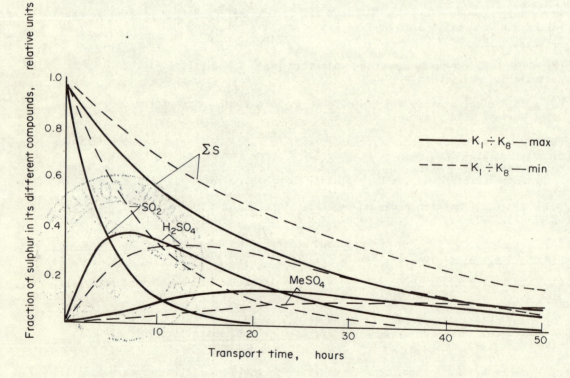

Fig. 2. Dynamics of removal, accumulation and transformation of different sylphur compounds in the
atmosphere at minimum and maximum values of the
$K_1 \div K_8$ coefficient

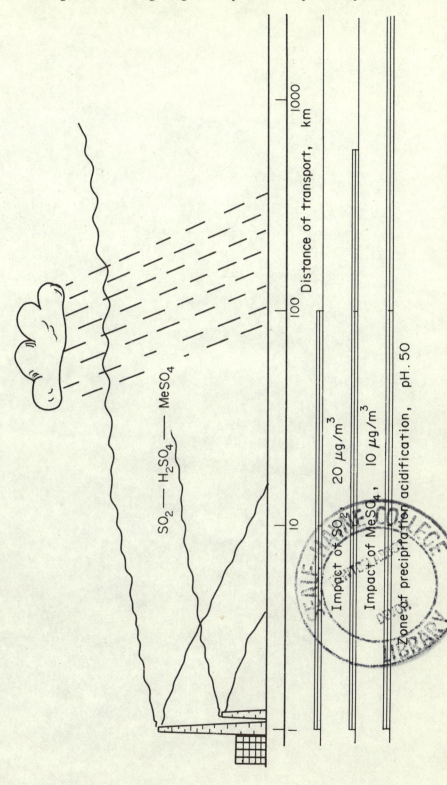

Fig. 3. Zone of impact of sulphur compounds on the environment at long-range transport

MANAGEMENT IN EDUCATION

Working Papers
in the social psychology
of educational institutions

by H. L. GRAY

Nafferton Books, 1980